Research Reports ESPRIT

Project 2071 · COMANDOS · Volume 1

Edited in cooperation with
the Commission of the European Communities

V. Cahill   R. Balter   N. R. Harris
X. Rousset de Pina (Eds.)

The COMANDOS
Distributed Application Platform

Springer-Verlag

Berlin Heidelberg New York
London Paris Tokyo
Hong Kong Barcelona
Budapest

Volume Editors

Vinny Cahill
Neville R. Harris

Roland Balter
Xavier Rousset de Pina

Department of Computer Science
O'Reilly Institute, Trinity College
Dublin 2, Ireland

Unité mixte BULL-IMAG
ZI de Mayencin, 2, rue Vignate
F-38610 Gieres, France

ESPRIT Project 2071 "Construction and Management of Distributed Open Systems" (Comandos-2) and its predecessor Project 834 "Construction and Management of Distributed Office Systems" (Comandos-1) belong to the domain Advanced Business and Home Systems — Peripherals (ABHS-P) of ESPRIT, the European Specific Programme for Research and Development in Information Technology supported by the Commission of the European Communities.

The project aims to facilitate the construction of large-scale, multivendor, distributed open systems by providing an integrated applications support environment for programming and using distributed applications that can manipulate long-lived data. The project was conducted in two phases. Comandos-1 started in 1986. The global architecture and the functional specification of kernel and system services were established and interfaces and language requirements defined. An integrated prototype of the overall platform was implemented and delivered. Comandos-2 started in 1989. The first release of the Comandos platform was used at several sites to construct new services and to develop distributed applications. A second release of the Comandos platform was designed and implemented providing enhanced facilities, additional services and tools, and better performance and reliability. This integrated version is now available.

CR Subject Classification (1991): D.4.7, D.1.5, D.1.3, H.2, J.1

ISBN-13: 978-3-540-56660-1   e-ISBN-13: 978-3-642-84954-1
DOI: 10.1007/978-3-642-84954-1

Publication No. EUR 15094 EN of the
Commission of the European Communities, Dissemination of Scientific and Technical Knowledge Unit,
Directorate-General Information Technologies and Industries, and Telecommunications,
Luxembourg

Typesetting: Camera-ready by authors
45/3140 – 543210 – Printed on acid-free paper

Preface

The last decade has seen an enormous change in the capability of information technology and also in the expectations of what that technology can provide. The personal computer revolution at the start of the 1980s brought computing power to the desktop in a way that, for the first time, non-technical users could understand and use in their everyday work. The invisible wall of mystique that had separated computers from their potential users for so long had been demolished, and the world of business would never be the same again.

As we entered the 1990s, a decade later, we witnessed the beginnings of another revolution. This revolution is not so obvious, but its implications are even more far-reaching. It is not so obvious because it is happening behind the scenes, in the communications and computing infrastructure that support the machines that can be seen sitting on office desks and, increasingly, being carried with business people as standard equipment along with a briefcase and umbrella. It is potentially more far-reaching for the following reason. The personal computer of the 1980s brought computing power to the user in a box that could fit on a desk. The revolution of the 1990s brings to the user computing power that is distributed across the whole planet.

The rise in networking that characterised the mid-1980s was the preface to a new era in advanced business systems. Interconnectivity of local, metropolitan, and wide area networks means that it is becoming increasingly the case that the business user can have access to computing resources connected to networks anywhere in the world. It does not matter if it is a microcomputer in Germany, a supercomputer in France or a minicomputer in Denmark, the user can have access to its data, programs and processing power from his or her own desktop.

The total computing resource available in this way is indefinitely large. Harnessing it in a form that the ordinary business or scientific user can use conveniently is not a trivial matter. The hardware and software attached to the various networks come from different vendors and the resulting systems and sub-systems are highly heterogeneous with respect to processors, operating systems, data structures and in many other ways. Also, the business user does not want to have to deal separately which each and every individual resource on the networks. That would be far too complicated. Neither would it harness the full potential of the resources involved. There is a saying that, "The whole is greater than the sum of the parts". It is like an orchestra. Each of the separate instruments by itself can perform well, each in its own particular way. But simply putting lots of them together does not realise their full potential. A room full of people playing musical instruments does not make an orchestra. Indeed, unless they are properly coordinated, with different aspects of the overall music properly and dynamically distributed among them, the resulting confusion can be worse than having just a single instrument playing.

The business user of the 1990s wants to be able to conduct an orchestra, not be confronted with a babel of separate instruments each competing for individual attention. The research and development carried out in Comandos brings that vision an important step nearer to commercial reality. The technical achievements made under Comandos have helped to put European industry in a world leadership position in the field of distributed systems, and have enabled some of the key European companies in the field to launch strategic new products, including the Distributed Computing Model announced by Groupe Bull in 1991.

Comandos reflects commitment from leading European companies, small and medium enterprises, and research institutes in seven different countries in the European Community who have cooperated over several years to develop the technologies necessary to make the advances required. Their continuing commitment during that period and the success of their efforts bear important testimony to the value of ESPRIT in providing a framework for European collaboration in strategic research and development.

The European Community is forming itself from great nations who have shown their resolution and ability to work together before, to successfully take on the challenges the world has presented. Past achievements in science and technology have demonstrated its creativity and inventiveness. Now it is using those qualities to invent new ways of turning Information Technology to advantage in building a business and social community that will provide economic, social and quality of life benefits to its citizens. During these harsh times and in the competitive world in which we live, the Community is finding ways to take advantage of its strengths, to pool resources and to move forward into the 1990s cooperatively and to boldly seize the opportunities that lie ahead. Comandos is an example of what can be achieved, and an example of which ESPRIT and the Community can be proud.

Attilio Stajano
Commission of the European Communities

Table of Contents

Brief History of the Project XIII

1 Introduction 1
   1.1 Rationale, Scope and Objectives 1
   1.2 Object-Oriented Approach 3
   1.3 The Comandos Model 4
   1.4 Programming with the Comandos Model 4
   1.5 Structure of the Comandos Platform 5
   1.6 The Comandos Virtual Machine 5
   1.7 The Comandos Virtual Machine Interface 7
   1.8 Application Services 7
   1.9 Management Tools 8
   1.10 Comandos and the Rest of the World 8
       1.10.1 Comandos and the Open Software Foundation 9
       1.10.2 Comandos and UNIX International 10
       1.10.3 Comandos and the Object Management Group 11
   1.11 What is Comandos Added Value? 12
   1.12 Road-map of the Book 13

I User's View of the Comandos Platform   15

2 Overview of the Comandos Platform 17
   2.1 Basic Features 17
       2.1.1 Transparent Access to Resources and Services 18
       2.1.2 Persistence 19
       2.1.3 Concurrency 21
       2.1.4 Atomicity 22
       2.1.5 Sharing 23
   2.2 Interworking Between Languages 23
       2.2.1 Manual Approach 24
       2.2.2 Automated Approach 25
   2.3 Data Management 25
   2.4 Security 26
   2.5 Management View of the Platform 27
   2.6 Interworking with UNIX 29
   2.7 Structure of the Platform 29

        2.7.1   The Comandos System   30
        2.7.2   Application Services and Management Tools   31

3   The Comandos Virtual Machine   33
    3.1   Object Model   33
        3.1.1   Comandos Objects   33
        3.1.2   Global Names   34
        3.1.3   Object Invocation   34
    3.2   Security Model   35
        3.2.1   Security Domains, Users and Groups   35
        3.2.2   Isolation   35
        3.2.3   Authorisation   36
        3.2.4   Security Levels   37
    3.3   Execution Model   38
        3.3.1   Job and Activity Operation   38
        3.3.2   Job and Activity Control   39
    3.4   Transaction Model   40
        3.4.1   Transaction Options   42
        3.4.2   Job and Activity Model for Transactions   42

4   Supported Programming Languages   44
    4.1   C++   44
        4.1.1   Type Model   45
        4.1.2   Distribution   46
        4.1.3   Persistence   47
        4.1.4   Concurrency   49
        4.1.5   Storage   51
        4.1.6   Transactions   52
        4.1.7   Exceptions   55
        4.1.8   Implementation   55
    4.2   Eiffel   56
        4.2.1   Type Model   56
        4.2.2   Persistence   57
        4.2.3   Distribution   59
        4.2.4   Concurrency   60
        4.2.5   Storage   61
        4.2.6   Transactions   61
        4.2.7   Exceptions   63
        4.2.8   Implementation   63
    4.3   The Comandos Object-Oriented Language   63
        4.3.1   Type Model   63
        4.3.2   Persistence   67
        4.3.3   Distribution   67
        4.3.4   Concurrency   67
        4.3.5   Transactions   69
        4.3.6   Exceptions   69
        4.3.7   Implementation   70

5   Development Tools   72
    5.1   The Distributed Debugger   72
          5.1.1   Printing the Content of an Object   73
          5.1.2   Execution Control   73
          5.1.3   Eliminating Non-deterministic Behaviour   74
    5.2   The User Interface Development System   75
    5.3   The Type Manager   76
          5.3.1   Canonical Type Model   77
          5.3.2   The Type Manager Architecture   80
          5.3.3   The Management of Units   81
          5.3.4   The Creation of Types   81
          5.3.5   The Storage and Retrieval of Type Information   82
          5.3.6   The Process of Language Registration   82
          5.3.7   The Process of Compilation   83

6   The Object Data Management Service   84
    6.1   Data Model   84
    6.2   Operational Model   87
    6.3   Structure   90
          6.3.1   The Aggregate Layer   90
          6.3.2   The Bulk Layer   90
          6.3.3   The Collection Layer   91
    6.4   The Programmer's Interface   91
          6.4.1   Basics   92
          6.4.2   The Data and Storage Definition Language   92
          6.4.3   The Data Manipulation Sub-language   94
    6.5   Summary   96

7   Management Tools   98
    7.1   The Distributed Directory Service   98
          7.1.1   Functional Model   99
          7.1.2   Directory Services   100
          7.1.3   The Distributed Directory Service Architecture   102
    7.2   Management and Administration Tools   103
          7.2.1   The System Observation Facility   104
          7.2.2   The System Control Facility   106
          7.2.3   User and Host Administration   108
          7.2.4   The Distributed Information System Designer   111
    7.3   Security Tools   114
          7.3.1   Protocol Data Analysis Tool   114
          7.3.2   Risk Management   117
    7.4   Relationships Between Tools   122

8   The CIDRE Application   123
    8.1   Description of the Pilot Application   124
          8.1.1   Functions   125
          8.1.2   Architecture   128
    8.2   CIDRE Design and Implementation   131

8.2.1   Use of the Type Model 131
8.2.2   Use of the Computational Model 133
8.2.3   Persistent Objects 134
8.2.4   Integration with UNIX 135
8.2.5   Use of Comandos Services 135
8.3   Evaluation 137
8.3.1   Model and Language 137
8.3.2   Architecture 138
8.3.3   Conclusion 139

II   Implementor's View of the Comandos Platform   141

9 Virtual Machine Interface 143
9.1   The Virtual Machine Architecture 143
9.2   Virtual Object Memory 145
9.2.1   Context Services 145
9.2.2   Global Services 147
9.3   Execution Sub-system 147
9.3.1   Job and Activity Management 148
9.3.2   Synchronisation Support 148
9.3.3   Exception Handling 149
9.4   Storage Sub-system 150
9.4.1   Container Management 150
9.4.2   Segments 150
9.4.3   Object Migration and Clustering 150
9.4.4   Ageing in the Storage Sub-system 151
9.5   Transaction Sub-system 152
9.5.1   Transaction Management 152
9.6   Communication Sub-system 152
9.6.1   Remote Invocation Support 153
9.6.2   Reliable Broadcast Protocol 153
9.7   Protection Sub-system 153
9.7.1   Authorisation 153
9.7.2   Secure Transmission 155
9.7.3   Auditing 156

10 Implementing the Virtual Machine 158
10.1   The Amadeus Platform 158
10.1.1   Basic Design Decisions and Assumptions 159
10.1.2   The Structure of Amadeus 161
10.1.3   Node Management 163
10.1.4   The Storage Sub-system 165
10.1.5   User and Extent Management 172
10.1.6   Context Management 175
10.1.7   Cluster Location 177
10.1.8   Cluster Fault Handling 180
10.1.9   Address Resolution 184

    10.1.10 The Object Manager 184
    10.1.11 Cluster Management 188
    10.1.12 Job and Activity Management 189
    10.1.13 Load Balancing 194
    10.1.14 Transaction Management 195
    10.1.15 Communications 198
    10.1.16 Thread Management 200
  10.2 Other Implementations 201
    10.2.1 CHORUS 201
    10.2.2 Mach 204

11 Interfacing a Language to the Virtual Machine 209
  11.1 The Generic Run-time 209
    11.1.1 Down-calls 210
    11.1.2 Up-calls 210
  11.2 The Eiffel Run-time 211
    11.2.1 Types and Objects 211
    11.2.2 Object Layout 212
    11.2.3 ERT Data Structures for a Class 213
    11.2.4 Object Creation, Access and Invocation 216
    11.2.5 Functionality Provided by the ERT 217
  11.3 Persistence 218
    11.3.1 Interfacing the ERT and GRT 218
    11.3.2 Down-calls 222
    11.3.3 Problems in the Implementation of Persistence 222
    11.3.4 Compilation 224
  11.4 Distribution 224
    11.4.1 Calling Mechanism 224
    11.4.2 Code Generation 226
    11.4.3 Up-calls for Distribution 229
    11.4.4 Problems in Distribution 230
  11.5 Concurrency 230
    11.5.1 Implementation 230
  11.6 Transactions 231
  11.7 Conclusion 232

12 Conclusions 234
  12.1 The Challenge of Distributed Computing and the Promise of the
     Comandos Technology 234
  12.2 Benefits of the Comandos Technology 235
    12.2.1 Main Benefits for the Application Developer 235
    12.2.2 Main Benefits for the End-user 236
  12.3 Industrial Achievements 236
  12.4 Research Achievements 238

Appendix   239

A Example Programs 241
   A.1 Specification of the SimpleMail Application 241
   A.2 C++ 243
        A.2.1 Application Mainline 243
        A.2.2 Class Mailer 245
        A.2.3 Class Mail_Directory 249
        A.2.4 Class Mailbox 252
        A.2.5 Class Message 254
        A.2.6 Utility and Library Classes 257
   A.3 Eiffel 259
        A.3.1 Application Mainline 259
        A.3.2 Class Mailer 261
        A.3.3 Class Mail_Directory 263
        A.3.4 Class Mailbox 265
        A.3.5 Class Message 266
        A.3.6 Utility and Library Classes 267
   A.4 Guide 273
        A.4 1 Class Mailer 273
        A.4.2 Class Mail_Directory 274
        A.4.3 Class Mailbox 275
        A.4.4 Class Message 277
        A.4.5 Utility and Library Classes 278

B Available Software 283

C Comandos Glossary 289

D Abbreviations 292

E Comandos Publications 295
   E.1 Papers and Reports 295
   E.2 Project Deliverables 305

References 307

Brief History of the Project

The overall objective of the Comandos (Construction and Management of Distributed Open Systems) project was to provide an integrated environment for the construction of distributed applications. The Comandos project was designed as a long-term initiative to produce a pre-industrial prototype of such a platform, based on innovative solutions. The project was conducted in two phases: Comandos-1 and Comandos-2.

The Comandos-1 project started in 1986, in the framework of ESPRIT-1. This first phase was mainly dedicated to a study of the feasibility of the construction of an object-based integrated distributed application support environment. This objective was achieved by the development of innovative solutions based on the integration of existing and emerging technologies.

Significant achievements have been obtained from this exploratory phase, in particular the definition of the Comandos object-oriented model for distributed computing and the Comandos architecture. A strategic result was the demonstration of various prototype implementations of the Comandos architecture, thus proving its feasibility on a number of underlying environments. This first release of the Comandos platform components was demonstrated at the annual ESPRIT Conference in Brussels in 1988 and again in 1989.

Started in 1989, Comandos-2 has exploited the results and experience drawn from the first phase to provide a full pre-industrial prototype of the Comandos platform. Comandos-2 involved two main streams of activity:

- The first release of the Comandos platform, delivered as a result of Comandos-1, was used at several sites as the basis for the construction of new services, and for the development of distributed applications.

- A second release of the Comandos platform was designed and implemented providing enhanced facilities, as well as better performance and reliability. In addition, services and tools developed on the first release were integrated within this release. This integrated version is now available and has been delivered to a number of sites for experimentation and evaluation.

In parallel with the implementation and integration work, the last two years of the project have also been dedicated to the promotion and exploitation of the Comandos technology. The Comandos technology is recognised by the industrial community as a major step towards providing a complete environment for distributed computing. The technology has been submitted to several international consortia and is likely to influence emerging standards in the area of distributed object-oriented systems. Furthermore, the technical achievements made under Comandos have helped to put European industry in a world leadership position, and has enabled some of the Comandos partners to launch new key products.

Objective of the Book

This book provides a general presentation of the Comandos distributed application platform.

It is structured into two parts. The first part provides a user's view of the Comandos platform. This part is mainly targeted at data processing managers, systems analysts, and application designers and programmers who have an interest in building distributed applications and services, as well as at the administrators of distributed systems. This part focuses on the description of the functionality provided by the platform, design choices and innovative aspects. The second part of the book gives an overview of the implementation of the platform.

This book does not give a complete technical description of the Comandos platform components. The interested reader is referred to the numerous published papers and Comandos deliverables which are publicly available.

Consortium

The Comandos-2 consortium involved fifteen collaborators from seven European countries including three leading European manufacturers, three software vendors, two telecommunications companies, two research laboratories and five academic institutions. The consortium consisted of five partners:

- Bull SA (France) (Prime Contractor)
- Instituto de Engenharia de Systemas e Computadores (Portugal)
- Siemens AG (Germany)
- Siemens Nixdorf Informationssysteme AG (Germany)
- University of Dublin, Trinity College (Ireland)

and ten associated partners:

- Applied Research Group Spa (Italy)
- Chorus Systèmes (France)
- Fraunhofer-Institut für Arbeitswirtschaft und Organisation (Germany)
- Gesellschaft für Mathematik und Datenverarbeitung MBH (Germany)

- Laboratoire de Génie Informatique-IMAG (France)
- Open Software Foundation – Research Institute (France)
- Service d'Etudes Communes des Postes et Télécommunications (France)
- Universitat Politecnica de Catalunya (Spain)
- Universität Stuttgart (Germany)
- University of Glasgow (United Kingdom)

In addition, International Computers Limited (United Kingdom), Istituto di l'Elaborazione dell'Informazione del C.N.R. (Italy), Nixdorf Computer AG (Germany) and Olivetti (Italy), participated in the Comandos-1 project.

Contributors

The objectives of the Comandos project could not have been achieved without the contributions of each of the following individuals.

For Bull SA: Abderrahman Abderrhaman, Roland Balter, Jacques Bernadat, Malcolm Bennett, Fabienne Boyer, Jacques Cayuela, Pierre Yves Chevalier, Francois Exertier, Andre Freyssinet, Serge Lacourte, Eric Paire, Christian Remy, Michel Riveill, Jean Luc Tesseron, Miguel Santana, Gerard Vandome and Xinxin Zhang.

For Instituto de Engenharia de Systemas e Computadores: José Alves Marques, Paulo Ferreira, Paulo Guedes, Nuno Guimares, David Matos, Jose Monge, Ricardo Nunes, Joao Pereira, José Pereira, Manuel Sequeira, Pedro Sousa, Cristina Videira Lopes and André Zuquete.

For Siemens AG: Johann Fichtner, Hermann Foltas, Joachim Katzer, Johann Lindmeyr, Thomas Mehlhart, Cornelia Persy, Frank Schalkowski, Winfried Weiss and Christian Wolff.

For the University of Dublin, Trinity College: Séan Baker, Ann Barry, Vinny Cahill, Donal Daly, Alexis Donnelly, Edward Finn, Yvon Gourhant, Neville Harris, Dominic Herity, Christopher Horn, Alan Judge, Stephen Kenny, Andre Kramer, Damien Lynch, Ciaran McHale, Colm McHugh, Maurice Martin, John Moreau, Anthony Murphy, Faris Naji, Joo Li Ooi, Annraí O'Toole, Mark Sheppard, John Slattery, Gradimir Starovic, Brendan Tangney, Paul Taylor, Bridget Walsh and Iseult White.

For the Applied Research Group Spa: Roberto Gagliardi, Gian-Domenico Oldano and Fausto Rabitti.

For Chorus Systèmes: Paulo Amaral, Didier Irlande, Michel Gien, Christian Jacquemot, Peter Jensen, Rodger Lea, and Adam Mirowski.

For Fraunhofer-Institut für Arbeitswirtschaft und Organisation and Universität Stuttgart: Wolfgang Clauss, Isabella Hofstetter, Gerrit Kerber, Helmut Meitner, Andreas Ness, Friedemann Reim and Alexander Roos.

For Gesellschaft für Mathematik und Datenverarbeitung MBH: Reiner Frings, Reinhold Kroeger, Frank Lange and Michael Mock.

For Laboratoire de Génie Informatique-IMAG: Dominique Decouchant, Andrzej Duda, Daniel Hagimont, Sacha Krakowiak, Herve Jamrozik, Patrick LeDot, Emmanuel Lenormand, Marie Meysembourg, Hiep Nguyen Van, Veronique Normand, Cecile Roisin, Xavier Rousset de Pina and Rodrigo Scioville.

For the Open Software Foundation – Research Institute: Youcef Laribi and James Loveluck.

For Service d'Etudes Communes des Postes et Télécommunications: Francois Bourdon, Jean-Marc Deshayes, Marcel Greard, Odile Lambert, Francois Merciol and Michel Milhau.

For the Universitat Politecnica de Catalunya: Cristina Barrado, Patricia Borensztjen, Francisco Jordan, Jesus Labarta, Manuel Medina, Ana Moreno and Mildred Sarmiento.

For the University of Glasgow: Steve Blott, Jack Campin, Daniel Chan, Richard Cooper, Colin Dunlop, David Harper, David Kerr, Moira Norrie, Francis Wai, Andrew Walker and Ray Welland.

Acknowledgments

Comandos was an ambitious project which required the integration of numerous skills and resources. Only the ESPRIT framework and spirit could provide the synergy required to carry out such a project. The Comandos consortium is thus grateful to the Commission of the European Communities for their support.

Special thanks are due to Attilio Stajano, Rosalie Zobel, John Beale, Ulrich Boes, Andrew Redman, Jan Roukens and Ralph Hansen of the European Commission for their support and for their assistance in the management of the project.

The consortium is also grateful to Dr. Mehmet Aksit, Dr. Jean Bacon, Dr. John Winterbotham, Dr. Christoph Steigner, Dr. Peter Linington, Dr. Jean Serge Banino and Dr. Radu Popescu-Zeletin for their many helpful suggestions and advice at various times throughout the course of the project.

Trademarks

The following trademarks used in this book are hereby acknowledged:

- CHORUS, CHORUS/MiX and CHORUS/COOL are trademarks of Chorus Systèmes.
- DPX and BOS are trademarks of Groupe Bull.
- DECstation and ULTRIX are trademarks of Digital Equipment Corporation.
- Apollo and NCS are trademarks of the Hewlett-Packard Company.
- POSIX is a trademark of the Institute of Electrical and Electronics Engineers.

- Eiffel is a trademark of the Non-profit International Consortium for Eiffel (NICE).
- OS/2 is a trademark of International Business Machines Corporation.
- Kerberos and X Window System are trademarks of the Massachusetts Institute of Technology.
- MS-DOS is a trademark of Microsoft Corporation.
- Object Management Group, OMG and OMG IDL are trademarks of the Object Management Group.
- Open Software Foundation, OSF, OSF/1, OSF/Motif and Motif are trademarks of the Open Software Foundation, Inc.
- SPARCstation is a trademark of SPARC International, Inc., licenced exclusively to Sun Microsystems, Inc.
- Sun Microsystems, Sun, Sun-3, Sun-4, Sun386i, SunOS, Network File System and NFS are trademarks or registered trademarks of Sun Microsystems, Inc.
- AFS is a trademark of Transarc Corporation.
- UI-ATLAS is a trademark of UNIX International.
- UNIX is a trademark of UNIX Systems Laboratories, Inc.
- X/Open is a trademark of the X/Open Company Limited.

1. Introduction

This chapter presents an overview of the Comandos distributed application platform. The first section presents the scope and objectives of the platform. Subsequent sections introduce the main concepts, design choices and overall architecture of the platform. In addition, the relationship with existing and emerging standards in the area of distributed processing is examined. Finally, the industrial interest in, and potential impact of the Comandos technology are summarised. The last section of this chapter presents a road map for the remainder of the book.

1.1 Rationale, Scope and Objectives

Today the growth in distributed systems is faster than in most other sectors of the computer industry. Their increasing use reflects both technological and organisational evolution. The emergence of local area networks (LANs), interconnected through high-speed worldwide networks stimulated the development of distributed applications as connection to the network became easy and inexpensive. Human organisations are often, by their nature, distributed, but with strong requirements for interworking and overall integration within the enterprise as demonstrated by the recent emergence of Computer Supported Cooperative Working (CSCW).

Computer users require a communications environment that will allow information to flow from wherever it is stored to wherever it is needed, without unnecessarily exposing the complexity of the network to the end user, the system administrator, or the application developer. To encourage and support the development of distributed applications, various computing models and architectures have been proposed over the last few years including the Distributed Computing Environment (DCE) issued by the Open Software Foundation (OSF) and the UNIX International (UI) UI-ATLAS framework. These architectural frameworks (as well as the earlier Open Systems Interconnection (OSI) standards) represent a major step forward in the evolution of distributed systems, as they allow inter-operability across heterogeneous environments.

However, the development and integration of application software is currently a labour and cost-intensive proposition, particularly for cooperative applications, in which large volumes of distributed structured data are shared by cooperative users. Methodologies and tools are needed to master the complexity inherent in heterogeneous distributed environments and in new application requirements.

The overall objective of the Comandos project was to specify and construct an integrated platform for programming and operating multi-vendor distributed systems. This platform is targeted at application programmers and system integrators, and aims to reduce the overall cost of the development, maintenance, and evolution of large distributed applications. The Comandos platform allows both the development of new applications, and the reuse of old-style (UNIX-oriented) applications.

Comandos is primarily targeted at the development and support of integrated (also described as tightly-coupled) distributed applications within a *cell* which constitutes the basic organisational and administrative component within the enterprise. A cell is basically composed of a set of cooperating workstations, servers and processor pools connected through a high-speed LAN. The goal is to present the distributed system as a coherent entity to its users despite the variety of its components. Wide area networks (WANs) are used for the interconnection of Comandos installations and for interworking with external environments. Figure 1.1 depicts a typical Comandos configuration.

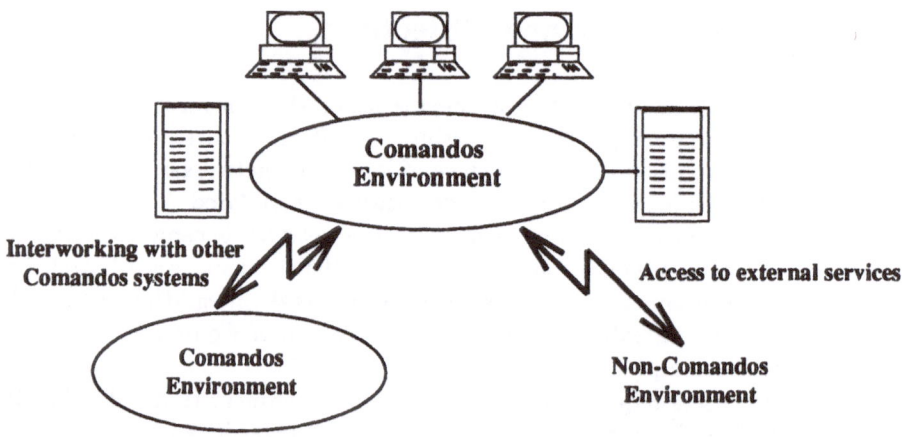

Fig. 1.1. A typical Comandos environment.

Although the Comandos project was initially targeted at office and business systems, the Comandos platform is also valuable as a basis for integrated information systems in such other application domains as computer aided design and software engineering.

The project itself has not provided substantial end-user applications, but rather a basis for the development of these. However, some moderate demonstrator applications have been implemented, in particular in the realm of document circulation and tracking.

For the development of these applications, the Comandos platform includes infrastructure supporting:

- concurrent distributed computations;
- storage and retrieval of persistent data;
- use of multiple programming languages including existing languages;
- reusable and extensible software modules;
- security and protection of data;
- on-line management, monitoring and control;
- access to pre-existing applications and information systems.

1.2 Object-Oriented Approach

The Comandos project adopted an innovative approach based on the integration of operating system, programming language and database technologies. A unified view is provided by a model and system architecture based on object-oriented technology, coupled with distributed persistent storage.

Object-oriented programming is now recognised as being a major breakthrough in productivity, reliability, and reuse of software components. Object-orientation was adopted in Comandos for a number of reasons. Abstraction is not only an important programming concept, but also aids in the construction of distributed applications by allowing the implementation and configuration of common services to be hidden from clients. Bundling executable code and data together into a single entity also aids the construction of such systems via the modularity which results. Accessing the same entity via different interfaces aids protection mechanisms. Code reuse and incremental development aid programmer productivity and also allow implementors and administrators to tailor and extend a common system to their own requirements. Finally, object-oriented data models provide a rich framework in which to capture complex structures, such as multimedia documents.

The object-oriented approach is also appearing in international standardisation activities such as the X/OPEN Object Management Layer (XOM), and the ISO/ECMA Open Distributed Processing (ODP) initiative. Today, this approach is receiving significant industrial support through the promotional activities of the Object Management Group (OMG), particularly in the area of distributed environments. Finally, the OSF and the UI consortium are both considering the evolution of their architectural frameworks based on distributed object management systems.

Within the Comandos project, the object paradigm provides an integrated view of application construction, and system management and control. Furthermore objects are the units of programming and data modelling, the units of addressing, and the units of storage.

1.3 The Comandos Model

Comandos provides a conceptual model of a distributed environment, encompassing both computation and data management. This model presents the functionality of the Comandos platform to application programmers and system administrators. This model is abstract in the sense that it does not require the use of any particular programming language. Technically it consists of two major components:

- A *computational model*, which allows distributed programs to be defined. This model provides the application designer with a multi-node multiprocessor virtual machine, in which parallelism is apparent and distribution is hidden.
- Common and extensible *type* and *data models*. The type model captures the type systems of various object-oriented programming languages, and allows inter-operability between them. The data model provides abstractions for modelling collections of objects, relationships between collections and classification structures.

1.4 Programming with the Comandos Model

To both facilitate the use of the Comandos model and to encourage its adoption, the model is provided to application developers through one or more programming languages. The uniformity of the Comandos model results in programming languages in which a uniform treatment of both transient and persistent data, of both passive and active entities, and, of both local and remote services are **all** potentially available.

This strategy differs from more classical approaches in which tight coupling of a programming language with support for persistence and distribution is **not** supported. Typically, in the classical approach, a set of languages is used for building programs where one language is used to describe the computation to be carried out, a different language is used to define storage types, and a further different language is used for interface definition and communication.

The Comandos model is provided through different programming languages. Moreover, a single application may be composed from parts written in different programming languages. The features of the model are particularly exploitable by object-oriented programming languages. Two approaches to the provision of language support have been followed: supporting existing languages, and providing a new language environment.

Two existing object-oriented languages are currently supported: C++ and Eiffel. The overall strategy is to enhance each host language with features of the Comandos computational model (mainly concurrency, persistence and distribution). Language extensions are supported using appropriate preprocessing, which generates necessary supplementary information. In some cases, restrictions are imposed on the use of standard features of the languages due to the distributed nature of the environment. However, in order to be consistent with the definition of each language, as well as to be able to support existing code, the number of such restrictions has been minimised.

The experience drawn from Comandos-1 convinced us that it is useful to provide a new language in which all the concepts of the Comandos model are faithfully reflected. The viability and usefulness of this new language have already been demonstrated by programming basic system services and a number of distributed applications.

1.5 Structure of the Comandos Platform

The overall structure of the Comandos platform is presented in Fig. 1.2. Basically, the platform consists of two main components:

- The *Comandos system*, which is itself structured in two layers: the *virtual machine*, which is independent of any supported programming language, and a set of one or more *language-specific run-time systems*.
- A set of *application services and management tools*, built as normal applications, which extend the functionality of the basic Comandos system.

A language-specific run-time system implements a specific extension of the basic Comandos virtual machine for a particular programming language. A given Comandos system provides at least one language-specific run-time in order to support objects programmed in the corresponding language; several language-specific run-times can coexist in the same system, thus allowing several languages to be used simultaneously.

1.6 The Comandos Virtual Machine

The Comandos virtual machine (c.f. Fig. 1.2) provides the basic mechanisms which are necessary for an object-oriented distributed system, supporting multiple language environments. This includes the management of persistent storage; the control of distributed computations; network communications; and transaction management.

The virtual machine provides a unified framework for the management of objects, which supports the viewpoints of both databases and general purpose programming languages. Programming languages frequently deal with transient entities – objects whose lifetime is limited to the execution of a program – while database languages deal with persistent ones, i.e. objects whose lifetime is independent from that of the programs which use them. The virtual machine supports both viewpoints in a uniform way.

Although the virtual machine provides full distribution transparency, such transparency is not always desirable and hence the virtual machine allows applications to be aware of the distribution of the objects which they manipulate if this is required.

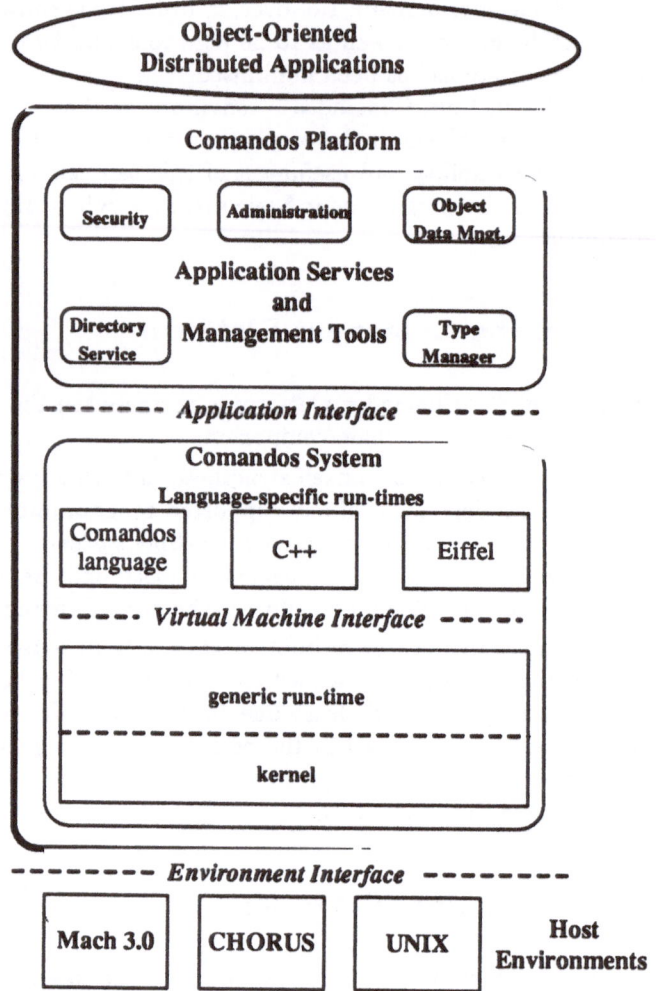

Fig. 1.2. The architecture of the Comandos platform.

At the upper level of the virtual machine is the *generic run-time* (GRT) (c.f. Fig. 1.2) which provides a language independent layer implementing distributed object invocation. The GRT is itself provided above the *kernel* layer which includes those components of the virtual machine which must be implemented in a protected way, and which interfaces directly with the underlying host environment.

The definition of the virtual machine is independent of any underlying system, and can be mapped onto various host environments. Two approaches have been used to implement the Comandos system. One implementation runs as a guest layer on top of an existing operating system (UNIX), without any modifications to this operating system. Other implementations are built directly on top of the OSF/1 MK and CHORUS distributed micro-kernels. All of these implementations provide full coexistence with a UNIX environment.

1.7 The Comandos Virtual Machine Interface

The Comandos *Virtual Machine Interface* (VMI) is the interface between the GRT and the various language-specific run-times (c.f. Fig. 1.2).

The VMI is intended to be used by compiler builders and basic service implementors. It provides a set of primitives which allow the interaction between application objects and the virtual machine. This interface has been standardised in order to allow easy portability of languages and services between various implementations of the virtual machine. This interface, as well as the overall Comandos architecture, has been widely publicised in order to encourage third parties to develop additional services and applications on top of the Comandos platform.

The VMI is the uniform view presented by the Comandos virtual machine to each of the various supported languages. As different languages have different calling semantics, a language-specific run-time must adapt the GRT primitives to the language-specific format. Moreover, as most of these primitives are based on manipulation of objects, whose format and model differ in each of the different languages, each language-specific run-time must also hide these language dependencies from the GRT.

To provide this flexibility and to make a minimum number of impositions on any language, Comandos adopted a general model in which the language may make calls to the GRT which depend on language-specific information. To handle such a call the GRT makes heavy use of up-calls, where an up-call is a call from a lower level to a higher one, using an entry point previously supplied by a regular call (down-call), to obtain the necessary information from the language-specific run-time.

This two-way interface between a language-specific run-time and the GRT allows objects of heterogeneous languages to be handled uniformly by the GRT. This scheme is sufficiently generic so as to allow easy portability of compilers and basic services between different implementations of the virtual machine.

1.8 Application Services

Application services include those facilities which are required at run time by a range of distributed applications or which are used in the development of distributed applications. Application services provided within the project include:

- Development tools to aid application designers in the design, construction and debugging of distributed applications;

- A Type Manager for the management of type information used in supporting interworking between different languages;
- An Object Data Management Service providing management of and associative access to (large) collections of objects.

1.9 Management Tools

Comandos also provides a number of management tools for the control and administration of a Comandos installation. These tools include:

- A Distributed Directory Service supporting symbolic naming of objects which conforms to the ISO/CCITT X.500 standards [CCITT 1988];
- A distributed System Observation and Control Facility;
- A system configuration and administration tool;
- Security tools for risk management and for the analysis of security data generated by the virtual machine;
- A tool for the design of a distributed office system.

In addition, existing tools can also be used, where appropriate, in a given Comandos environment. If the tool exists in a UNIX environment, then recoding of the tool is not required because of the coexistence of the Comandos and UNIX environments.

1.10 Comandos and the Rest of the World

Distributed systems trace their roots to the first computer communications, which were used to move information from one computer to another. As personal computers, engineering workstations, and LANs became cheaper and faster, various distributed computing implementations became popular. Notable examples include :

- the Domain system, developed by Apollo, which provides a uniform distributed storage system, and led to the Network Computing System (NCS) product.
- the Network File System (NFS), developed by Sun Microsystems, which extends the functionality of a UNIX file system to the network;
- the Andrew File System (AFS), developed at Carnegie Mellon University, which also provides the abstraction of a network-wide UNIX file system;
- the Portable Common Tool Environment (PCTE), developed within the ESPRIT program, which provides infrastructure for the construction of software engineering tools.

Comandos has borrowed ideas from these systems and has integrated them into a unified framework, through the intensive use of object-oriented technology.

Although it is premature to anticipate the impact of the Comandos project, the remainder of this section investigates how Comandos results and experiences could enhance the current state of the art in the area of distributed systems.

1.10.1 Comandos and the Open Software Foundation

1.10.1.1 Comandos and OSF/DCE. Distributed computing environments, integrating various enabling technologies into an architecturally coherent framework, are a recent development in distributed systems. The first of these was the OSF's DCE. DCE provides a set of fundamental services that support the development, use, and maintenance of applications in a heterogeneous distributed computing environment. The current components include a thread service, a remote procedure call and presentation service, a directory service, a time service, a security service, a distributed file system service, a diskless support service and personal computer integration.

A survey was carried out to help the OSF in charting its Open Road technical agenda by providing insights into members' priorities and their relative level of interest in specific computing technologies. The result of this survey [OSF 1991] showed that distributed operating systems and object oriented environments were the first two priorities. It is important to notice that both issues are fundamental aspects of the Comandos work.

Based on this survey, it is expected that OSF's long-term plans will include support for object-oriented environments. The OSF Special Interest Group on Distributed Computing Environments has launched a specific subgroup investigating the DCE enhancements necessary to support object-oriented environments. It is expected that Comandos results will greatly influence this evolution scheme as the OSF Research Institute is a member of the Comandos consortium.

Figure 1.3 depicts a possible scenario for enhancing a DCE environment with an object-oriented application platform based on Comandos. This approach allows the coexistence between applications developed using existing DCE tools and interfaces, and applications developed using the Comandos object model and programming environment. In addition existing services and applications may be accessed from the object-oriented environment through a simple wrapping mechanism based on the encapsulation of existing components into large objects.

A further ESPRIT project, HARNESS [HARNESS 1991a], has, as one of its objectives the integration of the Comandos platform within the overall DCE framework. To achieve this goal, HARNESS intends to use some of the DCE building blocks to implement the Comandos kernel (e.g. using the remote procedure call and naming services for network communication and the distributed file system for the implementation of persistent storage).

1.10.1.2 Comandos and OSF/DME. The OSF's Distributed Management Environment (DME) is intended to provide the building blocks required to develop and use management applications. It consists of a graphical user interface and application services – including software installation and distribution, software licensing, printing and user group management. These will be integrated into a management infrastructure with object and event services, management protocols, and application services.

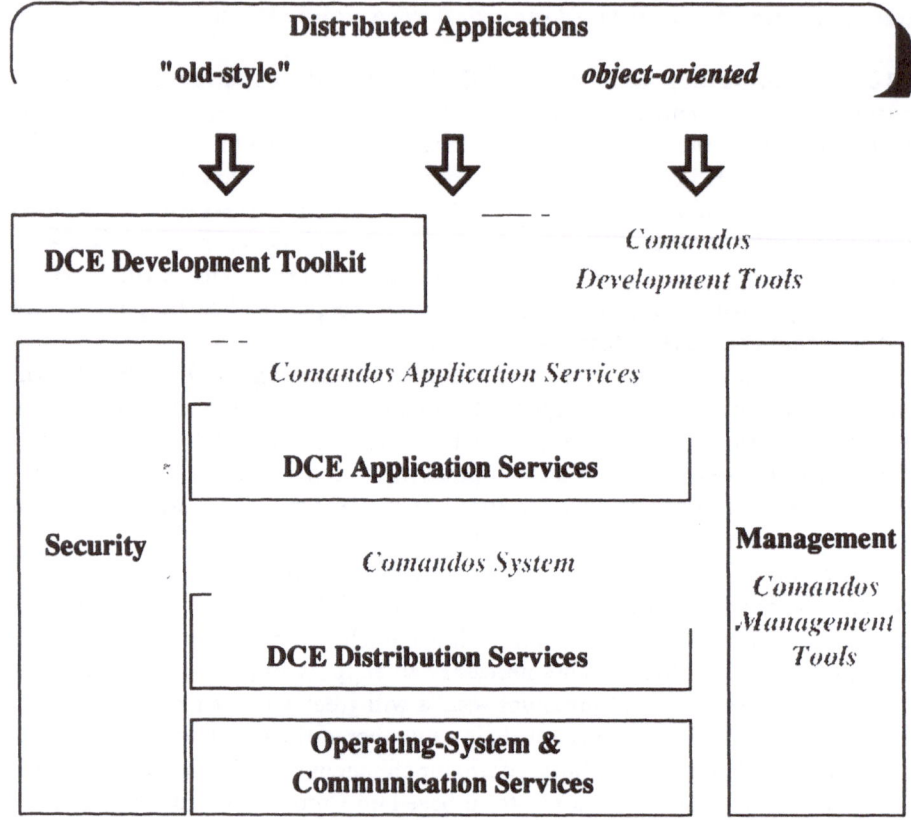

Fig. 1.3. A Comandos platform within a DCE environment.

The OSF/DME request for technology received forty-one initial responses. Submissions from twenty-seven vendors qualified for detailed evaluation – among them a submission by one of the Comandos partners. However the management applications submitted by Comandos turned out to be beyond the scope of the basic set of management applications required by the OSF at that time.

1.10.2 Comandos and UNIX International

More recently, the UI consortium announced the ATLAS framework, which intends to provide a coherent computing environment across a network of heterogeneous machines. From the architectural point of view, this framework is similar to that proposed by the OSF. Figure 1.4 describes a possible scenario for introducing an object-oriented application service based on Comandos within the ATLAS framework.

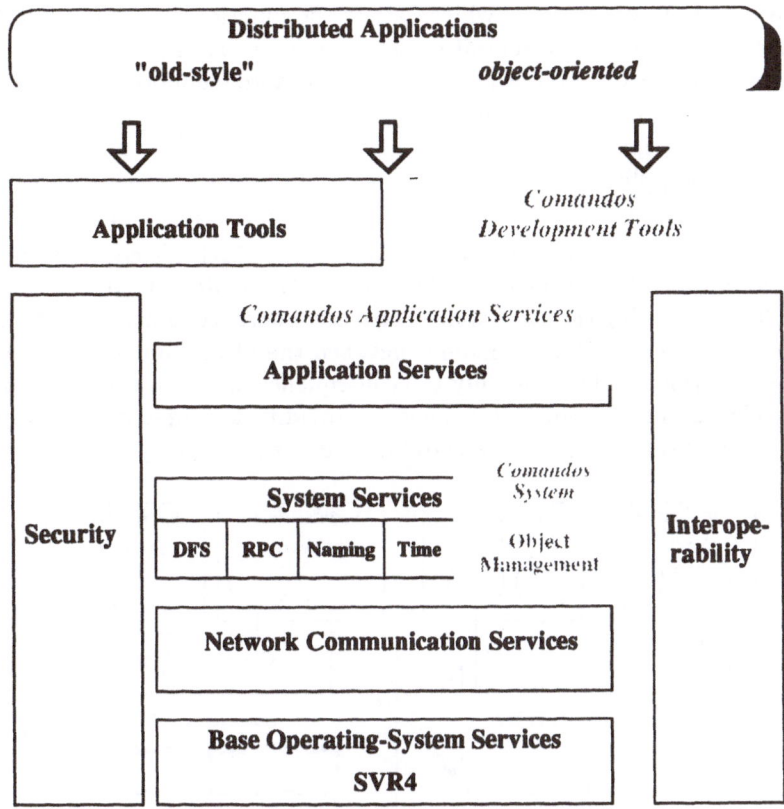

Fig. 1.4. A Comandos platform within an ATLAS environment.

1.10.3 Comandos and the Object Management Group

The OMG is an international consortium, created in 1990, which has as its primary objective the promotion of object-oriented technology throughout the Information Technology (IT) industry.

The OMG has published an Object Management Architecture (OMA) which describes the basic components of a distributed object-oriented environment and their relationships [Soley 1990]. The basic components of the OMA include:

- A core Object Model, with which each component should comply. The Comandos object model is fully compliant with the current definition of the core object model.
- An Object Request Broker (ORB) conforming to the OMG's Common Object Request Broker Architecture (CORBA) [DEC et al. 1991], which is the primary message delivery vehicle in an object-oriented distributed environment; it provides the mechanisms by which objects transparently make and receive requests and responses.

- A set of Object Services which extend the functionality of the ORB. Basic services include a repository for type information, support for object creation and deletion, a persistent object store, support for transactions and protection mechanisms.
- A set of design tools and common facilities for the development of object-oriented applications.

Although developed prior to the creation of the OMG, it should be noted that the Comandos architecture is very close to the OMG reference architecture, as shown in Fig. 1.5. This figure depicts the OMG architecture and the Comandos architecture using the same style. The main difference comes from the higher level of integration within Comandos between the ORB function and some of the object services. This is mainly the consequence of the integrated approach followed in Comandos, which was aimed at providing a complete object-oriented development environment, while OMG is focusing more on system integration.

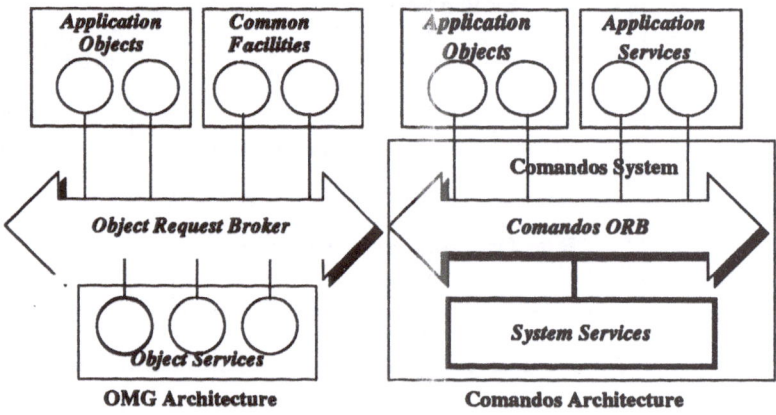

Fig. 1.5. OMG architecture versus Comandos architecture.

When the OMG issued a request for proposals for the ORB technology, one of the Comandos partners submitted a proposal based on the results of the Comandos project [Balter and Vandome 1991]. This technology was not, however, accepted by the OMG due to the lack of separation between the ORB and object services in the Comandos-based proposal.

Later, when the OMG issued a request for information concerning technology for object services, two responses based on the experience of the Comandos project were made [Puech and Trabelsi 1992, Cahill 1992].

1.11 What is Comandos Added Value?

Comandos has conceptualised, designed and, most importantly, implemented a vendor-independent platform for distributed processing which includes management of long-lived data, programming language support and on-line administration.

To date, no such vendor independent infrastructure incorporating all of these facilities exists. OSI may be used as a basis for interconnection of equipment from various vendors, but not as a common platform for the numerous interacting applications required in the integrated electronic organisation. The availability of such an integrated platform, operating in an environment of heterogeneous machines, would be a significant advance from current exploitations of OSI.

UNIX is an accepted vendor-independent system interface. Extensions to UNIX, such as NFS and AFS distributed file systems, or the PCTE Object Management System, extend aspects of the UNIX interface to distributed environments. More recently, the OSF's DCE and UI's ATLAS framework both provide an overall architecture and a set of basic services for the construction of distributed applications in the UNIX world. However, none of these systems integrate all of the facilities which characterise the Comandos distributed object system and programming environment. Therefore a Comandos platform is an appropriate enhancement of a DCE or ATLAS environment.

The object-oriented approach has been adopted as a central feature in the Comandos project. Object-orientation is now recognised as a leading-edge technology by the IT industry through the promotional activities of the OMG. Currently Comandos technology goes beyond OMG recommendations and thus the technical achievements and experience of the Comandos project should be a valuable input to future OMG activities.

Introducing the Comandos platform for the development of distributed applications should significantly increase productivity and competitiveness. Most of the Comandos partners have already launched advanced development programs with the aim of transferring the results of the Comandos project into products.

1.12 Road-map of the Book

The book is divided into two parts. The first part provides a user's view of the Comandos platform. It is mainly targeted data processing managers, systems analysts, and application designers and programmers who have an interest in building distributed applications and services, as well as at the administrators of distributed systems. It presents the basic functionality offered by a Comandos platform and shows how it can be used to build and operate distributed applications. This part is structured as follows:

- Chapter 2 gives an overview of the Comandos platform. It outlines the basic abstractions provided by a Comandos platform, and emphasises the role of the linguistic support for the design of distributed applications. This chapter also describes the structure of a Comandos platform in more detail.

- Chapter 3 describes the functionality provided by the Comandos virtual machine.
- Chapter 4 deals with the supported programming languages, C++, Eiffel, and the Comandos object-oriented language, showing how the functionality of the platform is reflected in each language.
- Chapter 5 describes the development tools provided to application programmers.
- Chapter 6 presents an overview of the facilities for data management provided by the Comandos platform.
- Chapter 7 describes the management tools provided to system administrators for the operational control of a Comandos installation.
- Finally in this part, Chap. 8 illustrates the use of the Comandos platform in the implementation of an application dealing with the circulation of documents within an enterprise.

The second part of the book provides an implementor's view of the Comandos platform. It is primarily targeted at those who are interested in the Comandos technology.

- Chapter 9 describes the VMI and the internal components of the Comandos virtual machine.
- Chapter 10 presents the principles of the implementation of the Comandos virtual machine. The reference implementation on UNIX is described in detail. In addition, this chapter presents the principles of the implementations on top of the CHORUS and Mach micro-kernel architectures.
- Chapter 11 shows how an existing language can be supported above the virtual machine.
- Finally, Chap. 12 presents some conclusions concerning the Comandos approach.

In addition, a number of appendices provide complementary information:

- Appendix A shows a simple distributed application programmed using each of the languages currently supported in Comandos.
- Appendix B gives a list of available software components.
- Appendix C is a glossary of terms used throughout the project.
- Appendix D lists the various abbreviations used in this book.
- Appendix E gives a list of published papers and reports concerning aspects of the Comandos project.

Finally, the book concludes with a list of references for works cited in the text.

Part I

User's View of the Comandos Platform

2. Overview of the Comandos Platform

This chapter gives an overview of the functionality provided by the Comandos platform to both the developers of distributed applications and to the administrators of distributed systems.

The fundamental goal of Comandos was to make available a platform providing the functionality necessary for the construction of sophisticated distributed applications. Moreover, the platform was to be independent of the use of any specific programming language for the development of these distributed applications. The platform is therefore designed to allow a range of different application programming languages to be supported. Hence, while the Comandos model describes the support provided by the platform in an abstract way, it is important to realise that the interface to the platform used by an application developer is typically provided through one of the supported programming languages. The model seen by a programmer may differ from the model implemented by the platform. For example, a particular language may restrict the visibility of certain features of the platform or, alternatively, enhance the functionality of the basic platform by adding extra support in its run-time system. Of course, the programming model provided by the Comandos programming language directly reflects the model provided by the platform.

2.1 Basic Features

To support sophisticated distributed applications any language should provide:

- transparent access to distributed resources (including data) and services;
- transparent access to persistent data;
- concurrent execution;
- controlled sharing of resources;
- support for fault tolerance.

In the following sections, the approach taken to supporting each of these features in Comandos is presented. The way in which these features are provided in the programming languages which are currently supported is postponed to Chap. 4.

2.1.1 Transparent Access to Resources and Services

One of the main requirements on the Comandos platform is transparency, i.e. the provision of a coherent and uniform view of all the resources (including data) and services provided by the system. In Comandos, all resources and services are modelled as objects. Transparency implies that the virtual machine provided to the user hides the distribution of objects and processing, as well as the possible heterogeneity of the underlying hardware. In addition, the system should provide user mobility, i.e. the ability for a user to access objects independently of being logged on to a specific workstation.

Transparency has many aspects: access transparency, in which both local and remote objects are accessed in the same way; location transparency, in which the location of an object is not apparent from its name; execution transparency, in which the execution site of a program may be easily changed, possibly in a dynamic way; environment transparency, in which the same program has the same effect independently of the site on which it is executed; failure transparency, in which a partial failure may be bypassed, so allowing programs to be fault-tolerant; and finally performance transparency, in which the costs of remote access are not generally degraded over those of local access.

Comandos supports access, location, execution and environment transparency. Although full failure transparency is not currently, supported a transaction mechanism (c.f. Sect. 2.1.4) is provided which allows an application to ensure that the data which it is accessing remains consistent even if the execution of the application is interrupted by a failure. Comandos also supports full user mobility.

In some cases, transparency is not desirable, and some applications may elect to be aware of the distribution of the objects which they manipulate. For such cases, the system primitives which allow the management of object location are made visible to the application programmer.

Thus the Comandos model defines execution structures which allow distributed programs to be defined. This model provides the application designer with a multi-node multi-processor virtual machine, in which distribution is (normally) hidden.

The central execution mechanism of the Comandos platform is object *invocation*, i.e. the execution of a specified method of an object by a process executing at some node. If the object happens to be present in virtual memory at the node, e.g. as a consequence of a previous invocation, the invocation is performed locally. If the object is not present in local virtual memory, it may be present in virtual memory at some other node, again as a result of a previous invocation. In this case a *remote invocation* will be carried out. Finally, it may happen that no node currently has an image of the object in virtual memory. In that case, the object must be located in secondary storage and will be *mapped* (loaded) into virtual memory at some node where the invocation will then be carried out.

An important consideration in the design and implementation of the object invocation mechanism was the separation between the mechanisms and policy used when an object is not already mapped into virtual memory. The function of the mechanisms is to locate the object and to map it at a selected node. The *execution policy* is concerned with the selection of the node on which to map the object.

The policy for the selection of the execution node may be static or dynamic. An example of a static policy would be to always bring the object to the invoking node; another example would be to always perform the invocation on the node at which the object is stored. An example of a dynamic policy is load balancing where the execution node is selected according to an evaluation of the current load on the nodes in the distributed system. In addition, it must be possible to allow the programmer to specify the node at which the object should be mapped. By default the Comandos platform employs a dynamic policy based on load balancing with the possibility of allowing the programmer to override the load balancing mechanism by specifying the desired execution node. Other policies can however be supported.

Note that each object resides entirely on a single node (either mapped in virtual memory or stored in secondary storage); however it can migrate to another node, either temporarily when mapped at that node, or permanently according to some administration criteria. Comandos does not support fragmentation of individual objects. This design choice results directly from the granularity of individual objects (usually small) and from the general approach in which large compound structures can be built out of object components. In the Comandos model a complex compound object and its various object components may reside on different nodes.

2.1.2 Persistence

In conventional programming languages, the lifetimes of most entities are bounded by the duration of the program run. External files are usually the sole exception, with the consequence that if a particular entity is to survive a program run, it must be inserted into a file (possibly requiring a change in its representation) and explicitly retrieved (and possibly rebuilt) at a later time. The disadvantages of this approach are well known [Atkinson et al. 1983]. In systems providing persistence, programmers can manipulate persistent entities without explicit I/O management.

In Comandos, persistence is defined via the reachability property of objects – that is, every object reachable by recursively enumerating the constituent objects from some specified set of root objects is guaranteed by the system to persist. Thus, there can be no dangling references to objects.

When not in use persistent objects are stored on secondary storage. When an attempt to access such an object is made, the object is automatically fetched from storage by the system and made available in virtual memory at an appropriate node. Hence it is unnecessary for the programmer to write code either to explicitly fetch the object from storage or to convert between the possibly different secondary storage and virtual memory representations of the object. Likewise, when the object is no longer required, the system automatically returns the object to secondary storage – there is no need for the programmer to explicitly store the object.

When an object is retrieved from storage other related objects may be retrieved at the same time and in the same I/O operation so that they are available for use should they be required. Such a group of related objects is known as a *cluster*. Such pre-fetching of objects improves performance by reducing the number of mapping and I/O operations required when related objects are used together.

2.1.2.1 Garbage Collection. Virtual memory and secondary storage are finite resources and a mechanism is needed to allow the space occupied by objects which are no longer required to be reclaimed. Note however that an object cannot be simply deleted, since Comandos guarantees that an object will not be removed from the system until the object is no longer reachable from some persistent root. Hence, in general, a garbage collection mechanism is required which verifies that no references to an object exist anywhere in the system, before deleting that object.

Garbage collection poses problems which are compounded in a distributed system. The number of objects in a production Comandos installation could be at least an order of magnitude larger than that found in current typical single-user object-based (virtual memory) environments. It would also appear unreasonable to rely on a single global garbage collector which required the entire distributed system to halt while it executed. Such a collector might take a long time to run, and require large quantities of memory in which to execute. Although it may be possible in some Comandos installations to halt the entire distributed system for garbage collection (e.g. overnight), this is unlikely to be generally acceptable because, for example, it may require that processing at some nodes halts until the next (overnight/over weekend) garbage collection once their stores are full.

The combination of distribution and persistence thus pose a challenge for garbage collection. In practice, a two level approach has been adopted in Comandos using garbage collection techniques within virtual memory and ageing within secondary storage. The ageing mechanism attempts to identify objects which are not used frequently and move them to archive storage rather than deleting them from the system. It is expected that the overhead of maintaining usage statistics for objects will be far less than the overhead associated with tracing references to objects needed for garbage collection.

2.1.2.2 Secondary Storage. Conceptually secondary storage in Comandos can be viewed as being divided into a number of *containers*. Each container usually holds many objects. A container corresponds to a disk volume or disk partition.

In practice a single container may be replicated: that is, a container is a logical entity, implemented by one or more physical containers as proposed in Locus [Popek and Walker 1985].

Each container in turn consists of a number of *segments*. A segment is a contiguous storage unit, and represents an integral number of disk blocks. Different segments within the same container need not be the same size. The disk blocks in a particular segment are assumed to be contiguous.

Segments are used to store objects and clusters. A particular object may be stored using exactly one segment, or may be stored in a cluster with other objects within a single segment. The two concepts are distinguished because a segment is a unit of secondary storage whereas a cluster is a unit of object grouping.

A side effect of retrieving a particular object from storage is to retrieve its associated segment, and hence any objects with which it is clustered. Allocation of objects to segments by higher-level components of the architecture is on the basis of hints to the storage system.

Objects may be migrated within persistent storage (i.e. between segments and/or containers) for one of the following reasons:

- Access optimisation, e.g. taking account of observed usage patterns to reduce the number of remote invocations. This may involve the co-location of objects which have a high probability of being used together.
- Administrative considerations, e.g. regrouping of data in a single container to take into account a reorganisation such as the merging of two projects.
- Security or availability considerations, e.g. objects may be moved off of a node which is being brought down for maintenance or withdrawn from service.

2.1.3 Concurrency

An important design decision was how to relate objects to processes. Two possible solutions were available:

1. Associate processes with objects, i.e. define active objects, in which every object contains a fixed or variable number of processes. This solution was used in previous systems such as Argus [Liskov and Scheifler 1983] and Eden [Almes et al. 1985].
2. Separate objects from processes, i.e. define passive objects which can be operated on by independently defined processes. This is the solution adopted in Clouds [Dasgupta et al. 1988], Amoeba [Mullender 1985] and SOS [Shapiro et al. 1989].

The active object model is conceptually simpler, since a single abstraction encompasses the concepts of resource and process. On the other hand passive objects contain less context information than active objects. Therefore object creation, invocation and migration can be implemented more efficiently than for active objects. Moreover, since the classes of application that Comandos supports typically involve creating many (usually small) objects, and building large compound structures out of object components, the passive object model is more appropriate.

In Comandos, a *job* represents the processing (possibly in parallel) of objects and consists of one or more sequential threads of control, called *activities*. A job is created by an activity of another job to invoke a specified method on some object. A new job initially consists of a single activity.

The execution of an activity consists of nested invocations of methods on objects. Each invocation may take place on any node in the system. At each invocation, the referenced object is located and, if necessary, loaded into virtual memory at some node. A remote invocation takes place if the node selected for execution is different from the node on which the invocation was requested. The choice of the execution node is determined by the execution policy in force.

An activity may, at any time, create one or more parallel activities within the same job. Therefore the model provides two levels of concurrency: between activities belonging to the same job (i.e. related computations within the same application); and between activities running in different jobs (i.e. independent applications). Asynchronous invocation can be implemented by creating a new activity (or job) to invoke a designated object.

2.1.4 Atomicity

Atomic transactions [Bernstein et al. 1987] provide a means of ensuring the consistency of data in the presence of concurrency and partial failure. In particular, transactions classically guarantee certain properties – atomicity, serialisability, isolation and permanence – for operations carried out within the transaction. Atomicity implies that the effects of a transaction are all-or-nothing. Serialisability ensures that each transaction will transform the system state from one consistent state to another consistent state even in the presence of concurrent transactions. Isolation guarantees that incomplete transactions will not reveal partial results to each other. Finally, permanence guarantees that once a transaction completes successfully, its results will not subsequently be lost.

In fault tolerant distributed systems it is common sense that the all-or-nothing property of computations should be provided. For some applications consistency of data is also required. However, providing the all-or-nothing property of computations and ensuring the consistency of the affected data are, at least in principle, orthogonal to each other. Consequently, a general backward error recovery mechanism which makes no assumptions about the synchronisation mechanism used should be provided. This enables the use of different and even no synchronisation mechanisms in the future without having to change the underlying recovery mechanism. As a first step in this direction Comandos provides a *generalised transaction mechanism*. This mechanism is based on a recovery layer which is able to manage dependencies between transactions. Thus, in contrast to traditional transactional systems, ensuring serialisability of transactions becomes possible without having to enforce the restrictive failure isolation property of transactions.

The Comandos transaction model (c.f. Chap. 3) is derived from that provided in the RelaX project [Schumann et al. 1989]. RelaX provides generalised distributed transactions extending the classical transaction model by supporting optional use of uncommitted data, extended nesting allowing the differentiation between recovery and synchronisation levels, and the separation of transaction commitment from completion. A transaction consists of a set of operations on objects which has the properties of atomicity, serialisability and permanence.

Since transaction mechanisms involve a certain overhead, these mechanisms apply only to a subset of all objects known as *atomic objects*. An object may be created as an atomic object or a non-atomic object can be promoted to be an atomic object (the reverse not being permitted). Hence the transaction properties are only guaranteed for operations on atomic objects carried out within a transaction. A transaction is entirely contained within a single job.

2.1.5 Sharing

There is no explicit communication through message passing between activities. Communication and synchronisation between activities (within the same job, or belonging to different jobs) is achieved through the sharing of objects.

Object sharing may be controlled in a number of ways, depending on consistency requirements for concurrent usage. Atomic objects are guaranteed to remain consistent despite concurrent access and partial failure of the underlying system.

Comandos makes no guarantees for the consistency of objects which are not atomic. Other objects (i.e. their class code) can maintain their own consistency in the presence of concurrent accesses by making use of primitive concurrency control mechanisms – such as semaphores – provided by the platform.

2.2 Interworking Between Languages

The functionality of the Comandos platform is provided to the application developer primarily through one of a set of supported programming languages. Moreover, since Comandos supports multiple object-oriented programming languages, a given distributed application can potentially be constructed from components written in different languages. Allowing such interworking between languages requires support to be provided in the platform.

Programmer productivity and system reliability are improved by the adoption of modern language designs. In particular, it has been found that languages which provide some kind of type system provide these benefits by early detection of errors and protection against data misuse. For these reasons all objects in Comandos can be typed. Comandos supports a variety of languages, including initially C++, Eiffel and the Comandos language, taking advantage of the type systems already in place in these languages, and yet providing freedom in the interworking of objects created using different languages.

Unfortunately, each of these languages provides its own individual type system, and varies in the degree of rigour with which it enforces the typing of values. Hence programs written in different languages need to access each other's values while each program needs to ensure the type security of its own operations. A central issue in supporting cross-language invocations is to achieve *type compatibility* so that entities – objects and methods – defined in one language can be accessed from another language in a consistent (i.e. type safe) way.

To achieve inter-language inter-operability, the primary concern is to allow an invocation on an object written in language A by an application written in language B. (Allowing the instantiation of objects of a class written in language A by an application written in a language B has not been considered). Two levels of inter-operability may be considered [Wileden et al. 1991]:

- The *Representation-level inter-operability* (RLI) defines type compatibility in terms of structure (representation), and provides a means for overcoming differences in the way that different programming languages (or machines) implement basic types. This is achieved by use of conversion procedures.
- The *Specification-level inter-operability* (SLI) defines type compatibility in terms of properties (specification), hiding representation differences for abstract types as well as basic types. This approach is based on the use of a common representation of types. SLI extends RLI in a way which provides a significant advantage, as it facilitates integration of cooperating programs by allowing them to communicate directly in terms of high-level abstract data types. Moreover, it prevents the misuse of shared data objects (i.e. the violation of the intended abstractions).

As a result of the object-oriented approach adopted in Comandos, inter-operability between languages was considered at the specification level. However, it should be noted that language inter-operability in a typed environment is a very complex issue, which goes far beyond the scope of the project. Therefore, a pragmatic but evolutionary approach was adopted in the time-frame of the project, which provided a simple but partial solution in a first step. This solution, described in Sect. 2.2.1, is not transparent and requires additional information to be provided by the application designer.

In parallel, an advanced approach is being investigated, which intends to provide a complete automated solution. This is based on the definition of a *canonical type model* to which the type systems of various languages can be mapped. This solution is described in Sect. 2.2.2.

2.2.1 Manual Approach

This section describes the current approach to supporting cross-language invocations between the supported languages. In this approach, the application programmer is aware of the existence of different type systems, and must provide additional information to allow cross-language invocations. Therefore this solution is not transparent. The approach can be described as follows:

- A common notation is adopted to describe language-specific types. This notation can be viewed as an interface definition language (IDL), which allows object interfaces to be defined in a standard way. The notation currently used is a subset of the OMG IDL [DEC et al. 1991].
- The programmer is required to (manually) define the interface of each type using the IDL. It is not necessary to provide such a definition for all types defined within a given language. Only types to be used in cross-language invocations have to be described using the IDL. Moreover, the definition can be restricted to the actual methods to be used in cross-language invocations. Types (or methods) which are not described using the IDL are not allowed in cross-language invocations.
- Given a description of a type in the IDL, a procedure (known as a *stub*) to convert each invocation from its format in a given calling language to that required by the target language can be generated
- At run time, cross-language invocations make use of these stubs to translate the parameters and results of each invocation as necessary.

This solution, meets SLI requirements for a subset of objects and methods, as well as RLI requirements for a subset of parameter types.

2.2.2 Automated Approach

A better and more transparent solution to the problem of translating invocations between the formats of different languages is based on the use of a canonical model of types to which the type systems of various languages can be mapped. Comandos provides such a model based on the theoretical work on type systems carried out by Cardelli [Cardelli and Wegner 1985] and others. The Comandos type model includes the ability to represent basic types (such as integer and string); constructed data types (including vectors, records, and variants); function types; existentially and universally quantified types; parametrised types; pointer types; dynamic types; and a variety of other types for particular kinds of objects such as exceptions. This set of types is described in Chap. 5.

Given a mapping from the type system of each supported language to the canonical type model, it is possible to generate the necessary stubs for cross language invocations without requiring the programmer to provide a description of the interface in a standard language. In effect the standardised description of the interface can be implicitly derived from the description of the language's type model.

2.3 Data Management

Comandos applications may involve large collections of objects of the same type. Hence, Comandos provides services for the management of such collections including associative access to objects belonging to collections. The Comandos data management model specifies the data modelling constructs supported in terms of the kinds of collections available, the operations on these collections and the kinds of structural constraints among collections that may be specified.

The overall aim of the data model is to provide a set of constructs that enables application programmers to model real world entities and the relationships between them with relative ease. The Comandos data management model, the Binary Relational Object-Oriented Model (BROOM), provides four kinds of collections which might be considered to be special forms of sets, sequences, bags and binary relations. These collections are provided through a number of generic bulk type constructors.

The inclusion of binary relations as collections is novel and therefore requires some comment. In recent years, the various forms of entity-relationship data models have been popular for data modelling. The basis of this approach is to model the real world in terms of entity sets and relationships between entity sets. Support for the direct representation of relationships is extremely beneficial in data modelling. A deficiency of the object-oriented approach is its inability to do just that. Therefore, the usual notions of the object-oriented data model have been extended to include direct representation of relationships between entity sets: this is achieved by introducing the binary relation as a kind of collection in the Comandos data model.

A further limitation of many existing object-oriented data models is that they allow only one collection of objects of a particular type. Thus, associated with a type there may be a collection which comprises the set of all current instances of that type. The notions of typing and classification have been separated. This permits several collections of objects to be associated with a given type. Collections are related by means of a classification structure. This approach provides a much more flexible modelling capability.

The classification structure is represented by means of structural constraints among collections. For example, an IS-A relationship between two set collections C and D says that every object that belongs to collection C must also belong to D and this may be represented by a subset constraint between C and D. Other forms of structural constraints supported correspond to partitions of collections, the intersection of collections, and cardinality and dependence constraints on relations.

2.4 Security

Maintaining the security of a computer system entails maintaining the integrity, availability and confidentiality of its assets (resources).

- *Integrity* means that the assets of a computer system can be modified only by authorised parties. In this context, modification includes changing, deleting, creating or changing the status of objects.
- *Availability* means that assets are available to authorised parties. An authorised party should not be prevented from accessing those objects to which it has legitimate access.

- *Confidentiality* means that the assets of a computing system are accessible only to authorised parties. The type of access includes reading, viewing, printing, or even simply knowing of the existence of an object.

The Comandos platform provides distributed applications running in the Comandos environment with facilities to keep objects secure. The ultimate goal of security in an object-oriented environment is to enforce the constraint that an object can always be manipulated only by authorised, authenticated and secure invocations of type-specific operations on that object. The mechanisms provided towards achieving this goal in Comandos are:

- Secure transmission of the arguments and results of each (remote) object invocation, by the use of encryption techniques to prevent play-back, copying or modification of messages;
- Authorisation checks on object invocations, achieved through the use of access control lists (ACLs), which are associated with each protected object. In this object-oriented framework, the access-rights can specify the set of operations that a user (or a group of users) can perform on the object.
- Isolation of objects at run time so as to protect against damage to an object by code of another object executing in the same address space.

In addition an audit service is provided which allows the system administrator to detect intrusion into or misuse of the system.

Note that while no authentication service is currently provided, it is expected that an authentication service such as Kerberos [Steiner et al. 1988] could easily be integrated with the Comandos platform.

These facilities are implemented by low-level mechanisms integrated within the virtual machine. High-level management tools for the overall administration of the security policies and procedures (e.g. user and group management, etc.) are also provided.

2.5 Management View of the Platform

Most approaches to organisational [Grochla 1982] and information systems design [Lockemann and Mayr 1986] are oriented towards a life-cycle model and a project organisation with phases for action. These approaches put most emphasis on the early stages of the life-cycle. However, these approaches tend to neglect the use and operation of an information system, or an organisation after implementation. This is certainly not the appropriate way of viewing an information system when one is concerned with its continuing performance over a long period of operation. Generally, a system is built within several weeks or months and used for many years.

The assumptions made about an information system and its environment during its implementation cannot be considered valid throughout its operation. For instance, the throughput can vary with the season or with market trends;

new products may emerge, and the size of the system may change. New technology is emerging at a rapid rate causing changes to the way a system is being built. Communication and networking are becoming more important, causing systems to grow dynamically and to become far more complex.

Hence, for the design and operation of a distributed system a new method should be followed. This calls for design and management approaches that explicitly surrender the assumptions underlying a phase-oriented approach [Floyd 1981]. Comandos thus adopts an evolutionary approach to system management.

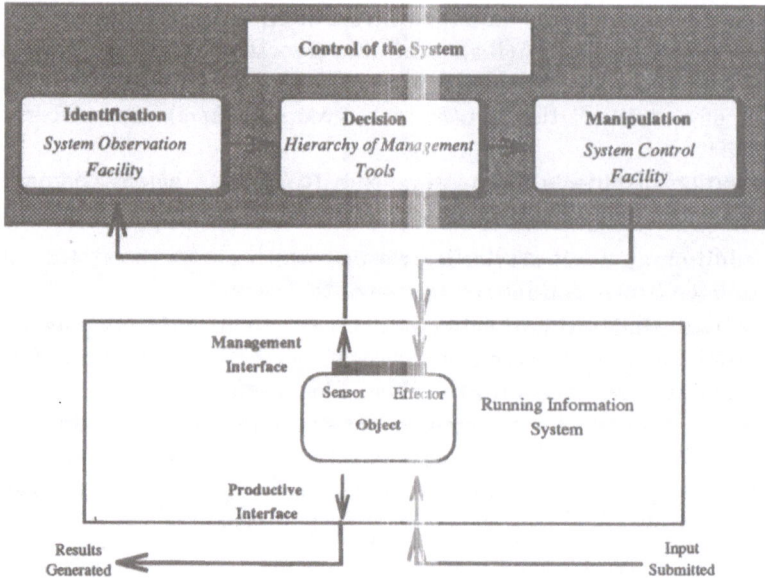

Fig. 2.1. Adaptive framework for system design and management.

The adaptive framework for the management of Comandos systems, described in Fig. 2.1, can be mapped onto three generic types of activities. *Observation activities* are concerned with collecting information while the system is running. The *decision activities* support the actual design, configuration and security management decisions. They are carried out by a human designer or manager using an interactive administration and management tool, specific to the task. The *control activities* realise a design or configuration decision, i.e. implement a change. These activities are supported in Comandos by a set of cooperating management tools.

2.6 Interworking with UNIX

One of the basic objectives of Comandos was to provide coexistence between the Comandos platform and the UNIX world. Interworking with other environments (e.g. OS/2 or MS-DOS), although recognised as being equally important, was not considered in the framework of the project. Interworking between Comandos applications and UNIX facilities and applications can be considered from two complementary points of view:

- Access to Comandos facilities from UNIX applications. This allows applications running on top of UNIX to take advantage of the support for persistence and distribution provided by Comandos.
  This is achieved by supplying an appropriate library on top of UNIX which provides access to the primitives of the Comandos VMI.
- Use of pre-existing UNIX facilities and applications in the implementation and operational control of Comandos applications. This is typically the case for:

  - input/output using the standard UNIX library;
  - user interface implementation based on the X Window System and OSF/Motif;
  - system management using pre-existing packages developed on top of UNIX.

The main problem to be solved in this case is to allow the UNIX application to make use of standard UNIX system calls. This can be solved in one of two possible ways depending on whether the Comandos platform is implemented as a software layer on top of UNIX or as a sub-system on top of a micro-kernel which also provides a UNIX sub-system.

In the first case, access to UNIX applications is theoretically simple to achieve as long as the Comandos execution structures (jobs and activities) are mapped directly on to UNIX processes. However, care must be taken with details such as the memory usage of the application.

In the second case, one of two approaches can be followed:

  - implement a special UNIX process which provides the interface between Comandos and the required UNIX facilities, or
  - provide the required UNIX facilities on top of Comandos.

For obvious reasons, the first solution has been adopted in Comandos.

2.7 Structure of the Platform

In this section the structure of the Comandos platform is described. A Comandos platform (c.f. Fig. 2.2) is composed of two basic components: a Comandos system, and a set of application services and management tools.

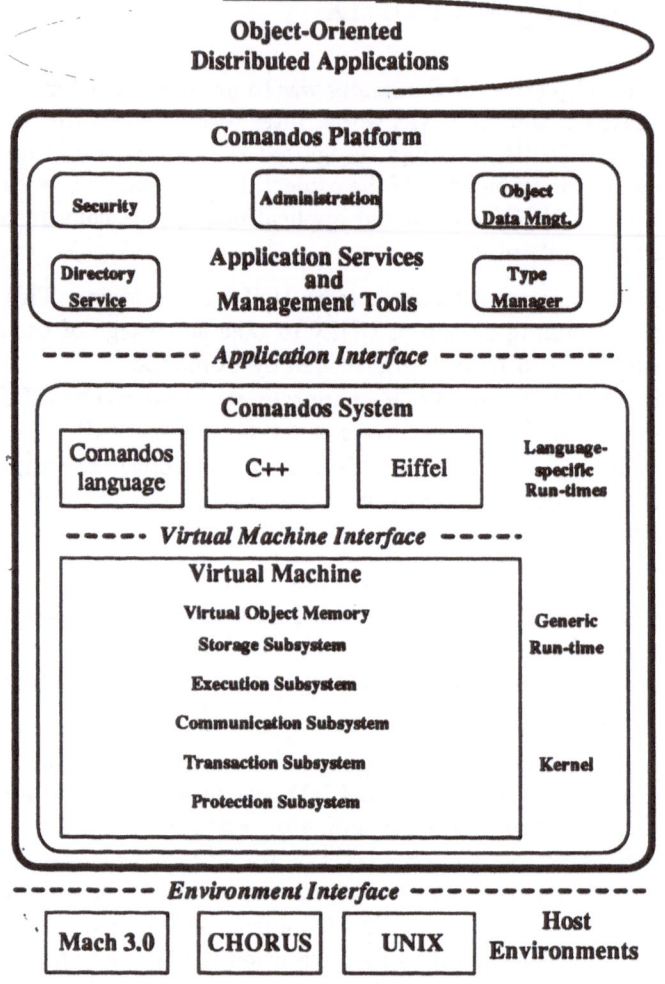

Fig. 2.2. The Comandos platform.

2.7.1 The Comandos System

As described in Chap. 1, a Comandos system is composed of the virtual machine and a set of language-specific run-time systems.

The Comandos virtual machine implements transparent distribution and persistence, concurrency, transactions, sharing and basic security services as described in this chapter.

The virtual machine consists of a number of functional components, which must be present in every Comandos implementation. These components are the:

- *Virtual Object Memory* which is responsible for implementing transparent access to distributed persistent objects and for all aspects of object management including object creation, low-level object naming, object location, remote invocation and the mapping and unmapping of objects to and from secondary storage.

- *Execution Sub-system* implements distributed concurrent processing and is responsible for job and activity creation and management, load balancing and low-level synchronisation mechanisms.
- *Storage Sub-system* provides distributed persistent storage.
- *Transaction Sub-system* implements the mechanisms necessary to support atomic objects and the transaction model.
- *Protection Sub-system* provides low-level security services including authorisation, secure transmission and generation of audit data.
- *Communication Sub-system* provides network communication services.

The virtual machine is composed of the kernel and the GRT. The GRT implements that functionality which can run in user mode while the kernel implements the functionality which, for security reasons, must run in protected mode – for example in a server or, where possible, in kernel mode.

The VMI provided by the GRT allows the functionality of the virtual machine to be easily adapted for any (object-oriented) programming language. Above the virtual machine a language-specific run-time provides the necessary mechanisms to adapt the functionality of the virtual machine to a particular language and to support additional features which are specific to that language. Each language-specific run-time provides extensions to the basic Comandos virtual machine. A given Comandos system must provide at least one language-specific run-time in order to support objects written in the corresponding language. However several language-specific run-times can coexist in the same system.

2.7.2 Application Services and Management Tools

The services and tools provided by the platform fall broadly into two categories: application services which are used in the development of distributed applications or which are required at run-time by a range of distributed applications, and management tools which are provided to assist in the management and administration of the system. Application services provided within the project include:

- *Development tools* to aid application designers in the design, construction and debugging of distributed applications. These development facilities include compilation tools, a distributed debugger and tools for the development of user interfaces.
- A *Type Manager* (TpM) is a repository of type information, which can be used by the languages available on a Comandos platform. During the process of application development or configuration, types can be created and registered in the TpM. Type information they may be read for the purpose of semantic checking either at build time or at run time. The

TpM's clients are thus compilers, preprocessors, language run-time systems and query processors. The TpM provides the basis for supporting the automated approach to interworking between languages described in Sect. 2.2.2.

- An *Object Data Management Service* (ODMS) for the management of and associative access to collections of objects. The ODMS is the component of the platform that performs database-like functions. The ODMS basically implements the BROOM data model facilities (c.f. Sect. 2.3). To achieve this goal the ODMS provides various forms of representation of collections, built-in operations on the pre-defined bulk data types of BROOM, and implements mechanisms for the efficient retrieval of objects from collections (e.g. indexing, part-of and inheritance hierarchy scanning, etc.) and optimisation of queries on collections.

The management tools provided include:

- A *Distributed Directory Service* (DDS) for symbolic object naming. The DDS is an implementation of the ISO/CCITT X.500-IS9594 standards integrated into the Comandos platform.
- A distributed *System Observation Facility* (SOF) which supports the observation activities of the adaptive framework for system management described in Sect. 2.5. Information collected by the SOF is passed to high-level management tools for processing (see below).
- A distributed *System Control Facility* (SCF) which supports the control activities of the adaptive framework for system management. Administration and reconfiguration decisions stemming from high-level management tools can be implemented using the SCF.
- A *system configuration and administration tool* which is bound to the SOF and SCF. System administrators are provided with graphical output showing statistics concerning system behaviour and can initiate configuration changes.
- *Security tools* for *risk management* and *analysis of audit data* generated by the virtual machine. Risks with respect to the integrity, availability, and confidentiality of information can be estimated on the basis of data provided by system observation and auditing as well as by simulation of system failures.
- A *tool for the design of a distributed office system*. Organisational designers are supported in the logical design of business processes and of the distributed information system used to execute these processes.

3. The Comandos Virtual Machine

This chapter describes, in detail, the functionality of the Comandos virtual machine and, in particular, how objects, distributed processing, transactions and security are supported by the virtual machine.

3.1 Object Model

Different object-oriented languages typically provide different object models. For example, some languages may allow access to an object only through an operation defined in the object's class. Other languages may allow the instance data of an object, or some designated subset of the instance data, to be read or written directly. Moreover, different languages typically use different methods of representing objects at run time, different forms of object references and different invocation mechanisms. An important goal of Comandos was to allow each supported language to retain its own object model and, as far as possible, its own execution structures while being extended to support the features of the Comandos model. Hence, the virtual machine makes no assumptions about the internal format or content of a language object, the format of object references used to refer to such an object in virtual memory or the way in which an object is accessed.

3.1.1 Comandos Objects

The virtual machine provides fine-grained passive data objects (which will be referred to, in this and subsequent sections, as *Comandos objects* or, simply, as objects). Comandos objects may be persistent and/or remotely accessible.

Objects, which, from the virtual machine's point of view, are simply contiguous blocks of memory, are used to contain and enclose language-level objects (referred to as *language objects*) containing both direct data and language-specific object references, and to which a supported language, through its language-specific run-time, may bind class code. Language-level object models can thus be built.

Supported languages can use language-specific forms of object references, such as virtual addresses or tagged pointers, to refer to objects mapped in the same address space.

The protocol between the virtual machine and language-specific run-time allows the virtual machine to perform a number of operations on objects, such as location of object references stored in a language object – which require language or object specific information. This protocol requires that each object must have a minimum set of methods, one for each basic operation which the virtual machine may request. The set of up-calls which must be supported by each object is described by the VMI and depends on whether the object is to be persistent or remotely accessible or both.

3.1.2 Global Names

A *global name* is globally unique, location independent name which can be used to refer to an object from anywhere in the distributed system. Unlike language-specific references, global names may be passed in remote invocations and stored on secondary storage along with the object which contains the name.

Each Comandos object is assigned a global name (when first required) which can be used to refer to and access the object when it is not mapped into the current address space.

When an object is stored on secondary storage, language-specific references stored within the object are translated to global names and translated back to the appropriate language-specific reference when the object is subsequently mapped in some address space. The translation is carried out by the virtual machine in cooperation with the language-specific run-time.

3.1.3 Object Invocation

Object invocation is the central feature of the Comandos execution model encompassing transparent handling of persistence, distribution and sharing.

Accesses to objects which are mapped locally are performed at language-specific run-time level. However, attempts to access objects which are not mapped in the current address space – *object faults* – must be trapped by the language-specific run-time and reported to the virtual machine.

At the virtual machine level, an activity can access any object in the address space in which it is currently executing either by directly reading and writing the object's instance data or by invoking any operation from the object's class. In effect, the virtual machine allows an activity unrestricted access to any object mapped into its current address space. A language may impose restrictions on the way in which a particular object can be accessed, as described earlier, however the virtual machine includes no mechanisms to allow a language to enforce these restrictions. Such mechanisms are not normally required since these restrictions are usually enforced at compile time.

An activity may access an object mapped in an address space other than its current address space only by invoking some operation from the object's class on the object i.e. the virtual machine provides no (other) mechanism to allow the instance data of an object mapped in another address space to be read or written. If the language allows direct access to the instance data of an object then such accesses must be translated to invocations at the virtual machine level.

Hence, in response to an object fault, the virtual machine either arranges to map the object into the current address space, or to carry-out an invocation on the object as required.

3.2 Security Model

This section introduces the entities relevant to the security model and the different levels of isolation, authorisation, secure transmission and audit supported by the platform.

3.2.1 Security Domains, Users and Groups

A *security domain* corresponds to one or more machines having a common security policy. Each security domain has a *security administrator* who is responsible for security functions.

A Comandos *user* is defined within a security domain. Each object is owned by a single user which may change over the lifetime of the object. Each job executes on behalf of a user. A job has the same access rights as the user on whose behalf it is running and is thus allowed to access only objects for which the user has the appropriate access rights.

A *group* is simply a set of individual users and/or other groups. Access rights may be specified for individual users or for groups.

3.2.2 Isolation

Protection of objects against damage by the code of another object executing in the same address space is achieved by allowing each user to use different *extents* to segregate those of the user's objects whose code may be untrustworthy from other objects and by ensuring that objects of different extents are always mapped in different address spaces.

In order to protect objects against faulty or malicious code of other objects which are being used by the same job, each object could be isolated within a separate address space and each object invocation required to cross a hardware enforced protection boundary. On conventional machines, and using fine-grained objects, this would lead to extremely poor performance, and hence objects must be grouped together such that not every invocation must cross a protection boundary. Objects which are placed together will not be (hardware) protected from one another: they may perhaps be software protected from one another, but this will obviously only be a discretionary protection and may be flouted.

Thus objects within the same grouping must *trust* one another not to (accidently or maliciously) damage their respective instance data and code.

Trust is a relation between an object and a set of classes. An object trusts its own class (and superclasses) but may be prepared to trust yet others. An extent is defined as a set of objects, with a common owner, which all mutually trust their respective classes. Thus an extent corresponds to a grouping of objects as described above. The objects to be grouped into the same extent is determined by the owner of the extent and the objects.

The objects existing in a Comandos system are divided into a set of non-overlapping extents where every object belongs to exactly one extent. Any object may be moved between two extents in a controlled manner, if the owners of the two extents agree. At any time some of the objects belonging to an extent may be stored in secondary storage while others may be mapped into virtual memory at various nodes.

A *context* is a dynamically varying collection of objects located at the same node (i.e a context is an abstraction of a virtual address space). Each context provides an addressing window on the global object space. A context may contain objects from one extent **only**. There may be only one context for a given extent at any given node. All objects belonging to an extent that are in use at a node are mapped into the single context for that extent at the node. This context is shared by all jobs using those objects.

If an activity invokes an object in a different extent from its current extent, i.e. a *cross-extent* invocation, a *cross-context invocation* is required to access the object.

New contexts can be associated with a given job in two cases: when an activity of the job invokes an operation on an object in a different extent or on an object at a different node. Both in turn lead to the concept of *diffusion*, in which a job subsumes additional contexts. The set of contexts and nodes used by a job can therefore grow dynamically. The set of contexts currently used by a job constitute its distributed virtual address space.

3.2.3 Authorisation

Authorisation in Comandos is based on the use of ACLs for designated objects. When authorisation is enabled, mandatory access checking is enforced on each cross-extent invocation. Not all objects need have associated ACLs, however, an object cannot be the target of a cross-extent call unless it has an ACL. It is expected that only a limited number of objects are visible from outside of any particular extent. These objects act as gateways to the extent.

Within an extent objects are assumed to have a relation of mutual trust. Access is thus by default unprotected. Of course, if two objects belong to the same extent and are mapped into the same context, one of them could circumvent any access control check by directly accessing the other object. However, as objects are only mapped together under the assumption that their class code is mutually trustable, this kind of unauthorised access is excluded by definition:

the class code is believed to operate correctly and is, per se, believed to access only objects to which it has a right. Thus accesses between objects in the same extent are not (necessarily) subject to authorisation checks so that an object's ACL is only mandatorily checked on a cross-extent invocation.

3.2.4 Security Levels

Every computer system has a *security level*, which reflects the degree to which each of the three security goals (c.f. Chap. 2) is met. The Comandos virtual machine supports a set of different security levels where for each individual security level, there is a corresponding combination of enabled security services. Lower values of security level imply a lower degree of security with fewer enabled services. The security level for each domain is determined by its administrator from the set of security levels supported by the virtual machine.

While all objects must belong to some extent and objects of different extents are always segregated at run time, different levels of authorisation, audit, and secure data exchange are supported. The specification of a level for each of these three services describes the security level of the distributed system.

3.2.4.1 Authorisation. The authorisation service protects against unauthorised access to an object. ACLs are used to specify which users (and/or groups) have the right to access each object. Three levels of authorisation can be supported by a Comandos system:

- 0: no authorisation control;
- 1: ACLs specify either total access or no access for each user or group;
- 2: operation based ACLs which specify the set of methods on the object which each user or group is allowed to invoke.

3.2.4.2 Audit. The virtual machine provides a *preselection* facility to turn on and off auditing and, more generally, to define which events should be audited. This is used to reduce the amount of audit data produced. Thus, the preselection facility can be used to restrict auditing to certain critical events, or to highly privileged users, but refrain from auditing normal users.

Many levels of audit are possible depending on the events which are to be audited. The security administrator selects the appropriate level of auditing via the preselection facility by selecting the events to be audited. Each type of event can be audited in one of three different ways: not at all, failed attempts only, all events of that type. A complete list of events which can be audited is given in Chap. 9.

Note that, while the generation and reporting of audit data is part of the virtual machine, a tool for the analysis of audit data is also provided as part of the platform (c.f. Chap. 7).

3.2.4.3 Secure Transmission. Secure transmission of data must be provided to guarantee the confidentiality and integrity of data in transit between the nodes of the system. The secure transmission service also guarantees that transmitted data is actually delivered. Four levels of security for data exchange are supported by Comandos:

- 0: clear transmission;
- 1: integrity guaranteed, i.e. protection against modification;
- 2: confidentiality guaranteed, i.e. protection against disclosure;
- 3: integrity and confidentiality both guaranteed.

3.3 Execution Model

The Comandos execution model describes both how transparent access to distributed and persistent objects and concurrent processing is achieved in Comandos. The execution model is based on jobs and activities which are the units of distributed processing of objects. Recall that an activity is a sequence of synchronous invocations on one or more objects possibly on different nodes and that a job is a set of one or more activities.

3.3.1 Job and Activity Operation

When a job is created it initially has a single activity, which starts its existence by invoking a specified operation on a specified object. Processing within an activity consists of synchronous invocations on objects (as well as direct reads and writes of the instance data of objects mapped into its current context). The initial activity may (recursively) create other activities. An activity terminates when processing of its initial operation is completed or when it is explicitly terminated. The job terminates when all of its activities, the initial activity and any other activities subsequently started within the job, terminate.

Activities within a single job communicate through shared objects. Communication between different jobs also takes place through shared objects.

When an activity invokes an operation on an object a number of different possible courses of action are possible depending on the extent in which the activity is already executing, the extent to which the target object belongs and whether or not the object is already mapped.

In the simplest case, the object belongs to the extent in which the activity is executing and is already mapped into the context where the activity is executing. This may arise either because the object is already being, or has recently been, accessed by some activity, or, perhaps because it is clustered with an object that has already been used by some activity. In any case, the attempted access can usually proceed immediately without the intervention of the virtual machine i.e. at language-specific run-time level. In practice this is likely to be the most common case.

Another possibility is that the object belongs to a different extent from that in which the activity is already executing but is already mapped at the current node (although, necessarily, in a different context). In this case the activity must perform a cross-context invocation in order to access the object. The cross-context invocation is to the single context representing the extent at the node. Such an invocation may result in the activity (and its job) diffusing to the new context if the context has not already been used by that activity (or any other activity belonging to the same job).

A further possibility is that the object is mapped at a remote node. In this case the activity must perform a remote invocation in order to access the object. The invocation is to the single context representing the extent at the remote node.

The final possibility is that the required object is not mapped at any node. In this case the object must be retrieved from secondary storage and mapped into some context at some node. The choice of node is determined by the execution policy in force (load balancing is the default policy) and the choice of context is dependent on the extent to which the object belongs. If there is no context for the target extent at the chosen node then a new context will be created for the extent, otherwise, the object will be mapped into the existing context for its extent at the chosen node.

When processing is transferred to a different context it is carried out exactly as in the original context and in particular it may subsequently be necessary to diffuse to yet another context, or even to transfer control to a previously visited context. In any case, once the operation is complete, the results will be returned to the original context where processing will then continue as before.

In general the latest version of any object must be used. An activity which attempts to invoke an operation on any object already in use must nevertheless have a consistent view of that object. Conceptually this is achieved as follows. When the target object is not mapped into the current context, the activity attempts to retrieve it from secondary storage. Every time a container receives a request to make some object available to an activity, it must first check to see if a copy of the object is already mapped into some context. If this is the case then rather than retrieving a new copy of the object from secondary storage, the activity is informed of the location of the mapped version of the object.

3.3.2 Job and Activity Control

The operations available to control each job and activity provide the ability to suspend and resume its execution; to terminate its execution before the initial invocation has completed and to query its current state. In addition, an operation to allow an activity to wait for the termination of another activity of the same job is also provided.

A job or activity may be in one of three possible states, **active**, **suspended** and **terminated**. An **active** activity is executing at some node of the system, performing object invocations. When an activity is **suspended** it is not eligible for execution until it is explicitly resumed. Activities are explicitly suspended and resumed by invocation of the corresponding primitives. An activity may suspend and resume another activity belonging to the same or to a different job, subject of course, to protection constraints. A job is `active` if any of its constituent activities is active and is suspended if all of its constituent activities are suspended.

3.4 Transaction Model

The transaction model describes how atomic transactions are provided in Comandos. As described in Chap. 2 the Comandos transaction model supports generalised transactions which have the properties of atomicity, permanence and serialisability.

In Comandos a transaction is started by specifying an operation on an object to be carried out as a transaction. In the course of this operation the transaction can then invoke operations on other objects which can be mapped at different nodes in the system. Consequently, transactions may span multiple nodes. Transactions may access atomic and non-atomic objects. Non-atomic objects may be accessed both inside and outside of transactions. They have no transactional properties, so that no assurances are made regarding the consistency of concurrent accesses or recoverability of updates to such objects within transactions. Atomic objects can only be updated inside transactions. However, they may also be read outside of a transaction, but with the risk of retrieving an inconsistent view of their values. Attempts to modify an atomic object outside of a transaction will lead to an exception.

A transaction terminates successfully when the operation invocation for which it was created completes normally. A transaction may be aborted when some undesired situation occurs. In this case the transaction leaves no effect in the system. The abort of a transaction may be initiated either by the user or by the system.

The fault model comprises transaction faults, node faults and context faults. Transaction faults occur when a transaction is explicitly aborted or as a result of an exception raised within the transaction. A transaction fault implies the system-wide abort of the transaction. Node faults occur when a node (or its operating system) crashes. Context faults occur when a single context fails. Context and node faults result in the loss of the volatile state of the contexts effected. On the surviving nodes, a node or context fault is mapped to a set of transaction faults for those transactions that visited the failed node or context. To ensure the all-or-nothing property of transactions, all uncommitted transactions that visited the failed node or context are aborted.

Two kinds of transactions are distinguished: *top-level transactions* and *nested transactions* (also known as *sub-transactions*). A nested transaction is any transaction started within another transaction – its parent. A top-level transaction is a transaction which is not started within another transaction.

Nested transactions abort independently from their parent and can be run in parallel increasing system performance. However, their effect only becomes permanent by committing the corresponding top-level transaction. Parent transactions can run concurrently with any of their sub-transactions. Note that a failure of the top-level transaction will always abort all the work done on behalf of this transaction, including the work of all sub-transactions of the transaction.

In Comandos it is also possible to create a sub-transaction for recovery purposes only. In this case the sub-transaction may abort independently from its parent, but is, from the concurrency control point of view, the same transaction. This approach gives the programmer a finer degree of control when defining a recovery region, and minimises the work that the programmer has to do in the event of the sub-transaction aborting. The sub-transaction runs at the same synchronisation level as its parent and so does not incur the overheads of nesting; it simply serves as a unit of work which can be independently aborted.

The transaction model allows the successful completion of a transaction to be separated from its commitment by introducing the additional transaction state *completed*. Thus several transactions can be committed within one commit protocol execution (i.e. in a so-called *group commit*). This approach reduces the number of commit protocol executions. According to reported measurements [Weinstein et al. 1985] transaction commitment incurs the major costs in running distributed transactions. The separation of the successful completion of a transaction from its commitment can therefore substantially reduce the overhead of running distributed transactions.

Synchronisation of transactions is achieved by using two-phase read/write locking. The model allows object fragments as well as whole objects to be locked. Such system-level read/write locking provides a good basis on which higher level concurrency control schemes like type-specific locking can be provided by mapping them to read/write locking of disjoint fragments of objects. For synchronisation of nested transactions a modified version of the locking rules presented in [Moss 1981] is used. With locking, deadlocks may arise which are detected using a timeout mechanism.

In the general version of the two-phase lock protocol each transaction is subdivided into a growing phase and a shrinking phase. During the first phase locks can only be acquired. After reaching its lockpoint, which can be indicated explicitly by the programmer or implicitly when the first lock is released, the transaction enters the second phase. From then on no further acquisition of locks by the transaction is possible but locks can optionally be released. Locks may therefore be released before the commitment of a transaction. This is particularly necessary for transactions of long duration which access hot-spot (i.e. frequently used) objects. Early release of locks may give rise to dependencies between transactions. If a transaction use an object released by an uncommitted transaction, then the transaction becomes dependent on the original transaction and cannot commit until the first transaction commits. Moreover, the abort of a transaction will cause the abort of all of its dependents.

3.4.1 Transaction Options

Given the model described above, a programmer may alter the behaviour of a transaction by selecting different options when creating a transaction. The options along with their default values are as follows:

- **commit:** normally when a transaction ends successfully all modifications are committed (i.e. made permanent). Turning this option off means that when the transaction ends, the modifications are not committed immediately but are deferred to a later time. (Default: on).
- **blocking:** if an activity running in a transaction cannot gain immediate access to an atomic object, the activity is blocked if this option is turned on, otherwise an exception is raised. (Default: on).
- **new_sync_level:** when creating a nested transaction, turning on the option means that the nested transaction runs at a different synchronisation level to that of its parent transaction, otherwise the nested transaction runs at the same synchronisation level. (Default: on).
- **committed_only:** if this option is turned on, the transaction may only access committed (as distinct from completed) atomic objects, otherwise both committed and completed objects may be accessed. Whether the transaction blocks or an exception is raised if this option is turned on, depends on the setting of the **blocking** option. (Default: off).
- **announce:** when turned off, dependencies arising between transactions are not noticed by Comandos. Turning this option off may lead to some unexpected results. (Default: on).

3.4.2 Job and Activity Model for Transactions

From a purely technical point of view, the notions of transaction and job are completely orthogonal to each other. In principle, a transaction may contain an arbitrary number of jobs and a job may run in different transactions simultaneously and/or sequentially. However, since in the Comandos model a job is the largest unit of work and therefore is not contained in some other computational unit, a transaction, including all of its sub-transactions, is restricted to being within a single job. Nevertheless, it is possible to create a new job inside of a transaction. This job will run outside of the creating transaction and may optionally create a new, independent top-level transaction.

Multiple activities per transaction per node are possible. Therefore, concurrency inside a single transaction is allowed without the overhead related to transaction-level concurrency control and recovery. Synchronisation of the activities running inside the same transaction is required in order to ensure the internal consistency of the objects used by the transaction. The transaction model provides multiple reader/single writer locks for synchronising such concurrent activities. Nevertheless, more sophisticated mechanisms may be provided at the language level.

Although the transaction model allows for multiple activities within a transaction, it basically supports synchronous remote operation invocations where every invocation has an explicit reply. The reply implies that all processing initiated by the remote invocation is terminated. This requirement avoids the need for a distributed termination detection algorithm. It can be implemented by delaying the return of an invocation until all activities created by the invocation have completed.

4. Supported Programming Languages

The provision of programming language support was a key aspect of the Comandos project. Two different approaches to the provision of programming language support were considered in the framework of the project: the use of existing languages, and the provision of a new language environment. The first approach allows the facilities of the existing programming environment to be exploited and existing code to be reused where appropriate. However, because of the constraints imposed by using (or modifying) existing compilers, some features of the Comandos model cannot be fully integrated within an existing language. In contrast, defining a new language allows full access to the facilities of the Comandos virtual machine to be provided. Both approaches are, however, complementary in that objects written in various programming languages can be combined within a given application.

This chapter describes the three programming languages currently supported by the Comandos platform:

- Two existing languages, C++ and Eiffel, which have been extended with various features of the Comandos computational model. The choice of these languages was motivated by their industrial and academic success.
- The newly defined Comandos object-oriented language.

Appendix A shows an example program, written using each of the three languages, in order to illustrate how to program an application which makes use of the features of the Comandos platform using each of these languages.

4.1 C++

C++ is an object-oriented programming language which is now widely used in industrial and academic environments. Refer to [Stroustrup 1987] for an introduction to C++ and [Ellis and Stroustrup 1990] for a complete definition of the C++ language. The following section assumes some familiarity with C++. Any discussion of specific features of the C++ language is based on the AT&T C++ Language System, Release 2.0.

The extended version of C++ supported by the Comandos platform is known as C**. C** provides the application programmer with support for using distribution, persistence, concurrency and transactions. Distribution and persistence are provided through extensions to the C++ language while concurrency and transactions are provided through library classes.

An important feature of C** is that not all C** objects need be potentially persistent or remotely accessible – the programmer is free to choose those classes whose instances are to be potentially persistent or remotely accessible. Instances of other classes behave as normal C++ objects and are not known to the underlying Comandos platform. A complete description of C** is given in [DSG 1992].

4.1.1 Type Model

C** extends C++ with support for distribution and persistence by the addition of new keywords to indicate those classes whose instances are to be remotely accessible or potentially persistent. This section describes how these changes effect the type model of C++.

New keywords were chosen so as to force the programmer to be explicitly aware of the use of these features given the extra costs incurred. This decision was motivated by the general C++ philosophy of making costs explicit.

In order to support distribution *global classes* and *global objects* were introduced. A global object is an instance of a global class. A class is global when one of the following hold:

- the class contains methods which are qualified by the keyword `global`;
- the class contains member objects which are global;
- or, the class inherits from a global class.

Global objects are the only objects in C** which may legitimately be mapped on a different machine (or in a different context) from those objects which hold pointers to them. Since member objects are never on a different node to their enclosing objects, remote access to an object must always be via a pointer.

C** imposes a number of restrictions on access to global objects. In particular, all accesses to global objects must always be via those methods of the objects' classes which have been qualified as `global`. This applies even if the target object is currently mapped locally, since a global object may migrate to another node at any time.

Similarly, global classes may not have `friends` since direct access to the data of a global object is not allowed. Access between peer objects of the same class is also disallowed; however, there is no way at present of preventing this, using C++ syntax, i.e. making data or methods truly private.

A global class can be derived (inherit) from a non-global class. A class can also inherit from a global class, in which case the global features of the parent class are inherited by the derived class i.e. the derived class is necessarily a global class. Note that allowing global classes to be derived from non-global classes implies that there is a single class hierarchy thus facilitating code reuse, and giving the programmer more flexibility. However, assignment of a pointer to a global object to a variable of one of its non-global super types is not allowed i.e. if a pointer to a local object is assigned as its value a pointer to a global object, then if the global object subsequently migrates, it could no longer be accessed by simply de-referencing the local pointer. The user can override these restrictions on assignment by assigning via a void* pointer, but this is not recommended.

In order to support persistence, the concept of a *persistent class* was introduced. Whether a C** object persists or not depends on two conditions – that its class supports persistence and also that it is transitively reachable from a persistent root. There is a certain overhead in supporting persistence, and in accordance with the C++ philosophy of making costs explicit, the user must identify classes which support persistence by using the keyword **permclass** instead of **class** in its definition, or else by deriving the class from an existing persistent class. Thus only instances of designated persistent classes – also known as *persistent objects* – are potentially persistent, and will persist only if they are reachable from a persistent root object.

Instead of maintaining two separate class hierarchies for persistent and non-persistent classes, a single class hierarchy including both normal C++ classes and persistent classes is supported. Thus a persistent class may inherit from a class, and a class may inherit from a persistent class (it is then a persistent class). The keyword **volclass** is used to distinguish classes which are non-persistent, regardless of what they inherit from. Again the main motivation behind allowing the hierarchies to interact is to facilitate code reuse. Note, however, that assignment between persistent objects and ordinary C++ objects is not allowed.

Member objects of persistent objects will implicitly persist since they are part of the data of the enclosing object even if they are not, themselves, instances of persistent classes. Pointers or references in a persistent object which point to other persistent objects will cause the referenced objects (since they are transitively reachable from the root) to persist. Objects of non-persistent classes to which a persistent object has pointers will not persist and hence such pointers are by default re-initialised as null pointers whenever the persistent object is mapped, although the user can override this.

4.1.2 Distribution

In order to describe how global classes are defined in C** an example of a simple class providing remote access to its instances – from any node at which pointers to such instances exist – is given below.

```
class system_wide_int {
    int value ;
public:
    system_wide_int(int Value=0) { value = Value ; };
    global int operator()() { return value; };
    global void inc() { value++ ; };
};
```

This C∗∗ class definition describes integer objects which have remotely invocable functions to return and to increment their values. Note that the global functions are required since remote access to the instance variable **value** is not allowed. Such an integer can be created as normal and a pointer to it can be obtained:

```
system_wide_int *i = new system_wide_int();
```

The pointer to the new object can subsequently be communicated to other nodes in the distributed system. The pointer can then be used to access the object from any node in the distributed system. For example:

```
cout << "i is " << (*i)() << "\n";
```

The use of a pointer to a remote object in C∗∗ is syntactically *identical* to the usual use of a pointer in C++: the current location of a (potentially remote) object is not apparent from a pointer to it. Indeed, the location of the object may change at run time, transparently to objects holding pointers to it.

In order to allow the programmer to exercise some control over the placement of objects at run time, C∗∗ supports the notion of a *preferred* node for each activity. The preferred node is the node at which objects to be used by the activity will be mapped if possible i.e. the preferred node is used as a hint to the underlying platform. A programmer can also explicitly request clusters to be mapped and unmapped.

The preferred node and the mapping and unmapping of clusters can be controlled using the standard operations listed in Table 4.1.

4.1.3 Persistence

As described previously, if the programmer wishes to make instances of a class potentially persistent, then the keyword **permclass** is used instead of **class**, or the class derived (directly or indirectly) from any other persistent class.

Since even an instance of a persistent class will only persist if reachable from a persistent root, some mechanism of specifying the persistent roots in the system is required. The standard operation **record** is used both to specify that an object is to be a root and to associate a symbolic name with the object. A program may subsequently use the standard operation **lookup** to obtain a pointer to the object at any time, even in a separate execution of the code.

Table 4.1. Operations to control mapping and unmapping

Operation	Description
int get_nodeid();	Get identifier of current node.
int get_prefnode();	Get identifier of current preferred node.
int set_prefnode(int n);	Set preferred node to be node n.
int mapcluster(int c);	Map cluster c at the preferred node.
int unmapcluster(int c);	Try to unmap cluster c.

For example, to create a (potentially) persistent integer, and ensure that it persists by making it a root, the following code is used:

```
permclass perm_integer {
    int value;
public:
    perm_integer(int Value=0)
            { value = Value ; };
    int operator()()
            { return value ; };
    void inc() { value++ ; };
} ;

main() {
    perm_integer *i;
    if (system.reset() || !(i=system.lookup("myinteger")) ) {
      i = new perm_integer();
      system.record("myinteger", i);
    }

    cout << "i is " << (*i)() << "\n";
    i->inc();
}
```

When this is run several times, it produces the following output (assuming that the program is called counter):

```
%counter -reset
i is 0
%counter
i is 1
%counter
i is 2
```

Note the use of the standard operation **reset** which indicates if the flag -reset has been passed to the program. The programmer may make use of this feature to allow the user to re-initialise persistent objects.

When a pointer to a persistent object is de-referenced, and the target object is not currently resident in memory, then some overheads are incurred while the target object is being fetched. Subsequently, all uses of that pointer incur no additional overheads beyond that of C++: the pointer refers directly to the target object in the usual way.

As a side effect of fetching one object from the store, the Comandos runtime may fetch further objects (in the same cluster), thus reducing the cost of subsequent object faults on the pre-fetched objects.

4.1.4 Concurrency

C∗∗ provides concurrency based on the model of jobs and activities. In C∗∗, this model is presented through the use of *futures* as in Multilisp [Halstead 1985]. Instead of invoking a member function synchronously, and waiting for its result, a new job or activity can be **forked** to execute the member function in parallel to the caller. At some later stage the caller can test for the termination of the job or activity, and recover the results of the asynchronous function call. Equally, the caller may choose to ignore those results and never synchronise with the job or activity. A job/activity can be suspended or resumed as often as is required. Moreover a job or activity can also be explicitly terminated.

Job and activity support is provided through a number of library classes. The following example shows how jobs and activities can be created. In the example, the operation to be invoked asynchronously is the **calculate** method of the **do_math** class: The code shows both an ordinary (synchronous) invocation of **do_math::calculate** as well as the creation of an activity to carry out the same invocation asynchronously.

```
call_calculate() {    // some function

    do_math *m_obj = new do_math();  // the target object
    glob_obj *obj = new glob_obj();  // some global object
    int result;

    // do normal invocation and get result
    int result = m_obj -> calculate(3, obj, 7);

    // create activity to do it asynchronously
    activity *act = new activity(m_obj, 0, ArgList+3+obj+7);

    // do other things...
    // ...perhaps suspending and resuming the activity
    act -> suspend();
    // ...
    act -> resume();
    // and then wait for the result
    int result = act -> wait_int();
};
```

The activity is created by calling the constructor from the **activity** class as follows:

- The first parameter to the constructor is the object on which the method is to be executed.
- The second is the operation number of the method to be invoked. Operation numbers are assigned to global operations defined in each class (not baseclass) consecutively starting from 0 in the order in which the opera-

tions are declared. Currently, there is no way of using the global operations defined in a base class as the initial operation of a job or activity.

- The third parameter is of the format ArgList + actual parameters in order. Default parameter values should not be used in the invocation.
- There is an optional fourth parameter, which is the identifier of a preferred node for the activity (as described in Sect. 4.1.2).

The constructor returns a pointer to an activity object which may be used to kill, suspend, resume and get status information for the activity. Finally, a call of the form wait_X on the activity waits for the result. Results may be of the type void, in which case act -> wait() is used, any of the basic types including floats, or a global void* pointer, in which case act -> wait_global_pointer() is used.

The interface to class job is very similar; suspending a job suspends all of its activities. Similarly, killing a job kills all of its activities. A simple wait() waits until all of the job's activities have completed – the other wait functions return the result of the job's initial activity, but only when all of the activities have completed.

4.1.4.1 Synchronisation. An activity is analogous to a lightweight process or thread. Programmers using activities need to take special care when sharing data between activities or when using UNIX system calls from a C** application.

Sharing data between activities simply requires synchronised access to the data, as outlined below. Standard UNIX libraries such as clib do not currently support multi-threaded execution. A number of other difficulties arise in the areas of non re-entrant system calls, the errno variable, signals and blocking I/O [Jones 1991]. Current thread packages – on which the implementation of activities is based – such as Cthreads or Sun's lwp package offer no real library support for multi-threaded programming although the Pthreads initiative, a part of the POSIX standardisation activity, intends to recommend solutions for these problems.

Shared Data Areas for Activities. C** provides the semaphore class, and a variation on it, called the acquiring class, which can be used to synchronise access to shared data. The definition of the semaphore class (from the C** library) is as follows:

```
permclass semaphore : public aon_semaphore {
public.
    semaphore():(1) {}          // binary semaphore
    semaphore(int i):(i) {}     // general semaphore

    global void wait();         // wait
    global void condwait();     // conditional wait
    global void signal();       // signal
```

Table 4.2. Operations to control storage and clustering

Operation	Description
int setlc(int l);	Make container l be the default container.
int getlc();	Get identifier of current default container.
int wherelc(int l);	Get identifier of node where container l mounted.
int setcluster(int c);	Make cluster c be the default cluster.
int newcluster(int s);	Create cluster of size s and return its identifier.
int objcluster(void* o);	Get identifier of cluster where object o is stored.

where the usual wait, signal and condwait (conditional wait) operations are defined. Note that such semaphores are both potentially persistent and remotely accessible.

To synchronise access to shared data a user program must wait on a semaphore before accessing shared data and signal the semaphore afterwards. Generally there is one semaphore per shared data section, however the programmer may opt for a finer granularity e.g. a semaphore per field of a shared data area so as to improve concurrency. The definition of the class acquiring is as follows:

```
class acquiring {    // Acquire semaphore for current scope.
   semaphore& s ;
public :
   acquiring(semaphore& S);  // wait on S
   ~acquiring();             // signal S
};
```

acquiring is used by simply declaring it at the beginning of a scope, initialising it with a semaphore and allowing the implicit constructors and destructors to operate.

4.1.5 Storage

The user can choose to be completely unaware of the underlying storage system, or can use the interface to the virtual machine to explicitly control or extract information concerning the storage or clustering of persistent objects.

The default policy for clustering particular groups of objects is determined by the underlying system, and implicitly, new clusters are created as needed.

The user may designate the *default container*, and within it the *default cluster*, which are used, by default, to store newly created persistent objects. However, these are essentially hints to the underlying system, and while in most cases they will be complied with, occasionally the system may override them.

The standard operations available to the C** programmer to control the storage and clustering of persistent objects are listed in Table 4.2.

4.1.6 Transactions

This section describes how transactions are supported in C**.

4.1.6.1 Atomic Objects. In C**, all instances of persistent classes are potentially atomic objects. Given an instance of such a non-atomic object, the object is promoted to being atomic with the standard operation `make_atomic`. Consider the following example:

```
#include <system.h>

permclass atomic_int {
    int value;
public:
    atomic_int(int);

    global int  read() const;
    global void write(int);
};

main() {
    atomic_int *i = new atomic_int(11);

    system.make_atomic(i);
    // ...
}
```

Object creation and atomic promotion can be combined into a single statement as follows:

```
atomic_int *i = new {ATOMIC} atomic_int(11);
```

Here, promotion is not performed immediately, but only when the object is next mapped. This may be used to create persistent atomic objects during the initialisation stage of a C** program (e.g. when the -reset flag is passed to the program).

When an object is created in a transaction and immediately promoted to being an atomic object, the operation `create_atomic` should be used instead of the operation `make_atomic`. For example:

```
// create new object
atomic_int *i = new atomic_int(11);
// promote object to atomic
system.create_atomic(i);
```

The `create_atomic` operation performs atomic promotion and also ensures the permanence of the creation in case the object is not otherwise modified during the transaction. This operation also has the side effect of acquiring a write lock on the object.

The transaction system supports non-strict, two-phase read/write locking. Hence, C∗∗ distinguishes between modifying operations and read-only operations. In the example class above, the operation **read** is a read only operation since the declaration of the operation is followed by the keyword **const**. The operation **write** is assumed to be a modifying operation and therefore may only be used inside of a transaction.

C∗∗ only guarantees the transactional properties for atomic objects so long as the objects are only accessed through operations which are declared as either **global** or **virtual**. Atomic objects should never be accessed via non-virtual or non-global operations and an atomic object's instance data should never be directly accessed. These restrictions are not enforced by the C∗∗ compiler or by the Comandos virtual machine so care should be taken to ensure proper use of atomic objects.

4.1.6.2 Creating Transactions. Transactions are created in a way similar to activities and jobs. The greatest difference is that while the activity and job interfaces are asynchronous, the transaction interface is purely synchronous. A transaction is created to perform an invocation on an object and the transaction ends when the invocation has completed successfully or when the transaction is aborted. Thus, there is no explicit operation for ending the transaction. Consider the following example:

```
#include ...

class interface {
public:
    global void start(int);
};

void interface::start(int i) {
    cout << "interface::start() i = " << i << "\n";
}

main() {
    interface *i = new interface();
    transaction T;

    T.begin(i, 0, ArgList+1968);
    cout << "Outcome of transaction is: ";
    switch (T.outcome()) {
     case TRANSACTION_COMMITTED: cout << "committed\n"; break;
     case TRANSACTION_COMPLETED: cout << "completed\n"; break;
     case TRANSACTION_ABORTED: cout << "aborted\n"; break;
     case TRANSACTION_ERROR: cout << "error\n"; break;
    }
```

As for jobs and activities, there is a special **transaction** class used in creating transactions. The operation for creating a transaction, **begin**, takes an object reference, an operation number and an optional list of arguments. In this example, when the transaction starts it invokes the operation **start** on the object referenced by i. Note that to be the initial operation of a transaction, the method **start** must be a **global** method. When the **begin** operation returns, the outcome of the transaction may be determined via the operation **outcome** which has four possible results:

- **TRANSACTION_COMMITTED**: the transaction committed.
- **TRANSACTION_COMPLETED**: the transaction completed.
- **TRANSACTION_ABORTED**: the transaction aborted.
- **TRANSACTION_ERROR**: some unspecified error occurred.

When creating a transaction, a top-level transaction is created if the current activity is not currently running in a transaction, otherwise a nested transaction is created.

4.1.6.3 Transaction Options. When creating a transaction, the programmer may effect how the transaction behaves by altering the value of some of the transaction options described in Sect. 3.4.1. Each option may be turned on or off or inspected via operations on the **transaction** class.

As an example, suppose a programmer wishes to create a transaction which only accesses committed data and which raises an exception instead of blocking. This may be done as follows:

```
transaction T;

T.set_committed_only();    // access committed only data
T.unset_blocking();        // non-blocking mode
T.begin(i, 0, ArgList+1968); // now create transaction
```

All of these options except for **new_sync_level** may also be turned on or off from within a transaction via the special operations described in the next section.

4.1.6.4 Transaction Operations. A number of standard operations are provided for manipulating transactions. The first of these is an operation **transaction_abort** to abort the current transaction. The outcome of an aborted transaction is **TRANSACTION_ABORTED**. Currently there is no way for a programmer to initiate the abort of a transaction other than the current transaction.

Since non-strict two-phase locking is supported, an operation **setlockpoint** is provided to specify that the current transaction has reached its lockpoint. Once a transaction has reached its lockpoint, the transaction may not acquire any more locks. That is, the transaction enters its shrinking phase and may only release previously acquired locks.

C** provides a way of explicitly setting and releasing locks on a given object by inheriting from a special class **atomic_lock**. The operations provided by this class are: **set_read_lock**, **release_read_lock**, **set_write_lock** and **release_write_lock**.

The operations **get_ts_options** and **set_ts_options** allow the programer to alter the behaviour of a transaction after the transaction has been created: The operation **get_ts_options** retrieves the current settings which may be then altered before calling the operation **set_ts_options** to change the current settings. All the available options are described in Sect. 3.4.1.

In order to determine if the current activity is currently running inside a transaction, the operation **in_trans** is provided. This operation returns nonzero if the current activity is running inside a transaction.

Given any object, it is possible to determine if the object is an atomic object or not. The operation **is_atomic** takes a reference to an object and returns nonzero if the object is atomic.

4.1.7 Exceptions

The current method of handling exceptions in C** is very simple. The user can specify one handler (essentially a function address) per activity, by using the standard operation **set_eehandler(handler_func)**.

The user can raise an exception using the operation **raisexc(exception)**. If the activity is executing in other than its initial context when the exception is raised then it exits and returns to its initial context. In any case, the handler originally specified by the user is invoked, passing it the exception identifier specified in the **raisexc** call.

If there is no user-supplied handler, the default system exception handler is invoked, which simply causes the activity to exit having displayed appropriate status information.

4.1.8 Implementation

C** is supported by a modified version of the GNU G++ version 1.37 compiler.

The compiler generates the up-calls for each persistent class necessary to allow instances of that class to be managed by the virtual machine. The up-calls are produced as the methods of an up-call class corresponding to each persistent class. An instance of the appropriate up-call class in embedded in the header of each Comandos object onto which a persistent object is mapped allowing the virtual machine to locate the up-calls.

The C** compiler supports distribution by generating additional code: this includes an additional method – dispatch – and a *proxy class* for each **global** class. An instance of this class, a *proxy*, is used to represent each instance of the class in any context where a pointer to the instance exists but the instance is not currently present. The proxy has the same interface as the real object and contains *stubs* for each of the global methods, to marshal parameters to be delivered to the target object via the virtual machine. At the remote side the virtual machine up-calls the dispatch method attached to the real object, which unpacks the parameters and invokes the required method. On return from the real method, dispatch marshals any results and returns these, via the virtual machine, to the proxy. This then unmarshals any results, and returns to the calling code.

4.2 Eiffel

Eiffel is a strongly typed, class based, object-oriented programming language which, together with its extensive class library, facilitates object-oriented design and software reuse.

A good introduction to the Eiffel language is contained in [Meyer 1988]. The complete definition of the Eiffel language is given in [Meyer 1989a] and the standard libraries (including the core KERNEL and SUPPORT class libraries) are detailed in [Meyer and Nerson 1990] The reader is assumed to be familiar with the Eiffel System (language and environment) and is referred to the above in any case. The discussion of specific language features and the Eiffel run-time environment is based on Version 2.3, level 4.

The extended version of Eiffel which exploits the facilities provided by the Comandos platform is referred to as Eiffel**. Support for using the main features of the Comandos platform – distribution, persistence, concurrency and transactions – is provided in Eiffel**. Unlike C** no changes to the Eiffel language were made to provide support for using persistence and distribution. In fact both persistence and distribution are normally transparent to the Eiffel** programmer – all Eiffel** objects are potentially persistent and distributed. Like C** concurrency and transaction support are provided through library classes. The Eiffel** programmer can interact with the Comandos virtual machine via the COMANDOS class interface.

4.2.1 Type Model

Eiffel is a typed language – every entity or function is declared as being of a certain type. The Eiffel type system is entirely based on the notion of class. An object's (or value's or instance's) behaviour is characterised by its associated class.

The Eiffel** type model is the same as the type model of Eiffel, except that the only features of an object that can be remotely accessed are its exported routines. Exported data items are not remotely accessible.

There have been no changes to the Eiffel language, making distribution and persistence transparent to the Eiffel** programmer. All objects in an Eiffel** system are potentially global and persistent. This decision was partly motivated by the issue of software reuse, a central feature of Eiffel, and partly by the extent of the run time information provided by Eiffel.

The Comandos type model distinguishes the notion of type, that is an abstract interface, and class, that is an implementation of a type. Each Comandos type can have potentially many (implementation) classes. In Eiffel, each type (class) has just one direct implementation.

Consequently, in Eiffel, the sub-typing and inheritance hierarchies are the same. The Eiffel term class applies both to a type and to its implementation. This approach is a restriction in terms of the overall Comandos type model, and hence presents no difficulties, when trying to map the Eiffel model on to the Comandos type model. Note also that the Eiffel information hiding mechanism is orthogonal to the inheritance structure. This allows an heir class not to export a parent's feature.

4.2.2 Persistence

Eiffel already provides support for persistence through its class library. In particular, object persistence can be obtained in one of two ways, in the current implementation of Eiffel.

Class STORABLE offers a simple explicit facility to store an object (and its dependents) to a named file. Any class X can make use of this facility simply by inheriting from class STORABLE. For example, given a definition of class X of the form:

```
class X export store_by_name, retrieve_by_name, ...
inherit
    STORABLE
feature
    <class_features>
end ;   --class X
```

An instance x of X is stored via the call:

```
x.store_by_name("some_file") ;
```

and can subsequently be retrieved via

```
x.retrieve_by_name("some_file") ;
```

Alternatively persistence may be obtained by use of an Eiffel *environment*. An Eiffel environment is a set of objects. Individual objects may be identified by a key with respect to the environment. Such objects, and all their direct and indirect dependents, are the *persistent objects* of the environment. An environment may be opened. All objects created thereafter will belong to the environment (until it is closed). Hence, class ENVIRONMENT provides an implicit facility to store a collection of arbitrary objects, with selective retrieval. A simple naming service is provided for object access. Any class of object may be stored in an environment (i.e. without having to inherit from any particular system class). The collection of stored objects can be queried, to discover e.g. the number of stored objects of a particular type. The environment as a whole is made to persist between Eiffel sessions, by storing an external representation of all the objects in a named file. When an object is retrieved from an environment all type information can be obtained, as this is stored along with the object representation that is written to the file. The reverse assignment statement can then be used to re-attach the object to a normal typed reference.

In both cases, when an object becomes persistent, all of its dependents are also stored since otherwise object references would, on retrieval, be meaningless. Shared references and cyclic dependencies are handled properly.

Three different approaches to exploiting the persistence facilities offered by the Comandos platform in Eiffel** programs are immediately apparent.

- All Eiffel** objects are created as Comandos objects and thus all objects reachable from a root (e.g. the default Name Service) automatically persist between different sessions. The support provided by Comandos could make the explicit object storage provided by Eiffel redundant. Any Eiffel** object which remains reachable from a root would then survive across program runs. The Eiffel** programmer would then no longer have to worry about explicitly ensuring that particular instances persist.

- Incorporate into the Eiffel** (language-specific) run-time, routines to emulate the performance of STORABLE and ENVIRONMENT. Consequently, from the Eiffel** programmer's viewpoint, there would be no difference between Eiffel** and Eiffel with respect to persistence. This has the advantage that normal language semantics are preserved, but the added functionality inherent to Comandos, is not fully exploited.

- A mixture of the above, i.e. provide modified implementations of STORABLE and ENVIRONMENT which mimic the simple naming service that they provide while using the standard Comandos facilities to provide persistence of individual instances. This would provide the Eiffel** programmer with conventional Eiffel persistence support and permit Eiffel** applications to directly use Comandos transparent persistence.

In fact the third method outlined above was chosen since it combines the advantages of both of the other alternatives. As an example, the following code shows how to create a (potentially) persistent integer in Eiffel**:

```
class EXAMPLE_INT export inc, val
feature
    v : INTEGER ;

    Create (i : INTEGER) is
      do v := i end ;

    inc is
      do v := v + 1 end ;

    val : INTEGER is
      do Result := v end ;
end ; --Class EXAMPLE_INT
```

```
class ROOT
inherit
    COMANDOS
feature
    p : EXAMPLE_INT ;

    Create is
      do
        if reset = 1
        then
            p.Create (1) ;
            record ("p.ns", p)
        end ;
        p ?= lookup ("p.ns") ;
        io.putstring("p is ") ;
        io.putint (p.val) ;
        io.newline ;
        p.inc
    end ;
end ; --Class ROOT
```

Note the use of standard operations **reset**, **record** and **lookup** described in Sect. 4.1.3. When this is run several times (with an instance of **ROOT** as the Eiffel system root object) the following output is produced:

```
$root -reset
p is 1
$root
p is 2
$root
p is 3
```

No additional code is generated to support persistence. Once a persistent object has been mapped in from secondary storage, there is no additional overhead attached to manipulating the object beyond that of Eiffel. An Eiffel** program that does not make use of any Comandos facilities incurs no additional overhead beyond the equivalent Eiffel program, except for some extra space taken up by the headers attached to each Comandos object in the system.

4.2.3 Distribution

The approach to distribution adopted allows all objects in an Eiffel** system to be remotely accessible. Thus, distribution, like persistence, is transparent to the Eiffel** programmer.

Hence, the class **EXAMPLE_INT** in the previous section not only describes objects which are potentially persistent but which are also remotely accessible.

Many users could run the integer program at the same time, possibly on different nodes, and it is completely transparent where the integer object is actually mapped. In this way, the integer object acts as a server capable of handling multiple client requests.

While distribution is normally transparent, the programmer can also exercise some control over the placement of objects and clusters at run time by specifying a preferred node for each activity and using the standard operations get_nodeid, set_prefnode, get_prefnode, mapcluster and unmapcluster described in Sect. 4.1.2.

4.2.4 Concurrency

Currently Eiffel retains the notion of a *program* which spans the execution of the Create operation of an instance of the ROOT class created for the program run. A single thread of control performs the sequence of object creations and method calls of the root class's Create operation. In effect, this corresponds to a Comandos job with a single activity.

The Eiffel** programmer's interface to concurrency is through a set of classes. The user can invoke an operation on an object asynchronously, and at some later stage test for the termination of the invocation, recover the results of the invocation and suspend and resume the call, through the appropriate class interface. The following example shows how an activity can be created in to call the calculate method of some class CALC:

```
calculate (a,b : INTEGER ; c : SOME_CLASS) : INTEGER
```

The call_calculate method takes an instance of CACL and invokes its calculate method both synchronously, and asynchronously as an activity:

```
call_calculate (c : CALC ; A_ref : SOME_CLASS) is
local
  act : ACTIVITY ;
    i : INTEGER ;
do
  c.Create ; -- Create CALC object
  i := c.calculate (1, 2, A_ref) ;
              -- Normal synchronous invocation
  act.Create (c, "calculate", 1, 2, A_ref) ;
              -- Create activity to do invocation
  i := act.wait_int ;
              -- and wait for the result
  end ;
```

The activity is created by calling the Create routine for the activity class passing it the object on which the method is to be executed, the name of the routine to be invoked, and finally the argument list for the method, which is a variable-sized list of parameters, any of which can be a reference to an object.

The full interface of the ACTIVITY class includes routines to kill, suspend and resume an activity as well as to wait for results of various types.

The JOB class interface is similar: as usual suspending or killing a job suspends or kills all of its activities, while the wait methods wait for all of the job's activities to complete before returning the result of the initial activity.

4.2.4.1 Synchronisation. Eiffel** provides the SEMAPHORE class to allow objects to synchronise accesses by multiple activities. The SEMAPHORE class provides wait, signal and condwait (conditional wait) operations as in C** (c.f. Sect. 4.1.4.1).

4.2.5 Storage

The Eiffel** programmer is by default unaware of the storage and clustering of objects, i.e the identity of an object's cluster or container, what other objects reside in the same cluster or where the cluster is stored.

As in C** the programmer may control the storage and clustering of objects by specifying the default container and default cluster. In particular, the standard operations setlc, getlc, wherelc, setcluster, newcluster and objcluster, described in Sect. 4.1.5, are also provided to the Eiffel** programmer through the COMANDOS class interface.

4.2.6 Transactions

Like persistence and distribution, the approach taken for transactions is that all objects in an Eiffel** system are potentially atomic. Making an object atomic in Eiffel** is a two step process, involving creating the object and subsequently calling the system to make the object atomic.

```
class USE_ATOMIC
inherit
   COMANDOS
feature
   i : EXAMPLE_INT

   use_i is
     do
       i.Create (1) ;
       make_atomic (i) ;
     end ;
end ; --Class USE_ATOMIC
```

A similar restriction to distribution applies in that access to an atomic object should only be through its exported routines.

The Eiffel** programmer's interface to transactions is through the TRANSACTION class interface. The transaction interface is synchronous, but in other respects it is similar to the job and activity interface, especially with regards to creating a transaction to perform an invocation on an object. The following example shows how to create a transaction:

```
class EXAMPLE export f1
feature
   f1 (i : INTEGER) : INTEGER
end ;

class USE_TRANSACTIONS
feature
 i : EXAMPLE ;
 T : TRANSACTION ;

 do_transaction is
   local
     r : INTEGER ;
   do
     i.Create (2) ;
     T.Create(i, "f1", 1973) ;
       --Create transaction to invoke method f1 on i
     io.putstring ("The outcome of the transaction is ") ;
     inspect
        T.outcome
     when Transaction_Commited then
        io.putstring ("commited")
     when Transaction_Completed then
        io.putstring ("completed") ;
        r := T.get_integer  --Get result of operation.
     when Transaction_Aborted then
        io.putstring ("aborted")
     when Transaction_Error then
        io.putstring ("error")
     end ;
     io.newline ;
   end ;
end ; --class USE_TRANSACTIONS
```

The means of starting a transaction on an object is similar to that of starting an activity to invoke a method on the object.

The TRANSACTION class also provides an interface to allow programmers to alter the transaction options described in Sect. 3.4.1 and thus to control the way in which the transaction behaves.

Finally, the COMANDOS class provides a number of methods which are expressly concerned with transaction management including, for example, the make_atomic method.

4.2.7 Exceptions

In Eiffel an exception can be triggered by the user, the system or by hardware signals, traps and interrupts. A single exception model deals with all possible exceptions. Exceptions can be triggered by:

- assertion violation;
- de-reference on void;
- operating system signals;
- failure of a called routine to meet its postcondition;
- programmer defined exceptions.

The exception handler can be associated at the routine or class level with uncaught exceptions propagating back through the activation stack. See Chap. 14 of [Meyer 1989a] for further details. The overall exception model in Eiffel is similar to that in the Comandos Language.

4.2.8 Implementation

The implementation of the Eiffel∗∗ language on top of the Comandos virtual machine is described in detail in Chap. 11.

4.3 The Comandos Object-Oriented Language

This section describes the facilities provided by the Comandos object-oriented language. This language has been designed to faithfully reflect all the facilities of the Comandos model. The Comandos language provides all the functionality described by the computational models and, in addition, provides extra functionality which is tailored for the construction of distributed object-oriented applications such as groupware. The Comandos object-oriented language is described fully in [Comandos 1991].

4.3.1 Type Model

Objects are the units of modelling and programming. An object encapsulates a set of data, the state of the object, and a set of operations, or methods, which operate on this data. Every object is an instance of a *type*, where the type describes the behaviour of that object (i.e. all the operations that the object can respond to, and all the attributes of the object that may be accessed by another object). Every object also possesses an *implementation* which describes the representation of that object and also the way in which the operations are carried out.

To create an object, a generic **New** operation is provided by all types. This operation creates a new object and returns a *reference* (i.e. unique system-wide identifier) for the object.

Objects are accessed through *variables*. Variables may be considered as place-holders for object references. More than one variable may be used to access the same object. A variables possesses a type; when accessing an object through a variable, only the interface described by the type of that variable may be used.

4.3.1.1 Basic Data Types and Type Constructors. All denotable values possess a type. The basic types of the type model are **Boolean**, **Integer**, **Real** and **Character**. Assignment and comparison are provided for all of these types. In addition each type has a set of type-specific operations, such as the arithmetic operations for **Integer** and **Real**, and the logical operations for type **Boolean**.

There is a special type **Top** which indicates a place-holder for a reference to an arbitrary object.

Complex objects may be defined from the basic data types by using a number of pre-defined *type constructors*: **String**, **List Of**, **Array Of**, **Record** and **Collection Of**.

4.3.1.2 User-defined Types and Classes. In the Comandos language, a type consists of three aspects:

- a name;
- an abstract description, which defines the behaviour of objects of the type; and
- one or more implementations of this abstract description.

The abstract description characterises the common interface to all objects of the type and is called an *abstract type* or, where context permits, just *type*. An implementation of this abstract type, a *class*, represents code and storage layout information.

A type specifies a behavior, that is common to all objects of the given type, in terms of the operations applicable to these objects; this is the usual concept of an abstract type. Each operation in a type description is defined by a *signature*, which specifies the name of the method, the type of its parameters, and whether each parameter is an argument (**In**), a result (**Out**), or both (**InOut**).

A type may specify that a component of the state of the object is visible. Such a visible component is also called an *attribute*. If **x** (a variable of type **t**) is an attribute of an object **obj**,two operations are implicitly defined: a function **x-val:t**, such that **obj.x-val** returns the value of **x**, and a procedure **x-set(In v:t)**, such that **obj.x-set(v)** sets the value of **x** to **v**. As a shorthand, these operations are expressed with the usual notations (e.g. **x:=v** for **obj.x-set(v)**), and the declaration of an attribute **x** of type **t** takes the usual form **x:t**. An initial value may be specified for an attribute. If a declaration (with initial value) is prefixed by the keyword **Const**, then the value of the attribute may not be modified (i.e. only **val** is provided).

A class specifies a particular implementation of a type. A class definition is common to all instances of the class. It includes a description of the internal state of the object, as a set of instance variables, and the code of the methods.

The attributes declared in the type definition are automatically included as instance variables.

An instance of a class is created by calling the method New of the class. The method New returns a reference to the created object. Thereafter, methods may be invoked on this object by calls using this reference.

4.3.1.3 Type Conformance. Generally, in classical typed languages, objects having different implementations, but which are of the same type as a variable, may be assigned as value to that variable. Object-oriented languages go one step further by allowing assignment of objects of different types to a variable. For instance, a variable in Smalltalk-80 can be assigned any object; however, no type checking is performed, and errors (e.g. non-existent method) can only be detected at run time. A goal of the Comandos language was to allow some of the flexibility of Smalltalk, while performing type checking at compile time as far as possible. This raises the following question: under what conditions may an object be assigned to a variable of a different type? Let ref be a variable of type T1. Then, an object of type T2 may be safely assigned to ref if T2 *conforms* to T1 so that subsequent operations on ref, allowed by its type T1, will be legal if applied on the object of type T2. Conformance is defined as follows:

- For each method defined in the interface of T1, there exists a method of the same name in the interface of T2.
- Each method of T2 has the same number of arguments (In parameters) and of results (Out parameters), and of InOut parameters as the corresponding method of T1.
- For each method m, the type of its arguments in T1 conforms to the type of its arguments in T2.
- For each method m, the type of its results in T2 conforms to the type of its results in T1.
- For each method m, the type of InOut parameters in T1 and T2 are the same.
- Every type conforms to itself.

This definition implies that for each attribute in type T1, there must exist an attribute of the same name and type in T2. This agrees with the notion of type extension [Wirth 1988], that applies to the special case where types T1 and T2 are records (i.e. they only specify attributes, and no explicit methods).

Note that conformance is a purely syntactic relationship that involves no semantic equivalence, since it only relates the signatures of the methods. Conformance has therefore no automatic implications regarding the actual behavior of the objects. However, in the special case of records, the only (implicitly defined) methods are val and set, whose semantics are well-defined; therefore, in this case, syntactic conformance guarantees consistent behavior.

4.3.1.4 Sub-typing. Sub-typing is a well-known way of specifying shared behavior between types. Informally, type T2 is a *sub-type* of type T1 (and T1 is a *super-type* of T2) if the interface of T2 provides at least the same operations (including attributes) as the interface of T1 (it may provide more operations). The sub-typing relationship defines a hierarchy between types. In the current design of the Comandos language, this hierarchy is simple, i.e. a type has only one super-type. Furthermore, it is specified, by definition, that a sub-type must conform to its super-type. As a consequence, methods may be overloaded in sub-types, provided that the conformance conditions are respected. Since the conformance relationship may be statically checked, the language is strongly typed.

Note that conformance and sub-typing are really two different concepts, although they have often been confused in the literature. Specifying that a sub-type must conform to its super-type in a language is a design decision which results from the requirement of statically checked type safety. However, some language designers have decided otherwise. The decision to allow non-conform sub-typing is usually motivated by the restriction imposed by the contravariant behavior [Cook 1989] of method arguments imposed by the conformance rule.

The restrictions imposed by static type checking may be alleviated by dynamic checking. Dynamic type checking is supported in the Comandos language, by the **Typecase** and **Assertype** constructs.

The sub-typing hierarchy is paralleled by a subclassing hierarchy, which allows reuse of physical properties (i.e. attributes and operation implementations) between objects that already share a common behavior. Let T2 be a sub-type of T1. If class C1 implements T1, a class C2 which implements T2 may be constructed by inheritance from C1 as follows.

- C2 inherits all the instance variable definitions present in C1.
- Additional instance variables may be defined in C2.
- C2 inherits all the methods defined in C1.
- An inherited method may be redefined in C2, as long as the conformance conditions are respected.
- Additional methods may be defined in C2, namely those which are part of the interface of T2 and which are not included in the interface of T1.

As usual, when an inherited method is overloaded, the overloaded method is still accessible within the new program (through a pseudo-variable **Super**).

4.3.1.5 Object Composition. The construction of complex structured objects is achieved by embedding references to objects within the state of other objects. This mechanism allows composite structures of arbitrary size to be built from component objects, and allows objects or sub-structures to be shared. Since references provide a system-wide naming scheme, composite structures, as opposed to individual objects, may be distributed on several nodes (although this distribution is not apparent at the programming language level).

Object composition is usually done through predefined constructors such as arrays, records, lists and collections which are the main building blocks for the construction of complex structures. For instance, the body of a document may be defined as a list of chapters, each of which is in turn a list of paragraphs, etc. Several documents may share a chapter (or a list of chapters).

4.3.2 Persistence

Every object in the Comandos language is potentially persistent. However, only objects which are reachable from a persistent root are made persistent by the run-time; other objects are garbage collected.

4.3.3 Distribution

Distribution is, by default, transparent. However, the language also provides constructs to force the creation or execution of an object to take place at a specified node. However, from the programmer's point of view remote and local invocations are indistinguishable. In particular, the public attributes of remote objects can be accessed in the same way as for local objects (unlike extended C++ and Eiffel which do not support this feature).

4.3.4 Concurrency

A job is created by an activity of another job using the primitive Start_Job. This primitive specifies a method to be carried out and creates an initial activity within the new job to invoke this method.

The execution of concurrent activities within a job may be controlled by the CoBegin .. CoEnd construct. Each object invocation enclosed between CoBegin and CoEnd is executed as a separate activity. The calling activity (i.e. the activity in which the construct is called) is suspended. Its resumption is controlled by the termination condition associated with CoEnd, which has the form of a boolean expression over the status (either terminated or not terminated) of the concurrent invocations. By default, if no termination condition is specified, the calling activity is resumed when all concurrent invocations have terminated.

4.3.4.1 Synchronisation Model. The Comandos language offers sophisticated facilities for the control of concurrent accesses to shared objects.

Object sharing must be controlled in order to guarantee that shared data remain in a consistent state. The approach taken in the Comandos language is to express synchronisation as a set of conditions associated with objects, rather than as primitives appearing within activities. This is fully consistent with the object-oriented approach, since the specification of the synchronisation constraints is concentrated in the class that describes the object instead of being spread out in methods that use the object. In addition, this synchronisation specification is shared by all instances of the class.

The only way for an activity to access or modify an object is to execute a method of this object. Therefore, synchronisation constraints are specified as a set of *activation conditions*, which form a control clause. Each activation condition is attached to a method and must be satisfied before the execution of this method may start. If no activation condition is attached to a method, then the execution of this method is unconstrained.

An activation condition is a boolean expression which may contain the following parameters: instance variables which represent the internal state of an instance, actual parameters of the method, and *synchronisation counters*.

Synchronisation counters are internal data which give, for each method of a given object, values such as the total number of invocations on the object, the total number of completed invocations and the number of invocations currently pending. These counters are automatically updated by the language. The synchronisation mechanism is fully described in [Decouchant et al. 1991].

The following counters are defined for each method m: `invoked(m)`, `started(m)`, `completed(m)`, `current(m)`, `pending(m)`. The three first counters count the number of times that method m has been invoked, started or completed respectively, and the last two count the number of activities currently executing m and currently waiting to execute m. The values of the last two counters can be calculated using the values of the first three.

Synchronisation constraints are illustrated by the following program, which implements a bounded buffer used for communication between activities. The types `ProducerConsumer` and `Element` are assumed to have been introduced elsewhere:

```
Class FixedSizeBuffer Implements ProducerConsumer Is
    Const size = <some constant>;
    buffer: Array [0..size-1] Of Element;
    first, last: Integer = 0;

    Method Put(In m: Element);
    Begin
        buffer[last] := m;
        last := last + 1 MOD size;
    End Put;

    Method Get(Out m: Element);
    Begin
        m := buffer[first];
        first := first + 1 MOD size;
    End Get;

    Control
            Put: (completed(Put) - completed(Get) < size)
                    and current(Put) = 0;
            Get: (completed(Put) > completed(Get))
                    and current(Get) = 0;
    End FixedSizeBuffer;
```

It should be noted that activation conditions are expressed using only boolean expressions. Modification of internal variables or more general algorithms are not allowed. As a consequence, some synchronisation schemes cannot be expressed directly, and must involve the use of additional methods.

4.3.5 Transactions

The Comandos object-oriented language provides a restricted transaction model. A transaction is started by using the **Transaction** primitive. A transaction terminates successfully when the operation specified in the call to **Transaction** completes. A transaction may be terminated unsuccessfully by invoking the primitive **AbortTransaction** when some undesired situation occurs. Transaction properties apply only to atomic objects. In the Comandos language, individual objects may be made atomic at creation time, or atomicity may be a property of a class, in which case all instances of that class will be atomic objects.

4.3.6 Exceptions

There are basically three kinds of exceptions. *User-defined exceptions* are raised at the language level. *System exceptions* report problems from the system (e.g. timeout during a remote call, abort of a transaction). *Hardware traps* are signalled by the processor (e.g. arithmetic exceptions or segmentation violation).

Although they are raised and reported differently, these various categories of exceptions are viewed and handled uniformly at the language level. In the Comandos object-oriented language, it is natural to express exception handling in terms of object invocation, in which any object invocation may terminate either normally returning a result or abnormally signalling an exception.

The main aspects of exception handling within the Comandos object-oriented language are summarised below:

4.3.6.1 Exception Declaration. Exceptions are identified by symbolic names – system exceptions and hardware traps have reserved names.

Exceptions are associated with object methods. The user-defined exceptions, potentially raised by a method, appear in the method's signature.

4.3.6.2 Exception Raising. User-defined exceptions may be raised using the **Raise** statement within the code of a method (provided that the corresponding exception is declared in the signature of the method). System exceptions and hardware traps are raised by the system.

A termination model of exception handling has been adopted: the interrupted method is stopped and execution is resumed at the level of the invoking method.

An unexpected exception is transformed into a pre-defined system exception

4.3.6.3 Exception Handling. Handlers are associated with method invocations. A handler specifies a specific procedure for handling expected exceptions (including pre-defined and user-defined exceptions). The keyword **All** specifies that a given routine handles all expected exceptions. A handler may also be associated with a class, in which case the specified handler is used for all methods of the class.

The keywords **Replace** and **Retry** specify fault recovery policies as follows:

- **Replace** provides an alternative result for the method which failed. Conformance between the replacement value and the one expected from the method is checked at compile time.
- **Retry** asks for a new execution of the method which raised the exception. To avoid the risk of recursive calls to the same handler, the system ensures that a given handler cannot be called again before terminating.

4.3.6.4 Restoration. Exception handling procedures allow alternative or retry policies to be implemented when a method fails. However this does not ensure that the invoked object is in a consistent state after it has raised an exception.

The **Restore** statement allows a restoration block, which is executed whenever a method exits abnormally by raising an exception, to be defined. This block is not executed if the method returns normally. As for handlers, restoration code may be provided at the method and class levels.

4.3.6.5 Inheritance and Conformance. Exceptions, being part of the signature of a method, are also part of the sub-types of a given type. Furthermore, the conformance rules between types have been extended to take exceptions into account.

Inheritance is also applied to handling and restoration code. A handler which is associated with a method is inherited as being part of the method; this means that either the subclass inherits the method and then automatically inherits the related handler, or it redefines the method and then must also redefine the handler. Handlers which are associated with a class are automatically inherited by its subclasses. The rule is similar for restoration blocks.

4.3.6.6 Concurrency. The CoBegin .. CoEnd construct allows concurrent activities to run in parallel. If the failure of a branch prevents the normal termination condition from ever being verified, then the remaining branches are stopped and a Join_failed exception raised.

4.3.7 Implementation

The compiler for the Comandos language is written in C and consists of approximately 30 000 lines of code. The compiler produces C which is in turn compiled by a standard C compiler. This approach allows the Comandos language compiler to be easily ported. The current version is able to generate C code which can be compiled on a wide range of target machines (Sun-3, Sun-4, and Sun386i; Bull DPX/1000 and DPX/2, Bull Zenith i386; DECstation 3100, and 5100)

For each type of compiler, the compiler produces a descriptor which is used during the compilation of other types and classes. For each class, the compiler produces the corresponding C code and a descriptor which is used in the compilation of further classes. Descriptors are stored in the UNIX file system. The output of the C compiler is post-processed to produce a Comandos binary, which is stored in the Comandos storage system.

The compiler runs in five passes:

- Pass 1 performs lexical and syntactical analysis of the source code, generating an appropriate tree structure using **lex** and **yacc** (or **flex** and **bison** from GNU).
- Pass 2 performs semantic analysis. The tree structure generated by pass 1 is decorated appropriately and a descriptor created. This step uses type and class descriptors created already.
- Pass 3 generates C code from the tree structure.
- Pass 4 compiles the C code and resolves external references.
- Pass 5 builds a Comandos binary from the UNIX binary and stores it in the storage system.

5. Development Tools

The Comandos approach is intended to remove the burden from programming distributed and persistent applications. Thus Comandos provides support for multiple programming languages. In addition to the compilation tools associated with each of the supported languages, other development tools are required at the various stages of the application life-cycle. However, although it was recognised as an important issue, the implementation of a complete development environment was not a primary objective of the project and hence only a limited set of such development tools has been provided within the project. This chapter describes the development tools provided by the project: a distributed debugger, a tool for the development of user interfaces, and a Type Manager which is a repository for type information that can be used by all the languages available on the Comandos platform. Further effort would be required to implement a development environment incorporating the necessary analysis and design tools, programming tools, debugging and tuning tools, and, configuration and maintenance tools.

5.1 The Distributed Debugger

Debugging a distributed parallel program is a difficult task because of the non-determinism caused by the concurrent execution of activities and by variable communication delays. An additional difficulty arises from interference with the program being debugged by the debugging tools.

The approach followed in Comandos is based on experience with an observation tool, the *Observer* [Jamrozik et al. 1991] which was developed in Comandos-1. Although the original purpose of the Observer was to provide a facility for displaying the objects and execution flow in a Comandos application graphically, it became apparent that this tool could be extended with debugging facilities. Thus the main features of the debugger are:

- Visualisation of application structure and execution flow.
- Provision of multiple views of the same application to show or to hide distribution. In the *job view* distribution is not visible – the execution is shown as if it was happening on a single machine. In the *node view*, individual views are connected directly to each node visited by the application

showing the execution of the application at that node. These two kinds of view are complementary for the observation of distributed applications.

- Selection of objects to be observed by class.
- Provision of debugging facilities including execution control and record and replay facilities.

The debugger follows the execution of a Comandos application through the sequence of elementary actions which it performs. The actions (or *events*) which can be monitored include:

- method call and return;
- object creation and destruction;
- object and class mapping;
- object migration;
- job and activity creation and termination;
- job and activity diffusion; and
- activity suspension and resumption.

Event tracing is done in close interaction with the language-specific run-time. The application is started in a special mode, in which all events generated by the application are reported to the debugger transparently to the application. Currently, the necessary extensions to the language-specific run-time have only been made for the Comandos language and hence the debugger is only available for use with applications written entirely in this language.

5.1.1 Printing the Content of an Object

During the execution of an application, the debugger can display the location and state of any object involved in the application. Given a reference to an object, the debugger can display the contents of the referenced object i.e. the values of its instance variables. These are displayed in a single window giving the name, the type and the value of each variable. References to other objects occurring in the instance data can be expanded by the user to display the object to which they refer.

Different objects can be designated by a single variable during the execution of an application. The debugger also provides a facility to show the evolution of a variable during the course of an application.

5.1.2 Execution Control

The debugging of an application is essentially an interactive task. Thus, it is important to give users some means for interacting both with the display and with the execution of their applications. The mechanisms provided by the debugger to control the execution of an application include:

- Suspension of the execution in order to examine the progress of the application and to analyse the current status of activities and objects. The execution can be terminated or resumed from this point as required.

- Tuning of the execution speed to allow the progress of the application to be followed in real time.
- Step by step execution i.e. suspension of the execution after each event.
- In addition, the user can select the components to be displayed and the update rate of the view.

5.1.3 Eliminating Non-deterministic Behaviour

An important and often difficult step in debugging programs is to actually locate the bugs. This is usually performed by executing the program and observing it at relevant points. In some cases (e.g. applications involving concurrency) this method cannot be used directly because of the effect of the tool on the execution i.e. the concurrent behaviour of the application is disturbed by the action of tracing, preventing the observation of its normal execution. The action of the debugger increases the non-deterministic behaviour of certain applications; for these applications, two executions may have different behaviours. A solution to this well-known problem in debugging parallel programs lies in adopting a two-phase approach, as proposed in [LeBlanc and Mellor-Crummey 1987] and [Miller and Choi 1988]:

- The *recording phase* (or execution phase): during the first execution of the program, the debugger records relevant events such as activity creation, suspension or resumption. Event selection can be restricted in order to reduce the amount of event recording. The trace contains a sequence of events, called a *history*. Data associated with these events are not recorded, in order to reduce the time and space used by recording; data are calculated for each execution during the second phase.
- The *replay phase* (or debugging phase): this second execution must replay the events recorded in the first phase without preserving timing constraints, but following the exact sequence of events recorded in the first phase. Debugging is performed in this second phase.

Using this approach, the same execution can be replayed as often as necessary, for debugging purposes.

The Comandos debugger provides two execution modes that correspond to the two phases described above. The first mode produces a history without supporting the debugging commands which are available in the second mode.

To reproduce the same behaviour, successive executions must follow the same execution path and use the same data. Therefore, some critical problems must be solved: management of the *execution context* and sharing of data with other applications. These two issues are addressed below.

During its execution a program uses a set of data known as its execution context. In a traditional system, the execution context of a program includes the temporary variables and files used by the program. To reproduce an execution, it is necessary to use exactly the same execution context; this condition is easy to achieve in a traditional system if:

- all variables used in a program are automatically initialised before each execution;
- a copy of each file to be written is taken before each execution and used by that execution;

In the Comandos system, there is not necessarily a distinction between temporary and permanent objects: all objects can be persistent and may be reused for successive executions. Thus there is a problem in distinguishing persistent objects which are effectively reused by successive executions of an application and objects created for each execution. Manual initialisation of objects to be used in different executions to the same initial state before each execution seems to be both tedious and error-prone when trying to reproduce the same execution. Hence the approach taken is to automatically rebuild the execution context of a program.

The debugger makes a copy of each object loaded by the application during the recording phase, and replaces it by a fresh copy before each execution during the replay phase. This requires support from the language-specific run-time such as the ability to copy mapped objects to replace an object by another.

The execution context of an application is composed of all the objects used during its execution. The copy mechanism is only used for a subset of the execution context of an application i.e. those objects used by the application but not created by it. All other objects are automatically created by each execution.

A consequence of this approach is that the execution must be isolated from the external world (i.e. objects normally shared between applications can no longer be shared due to the copy mechanism). The application is debugged in a particular mode, the *island mode*, disconnected from other applications, to ensure that there is no external interaction that can disturb the execution during the recording and the replay phases.

Application isolation is an important restriction for cooperative applications, which communicate by shared objects. There are two ways to deal with this problem. The first one is to group applications which share a set of objects and to debug them as a single application. The second approach consists of building a test program which simulates external actions on the shared objects.

5.2 The User Interface Development System

The objective of the User Interface Development System, known as the *INteractive GRaphical Interface Designer* (INGRID), is to provide a tool for the construction of interactive applications. In the design of the tool, three fundamental components were considered:

- A tool-kit that defines a comprehensive framework for user interface and application construction. This tool-kit (designated as the *4D tool-kit*) defines four main categories of objects:
  - *Display* objects correspond to the presentation component of the application and encapsulate Xt widgets.

- *Dialogue* objects encapsulate the processing of sequences of events and/or messages coming from Display objects.
- *Data* objects provide an interface between the interactive and the computational components of the application.
- *Driver* objects map particular Data objects to Display objects.

- A run-time system to provide support for interactive programming avoiding the need to integrate a complete interpreter inside the tool.
- A set of specialised editors, one for each of the object categories. The Display editor is currently the most sophisticated, allowing the construction of the graphical interface through direct manipulation operations.

As mentioned above, the user is presented with a set of dedicated editors for each of the user interface/application components, plus a higher level editor, called the *Organiser*, to establish the relations between objects.

The process of building an interface consists essentially of instantiation of tool-kit object and link operations, plus additional parameterisation of the created objects. Instantiation is mostly performed through direct manipulation operations. The link operations define the communication paths between objects, i.e. the recipients of the messages coming from either the user or the application. Parameterisation is done through per-class inspectors which are generated automatically from class definitions.

During the interface construction phase, if the application (computational) code is linked with the tool, the full application can be tested immediately, otherwise only the interface may be tested but no actual computation occurs.

An external representation of the objects, and the links between objects, allows the storage and retrieval of an interface during its design and construction. At the end of the construction phase, C++ code for the interface is generated which can be linked with the application code.

Use of INGRID with the Comandos platform allows the construction of interactive applications that manipulate persistent, distributed and shared data. However, the tool itself is independent of the Comandos platform although it is written in C++.

5.3 The Type Manager

The Type Manager (TpM) is the component of the Comandos platform which is responsible for the management of types. The TpM may be viewed as a database of type information which can be used from any of the languages supported by the Comandos platform. Basically the purpose of the TpM is twofold:

- to provide a uniform representation for types defined in the programming languages supported by the Comandos platform. This is achieved through the use of a *canonical model of types*, which is described in Sect. 5.3.1.
- to provide services for the storage and retrieval of type information. During the process of application development or configuration, types are created, named and registered in the TpM. Type information may be

read for the purpose of semantic type checking either at compile time or at run time. The architecture of the TpM is presented in Sect. 5.3.2. The management and use of type information are presented in subsequent sections.

Languages may access the TpM either by compiled-in calls to a standard library or by method calls to a standard TpM object. The TpM's clients are thus compilers, preprocessors, language-specific run-time systems and query processors. End users will not need direct access to the TpM's data although application programmers may.

5.3.1 Canonical Type Model

Objects managed by a Comandos system are typed. That is, they are classified into sets of objects such that all members of the set exhibit some common set of characteristics. A *type* consists of three aspects:

- a name;
- an abstract description, which defines the behaviour of objects of the type; and
- one or more implementations of this abstract description.

The abstract description characterises the common interface to all objects of the type and will be called an *abstract type* or, where context permits, just *type*. An implementation of this abstract type, a *class*, represents code and storage layout information. The provision of multiple classes for a single type is a requirement on a system such as Comandos which supports heterogeneous distributed applications – each machine architecture may require a different implementation of the same type. It also permits different representations of the same type to be used on the same node if this is appropriate.

Both the concepts of type and class are entirely intensional, in that there is no implication that a set of objects of the same type will necessarily exist or be available for access. It certainly does not imply that there is a single set of all the objects of a type.

Solely for the purposes of the TpM, types will be grouped into *kinds*, which bring together types which are similar at some higher abstract level. Thus for example there is the kind of basic types, the kind of procedure types, and the kind of existentially quantified types.

Finally, two different notions of one type being in some sense a more specialised form of another need to be specified. One abstract type, A, is said to be a *sub-type* of another abstract type, B, if any instance of A may be used wherever an instance of B is expected. The TpM will store code which checks sub-typing relations of this kind – the exact semantic details being different for different kinds and for different languages. The second notion is that implementation A, *inherits* from implementation B, if the code and storage structure information specified by B is reused by A. For simple situations, it would be expected that these two notions would be joined together.

The remainder of this section describes the kinds of type which the TpM can store and manipulate. This is specified as a type calculus which is essentially a development of [Cardelli and Wegner 1985]. For fuller details on all these matters, the reader is referred to [Comandos 1990b].

Basic Types The model assumes that there is a set of basic types, although which ones are included is matter of choice. The model assumes that each language possesses a set of basic types, but makes no assumptions about them. The set must be rich enough to allow the language to call and be called by the Comandos virtual machine – this requires that at least the primitive types integer, string and global name be available.

Constructor Types Five data constructor types are included in the model:

- Cartesian Product – a type of integer-indexed tuples;
- Record – a type of name-indexed tuples;
- Variant – a union of labelled typed fields;
- BoundedArray – an array with its bounds fixed at type definition time;
- FlexArray – an array where the bounds are not part of the type.

Function Types This allows the definition of the type of mappings from one type (or list of types) to another, given that the argument and result types have been defined.

Recursive Types Types which either refer to themselves or whose references form cycles are essential for the kinds of data models typically built in object-oriented systems. To define types recursively in a clean way, [Canning et al. 1989] is followed in introducing a fix-point operator, μ, as in:

$$\text{IntegerList} = \mu\, T \,.\, [\, \text{nil: Bottom} \mid \text{cons: } \{ \text{ hd: Integer ; tl: T } \} \,]$$

which defines **IntegerList** as a variant of either the **Bottom** type (whose only instance is **nil**) or the record type with the fields **hd**, of type **Integer**, and **tl**, of type **IntegerList**. This definition reads roughly that **IntegerList** is the type T, which will be fixed so that it can be used later in its own definition. Mutually recursive type definitions can be dealt with in the same way.

Generic Types Genericity is achieved by universally quantified types – type definitions which serve as templates for specific, instantiated types. They express collections of types with exactly the same structure. One example is the generalisation of the **IntegerList** type defined above to a generic **List** type, by combining recursion with parameterisation over the type of the elements:

$$\text{List} = \forall\, T \,.\, \mu\, S \,.\, [\, \text{nil : Bottom} \mid \text{cons : } \{ \text{ hd : T, tl : S } \} \,]$$

Here the generic type is defined as a fix-point of a variant type comprising either the unit type or a record type with the fields **hd** and **tl**. The type of **hd** is an arbitrary element type represented by the type variable T and the type of **tl** is the type of the fix-point of the recursion applied to the element type. Types such as **List of Integer** can be obtained by instantiating the type variable T with the type **Integer**.

Generic types provide sufficient syntax to express parametric polymorphism. For instance, a function returning the length of a list, for example, can be given the type:

$$\forall T. \ (List \ [T] \rightarrow Integer)$$

The type variable T is universally quantified over in this type. Its instantiation by a specific type – say Boolean – gives the type of a function returning the length of a list of booleans.

Abstract Types An abstract type defines a set of operations over a set of values. The set of values is the subject being abstracted over. Clients of an abstract type manipulate its values through the operations provided. So long as the interfaces to an abstract type remain unchanged, any implementation changes do not affect the clients. Mitchell and Plotkin, adopting a formalism of Girard's [Girard 1972], introduced the idea that abstract types can be expressed as existential quantification [Mitchell and Plotkin 1988]. For example, the Integer type can be expressed, in an object-oriented fashion, as:

$$\exists T. \ \{ \ add: \ T \rightarrow T; \ display: \ T \rightarrow String, \ ... \ \}$$

To introduce an existential type, we must have a type implementing the abstraction: the *witness type* or the *representation type*. This type is not visible outside the existential type's definition. To its clients, it is only known that a representation for the Integer type exists and that it can be used, for example, in an addition operation.

The division between abstract and representation types has been taken as the underlying mechanism for all Comandos types. However here we describe abstract types as being an explicit representation for object-oriented classes, since universal and existential types can be used in combination to model parametric abstract data types.

Top and Bottom Type systems that incorporate sub-typing organise their types into a lattice or partial order, which usually has a top element and, if it has multiple inheritance, may sometimes have a bottom one also. The Top type is a super-type of all types; all objects are instances of it. The Bottom type is a sub-type of all types; its only instance will be a polymorphic nil, where this is permitted.

Bounded Quantification Cardelli and Wegner add a further type construction facility to their system; the ability to construct universal or existential types where the parameter or witness type is constrained to be a sub-type of some other type. The abstract syntax for defining such a type looks like

$$\forall t \leq T \mid type - expression$$

or

$$\exists t \leq T \mid type - expression$$

This provides among other facilities, the ability to express inclusion polymorphism or IS-A relationships between classes.

F-bounded Quantification [Canning et al. 1989] extends bounded quantification by allowing the variable of quantification to occur in the constraint;

as described in their paper, this gives an increase in descriptive power particularly relevant to object-oriented languages.

Reference Types Almost all programming languages incorporate a pointer or reference type constructor which is a monadic function on types.

Exceptions Many modern programming languages have an exception model where raisable exceptions are declared in the interface specification of a function or procedure.

Dynamic Types Persistent programming systems need to handle long-lived data; this means that some programs may need to allow for types that have not been defined at the time they were written. Several language designs deal with this problem by introducing a special type for persistent data of unknown type; Dynamic in Amber [Cardelli 1984], pntr in PS-algol [PPRR 1986], any in Napier [Morrison et al. 1989]. All of these have slightly different semantics, which are in some cases different from Top – for instance, one might cover only user-defined types, while another covers all types, including basic types.

5.3.2 The Type Manager Architecture

Using the canonical type model described in the previous section, the types which arise in different languages can be described using a common formalism. In order to complete this process however, the TpM needs to contain specialised forms of operations to check type equivalence and sub-typing since different languages have different semantics for these operations. The mechanism for this and the general structure of the TpM are now described.

Types are grouped into a set of *units*, which gather together types which arise in a common context. There are two sorts of context, giving rise to two sorts of unit:

- a *language unit* holds the set of types intrinsic to a language – thus there will be language units for at least the Comandos Language, C++ and Eiffel;

- an *application unit* holds the set of types relevant to a particular application.

Application units are created in the context of an already existing unit (usually a language unit), thus forming the set of units into a hierarchy. In constructing a new application, the programmer creates a new unit for it and then, as the application is developed, the application-specific type information is housed in that unit. In developing the application, the programmer will have the current application unit available as well as any other unit above it in the hierarchy of units, but may also access the types in other units required by explicitly referencing them.

Access to types is therefore via a two-level naming scheme, in which a given type may be retrieved by providing the type name and the name of the unit in which it is stored. Type names are unique within units.

Table 5.1. Operations to manage units

Operation	Description
createLang	Create a new (empty) language unit.
lang	Retrieve a language unit by name.
createUnit	Create a new application unit.
removeUnit	Remove an application unit.
openUnit	Open an application unit for further use.
closeUnit	Close an application unit making insertions permanent.

In the following sections the functionality of the TpM is therefore described in terms of the management of units, the creation of types and the storage and retrieval of type information. Finally, the processes of registering a new language with the TpM and of compiling a program will be briefly described.

The implementation of the TpM is in the form of ODMS collections of types and units (c.f. Chap. 6). The descriptions which follow are thus in terms of the operations which are provided for the abstract types unit and type which underlie these collections.

5.3.3 The Management of Units

All types are stored in units. Operations are therefore provided which create and destroy units. Units are created in the context of some already existing unit – thus a hierarchy of units is created.

The process of inserting types into a unit follows a transactional approach. This approach has been chosen since all modules which store type information require the ability to make the insertion of a set of types atomic. For instance, during a compilation, either all of the types generated should be inserted or none of them. The situation in which a few of the types are stored before the compilation fails is to be avoided. Operations to open units for further insertions and to close them and confirm all the storage are provided. The full list of operations provided is given in Table 5.1.

5.3.4 The Creation of Types

Base types are created as special kinds of abstract types during the language registration process. All other types are created out of already existing types by calls to TpM operations. Each operation creates a type representation in the canonical form and then returns a reference to this representation. The operations use parameters which are either references to other types or contain information such as names. The constructor and function types are created by the operations cartesian, record, variant, array, flexArray, and function.

The construction of more complex types (recursive, quantified and abstract types) is achieved by more complex operations. Firstly, there is an operation

Table 5.2. Operations to create generic and abstract types

Operation	Description
subst	create an instantiation of a generic type
instantiate	create usable instantiations of abstract types
makeVar	
fixpoint	
universal	
existential	

Table 5.3. Operations to manage types

Operation	Description
putType	Insert the type into a unit.
unbindType	Remove the binding to a type from the unit.
getTypeByName	Retrieve a type dynamically.
getTypeByReference	Retrieve a type statically.

which creates type variables for use in quantified expressions. The result of this operation can then be used in constructing other types by being supplied wherever a type is expected. There is an operation which grounds recursively defined type expressions. There are operations to create generic and abstract types and to create instantiations of these (c.f. Table 5.2).

5.3.5 The Storage and Retrieval of Type Information

Once types have been created by the operations described in the previous section, they are manipulated in the context of the unit structure by the operations listed in Table 5.3.

The operations listed in Table 5.4 permit the retrieval of certain components of a constructor type.

Finally, the set of operations listed in Table 5.5 provides type checking and display facilities.

5.3.6 The Process of Language Registration

This section will briefly outline the steps with which a language unit is installed in the system, thus permitting a new language to use the TpM. A module must be written which proceeds as follows:

1. Create a language unit by a call to the operation createLang.
2. Install the base types by calls to the operation putType.

Table 5.4. Operations to retrieve components of constructor types

Operation	Description
getTupleField	Return type of a field of a cartesian product type.
getRecordFieldNames	Return names of the fields in a record type.
getRecordField	Return type of a named field of a record type.
getVariantFieldNames	Return names of the options of a variant type.
getVariantField	Return type of a named option of a variant type.
getArrayElt	Return element type of an array type.
getArrayBounds	Return bounds of an array type.
getFlexArrayElt	Return element type of a FlexArray type.
getFunctionArgs	Return argument types of a function.
getFunctionResult	Return result type of a function.

Table 5.5. Operations for type checking

Operation	Description
isNameEquivalent	Are the types derived from the same declaration?
isStructureEquivalent	Do the types have isomorphic type structures?
isSubtype	Do the types have compatible type structures?
display	Give representation suitable for screen output.

3. Install language specific versions of the code to perform type and sub-type checking. The operations, `isNameEquivalent`, etc. will call the appropriate version of these.
4. Close the language unit.

A language implementor wishing to use the TpM will need to have new user-defined types stored within it by using the operations described in Sect. 5.3.4: this may be done by modifying a compiler or by adding a preprocessing stage.

5.3.7 The Process of Compilation

The interaction between a language preprocessor or compiler and the TpM involves the following steps:

1. The processor opens the designated application unit in which all new types will be stored. It also recursively opens any units in which this unit is embedded as well as any other units which are specified.
2. As processing proceeds, types will be created by the operations described in Sect. 5.3.4 and then stored by the operation `putType`.
3. If the processor aborts, all of the insertions will be lost. If it succeeds, a call to `closeUnit` will make the changes permanent.

6. The Object Data Management Service

The Object Data Management Service (ODMS) supports the management of potentially large inter-related collections of persistent objects that typically arise in data intensive applications.

The ODMS data model, known as the Binary Relational Object-Oriented Model (BROOM), specifies the forms that collections may take and the ways in which collections may be inter-related by means of static constraints. An operational model is also supported by the ODMS in terms of a high-level query language based on a collection algebra. A description of the data and operational models are given in the first two sections of this chapter. These are followed by a description of how these models are realised within the ODMS and by a description of the application programmer's interface to the ODMS.

Further details of the ODMS and its underlying data model can be found in [Harper and Norrie 1991a], [Harper and Norrie 1991b] and [Norrie 1992]. The programmer's interface to the ODMS is described in [Glasgow 1992].

6.1 Data Model

It is important to emphasise that the ODMS has no control over the form of persistent objects contained in collections as this is determined by the type systems of the programming languages supported by Comandos. The ODMS was generalised to support collections of any form of data item supported by the system – not only objects. For example, it also supports collections of integers, strings and records. Hence the term *value* is used to mean any form of data item that can be described by the underlying type system whether it be a basic value such as an integer or string value, or a complex value such as a record or object value. Note that in the case of objects a value is in fact an object identifier: thus a collection of objects is in fact a collection of object identifiers.

The BROOM model specifies the ways in which values can be grouped into collections and how these collections can then be linked together to form a database.

Values are grouped into collections that correspond to the roles of those values in the application domain. Significant roles are identified by consideration of the envisaged use of the values. While the role of a value is clearly related to its type, this is not the sole determining factor. To illustrate this, consider a simple university database.

The university is interested in the various persons associated with the university and these are represented by objects of type **person**. Objects which are instances of type **person** may be grouped into a number of collections according to access patterns.

An application dealing with car parking permits might require access to all persons associated with the university and would therefore have a collection **Persons** with all existing **person** objects as members.

In addition, there may be an application which requires access only to persons who are registered as students in which case a collection **Students** could be formed. Further, if only staff members can be responsible for university projects, then the collection **Staff** might be formed. It is not necessary that the member objects of **Students** and **Staff** are of different types since these objects are classified by means of the membership of collections. Only in the event that it is actually required that the objects of one or other category have different properties, in terms of their form or behaviour, need specialised sub-types of **person** be created for students and staff.

Relationships between entities in the application domain are represented by mappings between collections of values representing these entities. In the university example, the relationships between staff members and the projects for which they are responsible could be represented by a relation called **Manages** which maps members of the **Staff** collection to members of the **Projects** collection. **Staff** is referred to as the *source collection* of **Manages** and **Projects** as the *target collection*. This relation can be represented by a collection of pair values of the form (s_i, p_j) where s_i is a member of the source collection and p_j is a member of the target collection.

Therefore, there are two forms of collections supported in the BROOM model. *Unary collections* are those which have atomic values as elements and, generally, represent collections of entities of the application domain. *Binary collections* are those which have pair values as elements and represent relationships between entities. Note that the source and target collections of a binary collection may be any form of collection; hence, a three way association may be represented by a binary collection which links a binary collection to a unary collection.

Collections (unary or binary) may exhibit set, bag or sequence properties depending upon whether or not the collection may contain duplicate elements and whether or not there is an ordering on the elements.

Collections may be linked together to form a *schema* which represents the dependencies among collections. There are two basic forms of dependencies among collections. Firstly, collections may be linked together into a *classification structure* by means of constraints which specify *collection families*. Secondly, each binary collection is linked to a source and target collection with associated cardinality constraints.

A collection family specifies one or more *parent collections* and one or more *child collections*. If there is a single parent and a single child, then there is a simple *sub-collection* relationship between the two collections. If a single parent has a number of children, then these children may have restrictions which indicate that they are *disjoint* and/or that they form a *cover* in which case every member of the parent collection must be a member of at least one of the children. If the children are disjoint and form a cover of the parent collection, then they are said to be a *partition* of the parent. If a collection is a child of two or more parent collections then it may be specified to be the *intersection* of the parent collections.

A classification structure is shown in Fig. 6.1 which is a simple example schema for the university database expressed in the graphical notation of BROOM. A unary collection is represented by a shaded rectangle with different shadings used for sets, bags and sequences. The name of the collection is given in the non-shaded part of the rectangle and the type of the members of the collection may be specified in the shaded part. A binary collection is represented by a shaded rounded-rectangle with the name of the collection inside.

A directed arc is used to indicate a parent of a family. Where a collection family consists of a single parent and a single child then a simple sub-collection relationship exists and there is a directed arc from the child to the parent with no constraint box. This can be seen in the case of the collection of research projects ResProjects which is a sub-collection of the collection Projects.

The collections of a collection family are linked together by means of arcs and constraint boxes. As described above, a collection family may satisfy conditions of disjointness, coverage, partitioning or intersection, and these are represented by a small constraint box containing d, c, p or i, respectively. The collections Students and Staff cover the collection Persons. Thus the collections Persons, Students and Staff form a collection family in which Persons is the parent and Students and Staff are the children. The collection Demonstrators is the intersection of the collections Students and Staff and this is indicated by a constraint box containing an i connecting the child collection Demonstrators to the two parent collections Students and Staff.

If a collection C_1 is specified to be a sub-collection of another collection C_2, then the type of the members of C_1 must either be the same as or a sub-type of that of the members of C_2.

The source collection of a binary collection is indicated by means of a grounded arc, i.e. an arc with a '•' at the source end, and the target collection is indicated by a directed arc. The cardinality constraints are written alongside the arcs. A cardinality constraint takes the general form $(i:j)$ where i indicates the minimum level of participation and j indicates the maximum level of participation, If the maximum level is given as n, then there is no maximum limit. In the example of Fig. 6.1, a staff member can be responsible for zero to six projects and each project must have exactly one associated member of staff.

An important feature of the BROOM model is its ability to represent multiple classification views. Consider the example of the staff in the university

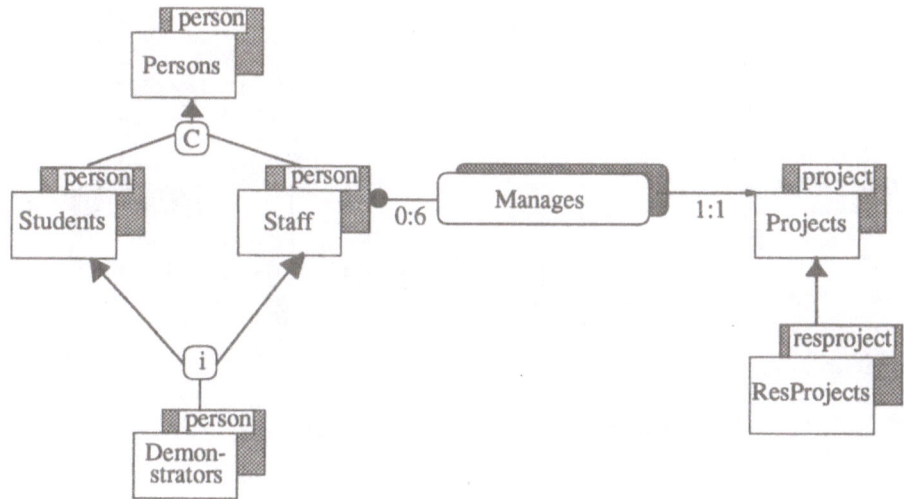

Fig. 6.1. An example schema diagram.

database. It is possible that one application processes staff who are European Community nationals in a different way from those who are not European Community nationals and it is therefore convenient to group staff into the two collections ECs and NonECs. However, another application may wish to group staff individuals according to whether they are academic or non-academic staff. In other words, the grouping of entities into significant roles is dependent upon the particular application. In BROOM, a collection may belong to any number of collection families and hence it is possible for different applications to have different classification views of application entities. A BROOM model for the above example is given in Fig. 6.2. Here Staff is both partitioned into the sub-collections ECs and NonECs, and, is also covered by the sub-collections Academics and NonAcademics. Supporting these multiple classification views is a powerful modelling mechanism which avoids the introduction of multiple sub-typing that would be required to model such situations in most other object-oriented data models.

6.2 Operational Model

The operational model of the ODMS specifies operations on collections. It is based on a collection algebra which can be thought of as a generalisation of the relational algebra to deal with general collections of values rather than the single form of collection given by sets of tuples.

The purpose and level of the collection algebra should be likened to that of the relational algebra. It defines operations on collections – but does not say anything about the implementation of these operations. A user may express

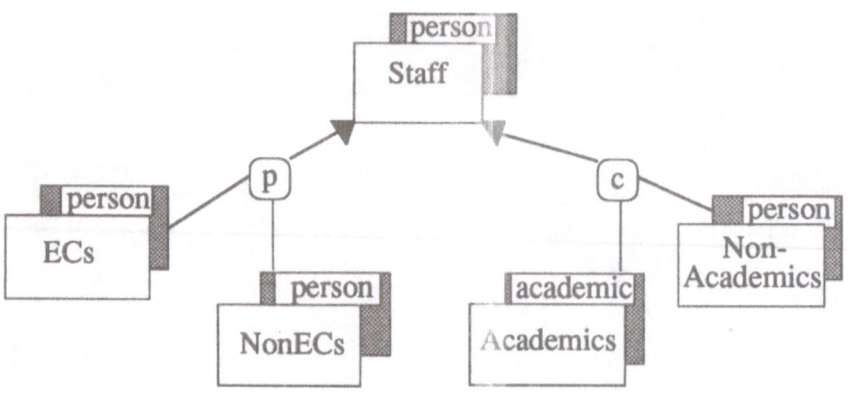

Fig. 6.2. Multiple classification views.

an operation on a database in terms of a high-level query expression purely in terms of the logical description of the data model. This means that it is more convenient for the user in that they need not know the physical representation of collections and further it means that these query expressions may be optimised. Such an algebra can provide the basis for the existence of a number of possible high-level query languages which may look more or less like the algebra in its pure form.

As outlined above, the BROOM model supports two forms of collection – unary and binary – and three kinds of collection – set, bag and sequence. While at first sight the possibility of six different sorts of collections might seem confusing, the uniformity of approach and the use of genericity keeps the model simple.

There are a number of operations which are available on all collections. Let C_1 and C_2 be collections, then

$$C_1 + C_2 \quad \text{union}$$
$$C_1 \char`^ C_2 \quad \text{intersection}$$
$$C_1 - C_2 \quad \text{difference}$$
$$C_1 \times C_2 \quad \text{Cartesian product}$$
$$C_1 @ M \quad \text{map method } M \text{ over collection } C_1$$
$$C_1 : P \quad \text{selection of values of } C_1 \text{ satisfying predicate } P$$
$$\# \, C_1 \quad \text{cardinality}$$

Each of these operations is specialised for each kind of collection. For example, if C_1 and C_2 are set collections, then in the expression $C_1 + C_2$ a set union operation will be performed on the sets of elements. If the operand collections are not of the same kind and form, then the conversion operations described later can be used to convert one or both collections so that they are of the same kind and form.

There are also a number of operations which are specific to a particular form or kind of collection. For example, sequence collections have operations which take account of the ordering of the elements.

In the case of binary collections, there are a number of specific operations some of which are given below.

$C_1 * C_2$ composition
inv C_1 inverse
C_1 **dr** C_3 domain restriction to the elements of collection C_3
C_1 **ds** C_3 domain subtraction of elements of collection C_3
C_1 **rr** C_3 range restriction to the elements of collection C_3
C_1 **rs** C_3 range subtraction of elements of collection C_3

Domain restriction reduces a binary collection by selecting all members which have a first element in the given set. Domain subtraction eliminates all those members which have a first element in the given set. Correspondingly, the range restriction and subtraction operations reduce a binary collection through consideration of the second elements of the member pairs.

In addition there are operations to convert between the three kinds of collections. These are **setify**, **bagify**, **seqify**. The conversions between the collection kinds are fairly natural. A sequence is converted to a bag by the elimination of ordering. A bag is converted to a set by the elimination of duplicates. A set is converted to a bag by taking the bag of elements of the set in which each element occurs exactly once. To convert a bag or set to a sequence requires an ordering to be specified.

A unary collection can be formed from a binary collection C either by taking the domain or range of C. The domain of C, **dom** C, is formed from the first elements of the member pairs of C. The range of C, **rng** C, is formed from the second elements of the member pairs. In both cases, the kind of the resulting unary collection will be the same as that of C.

A binary collection can be formed from a unary collection by the **relify** operation which constructs the corresponding identity mapping. For example, given the set $\{x, y, z\}$, then **relify** $\{x, y, z\} = \{(x, x), (y, y), (z, z)\}$.

Query expressions can be formed in terms of the operations of the collection algebra. As an example, consider a query expression to give the set of person objects who are managers of research projects with funds greater than 100 000 ECUs.

Seniors = **dom** (Manages **rr** ResProjects:funds > 100 000)

The expression on the right hand side of the equals is evaluated and the value is assigned to the collection **Seniors** which should be a unary set collection with member type **person**.

A brief flavour of the collection algebra has been presented but space limitations prevents a detailed description of the algebra and all of its properties being given. The algebraic properties of the algebra are important for performing transformations of query expressions for the purposes of query optimisation. Descriptions of the collection operations are given in [Glasgow 1992].

6.3 Structure

The ODMS provides a tool-kit of classes for the management of large (or small) collections of values. The library is layered: at the top level it implements the BROOM abstractions and at lower levels it provides access method aggregates such as dynamic hash tables and B+ trees.

The ODMS is portable – it is provided on several different platforms. At the time of writing these include Comandos, EXODUS [Carey et al. 1986], and several non-persistent C++ systems.

The following three subsections provide an overview of each tool-kit layer. These are most conveniently described from the bottom up. In that order, the layers provided are the *Aggregate Layer*, the *Bulk Layer*, and the *Collection Layer*. Full details of the ODMS can be found in [Glasgow 1992].

6.3.1 The Aggregate Layer

The *Aggregate Layer* provides basic access methods such as lists, dynamic hash tables and B+ trees. It also provides the model of a *storable value* used by higher levels. Storable values include all the base types of the programming language at hand, for example, integers, (restricted) strings and object references.

This layer is appropriate for application programmers who require sophisticated data storage structures. All the Aggregate Layer access methods support a unified interface. This increases the flexibility of use by the programmer.

The Aggregate Layer classes are used extensively by the higher levels of the tool-kit. By conforming to the interface conventions of the Aggregate Layer, additional specialised access methods can be provided for particular applications.

In addition to the basic access methods, the Aggregate Layer provides *Index Classes*. For each basic access method, there is a corresponding Index Class. So, for example, one can declare hashed or ordered indexes.

6.3.2 The Bulk Layer

The *Bulk Layer*, which is constructed on top of the Aggregate Layer, provides set, bag, sequence and relation abstractions. It is intended for use by programmers writing small stand-alone database applications.

Although appropriate defaults are employed, two levels of genericity are provided at the Bulk Layer. Firstly for sets and bags, the programmer may choose the underlying representation. For example, one set may require fast random access membership checks. In this case a hashed representation is appropriate. Another may require frequent scans over ordered sub-sets. In this case a balanced tree may be appropriate.

Secondly, for relations the representation can be a set, a bag, or a sequence. Combined with the flexibility above, the Bulk Layer provides, for example, hashed-set relations and sequence relations.

6.3.3 The Collection Layer

The *Collection Layer* provides the same abstractions as the Bulk Layer enhanced with multiple representations, intensional representations, constraints and query language support.

Collections have multiple representations: for example, a collection which is frequently accessed, in both a random and ordered way, may be sufficiently important to merit two implementations. If the collection stores information on particular Students, say, then one implementation may be a hashed index on student numbers, while another may be a B+ tree-based ordered index on the student names. Such representations are referred to as *extensional representations* as they are explicitly stored.

In contrast to extensional representations, *intensional representations* are "recipes" for the computation of the elements of a collection. More precisely, intentional representations are realised using query terms involving other collections. Thus a collection can have a number of intensional representations in addition to its extensional ones. For example, with reference to the example schema given previously, the set of Projects may have the intentional representation denoted by the term (rng Manages), that is, the range of the Manages relation. Intentional representations provide alternative access paths to data which are useful, for example, in query processing.

Each collection may have a number of extensional and intentional representations: the choice of these determines the space usage and efficiency of access to the collection on assorted properties. A collection with no extensional representations corresponds to that which is traditionally referred to as a *view*.

Constraints can be described and maintained between collections. For example, that the domain of the Manages relation above is equal to the Staff set may be declared to be a property to be enforced by the system. A notion of *semantic transaction* is introduced to encapsulate operations which are required to be atomic with respect to these constraints and recovery actions can be associated with each way in which a constraint can be violated.

A group of collections with multiple representations, some of which may be views, and with constraints declared between these collections, constitutes a database.

6.4 The Programmer's Interface

The ODMS programmer's interface enables application developers to program in terms of the BROOM data model and the associated operational model based on a collection algebra. Specifically it enables them to describe and manipulate BROOM databases comprising BROOM collections. Thus, the programmer's interface delivers the functionality provided by the Collection Layer of the ODMS tool-kit presented in Sect. 6.3.3. Specialised (sub-)languages are also provided for conveniently describing and manipulating BROOM databases and collections. Consequently, a data and storage definition language (DSDL) and a data manipulation sub-language (DML) are provided. It is intended that these languages be used in conjunction with any of the supported programming languages although initially C++ has been selected as the host language.

Application programmers wishing to program using the abstractions provided by the lower levels of the tool-kit, namely the Bulk and Aggregate levels, may do so using the C++ classes which implement these layers. For further details concerning these classes, the reader is referred to [Glasgow 1992].

6.4.1 Basics

An ODMS programmer must program at two levels; one involving objects which uses one of the supported programming languages, and the other involving collections with appropriate linguistic support for describing, constructing and manipulating collections.

In fact, all of the ODMS concepts are captured in the Collection Layer; thus there are C++ classes corresponding to the concepts of database, collection (of various forms), constraint, view and query. An ODMS application programmer could program directly using these classes. However, as observed earlier, specialised (sub-)languages are provided to describe and manipulate BROOM collections.

The DSDL is used to describe and construct a database in terms of the BROOM model. The result is a BROOM database containing BROOM collections and associated storage structures which can be populated with objects constructed using a supported language.

A DML for manipulating BROOM collections is also provided, and is embedded within a host programming language. The primary functions of the DML are to establish bindings between programming language variables and the collections of a database, and to enable querying of collections using a query language based on the collection algebra. The query language enables programmers to "program by querying", a programming style in which retrieval from collections is expressed declaratively. The ODMS is responsible for optimising and producing evaluation plans for these queries based on the representations of the collections.

The collections are populated with objects (and values) using operations provided directly by the ODMS collection classes.

6.4.2 The Data and Storage Definition Language

The DSDL enables a programmer to describe and create BROOM databases. The collections which comprise a database are described, and constraints over these collections are specified. For each collection, one or more representations are specified.

In the current version of the ODMS, DSDL programs are compiled into C++ which is compiled and executed. As a result, objects corresponding to the database and collections are created as persistent objects, and in the case of the database object named and made a persistent root.

A partial and simplified DSDL description of the university database introduced in the BROOM schema diagram of Fig. 6.1 is shown below. Partial type declarations for the types Person, Project and ResProject are also given.

```
database univDB;
 collections:
   Persons, Students, Staff, Demonstrators : set of Person;
   Projects : sequence of Project;
   ResProjects : set of ResProject;
   Manages : set of (Person, Project);
 constraints:
   Persons => cover [Students, Staff];
   intersection [Students, Staff] => Demonstrators;
   Projects => ResProjects;
   Manages <-> Staff (0:6) to Projects (1:n)
 representations:
   Persons index(hash) name;
   Staff, Students, ResProjects set(hash);
   Projects index(hash) pnumber, list;
   Manages domain index(hash);
end database.

/* Type declarations - not part of DSDL */
type Person
   name: string;
end;

type Project
   pnumber: integer;
   title : string
end;

type ResProject subtype of Project
   fundingbody : string;
   budget : integer
end;
```

Collections in the database are described by *collection schemes*. Each collection scheme gives a description of a collection comprising of its name, the type of its members and its behaviour. The collection schemes give the name space of the database in that they bind names to collections.

There are two forms of constraint statement – one for collection families and one for relationships. The constraint

$$\text{Projects} => \text{ResProjects}$$

specifies that ResProjects is a sub-collection of Projects. In general, the parent collection (or list of parent collections) is given on the left of => and the child (or list of children) on the right. If a list of collections is supplied then the list may be qualified by a constraint condition. In the case of parent collections this condition may be intersection. In the case of child collections the condition may be one of disjoint, cover or partition. The constraint

$$\text{Manages} < - > \text{Staff} \ (0\!:\!6) \ \textbf{to} \ \text{Projects} \ (1\!:\!n)$$

specifies that relation Manages has source collection Staff and target collection Projects with the associated cardinality constraints.

The application programmer may choose appropriate representations for each collection depending on the data accessing requirements of the applications expected to execute against the database. The choice of representations correspond to access methods provided by the Bulk and Aggregate layers described in Sect. 6.3. Representations may either be direct representations of a collection, e.g. set of persons, or indexed representations, e.g. name index over persons.

For the Persons unary collection, a hashed index over the name attribute of person objects in the collection is specified. In this case, the programmer expects to access individual persons by name rather than accessing persons in name order.

For the Projects unary collection two representations are specified, a hashed index over project number, and a direct representation which is a list of projects (actually project identifiers).

For the Manages binary collection, a domain-to-range hashed index over the domain values (persons) is specified which enables fast access to projects managed by a given person. This kind of index is similar to the join indexes proposed for relational DBMS. Other representations for binary relations are being investigated including the usual representations used in object-oriented databases namely embedding references directly within objects. In addition to the stored representations described thus far, representations can be views expressed using queries.

6.4.3 The Data Manipulation Sub-language

The DML in combination with its host language enables an application programmer to query and update collections in a BROOM database.

The DML will be introduced by way of a simplified transaction, in which a new project is added to the university database. The C++/DML program which implements this transaction is shown below. The line numbers appearing in the program text will be referenced in the description below.

```
1: main() {

2:   dml useDatabase univDB;

3:   char* PName= getString();

4:   Person* aStaff= [/ one ( Staff : name==PName ) /];

5:   Project* aProject= new Project();
6:   Projects->insert(aProject);

7:   if [/ count ({aStaff} dr Manages) /] < 6
8:       Manages->relate(aStaff,aProject);

9:   Set* PNames= [/ rng ({aStaff} dr Manages) map title /];
10: }
```

The DML useDatabase statement (line 2) establishes bindings between programming language variables and the collections in the specified database. By default, each collection is bound to a variable of the same name of the appropriate type, e.g. a variable Projects of type UnaryCollection* is introduced.

The query language component of the DML is closely modelled on the collection algebra introduced in Sect. 6.2. Queries extend the expression syntax of the host programming language and are strongly typed. A query expression of a given type may appear anywhere that an expression of that type may appear. Query expressions are delimited by special brackets [/../].

In line 4, the set of persons with name PName is selected from the Staff collection, and assuming that set contains just one person, the query evaluates to a single person. The type of this query is Person*. The query in line 7 counts the number of projects managed by a particular person (aStaff) and the expression is of type int. Set literals are introduced between the brackets {..}. The query in line 9 evaluates to the set of titles of projects managed by the given person (aStaff).

Collections are updated by invoking operations provided by the corresponding collection class (a C++ class). For example, a project is inserted in the unary collection Projects in line 6. In line 7, the binary collection Manages has a new pair (aStaff, aProject) inserted. Other operations are provided to delete individual objects and groups of objects from unary collections, and analogous operations are provided for binary collections.

Programs written in C++/DML are preprocessed to produce C++ programs. Each embedded query expression is extracted from the program text, parsed, type-checked and then a corresponding query object is constructed and saved in the Comandos storage system. Such a query comprises a parse tree, corresponding to the query expression, and an execution plan for evaluating the query that results from query optimisation. Embedded query expressions are then replaced with C++ text which fetches the corresponding query object from the storage system and evaluates it. Queries are "active" objects in the sense that they are self-optimising and self-evaluating.

The application programming interface described herein has been developed to meet the requirements of programmers using programming languages such as C++. Consequently, DML extensions to the host language have been limited to the minimum necessary to exploit the functionality provided by the ODMS. However, it is clear that the ODMS provides a foundation on which very high-level database programming languages and supporting systems can be built.

6.5 Summary

The Comandos ODMS augments the services provided by the Comandos kernel with appropriate support for programming database applications which typically involve large collections of data. The Comandos kernel provides for the persistent storage of typed objects, and the ODMS adds facilities for the management of potentially large inter-related collections of such objects. These facilities are based around the structures and operations of the ODMS data model.

The structural part of the ODMS data model, BROOM, is designed to describe collections, and classification structures over them, by means of static constraints. Recall that these collections describe logical groupings of objects which may have one or more physical representations. A programmer expresses operations in terms of logical collections, and the ODMS is responsible for mapping these operations to the corresponding physical representations thus realising the database concept of physical data independence. Static constraints are used to capture the semantics of the application system and the ODMS is then responsible for checking database consistency with respect to these constraints. However, these can be used to support a notion of "programming by constraints" where update rules are attached to constraints and the ODMS maintains consistency through update propagation.

The operational part of the ODMS data model is based on an algebra of collections, and this algebra in turn provides the basis for developing query languages. A particular query language has been realised in Comandos as an embedded sub-language within C++ (c.f. Sect. 6.4.3). This approach enables associative access to collections of data and thereby supports a declarative style of programming which has been referred to as "programming by querying". By focussing on the provision of higher-level programming abstractions, the ODMS extends the repertoire of programming styles available to the Comandos application programmer. In these respects, the ODMS differs markedly from other proposals for integrating database functionality within persistent object systems. Rather than simply providing a set of container types, a collection-based data model which captures conceptual dependencies between collections has been developed.

A complete prototype of the ODMS has been implemented. The ODMS C++ class library, which is the basis of the services, was constructed in accordance with an open, layered implementation architecture. The resultant services are effective for programming, efficient in operation, and extensible in meeting new data management requirements.

The experience gained in designing and implementing the ODMS for Comandos should provide useful guidelines to the developers of future data management services for distributed open systems.

7. Management Tools

The Comandos platform includes a set of cooperating management tools for the overall control and administration of a Comandos installation. Since the dynamics of the environment also affects the administration and management tasks, the tools themselves must be implemented in a highly flexible, reusable way. Existing UNIX tools can also be reused, where they appear to be appropriate for a given Comandos environment, as a result of the coexistence of the Comandos and UNIX environments.

This chapter describes the three categories of management tools developed in the project:

- The *Distributed Directory Service*, presented in Sect. 7.1, is an implementation of the X.500-IS9594 standards [CCITT 1988] integrated into the Comandos platform.
- Section 7.2 describes a set of administration and configuration facilities, which allow the operational control of an installation.
  - The *System Observation Facility* allows management information to be collected dynamically from *sensors* built into managed objects.
  - Administration and reconfiguration decisions stemming from the management tools are then implemented by the *System Control Facility*.
  - The *User and Host Administration* tool supports the management of users and hosts.
  - In addition, Comandos provides a related tool which supports the design of distributed business systems.
- Section 7.3 describes a set of security tools which include:
  - A *Protocol Data Analysis Tool*, which is responsible for the analysis of the audit data generated by the running system.
  - A *Risk Management Tool* which assists with the assessment of risks to the operation of the system.

7.1 The Distributed Directory Service

A directory service is basically an application which, given a resource name, returns information about the corresponding resource. It is used by other tools, services and applications to convert symbolic names for objects to the global names of the corresponding objects, and to obtain additional information concerning the object. Any application may use the directory assuming that the information it needs was registered with the directory.

The Comandos *Distributed Directory Service* (DDS) is a distributed application built in conformance with the X.500 ISO-CCITT recommendations [CCITT 1988], which define OSI application layer entities, a data model, a functional model, services and protocols.

In the following sections, an overview of the DDS architecture is presented. This description focuses on the functional model of the DDS and the directory services supported.

7.1.1 Functional Model

7.1.1.1 Information Model. A resource name is a hierarchical name, called a *Distinguished Name* (DN), allowing unique and unambiguous identification of the resource.

The information concerning a resource is composed of a set of *attributes*. This information is grouped and organised into the *Directory Information Tree* (DIT). In a Comandos distributed system, the DIT is itself distributed on several nodes.

The Directory Information Tree. A directory is logically structured as a tree in which nodes and leaves form directory entries (c.f. Fig. 7.1). The top of the tree is called the *root*. Two kinds of entries are possible: *object* entries which hold the information describing an object; and *alias* entries hold references to object entries.

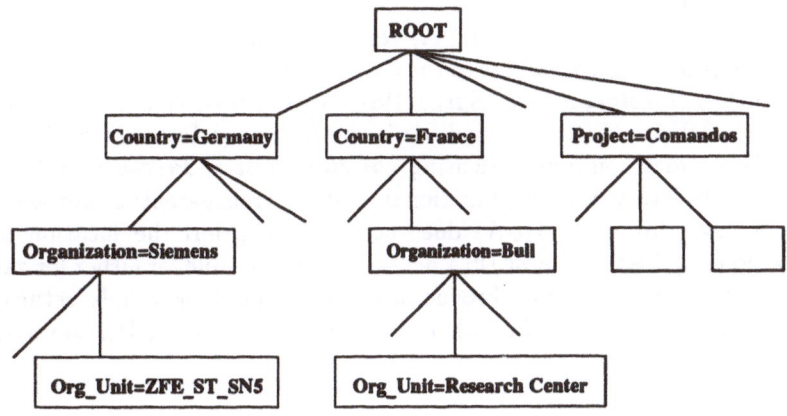

Fig. 7.1. Structure of the DIT.

A directory entry is structured as a set of attributes where each attribute has an attribute type and can be multi-valued. At least one of the attributes of the entry is said to be *distinguished* – its type and value forming the name of the entry. The DN of an entry is obtained by concatenating this attribute type and value couple to the DN of its parent. An example of a DN for an Org_Unit entry in the tree of Fig. 7.1 might be:

{Country = Germany/Organisation = Siemens/Org_Unit = ZFE_ST_SN5}

Objects and Object-classes. All entries containing the same kind of information have their format defined by an *object-class*. An object-class contains a list of mandatory and optional attributes. Attributes can be single or multi-valued. A set of selected object-classes is pre-defined in the X.500 standard. For instance, the Person object-class has the following ASN.1 definition:

```
        Person OBJECT-CLASS SUBCLASS OF top
               MUST CONTAIN {
                      commonName,
                      surname }
               MAY CONTAIN {
                      description,
                      seeAlso,
                      telephoneNumber,
                      userPassword }
```

The rules for DN formation, composition of object classes, and attribute types constitute the *Directory Schema Information*. In a distributed system, the DIT can be spread over multiple nodes. The information used to locate an object entry given its DN constitutes the *Knowledge Information*.

7.1.1.2 Operational Model.
The structure of the DDS is based on the client-server model (c.f. Fig. 7.2).

The *Directory User Agent* (DUA) represents the client part and provides application processes with access to the directory service. The actual services are offered by the *Directory Service Agent* (DSA) at the server side. Communication between the DUA and DSA is supplied via the *Directory Access Protocol* (DAP). Several DSAs may communicate using *Directory System Protocol* (DSP).

For the directory user this functional model is transparent: a user accessing the directory (through a DUA) does not know a priori the location of the information required. The first DSA accessed is responsible for either forwarding the request to another DSA, broadcasting the request or simply returning a referral giving the address of another DSA and allowing the DUA to reissue its request.

7.1.2 Directory Services

The services provided by the DDS may be divided into three categories:

- The *white pages service* allows direct look-up in the directory as in the white pages of a telephone directory. The user provides the DN of an object

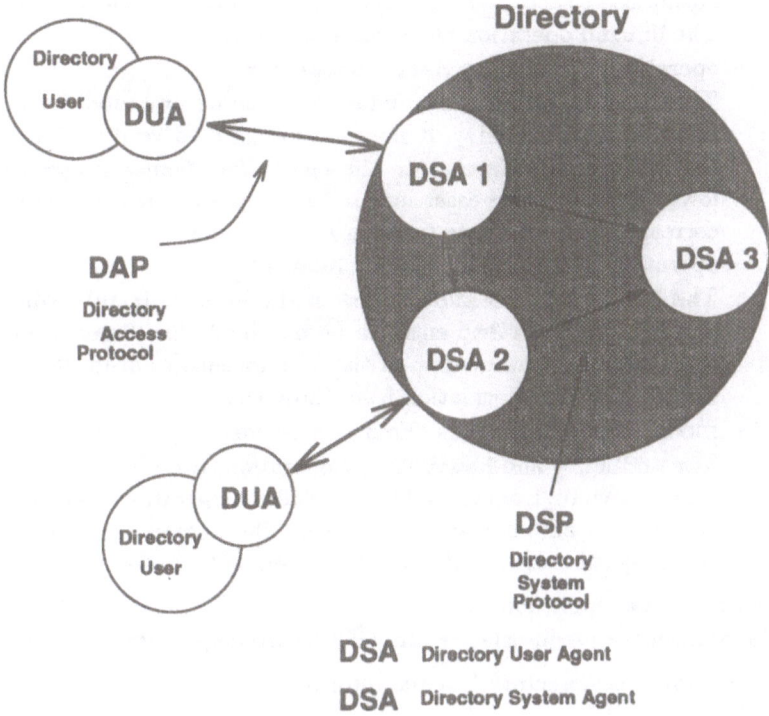

Fig. 7.2. Structure of the DDS.

entry together with the names of the attributes of the object required. The DDS returns the values of these attributes of the specified object.

- The *yellow pages service*, like the yellow pages of a telephone directory, allows objects to be looked-up based on the values of their attributes. The search is carried out relative to a designated starting node. In order to select the required objects, the user can specify a *filter* which is given in first order logic. To control the search process it is possible to specify criteria for the search space and the number of results required.
- Sometimes it is possible that a user does not know the DN of the particular object required. In this case it is necessary to have a mechanism which supports finding the desired naming path. Such a mechanism is offered by the *browsing service*.

Two sets of operations constitute the interface to the DDS: one which is accessible to all users, and one which is restricted to system administrators.

- The user interface is composed of the following operations:
    - operations to connect to the directory service: `Bind`, `Unbind`;
      The `Bind` operation is used by the DUA to establish an association with a DSA prior to any further operation. The client is identified and

authorised to access the directory, based on the credentials presented. The `Unbind` operation closes an association.

- operations for reading: `Read, Compare,`;

  The `Read` operation allows information to be extracted from an explicitly identified entry. It may also be used to verify a DN, and to get an internal reference to the entry. The `Compare` operation allows attribute value assertions to be compared with the value of the corresponding attribute types in a given entry.

- operations for searching: `List, Search`;

  The `List` operation allows a list of the immediate sub-ordinates of an explicitly identified entry to be obtained. The `Search` operation is used to search a portion of the DIT for entries of interest, and to return selected information from those entries.

- modifying operations: `AddEntry, RemoveEntry, Modify, Rename`;

  The `AddEntry` and `RemoveEntry` operations are used to add/remove a leaf entry to/from the DIT. The `Modify` operation allows information within an entry to be modified. The `Rename` operation is used to change the relative distinguished name of a leaf entry in the DIT.

Most of these operations have the target entry DN as first argument.

- An administrative interface is provided to privileged users allowing for:
  - update of Directory Schema Information;
  - update of Directory Knowledge Information;
  - user registration;
  - authorisation and security management.

7.1.3 The Distributed Directory Service Architecture

As shown in Fig. 7.3, the architecture of the DDS is layered in four levels.

- At the upper level is the user interface. A graphical interface, using the X Window System and OSF/Motif, is provided to the directory user; the administrative interface is offered only through a classical text-based interface.
- The second layer consists of the main components of the DDS :
  - *Schema Management* – The task of the Schema Manager is the management of directory meta-information. The Schema Information is a special part of the DIT and can only be manipulated by the administrator via the Schema Management interface.
  - *Knowledge Management* – The task of the Knowledge Manager is to manage information about the distribution of the DIT. This knowledge is the basis for the mapping of an entry name to its location within a fragment of the DIT.
  - *Directory Services* – The Directory Services have already been described above.

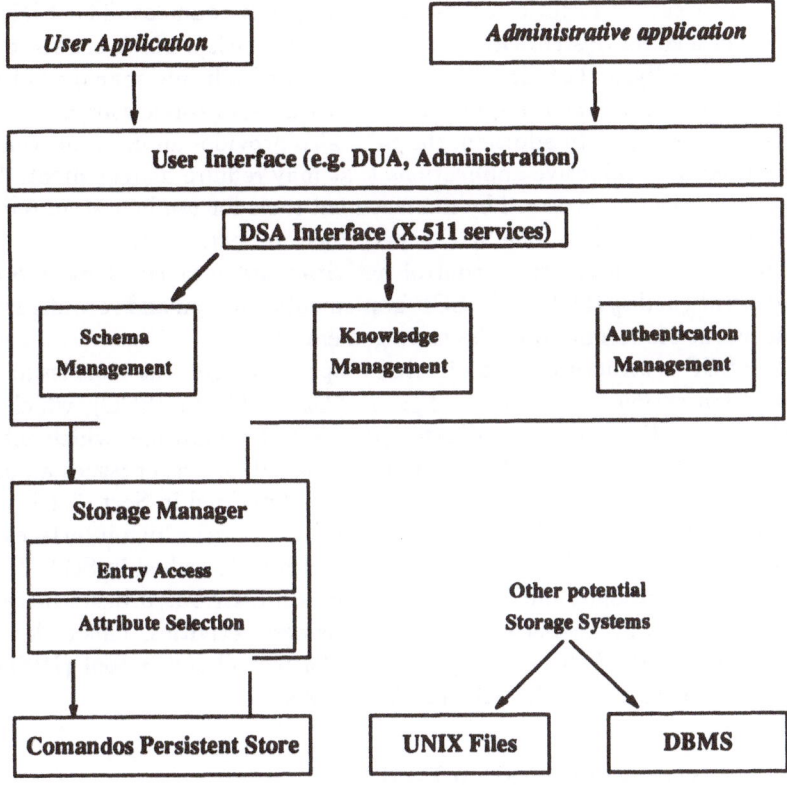

Fig. 7.3. Architecture of the DDS.

    – *Authentication Management* – The task of the Authentication Manager is to control and supervise access to the directory.
- The modules described above are supported by the Storage Management package which manages access to the underlying data storage system.
- Finally, the bottom layer implements the Management Information Base, that is the set of managed objects. The architecture allows different implementations of this layer to be provided using simple UNIX files, databases, or, as in Comandos, persistent objects.

7.2 Management and Administration Tools

The Comandos approach to system management was introduced in Chap. 2. It is based on an evolutionary approach which is mapped onto three generic types of activities: *observation, analysis and decision, and control.*

- The observation activities in the running system are performed by a *System Observation Facility* (SOF). The SOF is itself a distributed service which uses the facilities of the underlying environment. The SOF consists of a set of *System Observation Centres* (SOCs), which are structured hierarchically, and of *typed sensors*, which are built into managed objects. The SOF collects *alert* requests and statistics from application objects and from the system. In addition, the SOF also provides an interface that can be used by productive applications that may require management. These statistics can be accessed by management tools for use in system redesign and reconfiguration. The SOF is described in Sect. 7.2.1.

- Like system observation, control activities are performed by a *System Control Facility* (SCF). The SCF implements redesign and reconfiguration decisions stemming from the management tools.

  The SCF is structured as a directed graph. Management tools issue modification action demands to a *System Control Centre* (SCC), which then either directly accesses an *effector* (the part of a controller which actually implements the control decision) in a managed object, or issues an action demand to a lower-level SCC. The SCF is described in Sect. 7.2.2.

- A tool for *User and Host Administration* (UsrAdm) which interfaces with the SOF and SCF is also provided. UsrAdm is described in Sect. 7.2.3.

- The organisational and technical design of a distributed business system is based on a process-oriented view of business activities. This task is supported by the *Distributed Information System Designer* tool (DISDES). The DISDES tool is described in Sect. 7.2.4.

7.2.1 The System Observation Facility

The SOF carries out the observation function of the adaptive approach to system design and management. The SOF is a distributed service which gathers, aggregates and makes available information needed for the management of the system. This information is generated by the running system and describes the actual state of the system. Based on the information gathered by the SOF, changes in the configuration of the system can be identified. The SOF consists of three types of components:

Sensors are attached to managed objects to generate information. Sensors are defined by the type of information to be generated.

System Observation Centres collect, store and aggregate the information received from the sensors. The number of SOCs is variable and a hierarchy of SOCs can be built.

The Bidirectional Communication Service (BCS) transmits information from the sensors to the SOCs as well as between SOCs.

For example, a sensor could be installed on every host in the system which periodically generates information about the disk usage of various users. This information could then be sent to a SOC located on one host in the system which collects the information, aggregates it to a time series, and stores it. The transfer of the data between the sensors and the SOC would be done by the BCS.

The SOC provides a standardised interface through which any management tool can query the stored information. For example, the management tool UsrAdm (c.f. Sect. 7.2.3) queries such data and provides graphical output.

Figure 7.4 depicts the internal structure of a SOC. Information can be received both from the objects being observed and from other SOCs which are positioned lower in the SOC hierarchy. Alarms to the operator are produced according to pre-defined alarm conditions; statistics are delivered to higher level SOCs, and a query interface to management tools is provided.

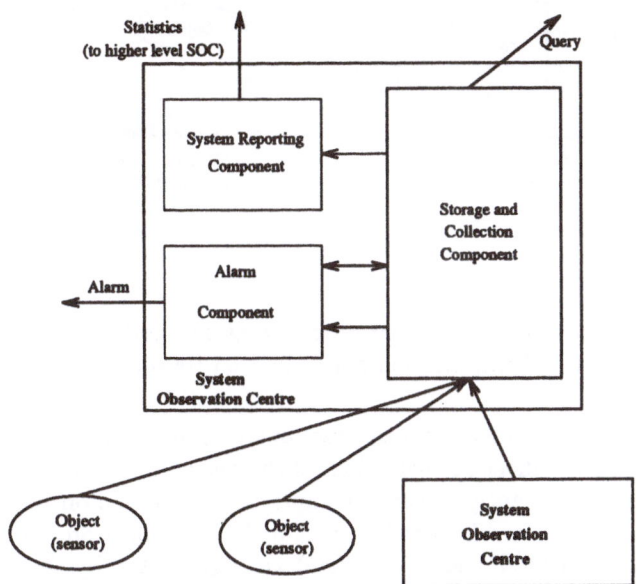

Fig. 7.4. Structure of a SOC.

At least one SOC is required in each system, but a hierarchy of SOCs can also be installed. This hierarchy reflects the level of aggregation of information required. Low level SOCs receive information from sensors and report it, possibly aggregated, to the next higher level. Additionally, every SOC in the hierarchy can receive information from sensors and provide information to other tools. Figure 7.5 shows these relationships. The solid arrows depict the reporting of information to a SOC; the dashed lines depict the querying of stored information by management tools. The reporting structure is built up as a directed graph, whereby a SOC can report to other SOCs. Information flow is directed in one direction, closed loops are not possible.

Every sensor in the distributed system is identified uniquely and reports to exactly one SOC. When installing a sensor, the name of its SOC (receiver) must be known. This name is unique in the management domain and is maintained in the DDS (c.f. Sect. 7.1).

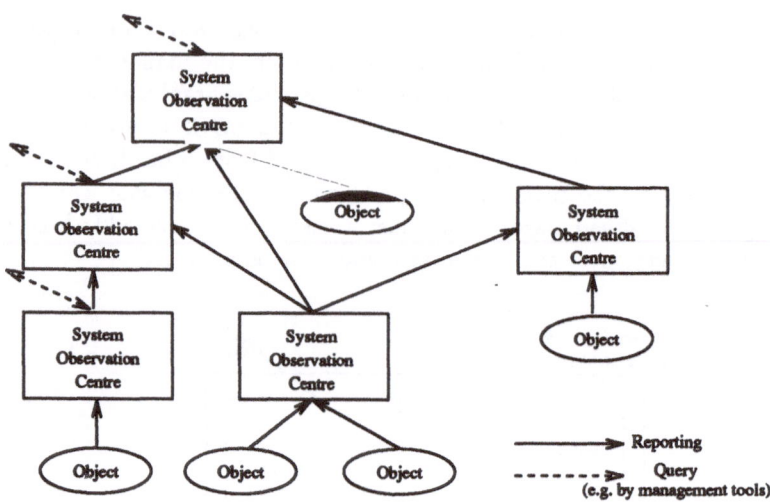

Fig. 7.5. The hierarchy of SOCs.

Within the SOC, data from the sensors is aggregated and transformed to one of two different types of information depending on its purpose. The types of information are:

Statistics are information which are measured routinely and produced through data aggregation to reflect the behaviour of the distributed system. Statistics are stored permanently in the SOC and can be queried on request.

Alarms describe a condition which requires immediate action from an operator. Alarms are initiated if some specific data is generated by the sensors and sent to the SOC. Pre-defined alarm conditions in the SOC are checked. An alarm is produced and reported immediately to the operator through the alarm mechanisms. Furthermore, statistics are produced to describe the occurrence of the alarm which are handled as discussed above.

For further information on the SOF see [Comandos 1990a].

7.2.2 The System Control Facility

The SCF is a distributed service which allows the distributed system to be reconfigured. System management defines these modifications as structural changes to the information system. Such changes can be composed of several steps and effect various objects in the distributed system. Examples of such changes are: relocation of a user's directory or an application from computer A to computer B; relocation of printer resources; or the registration or deletion of a user.

The SCF is composed of three kinds of components: *effectors, System Control Centres* (SCC) and a distributed service for command transfer. The SCF is structured as a directed graph. Management tools issue modification action demands to a SCC, which either accesses an effector in a managed object directly or issues an action demand to a lower-level SCC. These commands generally involve several changes to different objects which depend on each other. This implies that such a command (and its sub-commands) has to be executed as a transaction. The individual components of the SCF are described below (a detailed description may be found in [Comandos 1990c]).

7.2.2.1 Effectors. Effectors are the components of the SCF that are integrated into the objects to be managed. Effectors perform the modifications to an object requested by a control command from an SCC. An effector receives commands from only one SCC. This ensures that conflicting commands cannot occur.

Three threads of control can be distinguished in the SCF. One is within the managed object itself. This is the most important since it is related to the object's productive service. Another is within the SCF and is concerned with the execution of commands in the SCCs and effectors. The third is within the management tool and is concerned with the determination of change commands.

7.2.2.2 System Control Centres. An SCC consists of several components which are presented in Fig. 7.6. The figure shows that a SCC can receive action demands from various SCCs. It can submit demands to effectors as well as to lower level SCCs.

The four types of commands provided by a SCF allow the activation of a control operation of an object, initialisation of a new control operation in the SCC, update of the state of the SCC, and removal of a control operation from the SCC.

7.2.2.3 Hierarchy of the System Control Centres. The SCCs are arranged hierarchically reflecting the level of control required in the distributed system. The command structure of the SCCs is a directed graph, whereby one SCC can issue commands to several lower-level SCCs and can receive commands from higher-level SCCs. Closed loops are not possible.

Figure 7.7 shows the hierarchy of the SCCs as a directed graph where the arrows show the transfer of commands.

7.2.2.4 Distribution of the SCF. Effectors and SCCs are not themselves distributed. Effectors as well as SCCs can be present on every computer in the distributed system.

On one computer there may be several effectors, each handling a different task. The same holds for the SCCs where one SCC may be responsible for only one kind of modification task, e.g. one control centre may be responsible for handling the relocation of user directories and another for handling the parameterisation of an application. However, for reasons of simplicity, the designer of the SCF will not usually position more than one SCC on one computer. In this case the SCC controls all the different modification activities.

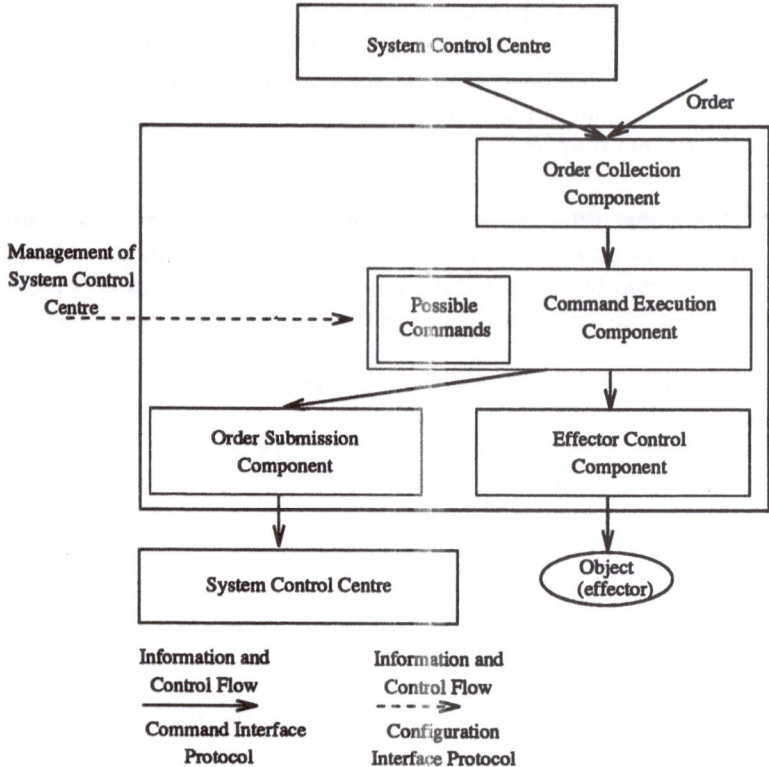

Fig. 7.6. Structure of a SCC.

7.2.2.5 Distributed Command Service. The distributed command service is used to execute a control command on a remote host. Depending on the implementation of the control command different mechanisms are used.

7.2.3 User and Host Administration

The tool for user and host administration (UsrAdm) encompasses three functions:

- generation and representation of a model of the relevant features of the existing distributed system,
- integration of statistics on hosts and users into the model based on data from the SOF (c.f. Sect. 7.2.1), and
- implementation of system changes using the SCF (c.f. Sect. 7.2.2).

The System Administration Model comprises people, users, groups, accounts, hosts, and home directories. Figure 7.8 shows the relationships between the model elements.

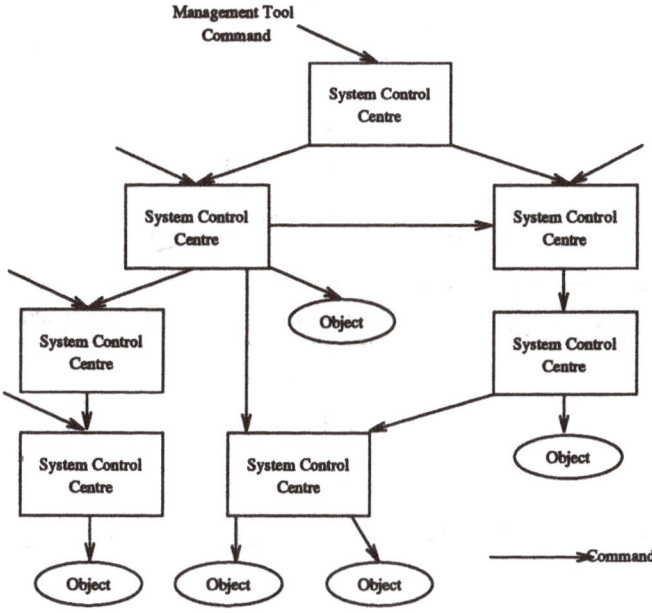

Fig. 7.7. Hierarchical structure of the SCCs.

UsrAdm supports the system administrator in modelling the system and improving the system configuration. Representation and manipulation of the System Administration Model is supported, and active advice is given on possible improvements to the system configuration. Support is provided for testing and evaluating the solutions generated with respect to the goals of the design. For example, work load and the usage of storage on different hosts have to be balanced. Users have to be combined in groups corresponding to organisational needs.

Different views of the system model, such as a host view, a user view, and a group view are possible. The host view presents all hosts and their characteristics. The user view gives the relations between users and their accounts. The grouping of users is shown in the group view. In each view **add** and **remove** operations are available to modify the model. Besides the model of the actual system, several alternative models can be maintained.

On the basis of the above model, statistics concerning users and hosts can be produced. Since it is possible to build models which do not correspond to the actual state of the distributed system, statistics can only be given, if the model and the actual state correspond. Information on users and hosts is gathered and stored by the SOF. To retrieve the information, UsrAdm sends queries in a pre-defined format to the SOF, which replies with the required information. For the host view, information on the processor load, the use of disk space, and the calls to the storage system can be displayed for selected hosts. The user view

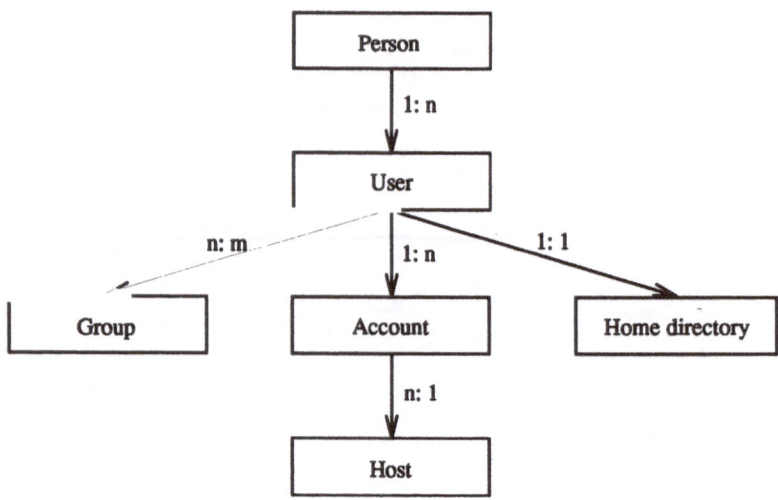

Fig. 7.8. The System Administration Model.

provides information on user activities on hosts in the system and on the size of the user's home directory.

Based on the model and the retrieved statistics, modifications to the configuration of the distributed system may be desired to increase its effectiveness. Modifications may be required at the host, user, or group level. The SCF is used to implement the changes in the running system.

The structure of the UsrAdm tool reflects the functional components of a decision support tool. The components of UsrAdm are structured according to the functional decision component they support. At the top level, the organisational designer interacts with the Functional Component Manager which allows the designer to switch between generating solutions, assessing solutions, system observation and implementation of a design solution. Figure 7.9 depicts the architecture of the UsrAdm tool and identifies its components.

The Intelligence Manager provides a host view and a user view allowing statistics based on the information provided by the SOF to be viewed.

The Generation Manager supports the system administrator in understanding the problem and improving the configuration by building the System Administration Model. The tool components for generating solutions are the Generation Manager, a Graphical Model and View Editor and element editors. A host view, a user view and a group view of the model are supported by the Generation Manager.

The Assessment Manager supports the system administrator in testing and evaluating the solutions generated with respect to the goals of the design. It provides information about the design of the system by analysing the model.

The Implementation Manager realises a given model by modifying the actual system. Modifications within the running system can affect hosts, users, or

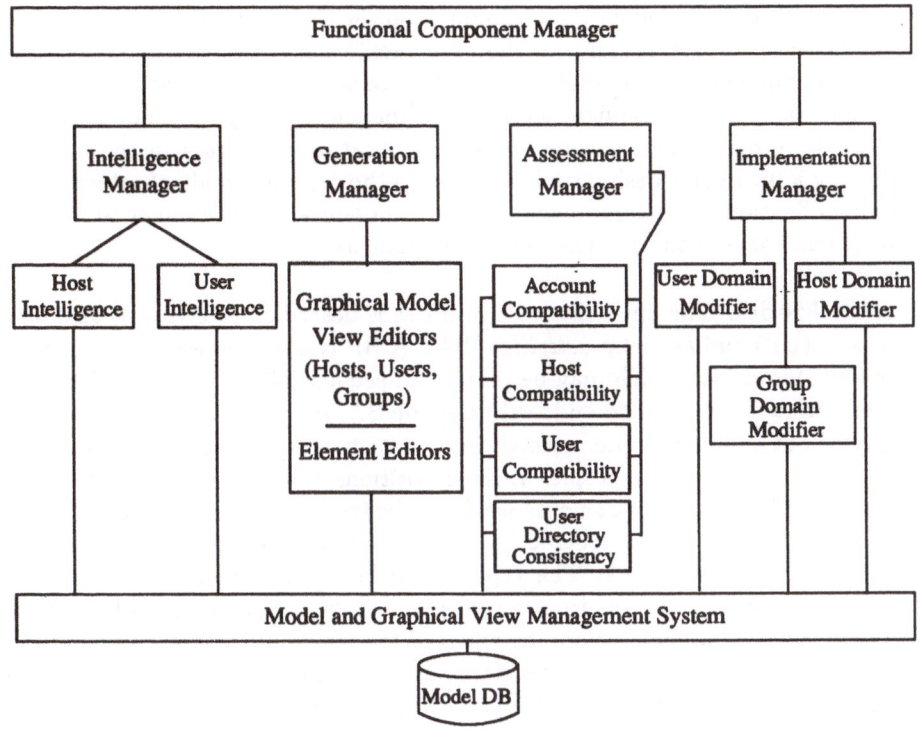

Fig. 7.9. Architecture of UsrAdm.

groups of users. To implement the changes in the running system, the Implementation Manager uses the SCF.

7.2.4 The Distributed Information System Designer

The Distributed Information System Designer (DISDES) is a computer-based tool which supports an organisational designer in the logical design of a distributed information system and, partially, in the organisational design of business processes. DISDES does not automate these tasks but rather assists the human organisational designer in carrying them out.

DISDES provides interactive support for the organisational designer. The design process is driven by the user of the tool. Thus the tool in not intended to provide complete solutions. The organisational designer is expected to modify and augment the partial solutions proposed by the tool.

Central to the tool is the *model base* which stores a model of the current system and possibly several alternative system models used by the organisational designer. Two categories of tool components operate on this model base: those for generating solutions and those for assessing solutions. In addition to these there are components for communication with the running system – for observation of the system and for the implementation of design decisions.

The components of the tool can be split into two groups: the solution mode components, and the modification mode components. The purpose of the solution mode components is to support the organisational designer in the process of solving a particular design problem. This is the primary mode of interaction. The modification mode components allow the organisational designer to modify and extend some of the solution mode components.

7.2.4.1 Model. The operation of a business is described in terms of *business processes* (BP) and *business activities* (BA). A BP is a sequence of BAs or business (sub-)processes which may be performed sequentially or in parallel. A BP begins with a single BA and ends with a single BA. A BA is an atomic task that is carried out completely (i.e. without interruption or suspension) by a *position*. Positions can be held by *people*. Various positions can be aggregated to form *groups*. A BA is a unit of *business work*. A hierarchy of types of business work exists but each BA is of a specific type. So-called *function software* is required to carry out business work. The type of the function software describes the functionality of the software from a user point of view. A hierarchy of function software types is possible where instances of the leaves of the hierarchy are individual *software components*. These are real components including application programs and data. The relationships between the elements of the model are shown in Fig. 7.10.

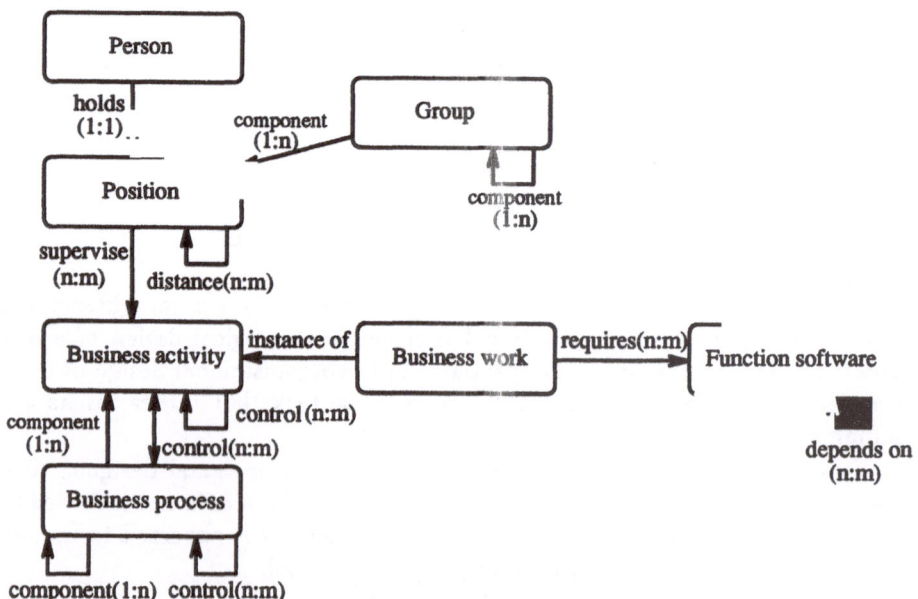

Fig. 7.10. Relationships between the elements of the DISDES model.

7.2.4.2 Solution Mode Components. Figure 7.11 shows the architecture of
DISDES and identifies the components and sub-components of the tool. At the
top level the organisational designer interacts with the Functional Component
Manager which allows him to switch between generating solutions, assessing
solutions, system observation and implementation of design solutions.

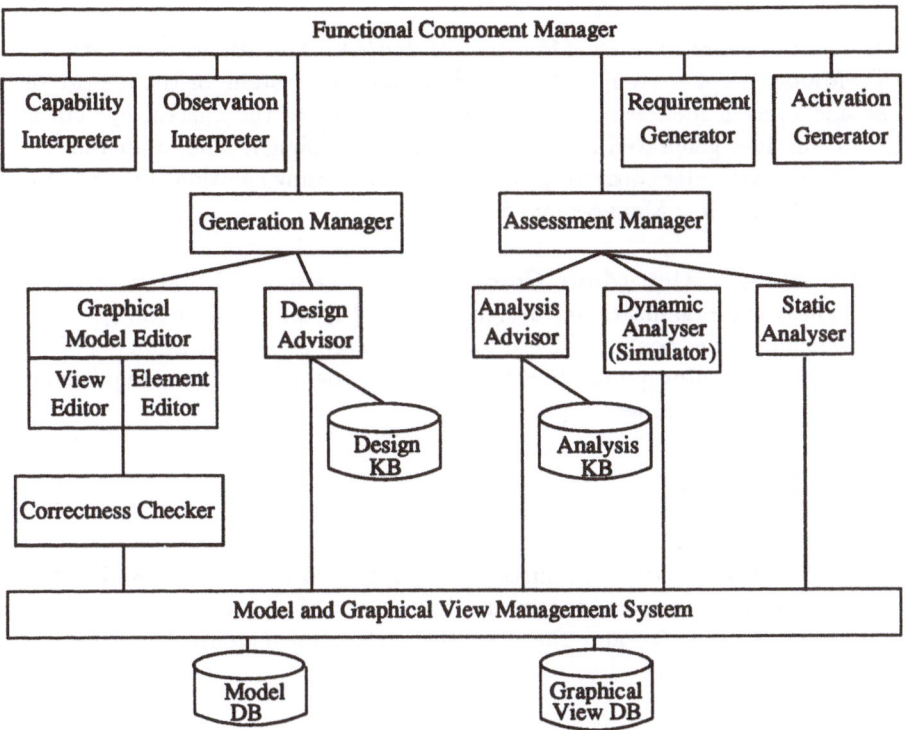

Fig. 7.11. Architecture of DISDES.

Generation Components. The generation components support the organisational designer in modelling and improving the organisation and system design.
Representation and manipulation of an organisation model is supported and
active advice given on how to carry out the design.

The main tool components for generating design solutions are the generation
manager, a graphical model editor, a correctness checker, and a design advisor
which possesses a design knowledge-base.

Assessment Components. The assessment components support the organisational designer in testing and evaluating the solutions generated with respect
to the goals of the design. They provide information about the design of the

organisation and system by analysing the model generated using the generation components.

Several ways of analysing the model support a variety of possible assessment goals. Depending on the kind of analysis, different features of the model or different effects of its simulation are accounted for. The organisational designer is supported in interpreting these results.

Model and Graphical View Management System. The Model and Graphical View Management System is the underlying storage system for the logical business and system models including both the model of the current system and the alternatives generated by the organisational designer. The other tool components, in particular those for generating and assessing solutions use the Model and Graphical View Management System.

7.2.4.3 Modification Mode Components. The modification mode components allow the organisational designer to modify and extend the generation and assessment components. These components are implementation dependent. In the current prototype modifications to the program code are required, e.g. the addition of new object types.

7.3 Security Tools

The work of the security administrator is supported by a set of security tools. Two such tools were provided in the framework of Comandos – one for the analysis of audit data, and the other for risk management. These tools are described below.

7.3.1 Protocol Data Analysis Tool

Computer systems satisfying criterion C2 or higher of the U.S. Department of Defence Orange Book [DoD 1985] must have an audit mechanism which records every security relevant action. The Comandos virtual machine provides such an audit service. However, the amount of data produced by an audit service can be so large that it is impossible to analyse by hand. Hence, most audit mechanisms are delivered with some kind of analysis tool – indeed the NCSC guide to auditing [NCSC 1988] requires this. However, the functionality of these tools is usually very restricted. They support only data analysis on a record-by-record basis.

The Comandos *Protocol Data Analysis Tool* (PDAT) attempts to analyse protocol data generated during the auditing of secure computer systems very thoroughly. Moreover, since secure computer systems from different manufacturers generate audit data with very different formats, a major aspect of the design of PDAT was its configurability. Hence PDAT is able to analyse protocol data from different systems running in different environments.

7.3.1.1 The Operation of PDAT. Audit data is received by PDAT in the form of audit records. Each record contains all logical information about a single security relevant event carried out by the system. Audit data received by PDAT are transformed into an internal format and then analysed by applying criteria which have been defined previously and stored in a database. Satisfaction of any criterion leads to the initiation of an operator defined action. This action can be different for each criterion. Criteria and actions can be defined by the operator and stored using names. In principle the action can consist of calling any application.

7.3.1.2 Architecture. PDAT consists of two types of components:

- An *Evaluation Unit* (EU) runs on each host where audit data is produced. It reads and evaluates protocol data and sends the results to the PDAT Control Unit. An EU consists of three layers: the Audit Trail Interface, the Audit Analyser and the Network Protocol Interface (c.f. Fig. 7.12).
- The *Control Unit* (CU) runs on the auditor's workstation and is connected to all the EUs in the distributed system. It configures all EUs with a set of search criteria. It can start, suspend, resume and cancel audit runs and reports the results of the analysis to the auditor. The CU also consists of three layers. The User Interface maps user input to commands for the Command Layer. Output from commands is displayed in windows and forms. Commands to control EUs are transformed to an internal format required by the Network Protocol Interface and sent to the appropriate EU.

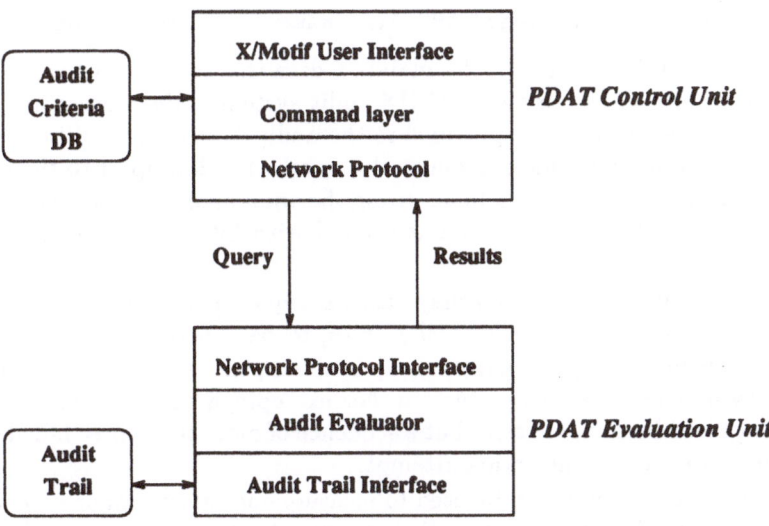

Fig. 7.12. Architecture of PDAT.

The Audit Trail Interface. The *Audit Trail Interface* reads the protocol data from an audit trail and transforms it into an internal format. The audit trail consists of a sequence of audit records where each record contains the information concerning one security event. The record format is similar to a C structure with variant parts. It consists of a number of fields representing the parameters of the event. Possible field types include String, Integer, Float and Timestamp. Each record has a fixed part containing at least the event type, event class, timestamp and a return code, and a variable part which depends on the event type. The Audit Trail Interface maps the field contents to internal field variables. The field names are user definable.

The Audit Evaluator. The *Audit Evaluator* analyses the audit records according to the search criteria set by the CU. The results are collected in buffers and sent to the CU when requested. Four methods of analysing protocol data are supported:

- The simplest method is record-wise selection. Each record is checked to determine if it fulfills some filter condition. Filter conditions are built up from arithmetic, logical and relational operators applied to the fields of the audit records. A LIKE operator may be used to compare fields with regular string expressions. The operators YEAR, MONTH, DATA, TIME and DAYOFWEEK can be used to access the components of a timestamp value. The example below shows a filter to identify accesses to the password file at weekends.:

  ```
  DAYOFWEEK(time) IN (Sunday, Saturday) AND type='open' AND
      event='data_read' AND file_name LIKE '/etc/.*passwd'
  ```

- Dynamic tables and variables maintain data that is relevant to more than one record. For example, in UNIX audit systems only process identifiers and file descriptors are provided in the audit data instead of full process or file names. The information used to map a file descriptor to the full file name must be stored in a table within the audit analysis tool. Actions that operate on the tables can be associated with filter conditions in update rules.

- A security relevant action may cause a sequence of logically related audit records, called a *behavioral pattern*, to be generated. The individual records making up the pattern may be unsuspicious, but the combination may indicate a security violation. For example, a single failed login may be caused by a typing error but a sequence of more than three failed logins may indicate a penetration attempt.

- Statistical methods can be used to measure normal system or user behavior and to detect anomalies. For instance, the rate of unsuccessful login attempts among all login attempts can be compared with a certain value. If this rate suddenly increases considerably, an attempt to break-in by guessing passwords is almost certain.

The Network Protocol. An EU acts as a server in that it responds to requests sent by the CU. Examples of such requests are the configuration of the EU with a set of search criteria or the request to send back the results of the analysis.

The Command Layer. The Command Layer provides a parser for audit configuration specifications, maintains the analysis results and interprets the user command input. Commands referring to an EU are transformed to the network protocol format. Audit configuration is specified using a special query language – PDATQL – which provides a means to determine:
- the names and types of the audit record fields;
- the search conditions on the audit data;
- the actions that update variables and dynamic tables;
- the operations to start system specific jobs or to output warning messages;
- the formats of the analysis reports output, and
- the rules that associate search conditions with actions and operations.

PDAT also provides different views of the analysis results. The auditor can concentrate on the essential data. PDAT can provide a list of all events, a table of events of one kind or print data for single events. For each criterion, a subset of the fields of a record can be selected to be printed by the report module.

7.3.2 Risk Management

A *risk* exists if there is some probability that some *threat* can cause *damage* to some *asset*. An asset can be any object in the distributed system including a BP, node, program or data. Threats to these objects include failure, theft, disclosure and falsification. The focus in Comandos is on the analysis of distributed systems. The analysis can be made for an existing configuration of the system or for possible alternative configurations.

Although the general risk management approach is broader, risk management in Comandos concentrates on determining the impact of system component failures on the continuation of BAs and BPs designed with DISDES. Therefore the elements of the DISDES model (BPs, BAs, business work, function software and software components) are also known by the risk management tool. Software components depend on hardware components in order to operate. Hardware components are physical entities like processors, disk partitions and transceivers. Hardware components can be defined at different levels of abstraction. For example, a host can be considered as a hardware component consisting of a processor, main memory and disk partitions (c.f. Fig. 7.13).

7.3.2.1 Risks in a Business Environment. BPs and BAs are considered as assets. An asset is a valuable object and has an associated profit loss value indicating the loss caused by unavailability or destruction of the asset.

Assets can be endangered by threats. Failure of software or hardware components are considered as threats since they may lead to the failure of a BA.

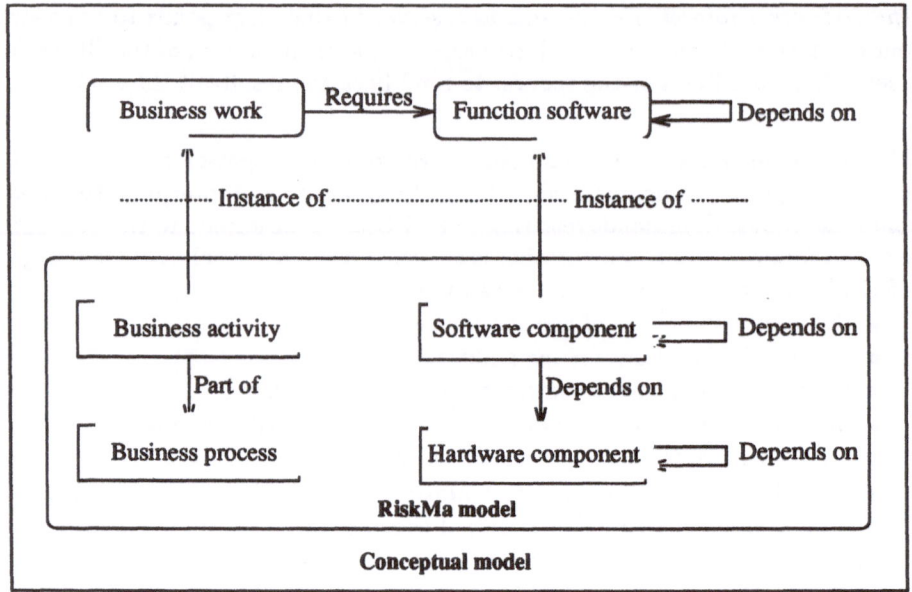

Fig. 7.13. Relationships between the elements of the RiskMa model.

The relationship between assets and threats is many to many. One threat may endanger several assets and an asset may be endangered by several threats.

Because a threat can endanger several assets, the damage caused by a threat is calculated by summing up the damage caused to each asset. The *severity* of the damage gives the degree to which an asset is endangered by a threat. In the case of failure, the duration of the failure can be regarded as its severity.

For risk evaluation an annual loss expectancy is calculated. The annual loss expectancy is calculated as the product of the value of the asset, the likelihood of the threat, and the severity.

To diminish a risk, countermeasures have to be taken. A risk can be diminished by reducing the damage, the probability of the damage occurring, and/or the severity. For example, reduction of the probability of a software component failure can be achieved by increasing the degree of redundancy of that component.

7.3.2.2 The Risk Management Tool. The Risk Management Tool (RiskMa) is concerned with assessing the dependability of system components. The main components of RiskMa are depicted in Fig. 7.14. The Functional Component Manager provides access to dedicated managers supporting part of the decision process in risk management.

Information on the running system is provided by the intelligence components. A Graphical Model Browser allows a graphical representation of the system model to be examined. Several views of the model can be selected and dependability statistics can be requested. The statistics on dependability are provided by the SOF. The statistics on hardware and software components provided by the SOC include the number of failures, mean failure duration, mean time between failures, and availability.

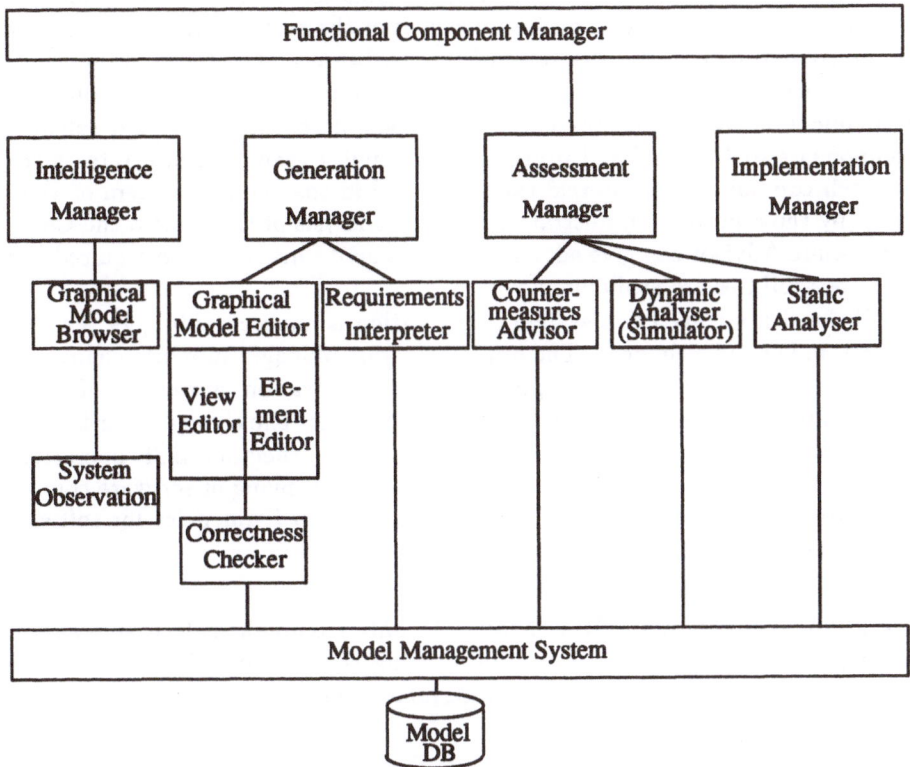

Fig. 7.14. Architecture of RiskMa.

The Generation Manager supports the asset analysis and threat analysis tasks. It provides access to the Requirements Interpreter and the Graphical Model Editor. The Requirements Interpreter is the interface to the DISDES tool. Information on BPs, BAs, business work, and function software is retrieved from the DISDES model base. Not all attributes of these entities are relevant for RiskMa. Therefore only part of the information contained in the DISDES model base is used. The Graphical Model Editor provides different views of the RiskMa model. The hardware component view shows the relationships between the hardware components. The software component view shows the relationships between the software components and the hardware components, and the relationships between the software components themselves. The process flow view shows the relationships between the BAs and the software components. In each view, a view editor and element editors are provided. The view editor allows the view to be modified by adding or removing elements of the view. The element editor is used to define the attributes of the entities described in the dependability model. For hardware and software components the status (up or down) can be modified. The correctness of operations with the view and element editors is checked by the Correctness Checker.

The Assessment Manager allows a risk evaluation to be performed for specific assets and gives advice on improvement of the system configuration. The Static Analyser evaluates the state of the hardware and software components with respect to the component states defined during model generation. The Dynamic Analyser allows the state transitions of the hardware and software components to be simulated using a dependability graph. Failure rates given for each component can be real rates observed in the running system or rates given by the security administrator. After an analysis of the system the Countermeasure Advisor can give advice on where countermeasures are required and what possibilities are available.

If the risk involved in a system configuration is unacceptably high the configuration has to be changed. The Implementation Manager supports changes to the system configuration, e.g. replication of an application, movement of application software, or making other resources redundant. The change order is given to the SCC which realises the change by triggering effectors. SCF operations include, for example, moving software components, copying of software components to increase redundancy, and increasing backup frequencies for software components.

7.3.2.3 Comprehensive Risk Management. Comprehensive Risk Management (CRM) is an important task in assuring the security of an information system. Two basically different, but interrelated phases of CRM can be identified:

- During system (re)design, the assets and risks and their corresponding costs are identified. Based on this information, measures are proposed which assure a specified level of security within established cost limits.
- During system operation, actual risks are identified to allow for appropriate action. An example is the tracking of intrusion attacks by audit analysis tools in order to allow immediate countermeasures to be taken.

Both tasks are closely related because the identification of actual risks can lead to a re-evaluation of the security of an installation requiring new or different countermeasures to be deployed. The security administrator of a distributed system needs on-line support for assessing actual risks and for selecting and implementing cost-effective security measures.

The Security Control Centre. For these reasons a Security Control Centre (SecCC) which allows effective on-line risk management is essential. Using both risk-relevant information provided by the Comandos system and additional human expert judgement, the SecCC refines the available information by applying mathematical models. Thus an improved insight into the security related properties of the system is obtained. These general models provide the basis for risk assessment models which in turn provide an input for decision support models.

The current version of the SecCC concentrates on information gathering, system modelling, and risk assessment. In later versions appropriate security measures could be selected automatically and presented to the security administrator or be applied directly by the SecCC if the security administrator is not available.

Architecture. Figure 7.15 shows the structure of and the data flow within a SecCC. Part of the information necessary for risk assessment is gathered by the SOF (c.f. Sect 7.2.1); further information is extracted from the audit data (c.f. 7.3.1). Other information sources within the observed system are conceivable (e.g. network management information), but were not considered in detail in the Comandos project.

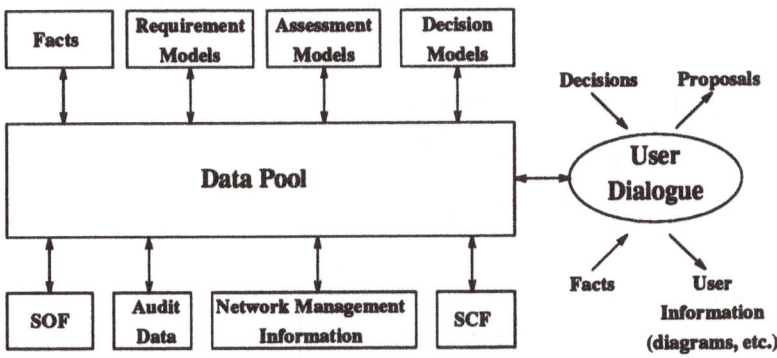

Fig. 7.15. Architecture of a SecCC.

In addition, the security administrator has facilities to enter judgements and facts not available within the system (e.g. on the environment, on users or on the possible financial consequences if security violations occurred).

Central to the SecCC are the models, which support the security administrator in:

- understanding security relevant facts within the system (e.g. structure of rights, remote access);
- assessing the degree to which security requirements are met (e.g. the availability of BPs);
- evaluating risks in real or hypothetical situations;
- deciding on security countermeasures.

These models receive their input from and write their output to a common data pool. This allows incremental development of the different models as part of an open modelling approach.

Since, for the foreseeable future, the security administrator will be required to take the most important decisions personally, an appropriate and modern user interface is necessary. Through this interface the user enters facts and knowledge, receives information – in graphical form – and proposals for security measures. Finally, the user interface supports the user in implementing his decisions.

7.4 Relationships Between Tools

Figure 7.16 shows the relationships which exist between the management tools and the security tools.

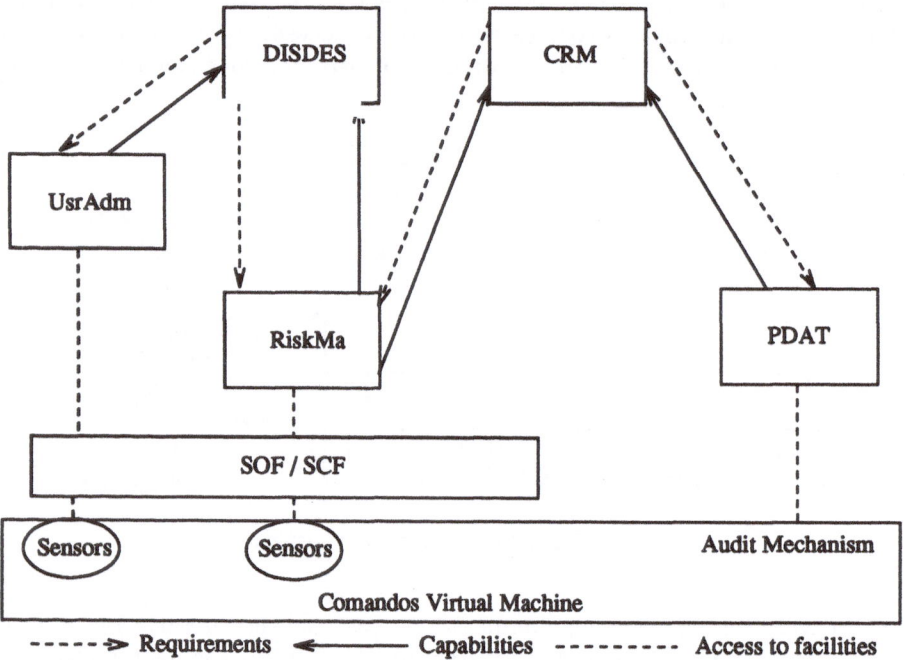

Fig. 7.16. Relationships between administration and security tools.

- The input data for RiskMa comes from the SOF/SCF.
- PDAT takes the audit data as input and can use the output data from RiskMa.
- CRM uses the output from RiskMa and PDAT to decide about the current security state of the system.
- DISDES uses information from RiskMa and UsrAdm to describe the current state of the distributed system.

8. The CIDRE Application

This chapter describes an example of a real-world distributed application built using the facilities provided by the Comandos platform. This application was used in Comandos as a test bed to:

- evaluaté the Comandos architecture and prototype implementations, and
- demonstrate the capabilities of Comandos.

The primary pilot application for Comandos was the CIDRE (Circulation Intelligente de Dossiers REpartis) application developed at SEPT. This application was chosen for several reasons:

- This is a real-world large-scale application which is typical of the office environment. Furthermore it is intended to distribute this application to a number of pilot sites, in early 1993, as part of the AMBIANCE project. AMBIANCE is a France Telecom project, addressing group office communication, and aimed at providing packaged products and value added services such as document circulation, cooperative editing, and document filing and retrieval.
- CIDRE was originally designed using the object paradigm; the first implementation of CIDRE was carried out on top of the CHORUS/COOL v1 platform – an experimental object-oriented platform resulting from cooperation between INRIA, Chorus Systèmes, and SEPT – which provided basic support for distributed C++ programming on top of the CHORUS micro-kernel.
- The CIDRE application is sufficiently large and complex to take advantage of the various innovative features provided by Comandos. However, it was not expected that a single application would allow all the functionality provided by the Comandos platform to be tested. Therefore additional demonstration applications were developed in the framework of the project for the purpose of testing and demonstrating specific features. These applications are not described here.

The first section of this chapter summarises the main characteristics of the CIDRE application: its objectives, functionality and architecture. Subsequent sections describe the design of the CIDRE application using the Comandos model and architecture, and present an overall evaluation of this experiment.

8.1 Description of the Pilot Application

CIDRE is a CSCW application targeted at industrial, business and administrative environments. The CIDRE office system is a sophisticated communication tool based on documents, which can be used within an enterprise, or between several related enterprises, to support cooperative working.

In the CIDRE office framework, an *office procedure* is described by a *folder* which can be viewed as a set of related *documents*, and their synchronisation rules. Each document is defined by: its *content*, a *circulation scheme*, a *history* and a set of *actions*. The circulation scheme describes the sequence of steps (and workers) involved in the execution of the office procedure. Actions represent individual tasks to be performed on a given document.

The main goal of CIDRE is to provide automatic circulation of folders between networked workstations. It provides facilities to help office workers participating in office procedures by recording and maintaining circulation rules, and managing distributed folders. Another key aspect of the CIDRE system is the way in which knowledge about an organisation is managed in order to provide intelligent services such as access control, approval and disapproval mechanisms, delegation facilities, and exception handling. All of these services are accessed by means of a unified user interface known as the CIDRE *Electronic Desk*.

Folders are created by the CIDRE *administrator* and registered in the CIDRE environment. To actually launch an office procedure, a user creates and initialises an instance of the appropriate folder. At this time the user can interact with the various documents belonging to the folder, either directly (e.g. by consulting its contents), or through the actions associated with the document. Additional information concerning the documents may be retrieved from their histories and circulation scheme (e.g. the names of the users involved in the office procedure).

When a user terminates a task on a given document, the system automatically determines the next office worker from the circulation scheme, and then migrates the document to the corresponding workstation where it is made available to a new user through that user's Electronic Desk. All interactions carried out on a given document are recorded in its history.

Additional mechanisms are provided by the CIDRE environment to help users to solve problems which may be encountered in the execution of an office procedure (e.g. substitution, delegation and negotiation when a conflict occurs). At any time, users may consult the state of a circulating document (including its content and history), provided that they have the appropriate access rights.

On the user's workstation, a typical CIDRE configuration includes an Electronic Desk supporting the circulation service, a directory service, a delegation service, and a negotiation service. Optional services may include a mail service, a print service, and local tools (e.g. a word processor or a local database system).

8.1.1 Functions

8.1.1.1 Basic Concepts. The CIDRE application was originally specified and developed in an object-oriented way. The objects described below were defined for the specific purposes of the CIDRE application. The Comandos approach allowed, thanks to its fine-grained object model, an easy mapping between CIDRE objects and Comandos objects.

- **Office object**: an active object obeying environment constraints and conveying information on a network of computers. Two main categories of office objects are handled by the CIDRE system: structured documents and distributed folders. These objects are described below. Other types of office objects, such as services and tools will be considered later in this chapter.
- **Structured document**: a document with both a logical and a physical structure attached to it. The logical structure defines logical parts (e.g. logical atoms and fields) with access rights for various workers' functions. Such a document represents the electronic counterpart of a paper document as naturally as possible.
- **Distributed folder**: a set of structured documents and their relationships. The description of these relationships (e.g. synchronisation constraints) is part of the folder. Parallel processing on several documents belonging to the same folder, across the network, is allowed.

The circulation of an object is performed by CIDRE according to directives (composed of circulation rules and a resulting execution scheme) attached to the object and external events which can modify the circulation.

When a conflict between office workers occurs, CIDRE tries to help them to solve the problem by determining precisely the context of the conflict and examining the knowledge acquired from similar situations in the past. For example, this could lead to the computation of a new circulation scheme.

8.1.1.2 Circulation Schemes. Circulation schemes are the backbone of the CIDRE application as they allow cooperative working on documents (or parts of documents) to be controlled. A circulation scheme is computed by an expert system from the control information provided by the CIDRE administrator. This information consists of a set of constraints on actions to be performed on documents (or parts of a document) belonging to a given folder. These constraints allow the data flow involving documents and users, as well as the ordering of actions and synchronisation to be determined.

The CIDRE administration workstation provides tools allowing :

- access rights to be attached to parts of a document,
- actions which are to be performed by different office workers on these parts of the document to be defined,
- precedence constraints applying to this set of actions to be collected,
- the resulting circulation scheme to be designed in the form of an Information Control Net. (ICN), which is an extended Petri Net.

An example of a circulation scheme associated with a training registration procedure is presented in Fig. 8.1.

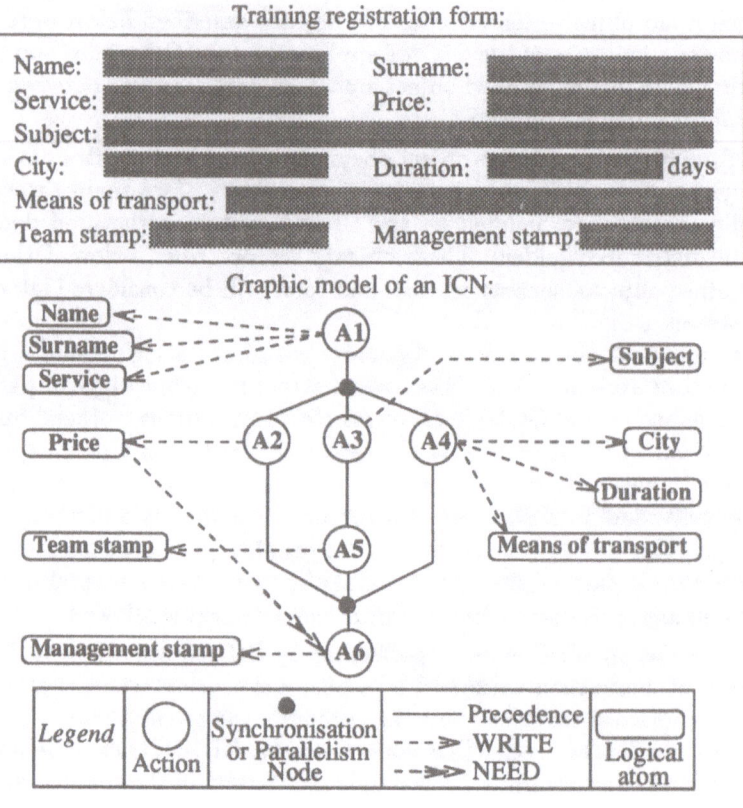

Fig. 8.1. Example of a circulation scheme.

The top part of the diagram shows the registration form associated with the registration procedure. This document circulates amongst the various workers involved in the registration procedure. In order to create the circulation scheme associated with this document, the CIDRE administrator defines the actions (noted Ai) and the precedence relationships between them. The following actions are defined:

```
A1 = initiator WRITE Name, Surname, Service
A2 = initiator WRITE Price
A3 = initiator WRITE Object
A4 = initiator WRITE City, Duration, Means of transport
A5 = team leader WRITE Team-stamp
A6 = manager WRITE Manager-stamp
```

The first parameter (e.g. initiator or team leader) indicates the role associated with the given action. The second parameter (e.g. WRITE) gives the type of operation to be applied to the fields specified in the remaining parameters.

Action ordering and synchronisation rules are expressed as follows:

```
A1 IS-BEFORE All-actions
A4 IS-BEFORE A6
A5 IS-BEFORE A6
A3 IS-BEFORE A5
A6 NEED Price
```

This set of declarative rules is handled by an expert system which proceeds in two steps. First it checks the consistency of the overall schema (e.g. detection of ambiguities and cycles); this step may involve a dialog between the expert system and the administrator. The second step consists of producing the circulation scheme for each document involved in the office procedure (each document may be handled separately). In addition, the set of declarative rules is also stored in the folder associated with the office procedure to allow recomputation of the circulation schemes if necessary (e.g. when a conflict occurs during the execution of the office procedure).

8.1.1.3 Delegation and Substitution. Delegation and substitution are two important situations which must be handled in a real-world office environment.

A short absence, for which only the initial time is known precisely, causes a systematic *delegation*. Use of a functional directory service allows another worker to be found who has the same function in the enterprise.

A longer absence, for which the start and end times are known, requires a *substitution* request. Several possibilities are offered to a user who requests a substitute:

- give the name of the substitute explicitly,
- give the function of the substitute, and allow the substitute to be chosen through the functional directory service,
- force the next worker in the office procedure to be the substitute – this worker will not then be able to find another substitute,

The delegation service checks the time consistency of the proposed request, and prevents the delegation of one function to several workers at the same time.

Other delegation mechanisms are taken into account; an example is "once-off" delegation, which allows a new step to be added to the initial circulation scheme, by temporarily adding a new worker to the existing ones.

After determining the corresponding worker for each possible action, CIDRE makes the appropriate documents available to him, by putting them on the corresponding desk.

8.1.1.4 Document Tracking and Enquiry. After initialisation of an office procedure (by means of a folder instantiation), an office worker may enquire from CIDRE the global state of the procedure. This global state is composed of the state of each document (i.e. its content and its position in the circulation process).

8.1.1.5 Negotiation. CIDRE helps office workers solve problems which may occur during document circulation, and which may not have been foreseen by the CIDRE administrator; workers may, in such situations, open an extended talk service that allows:

- direct interaction between the workers taking the form of a question and answer session or a discussion of a common object (e.g. a document shared by the users and visible on both workstations at that time).
- decisions that have been taken to be registered and validated on the circulating document (e.g. by updating its contents or circulation scheme).

8.1.2 Architecture

The overall architecture of the CIDRE system on top of the Comandos platform, is depicted in Fig. 8.2. The main components of the architecture are described below.

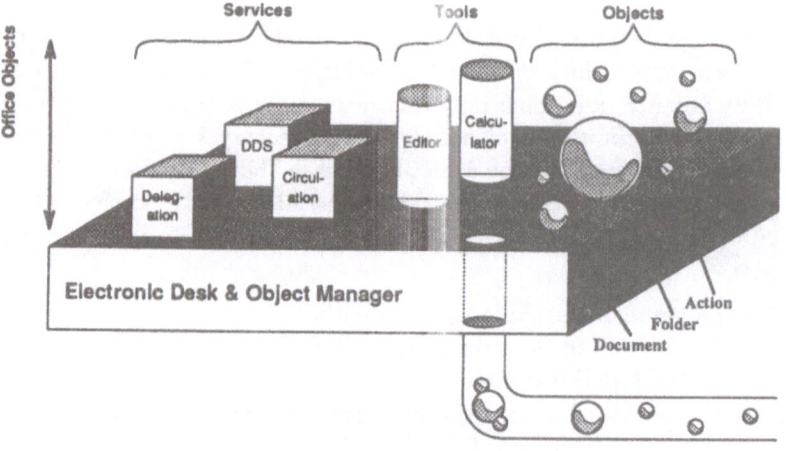

Fig. 8.2. Architecture of CIDRE.

8.1.2.1 The Electronic Desk. Office workers access all the components of their working environments by means of a unified interface called the Electronic Desk. This interface provides a natural way of interacting with office applications and office objects.

The Electronic Desk layer provides support for the management of all office objects. It allows direct communication between remote and local offices.

The Electronic Desk is the interface between an office worker and office applications. It contains an Object Manager (OM) which has two main functions: the storage and management of office objects belonging to the local user, and communication with other remote OMs. Any office object to be manipulated on a given workstation (through the use of the corresponding Electronic Desk) is registered with the local OM. OMs represent an additional communication layer above the Comandos platform.

The CIDRE experience has shown that the Electronic Desk layer could be reused as a generic desk-top for other office applications. The detailed evaluation of the Comandos implementation of CIDRE revealed that this layer takes particular advantage of Comandos features.

8.1.2.2 Office Objects. As already mentioned, office objects are the entities managed by the CIDRE system. In other words, all types of objects managed in a CIDRE environment can be viewed as specialisations of the basic office object type. The relationships between the various object types involved in a CIDRE environment are depicted in Fig. 8.3 (in this picture, a link between two round boxes describes a specialisation relationship). Consequently, all objects throughout the system provide a standard behaviour which is defined by the type `OfficeObject`. In addition, different types of objects may provide additional functionalities which are specific to their type. The various categories of office objects are described below.

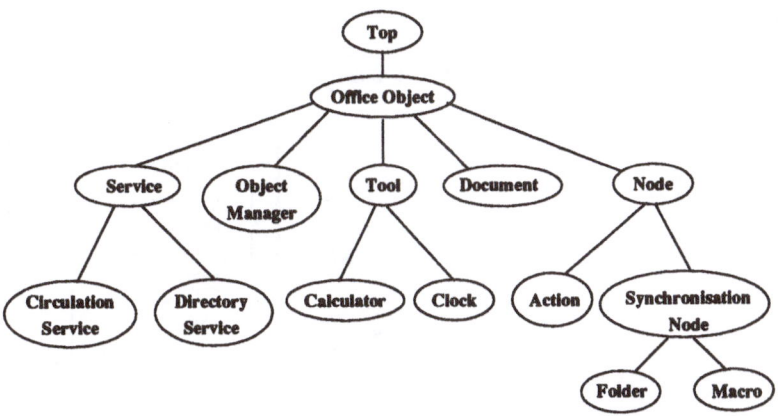

Fig. 8.3. Office objects tree.

Documents. CIDRE documents are composed of three parts:

- the content, which is collaboratively edited during the circulation of the document. The content type provides a logical view of the document. The content is composed of *logical atoms*, which are in turn composed of several fields. Implementation choices (such as the document format) are hidden at this level of description.
- the circulation scheme is embedded in the document in order to allow autonomous circulation of the document. The circulation scheme regis-

ters actions (see below) which have been completed, actions which are in progress, and computes the actions which become possible.
- the history part of the document maintains information concerning the implementation of the circulation scheme (such as the names of the workers who performed actions and the effective time ordering of the actions).

Folders. CIDRE folders have two main purposes:
- to synchronise the circulation of their own documents (i.e. the documents which are registered within the folder). This function is by nature distributed.
- to provide, at any time, a consistent view of the state of each document.

Figure 8.4 depicts a set of related folder and document objects. Although they are referenced by the same folder, different documents are distinct entities which can be manipulated or migrated independently of each other.

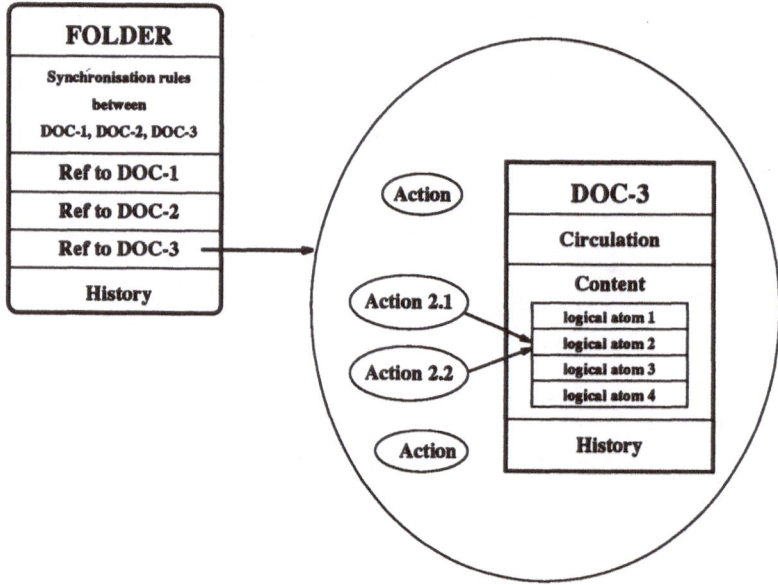

Fig. 8.4. Folder and document objects.

Actions. CIDRE actions allow office workers to handle documents. Action objects represent logical operations which can be performed on the logical parts of a document, provided that the office worker has the corresponding access-right.

Services. A CIDRE *office service* is a distributed office application, shared by several users. Typical office services include the circulation service, the negotiation service, the delegation service, the diary service, and the directory service.

Additional services provided by UNIX can be used within the CIDRE environment (e.g. mail and print services).

Tools. A CIDRE *office tool* (such as a word processor or a calculator) is an individual application located on a user workstation. CIDRE services and tools are office objects which provide additional functionality to office workers. The CIDRE environment allows dedicated services, and tools to be built and existing services and tools which are available in a UNIX environment to be reused.

8.2 CIDRE Design and Implementation

In the framework of the Comandos project, the CIDRE pilot application was redesigned using the facilities of the Comandos computational model. The development of the actual prototype was carried out using the Comandos object-oriented language. In addition, the application uses other facilities provided by the Comandos platform such as the DDS (c.f. Chap. 7). Finally, existing UNIX tools and services were reused, where it was appropriate (e.g. the user interface is implemented using the X Window System and OSF/Motif).

8.2.1 Use of the Type Model

The Comandos language type model allowed a simple mapping between CIDRE objects and Comandos objects.

8.2.1.1 Types and Classes. The example below shows an extract from the Comandos language type definition for the generic CIDRE office object - recall that all CIDRE objects provide at least the functionality of `OfficeObject`.

```
TYPE OfficeObject IS
 Name : String[MAXNAME] = "";
 MyOm : REF Om = NIL;                /* Current OM
 OmName : String [MAXNAME] = "";
 ObjFather : REF OfficeObject = NIL;
 UserName : String [MAXNAME] = "";    /* Current owner
 AutoMigration : Boolean = TRUE;      /* Migration allowed

 METHOD Init(IN name : String; typ : String);
 METHOD Register(IN REF Om); /* Register object in current OM
 METHOD CancelMigration;
 METHOD Session;
 METHOD Migration;
 METHOD Clone: REF OfficeObject;
 METHOD Kill;
 METHOD Print;
 METHOD Execute;
END OfficeObject.
```

8.2.1.2 Type Hierarchy and Sub-typing. Sub-typing is a natural way of implementing the office object tree described in Fig. 8.3. The example below illustrates the use of sub-typing to define a service object as a specialisation of an office object.

The Service type is defined as a sub-type of the OfficeObject type as follows. New public variables (e.g. Site, Info, MyPrivateOm) appear in the definition of the Service type. The Init method of the original office object type is overloaded. In addition, new methods are added: Modif, Run, ObjectIn, ObjectOut.

```
TYPE Service SUBTYPE OF OfficeObject IS
   Site : String[MAXNAME] = "";
   Info : String[MAXSTRING] = "";
   MyPrivateOm : REF OmP = NIL;

   METHOD Init (IN REF Desk; REF Om): Boolean;
   METHOD Modif (IN REF List OF REF TypeObject;
                    REF List OF REF Reflect);
   METHOD Run;
   METHOD ObjectIn (IN REF OfficeObject);
   METHOD ObjectOut (IN REF OfficeObject);
END Service;
```

In the same way the type Document is also defined as a sub-type of OfficeObject as follows:

```
TYPE Document SUBTYPE OF OfficeObject IS
   MyContent : REF Content = NIL;
   MyStory : REF Story = NIL;
   MyCirc : REF Circulation = NIL;

   <additional methods>

END Document.
```

The Electronic Desk makes use of conformance to manage office objects in a uniform way. All objects that are sub-types of office object are seen and handled by the Electronic Desk through the basic interface specified by the type OfficeObject (shown in the example above).

8.2.1.3 Object Composition. As shown in Fig. 8.4, documents and folders are compound objects. A folder holds references to the documents it manages. A document is, in turn, composed of internal objects such as MyContent or MyCirc. This composition scheme is expressed in the Document type described above as a set of references to objects. The objects that are part of an entity such as a folder can be located on different sites. Objects contained in a document (e.g. an action object or the history), may be accessed and managed by the Electronic Desk independently of the document itself. The CIDRE application often uses compound objects.

8.2.2 Use of the Computational Model

8.2.2.1 Jobs and Activities. In CIDRE a Comandos job is associated with a user session, being started when a user connects to the CIDRE environment and opens the Electronic Desk. The job terminates when the user leaves the CIDRE environment. The initial activity of each job launches two parallel activities: one for the user interface, and another to update graphical objects to reflect changes to application objects asynchronously.

A given job may diffuse to several nodes if the Electronic Desk attempts to use remote objects. On the other hand some office objects (e.g. documents or parts of documents) can be shared between jobs belonging to different users.

8.2.2.2 Distribution. An important issue in distributed applications such as CIDRE is the location of different services or specific objects. Objects must migrate from one site to another without disturbing running applications.

Distribution transparency is achieved at two levels. From the end-user point of view, objects can be accessed independently of their location (depending on the rights of the office worker). Thus, the user has a global and uniform view of the distributed system. From the programmer's point of view, object location is managed as follows:

- Given the CIDRE name of an office object, a request to the local OM allows the global name of the object to be obtained (this may involve a protocol with remote OMs).
- Given its global name, an object may be accessed, whether it be local or remote. It is the responsibility of the Comandos virtual machine to retrieve the target object and to execute the required operation.

8.2.2.3 Synchronisation and Communication Through Shared Objects. In a distributed application like CIDRE many objects can be shared. For example, documents or services may be accessed by different users at the same time. Furthermore, office objects may have several different graphical interfaces running simultaneously.

The Comandos language provides facilities to express concurrency control and execution conditions at the level of each method. The example below illustrates the use of this facility for expressing mutual exclusion between two methods Append and Remove of the OM. This condition prevents objects being simultaneously removed from and added to a given OM.

```
CLASS Om SUBCLASS OF OfficeObject IS
  METHOD Append(IN obj : REF OfficeObject);
  METHOD Remove(IN obj :REF OfficeObject):Boolean;

  CONTROL
    EXCLUSIVE (Append,Remove);
END Om.
```

Object sharing and concurrency control allow the handling of synchronisation inside of the object. This allows the possibility of visualising updates to shared office objects immediately from the graphical user interface.

8.2.3 Persistent Objects

During a session, users open their Electronic Desks, create objects (e.g. documents and messages), execute actions on those objects, and modify their own environments. As users log out, closing their Electronic Desks, part of the modified information must be saved so that they will find their environment in the same state at the beginning of the next session. This is achieved by making the objects managed by the Electronic Desk persistent. In CIDRE, this can be achieved in one of two ways.

1. Persistence is provided implicitly by the Comandos virtual machine. Within the CIDRE application, the Electronic Desk and the OM are made persistent roots so that any office object managed by an Electronic Desk or an OM automatically persists. For example:

```
/* This method of class OfficeObject registers an object
/* in an OM, thus implicitly making the object persist.
METHOD Register(IN  om : REF Om);
BEGIN
  MyOm := om;
  OmName := om.Name;
  MyOm.Append (SELF, SEEN);
END Register;
```

2. Another way to make objects persistent is to register them in in a directory using a naming service, as shown below.

```
CLASS Om SUBCLASS OF OfficeObject IMPLEMENTS Om IS
  LocalDirOMs : REF Catal = NIL;

  METHOD Init(IN name:String; desk:REF Desk; om:REF Om);
  BEGIN
    UserName := name;
    /* Search for another object with the same symbolic name
    IF LocalDirOMs.Search (UserName) # NIL
    THEN
        Message("Om already exists");
        SELF.Destroy;
        RETURN;
    END;
    /* Insert the OM's name and reference into the directory
    LocalDirOMs.Insert (UserName, SELF);
  END INIT;

END Om.
```

Persistent programming is a major advantage for application development as it removes the burden of saving and restoring persistent data explicitly. The application programmer only has to focus on a few objects which should be registered with the naming service. The object composition mechanism ensures that all component objects automatically persist.

8.2.4 Integration with UNIX

Since the Comandos platform is available on top of UNIX, interworking with existing UNIX services and applications was easily supported. Two examples of the use of this interworking capability are described below.

8.2.4.1 Access to Existing UNIX Applications. Existing UNIX applications have to be supported in order to provide users with their usual environment as well as the new environment. Coexistence with the existing UNIX environment is a condition for future acceptance by customers.

The CIDRE Electronic Desk provides access to office tools which already existed on top of UNIX (e.g. calculators and word-processors). This is achieved by simply embedding the target UNIX tool into a specific office object type, as shown in the following example (the method Run simply allows the UNIX program to be run):

```
TYPE Tool SUBTYPE OF OfficeObject IS
  METHOD Init;
  METHOD Run;
END Tool.
```

8.2.4.2 The User Interface. A CIDRE environment, as for any office environment, must provide the office worker with a high level graphical interface. The Comandos platform provides a complete OSF/Motif library embedded within the Comandos language.

The development of the CIDRE graphical user interface made intensive use of the mechanisms and tools offered by the Comandos language to build interactive applications based on the OSF/Motif toolkit [Normand 1990].

8.2.5 Use of Comandos Services

The CIDRE application uses the DDS for the description of the organisational structure of the office environment. This description includes primarily the individuals, departments and activity domains involved in the office environment, as well as their attributes (e.g. a person has a name, a password, a function within the enterprise and some access rights).

Calls to the DDS allow information associated with a given entity to be retrieved for application-level security control (such as password checking at user log in time or checking of the access rights on a document), and to get additional information required by a service (such as the role and name of a user who creates a document). The interface to the Comandos DDS is specified in the Directory class which is described below:

```
CLASS Directory SUBCLASS OF Service IMPLEMENTS Directory IS
  dsa : REF Dsa = NIL;
  dsaChan : REF DirChannel= NIL;
  /* dsa and dsaChan are DDS objects conforming to the X500 model.

  /* In the following method, the Directory class uses the DDS
  /* to access and manipulate the data stored in the directory.
  METHOD CheckPers(IN name:String; sname:String; pass:String):Integer;
      dn : REF DistName;
      ok : Boolean;
      ava : REF Ava;
      strval : REF StrVal;
      result : REF List OF REF DistName;
      err : String[80];
  BEGIN
      /* Creation of the objects which are known by DDS service :
      /* dn is the distinguished name of the target entry;
      /* ava is the structure which allows the attributes of
      /* the target entry to be described.
      dn := DistName.New;
      ok := dn.Init("/O=STAFF", g_codes);
      ....
      ava := Ava.New;
      strval := StrVal.New;
      strval.Init(name);
      ava.Init(3,strval);

      /* Open a communication channel with the DSA
      dsaChan := dsa.Bind("/O=SEPT",err);

      /* Call the DSA to search the entry corresponding to a person,
      /* given their name.
      result := dsaChan.Search(dn,ava,err);

      /* Call the DSA to check attributes of the given entry
      /* (password, etc.).
      ok := dsaChan.Compare(dn, ava, err) ;

      /* Close the communication with the DDS.
      dsaChan.Unbind;
  END CheckPers;

END Directory.
```

8.3 Evaluation

The redesign and implementation of CIDRE on top of the Comandos platform was carried out by three people (already trained in the use of object-oriented languages, but not in the specifics of the Comandos model and language). The current prototype includes about 30 000 lines of Comandos language source code corresponding to 90 classes. This is only a subset of the full CIDRE application (i.e. some services have not yet been implemented on the Comandos platform)

Due to the natural mapping between application objects and Comandos objects, the CIDRE redesign was performed easily. The main aspects of this mapping have been described in the sections above. This section summarises the main lessons learnt from the use of the Comandos platform for the redesign and implementation of the CIDRE system.

8.3.1 Model and Language

The Comandos model and language appear cleaner than C++, mainly in the following aspects:

- Distinction between types and classes. Although it was not used intensively, this feature was particularly useful for adapting some application components to specific user requirements. An example is the coexistence of several implementations of the type Document allowing the use of private facilities to fill in the fields of document representing forms (e.g. manually or by retrieving data from an internal database). By comparison, a classical approach would consist of using the inheritance mechanism to build the corresponding facility.
- Inheritance and conformance. The strongly typed approach combined with conformance, which is implicitly associated with inheritance, allow early detection of programming errors, and thus provide a safe programming framework.
- Global object identification (by references rather than by pointers) which is independent of object location policy.
- Syntactic constructs for concurrency control. The CIDRE experience revealed two major advantages provided by the declarative approach of the Comandos language:
    - the application programmer does not need to implement an explicit distributed monitor facility which is itself a complex software component.
    - the code which implements concurrency control is kept separated from the actual code of the methods; this allows the synchronisation policy to be changed without affecting the method's code.
- Support for parallelism.
- Exception handling.

The Comandos language provides the ability to clearly and quickly use the features of the Comandos model. However, some limitations still exist, such as the lack of multiple inheritance, and more sophisticated data modelling facilities (the ODMS not being available in the prototype used to implement the CIDRE application).

The development process suffered from the unstable state of the Comandos language compiler (developed in parallel by a Comandos partner), and, more importantly, from a lack of development tools to assist the programmer in designing, programming and debugging code.

8.3.2 Architecture

8.3.2.1 Distribution Transparency. Location and access transparency are key issues in designing and implementing an application like CIDRE. Most of the time, the application designer is relieved of the burden of managing remote invocation (including object location, marshalling and unmarshalling and communication) explicitly. In comparison with the experience drawn from the first implementation of CIDRE (in C++ on CHORUS/COOL), the distribution transparency provided by the Comandos virtual machine is a considerable advantage.

However, some specific situations encountered in CIDRE require that a given object (i.e. document or part of a document) be on a given workstation for protection or efficiency reasons. This is the case, in particular, when the circulation scheme requires the migration of a document to a given workstation. Thus, management of location information may still be desired at some level; this leads to the concept of full, but controlled, location transparency. This facility was missing in the early version of the Comandos language, but is now available.

8.3.2.2 Persistent Data Management. Given the large number of object types in the application, automatic persistence, which avoids the need to develop private data structures to store each kind of object, resulted in a valuable saving in development resources. It should be noted that this gain not only occurs in the first development stage, but also, and this is certainly more important, when the software evolves: the developer does not have to maintain these private storage structures in parallel with the classes.

8.3.2.3 Integration Facilities.
- **Other Comandos applications, services and tools:** The adoption of a common object model made the integration and use of the DDS, developed by another team, easy and efficient.
- **UNIX applications:** Communication between Comandos and UNIX is easy. This allowed, for instance, some standard X Window System tools to be made available within the CIDRE Electronic Desk.
- **Window environment:** OSF/Motif resource files can be reused.

8.3.3 Conclusion

The CIDRE application was a very constructive way of validating the Comandos approach on a state-of-the-art application, and of learning from the experiences of the application developers. In this sense these objectives of the CIDRE application development have been achieved successfully.

- The current CIDRE prototype represents a powerful demonstration application, which is typical of the distributed office environment. The prototype has already been demonstrated publicly on various occasions.
- Although the CIDRE application could not allow all of the features of Comandos to be evaluated, it allowed the usefulness of the major design choices and innovative aspects of the Comandos platform to be demonstrated in the construction of a large distributed application including:
  - the object-oriented approach supported by linguistic constructs,
  - distribution transparency and persistent programming,
  - interworking with a UNIX environment,
  - incremental and rapid development, based on the reuse of software components (class libraries and other Comandos services).

Based on this experience, and on earlier experience with CHORUS/COOL-1, SEPT has decided to adopt the distributed platform approach for industrial projects in the office area, and to use an industrial implementation of the Comandos virtual machine as the underlying technology.

Part II

Implementor's View of the Comandos Platform

9. Virtual Machine Interface

This part of the book is concerned with the implementation of the Comandos platform – in particular, the Comandos system. The aim of this part of the book is to provide the interested reader with an overview of the implementation and a feeling for the complexity of the system. Further details concerning the design and implementation of the system can be found in the many published papers listed in App. E.

This chapter describes the main principles of the VMI together with the major routines (both up-calls and down-calls) which make up the VMI. This chapter also describes the architecture of the virtual machine and the role of each of its main components.

Chapter 10 describes the implementation of the virtual machine. Chapter 11 describes the implementation of a language-specific run-time which interfaces to the Comandos virtual machine.

9.1 The Virtual Machine Architecture

The Comandos virtual machine implements the basic functionality necessary to support transparent distributed processing. The VMI presents a uniform view of the Comandos virtual machine to each of the supported programming languages. The VMI is provided as a set of primitives implemented by the GRT which itself makes use of the services of the underlying Comandos kernel. The kernel includes those components of the virtual machine which must be implemented in a protected way.

However, as different languages have different calling semantics, a language-specific run-time must adapt the GRT primitives to the language-specific format. Moreover, as most of these primitives are based on manipulation of objects whose implementation differs throughout the different languages, each language-specific run-time must also hide these language dependencies from the GRT.

To provide this flexibility and to make a minimum number of impositions on any language, Comandos supports a general model in which the language may make calls to the GRT which depend on language-specific information. To handle such a call the GRT uses up-calls to the language-specific run-time to obtain the required information.

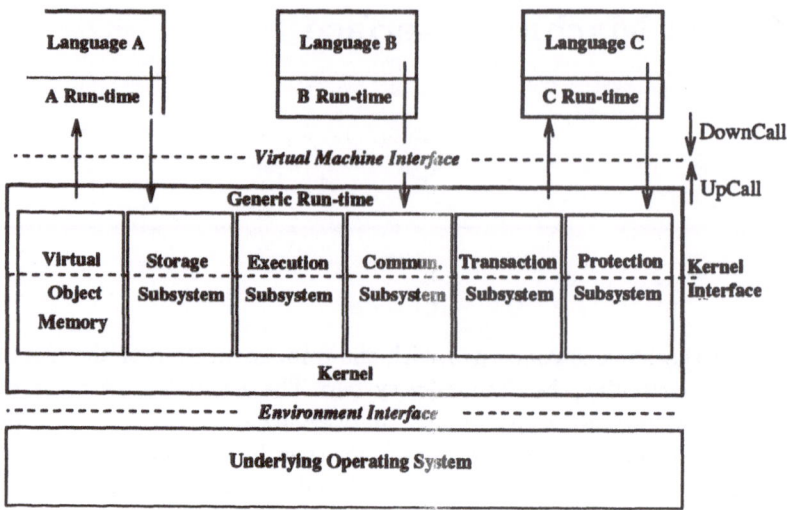

Fig. 9.1. The internal architecture of the Comandos virtual machine.

This two-way interface between a language-specific run-time and the GRT allows objects of different languages to be handled commonly by the GRT and allows the latter to be commonly accessed by different languages.

The Comandos virtual machine is internally composed of six components:

- the *Virtual Object Memory* (VOM) handles all operations related to the management of contexts and the objects mapped into those contexts.
- the *Execution Sub-system* (ES) provides support for object execution, and implements jobs and activities;
- the *Storage Sub-system* (SS) provides storage for persistent objects;
- the *Transaction Sub-system* (TS) supports atomic objects and transactions;
- the *Communication Sub-system* (CS) is responsible for providing a generic RPC interface independent of the underlying protocol stack and for all communication between kernels;
- the *Protection Sub-system* (PS) provides low level security mechanisms.

The implementation of these components is split across three interfaces (c.f. Fig. 9.1):

- the *Virtual Machine Interface* – the interface across which the GRT and a supported language communicate;
- the *Kernel Interface* – dividing those parts of the virtual machine which are accessible directly by applications (i.e. running in user mode) and those which are accessible only in a privileged mode;
- the *Environment Interface* – the interface between the Comandos virtual machine and the underlying host environment: UNIX, CHORUS, or Mach for example.

9.2 Virtual Object Memory

The VOM implements the distributed object space manipulated by jobs and activities, and thus by application programs.

The VOM provides two types of services – *context services* and *global services*. Context services are provided within each individual context and are mainly concerned with management of the objects mapped in the context. Global services are concerned with issues such as context creation and deletion (to support extents); sharing of objects between contexts as necessary, and object location in the distributed system. While context services are implemented by code running in user mode within each context, global services may be implemented in kernel mode or by specific VOM servers as well as in user mode within a context, depending on the underlying environment. In this section an overview of the basic functionality of the VOM is presented.

9.2.1 Context Services

The VOM provides generic support for management of Comandos objects (c.f. Chap 3), including their creation and possible garbage collection. In the following, Comandos objects are referred to simply as objects.

The following sections give an overview of how the VOM manages objects. The set of up-calls which must be supported by each such object is described by the VMI class Object. and is described in detail in Chap. 11 together with the down-calls related to object management which are described by the VMI class Context.

9.2.1.1 Object Creation and Promotion. Objects are brought into existence by calling the VOM. The VOM allocates space, which is untyped, and can be used by the language-specific run-time as a repository for language objects.

Any object created in this way is known as a *volatile.* Such objects exist and are known only within the context in which they were created. Objects may become known outside of their context of creation (either because a reference to the object has been passed out of the context, or because the object itself migrates out of the context). If this happens, the object is *promoted* to being a globally known object.

9.2.1.2 Object Global Naming. Objects are assigned global names only when they promoted. Thus a location independent form of naming is used to transmit a reference to an object outside of the context in which the object was created. Global names may be passed in remote/cross-context invocations and stored in the SS.

The VOM interacts with the SS in allocating global names since a global name consists of a container identifier and a generation number which is unique within that container. The container identifier names the secondary storage container initially specified for the object. If the object migrates between containers, then its initial container must keep track of the object's current storage location.

9.2.1.3 Object Invocation. Object invocation is the central feature of the Comandos model encompassing all the features related to transparent handling of persistence, distribution and sharing.

Invocations on objects mapped locally are performed at language-specific run-time level. However, attempts to access objects which are not mapped in the current context – object faults – must be trapped by the language-specific run-time and reported to the VOM. The VOM either arranges to map the object into the current context, or to carry-out a cross-context or remote invocation as required. The VOM may interact with the PS, SS and AM in determining how to handle the object fault. The following paragraphs introduce the basic mechanisms within the VOM to handle object faults.

9.2.1.4 Object Mapping. When mapping an object, the VOM must first allocate memory for the object. The VOM translates global names contained in the mapped object to direct addresses by up-calling the object's language-specific run-time. This translation may be delayed until the object is actually used (e.g. being invoked) if the object was pre-fetched.

Groups of objects, i.e. clusters, form the actual unit of transfer between the VOM and the SS. Since objects are retrieved in clusters, the VOM must handle demand loading of one object and pre-fetching of the others. Pre-fetched objects are simply registered in the faulting context.

9.2.1.5 Remote and Cross-context Invocation. When the resolution of an object fault requires that a remote or cross-context invocation is carried out, the VOM is responsible for initiating the transmission of the parameter frame to the target node. The parameter frame is provided by the language level and is not normally interpreted by the VOM. At the target node the VOM will provide the parameter frame to the target object via an up-call i.e. all objects must be prepared to receive incoming invocations in a standard form.

9.2.1.6 Local Garbage Collection. The creation of new objects may lead to exhaustion of memory. To recycle unused memory the VOM incorporates a local (intra-context) garbage collector which, taking promoted objects as part of its root, collects volatile objects which have become garbage.

As the VOM imposes no parameter frame formats the collector must be conservative when scanning stacks. However, local garbage collection uses the up-call mechanism to locate object references held by objects. Note that garbage collection can be compacting only if dynamic object movement is supported by the language and its language-specific run-time.

9.2.1.7 Clustering. A cluster consists of a header, a list of the objects contained in the cluster and a set of objects. Each cluster contains a set of persistent objects which are mapped into one contiguous region of virtual memory.

New (volatile) objects are allocated in the creating context's heap by the VOM and only inserted into a cluster if still referenced by a promoted object at the time that the context is being deleted. Since a large proportion of objects do not survive to context deletion time the cost of copying objects into clusters on unmapping is preferable to the complexity of cluster heap management, which is needed if all objects are created in a cluster. On context deletion any volatile objects that are to be stored are placed in a default cluster (a new or existing cluster) by the VOM, and the SS is informed.

The overhead of a cluster imposed on a single large persistent object is low, and hence all persistent objects reside in clusters.

9.2.2 Global Services

At each node the VOM also provides global services such as context creation and deletion, and object location.

9.2.2.1 Context Management. Contexts are created when jobs and activities invoke operations on objects from different extents for which no appropriate context already exists on the node. Contexts are deleted when there is no further job or activity actively using the context.

9.2.2.2 Remote Object Location. In the handling of an object fault, the global part of the VOM is responsible for locating the target object. The object may be located either in another context at the same node or in some context at another node.

At each node of the distributed system the VOM maintains a mapping for each globally known object which is mapped at that node, giving the context into which the object is mapped.

In order to locate objects mapped on other nodes the VOM keeps another mapping giving the location of each object (actually cluster) that is mapped anywhere in the distributed system. This table is partitioned so that the entry for each cluster is stored at a single node.

9.3 Execution Sub-system

The ES provides support for the execution model described in Chap. 3. It is mainly responsible for job and activity management including the creation, control and diffusion of jobs and activities as required. The ES is also responsible for providing low level synchronisation mechanisms. These facilities appear as pre-defined system classes (job, activity and semaphore) in the VMI and are described as such in the following sections. Support for exception handling is also provided by the ES.

9.3.1 Job and Activity Management

A new job is created by invoking the constructor from the Job class, passing as a parameter a description of the initial operation to be carried out by the job including its parameters. An additional optional **node** parameter allows suppression of the distribution transparency provided by the system by specifying the node at which the job is preferred to execute. A **priority** parameter can also be given when a job is created. This priority is associated with all activities within the job. A global name for the job is allocated when the job is created. This global name contains the identification of the node where the job was created.

Parallelism within a job is provided by creating parallel activities. A new activity is created by invoking the constructor from the **Activity** class. An initial operation, and its associated parameters, on an initial object are specified. As for jobs, an additional optional **node** parameter allows the preferred execution node of the activity to be specified. A **priority** parameter can also be given when an activity is created. A new activity is always created within the current job. A global name is allocated and returned for each new activity. An activity can be created in the **active** or **suspended** states. If **suspended** it becomes **active** when the **Resume** operation is invoked.

An active activity can be explicitly suspended by any other activity by means of the **Suspend** operation. When in the suspended state, it can be resumed by any other activity by means of the **Resume** operation. An activity can also wait, using the **Join** operation, for the termination of another activity of the same job.

An activity can be killed using the destructor. The activity cannot be restarted and all of its resources are released.

The **Status** operation returns the current state of the activity (either **active**, **suspended** or **terminated**) and general information about the status of the activity. All activity operations can be invoked on any node, not only nodes visited by the activity.

Similar operations are provided for job control including the ability to suspend, resume, kill and query the state of a particular job.

9.3.2 Synchronisation Support

The ES also supports the basic synchronisation mechanism provided by the VMI – semaphores. Higher level synchronisation mechanisms can be provided by supported programming languages (c.f. Chap. 4) using this basic mechanism.

Semaphores are system objects which are identified by global names. They are created on a given node, but can be accessed from any node using the standard object invocation mechanism. Semaphores are potentially persistent, however, a semaphore can only be unmapped if no activity is currently blocked on it.

A new semaphore is created by invoking the constructor from the Semaphore class. A global name, which is used to identify the semaphore on any node, is allocated and returned. The standard P (wait) and V (signal) operations can then be invoked from any node by any activity.

9.3.3 Exception Handling

There are three categories of exceptions recognised by the virtual machine:

- hardware exceptions which are detected by the hardware;
- virtual machine exceptions which are detected by the virtual machine; and
- user-defined exceptions which are language-specific.

The ES provides mechanisms allowing each supported language to report these three exception categories to programmers according to its own exception model.

9.3.3.1 User-defined Exceptions. It is assumed that user-defined exceptions are processed either within the invoked object or within the invoking object. If both objects are within the same context these exceptions are not visible to the virtual machine, and are completely processed within the language-specific run-time. If both objects are not within the same context, it may be necessary to propagate the exception and any associated information from the current context to the context of the invoking object. This is done by allowing additional information to be returned with the parameter block of each cross-context invocation.

9.3.3.2 Virtual Machine Exceptions. These are failures of object invocations carried out through the virtual machine, for example, node or communication failures. All such events are detected by the virtual machine during the processing of the invocation. These events are returned as errors from the current call to the virtual machine. For example, a communication failure during a remote object invocation will be reported as an error to the language-specific run-time.

The language-specific run-time propagates these errors according to the language-specific exception model.

9.3.3.3 Hardware Exceptions. Hardware exceptions are detected by the underlying system and reported to the ES by whatever means are provided by the underlying environment e.g. signals in UNIX. Hardware exceptions are propagated to the language-specific run-time which will process them according to the language exception model.

9.4 Storage Sub-system

The SS implements a distributed object repository (persistent store), in which storage containers can be distributed amongst different nodes in the system.

Since large collections of relatively small objects are to be stored and retrieved, actual storage and retrieval is performed in groups of objects held in *segments*. This both optimises storage and retrieval and allows locality of reference between objects to be exploited by the VOM.

9.4.1 Container Management

A container is a physically or logically contiguous area of secondary storage corresponding to a disk partition. Each container stores some control information together with a set of segments.

More than one container can be mounted on a node. The SS maintains a mapping from container identifier to node, and keeps enough information to locate any object stored in a container despite the possibility of object migration.

9.4.2 Segments

From the SS point of view the unit of transfer between the VOM and the SS is a segment. Note, in particular, that it is possible to fetch a segment from a container which resides at another node.

A segment is a contiguous storage unit consisting of a number of disk blocks. A segment may be logically contiguous, if for example the Comandos storage system is implemented using UNIX files, or physically contiguous, if for example the storage system is implemented directly on a raw disk interface.

9.4.3 Object Migration and Clustering

Cluster reorganisation is performed internally to the SS. Once made persistent, objects may be migrated between clusters by the SS as a result of user level directives or other reference information available e.g. from the VOM. In particular, a down-call is provided by the VMI to allow languages, and thus applications, to apply grouping primitives to objects. These calls are taken by the SS as grouping hints which may place the named objects in the same cluster. Grouping directives may however conflict across applications.

In addition, object migration between containers is supported independently of clustering.

The global name (c.f. Chap. 3) of a persistent object is used to identify both its host container and the position of the object within the container. When an individual object moves in secondary storage, it is usually not possible to update all references to this object, since they may have been widely distributed and copied. Object migration between clusters in the same container simply involves updating internal mappings, but migration between potentially distributed containers requires a separate mechanism. The classical solution to this problem relies on the use of forwarding pointers. These pointers may possibly form a chain; however, speed-up techniques are used to prevent following such chains by caching the last known position. In the last resort, the identity of the object can be broadcast to all the nodes. Since object movement in secondary storage is likely to be exceptional, it is expected that most relocation problems will be solved by forwarding pointers and that searching by broadcast will almost never occur. Volatile forwarding information may be used to accelerate a search, but may be out of date or incomplete due to node crashes.

9.4.4 Ageing in the Storage Sub-system

The SS is layered much in the same way as modern virtual memory systems use main memory and disk space. In the simplest case this can be seen as the difference between disks and tapes, or within the distributed system it can be mirrored as a local disk, remote disk and archive disk. As the use of an object tapers off it is removed from its prime secondary storage and written to some other container. When an aged object is reused it is automatically brought back into prime storage, where it will remain until it once again goes stale.

It is impractical, and indeed undesirable, to preserve for all time all objects ever created in the system. Accordingly, sufficiently old objects are eventually deleted at some point in time. Thus the system only guarantees that objects are maintained as long as they are in use.

In Comandos this layering of storage is implemented by organising containers into hierarchies. Each container knows its (unique) parent, and aged objects are passed to it. The hierarchies can be of any height and there can be any number of independent hierarchies in the system. On attempting to retrieve an object from its container the request is passed on to the parent if the required object is not found locally. This request is propagated back up the hierarchy until the object is found and brought back into its original prime container, or the root is reached. Depending on the system administration, the root may well be archival storage such as magnetic tape or an optical disk. If the object is not found in the root then it has been deleted, and its global name is a (detectable) dangling reference. This is acceptable because in general the system only guarantees to retain an object while it is being used within some period of time.

The process of locating an object requires that each container knows its parent. This enables the ageing tree to be traversed from any leaf up to the root. Traversal in the opposite direction is not required as an object's prime container can be derived from its global name, which never changes. Obviously retrieving an object which is not in its prime container will be slower, but this is also acceptable, just as in a memory swapping system the working set is in prime storage and the rest, which is accessed less frequently, is on secondary storage.

Some objects may be marked by system administrators as *permanent* so that they will never be deleted. Such objects will age as usual if they are not used, but would never be deleted from their root container.

9.5 Transaction Sub-system

The transaction model (c.f. Chap. 3) is realised by the TS.

9.5.1 Transaction Management

The operations available to manage transactions are described by the **Transaction** and **Lock** classes.

A transaction or sub-transaction is started by using the constructor from class **Transaction** to specify the initial operation of the (sub-)transaction. This operation is a local synchronous operation which does not return until the transaction is complete.

A transaction terminates successfully when the operation invocation for which it was created completes normally. Hence there is no need for an explicit **EndTransaction** operation and none is provided.

A transaction may be terminated unsuccessfully by invoking the **Abort** operation when some undesired situation occurs.

The **CheckAccess** operation is called to acquire locks and create recovery points for atomic objects before accesses to those objects proceed. It can be used by a language-specific run-time implementing implicit concurrency control.

The **SetLockpoint** operation can be used to explicitly indicate that the lockpoint of the transaction has been reached.

The **MakeAtomic** operation is used to promote an object to atomic.

Finally, the **State** operation can be used to obtain the state of the transaction at any time.

Locks can also be acquired explicitly by using the **Set** operation from class **Lock** and released using the **Release** operation. The lockpoint of a transaction can be reached implicitly by executing the first **Release** operation.

9.6 Communication Sub-system

The CS provides transparent communication between every node in a Comandos installation. It offers two basic services:

- support for the remote invocation and for communication between kernels on different nodes through the Generic Remote Procedure Call (GRPC) interface;
- support for the TS and other components through the Reliable Broadcast Protocol (RBP).

9.6.1 Remote Invocation Support

The platform should be able to use any RPC package with minimal implementation effort, for example SunRPC or DCE RPC or any other package which offers the required features.

The functionality required by the higher levels – in particular the VOM which is responsible for managing remote invocation – is described by the GRPC interface. That is, the GRPC can be seen as an abstract interface to the underlying communications services provided by the host environment or provided by a standard RPC package as indicated above.

The GRPC supports different types of communication including:

- Announcements, for which no reply takes place;
- Reliable communication between distinct kernels, with at-most-once semantics, and without any limitation in time between the request and the reply.

For remote invocations, as described previously, the VOM, in cooperation with the appropriate language-specific run-time, is responsible for managing the stack-frames and marshaling parameters. Exactly which types of data can be passed is therefore language specific. The CS only provides a basic communication mechanism to the higher levels.

9.6.2 Reliable Broadcast Protocol

The Reliable Broadcast Protocol (RBP) is the underlying communication protocol used by the TS. It ensures that a sequence of messages from one sender is received at all nodes in that order, and furthermore, that the total sequence of received messages from all nodes is the same at every receiving node (global ordering). Detection of node faults, reformation after a reintegration request of a recovering node and reporting of these events to the surviving nodes are handled by the RBP. Corresponding indication messages are inserted into the global sequence of messages.

9.7 Protection Sub-system

The PS provides support for the security model which was described in Chap. 3. It is responsible for authorisation, secure transmission and auditing. Each of these topics is described below.

9.7.1 Authorisation

There are two major goals of the authorisation control mechanism:

1. protection against unauthorised access to an object;
2. protection against damage to an object by the malicious or fault code of another object (since objects can be co-resident in the same context).

While related, protection against unauthorised access via checking of ACLs, and protection against bad code via the use of separate extents, are orthogonal issues. However both functions are provided by the authorisation service.

The authorisation service provides the mechanisms to administer users and groups; to connect an ACL to an object and to modify existing ACLs; to manage extents and to change the ownership of an object. As usual these facilities are described by a set of VMI classes.

9.7.1.1 User and Group Management. A user is represented within the system by an object of a pre-defined class. A user object contains information such as the user's name, address, phone number and accounting data.

A group is represented within the system by an instance of a pre-defined class which contains information such as the name of the group, the list of individual users belonging to this group, etc. A group is identified by the global name of the corresponding group object.

The main operations on group are AddUser (to add a new user to the group), RemoveUser (to remove a user from the group), AddGroup (to add a new child group to the group), RemoveGroup (to remove a child group from the group).

9.7.1.2 Extent Management. Extents are visible to application programmers and to system users. Extents are named entities which may be created by users. The owner of an extent is its creator. A user may own more than one extent.

The owner of an extent defines the set of classes which may have instances in the extent. This set of classes may be mapped into the extent for execution. A class can obtain instances in an extent in two ways:

- an instance of a class may be created by another object in the extent under the control of the programmer;
- an object may be migrated between extents with the consent of the owners of both extents who, in practice, may actually be the same user.

9.7.1.3 Access Control Management. An ACL for an object gives a list of typed operations which can be invoked upon the object. For each operation in the list either a single user, a group of users, or an extent is specified.

The use of the user and group identifiers of the requester allow authorisation based on real users. Use of the identifier of the calling extent allows a trusted service to make use of another. This mechanism provides a controlled means of gaining privilege, allowing an invoked object to perform actions for which the requesting user has no direct right.

Note that the programmer can control which operations can be made visible outside of the extent and can enforce application-specific checks on actual parameters, in addition to the basic ACL check.

9.7.2 Secure Transmission

The Secure Transfer Service (STS) provides for the security of data during transmission over network communication channels. The STS allows both the components of the virtual machine and application objects to send private messages to their remote peers, while maintaining security.

The quality of the service depends on the system security level chosen by the security administrator – usually it will depend on the significance of the data to be transferred.

The communication security level component of the system security level allows a particular transfer procedure to be chosen. Each transfer procedure uses different sets of security mechanisms to reach the requested security level.

The communication security level can take any of the following values [Medina and Morena 1991]:

1. Level 0. The STS transmits data as clear text, without any protection.
2. Level 2. The STS transmits data protecting it against modification (including substitution, insertion or deletion). This level provides data integrity.
3. Level 1. The STS transmits data as cipher text, protecting it against monitoring. This level provides data confidentiality.
4. Level 3. The STS transmits data protecting it against monitoring and/or modification. This level provides data confidentiality and integrity.

9.7.2.1 STS Modules. The STS is composed of four basic modules: the Authentication Module (AuM), the Security Context Management Module (SCMM), the Secure Protocol Module (SPM) and the Security Transport Interface Module (STIM).

1. *The Authentication Module* is responsible for initiating authentication of two entities (identified by their transport – or other – addresses), which want to establish a connection for future data exchange. The AuM verifies the identities of the entities involved in the communication. Such authentication is mandatory if secure communication is desired.

   Two entities wishing to communicate over a trusted channel have to authenticate themselves through a third party entity: the Authentication Server. After the authentication process has been carried out, the two communicating entities exchange information in order to negotiate or to establish a common agreed security context. A security context is defined by a set of parameter values which specify a data exchange quality of service. The most important security parameters include: the security level (confidentiality and/or integrity); the confidentiality and integrity algorithms; the key granularity; the encryption keys and the transport addresses.

   The security context unambiguously relates two entities that reside in the same security domain and that are accessible via their transport addresses. The security context holds the information used by the Secure

Protocol Module in order to build secure transport protocol data units. SP4 [ISO 1991] is used in the implementation of the Secure Transport Protocol.

2. *The Context Management Module* is formed by a set of routines whose purpose is to maintain and to manage security contexts negotiated during authentication. The SCMM registers and removes security contexts in the Security Data Base when required.

3. *The Secure Protocol Module* converts Transport Protocol Data Units (TP-DUs) received from the Transport Layer to STPDUs (Secure Transport Protocol Data Units) before it sends them to the Network Layer. This module implements the Transport Level Security Protocol defined by ISO ([ISO 1991, ISO 1989]) that supports both connection-oriented and connectionless protocols. The protection achieved by this protocol extension depends on the proper operation of security management including key management.

   In the implementation, key management is performed by the Authentication Module and the Security Context Management Module. The protocol implemented supports both integrity and confidentiality of the exchanged data.

4. *The Security Transport Interface Module* defines a set of routines which provide the secure transport services in addition to the basic transport functionality.

9.7.3 Auditing

While the analysis of audit data is essential in every system, the threats encountered by a distributed open environment lead to special requirements for both the generation of audit data and their analysis for security-relevant patterns. These requirements are partially due to the object-oriented approach of Comandos, where the access to objects is the fundamental right of a user or of another object.

The Comandos virtual machine provides PDAT (c.f. Chap. 7) with a stream of audit data especially adapted to the requirements mentioned above. PDAT then processes the audit data by applying the currently defined criteria set. Finding any criterion satisfied may result in starting an activity to react to the perceived threat. System auditing must be done at the virtual machine level, so that users cannot avoid auditing. Thus the audit mechanism must be an integral part of the virtual machine.

Table 9.1 lists the most important events which may be audited. Further application-specific auditing is possible.

Depending on the security request one of three different levels of auditing may be chosen:

- No auditing.
- Audit only failed events.
- Full auditing (all events).

Table 9.1. List of audit events

Type of Event	
object:	creation
object:	deletion
object:	change of owner
object:	change of ACL
object:	invocation
extent:	creation
extent:	deletion
extent:	change of owner
extent:	change of ACL
extent:	cross invocation
job:	creation
job:	deletion
job:	termination
activity:	creation
activity:	deletion
activity:	termination
use of secure transmission	

Furthermore the audit data generation may be divided into several priority classes, so that not all events are always audited (assuming that auditing is enabled).

In general the audit information contains at least a time stamp, the invoking user and job, the type of the invocation and a field indicating success. Any other information depends on the type of the audited information, e.g. for an extent deletion the name of the deleted extent is provided.

10. Implementing the Virtual Machine

A strategic result of the Comandos project is the implementation and demonstration of a number of operational prototypes of the Comandos virtual machine, thus proving its feasibility in multi-vendor environments. Two basic approaches to the implementation of the platform were considered in the framework of the project:

- The first approach consisted of implementing the virtual machine as a guest layer on top of UNIX, without any modification to the UNIX kernel. One such implementation, Amadeus, was designated as the *reference platform* for the project. Therefore it was the basis for the integration of the numerous system components, application services and management tools developed throughout the project. This implementation is detailed in Sect. 10.1 below. The other major UNIX-based implementation of the virtual machine, IK, is described in [Sousa et al. 1993]. One of the objectives of the ESPRIT HARNESS project is to integrate this implementation of the Comandos platform with the DCE environment [HARNESS 1991b].
- The other approach followed was to implement the virtual machine directly on top of a micro-kernel. The motivation for this approach stemmed from the belief that the micro-kernel technology would be better able to support the Comandos abstractions, especially as far as distributed shared objects and protection were concerned. Note however that the target environments must, nevertheless, provide full access to UNIX applications. Two prototypes have been implemented using micro-kernel technology and are briefly described in Sect. 10.2 below:
  - one implementation runs on top of the CHORUS micro-kernel,
  - one implementation runs on top of OSF/1-MK.

These prototypes implement the VMI so that it will be possible to port a given language-specific run-time or service from one prototype to another. Full interworking of the various prototypes was beyond the scope of the project.

10.1 The Amadeus Platform

The Amadeus platform is the reference implementation of the Comandos virtual machine. Following the Comandos architecture, Amadeus consists of two main components: the GRT and the kernel. The Amadeus kernel is implemented as a collection of servers at each node, while the GRT is implemented as a library which must be present in every context. As a general rule, functionality is placed in the GRT whenever possible so as to maximise performance by avoiding inter-process communication and extra context switching. Functionality is assigned to the servers only if it must be protected. In effect, the servers provide the minimum functionality that would be implemented in protected mode if Amadeus were implemented on bare hardware or using an underlying micro-kernel.

The Amadeus kernel is a trusted component implemented by a number of servers. The so-called kernel server is responsible for cluster fault handling and extent management. On a cluster fault the kernel server is responsible for determining the extent, node and context in which the attempted invocation should be carried out and for forwarding the request to the target context as necessary. Thus the kernel server is responsible for maintaining the mapping between a cluster and its extent, for cluster location, and for extent activation and context creation. In addition to the kernel server, the RelaX Transaction Manager (TM), which is responsible for the execution of the distributed transaction coordination protocols, is implemented as a server at every node (c.f. Sect. 10.1.14). The TM and kernel servers make use of a totally ordered atomic broadcast protocol – the Reliable Broadcast Protocol (RBP) – which is implemented by another server at each node. Finally, each node may support a collection of storage servers managing different types of containers.

The GRT is mainly responsible for generic object management, job and activity management and for cluster mapping and unmapping including interfacing to secondary storage. The GRT also has a role in cluster fault handling – enabling the kernel to be by-passed where allowable. Finally, the GRT is responsible for the synchronisation of accesses to and recovery of atomic objects,

Section 10.1.1 gives an overview of the main design decisions taken in Amadeus. Section 10.1.2 describes the internal components of the Amadeus kernel and GRT. Subsequent sections describe the design and implementation of these components of Amadeus. In the space available only an overview of the design can be given – the interested reader is referred to [Cahill et al. 1992] for a more detailed description of the design.

10.1.1 Basic Design Decisions and Assumptions

This section outlines some of the global design decisions taken in the implementation of the system and in particular explains how concepts such as user, context and container are mapped onto the facilities provided by typical UNIX systems.

Amadeus has been designed to run in a tightly integrated network of UNIX workstations connected by a local area network.

Each Amadeus user maps onto a specific UNIX user. It is assumed that each user has the same UNIX user identifier on all nodes in the network[1] and

---

[1]For example, because the UNIX network has a single password file shared by all nodes.

the same user identifier is used for the Amadeus user as for the corresponding UNIX user.

Although ideally an extent is defined in terms of a set of classes, in practice, in this UNIX implementation, each extent is defined by a text image which includes all of the classes which are permitted in the extent. A text image is associated with each extent when the extent is created (c.f. Sect. 10.1.5). In principle, a user can request different applications to be run in any extent. In practice, without dynamic linking, a user can only ask to run one application in any extent – that corresponding to the text image for that extent.

Each Amadeus context is implemented as a UNIX process known as a *client*. A client can be created either as a result of a user starting an application or because of a cluster fault by an existing application. The UNIX text image to be run by the client is determined from the extent represented by the client. When an application is started in the extent, the mainline of the image is run. However, when a client is forked as a result of a cluster fault, the client idles waiting for the cross-context invocation request rather than executing the application mainline. Note that there may be many client images available in any Amadeus system and many jobs executing simultaneously and running the same or different images in the same or different extents.

The kernel servers are also implemented as UNIX processes. Moreover, in order to be able to implement the necessary security mechanisms, at least the kernel server must run with UNIX root privileges e.g. to make use of the UNIX setuid system call.

Although activities may share objects there is no physical sharing of memory in the current implementation. Each cluster appears in only one context and shared objects are accessed only by cross-context invocation. The decision not to share objects between contexts was motivated by the desire to support the use of virtual addresses as object references in language level objects. An alternative to the use of multiple contexts might have been the use of a single context per node. However this was rejected for security reasons, because of the limitations on the size of virtual address spaces that can be sufficiently supported by standard UNIX systems and to increase failure isolation when applications crash.

Activities are represented by threads in each visited context.

The current version of Amadeus assumes an underlying distributed file system which is shared by all the nodes in the Amadeus system and is used to make control information which is required by the various kernel components globally available. Although the SS allows different implementations of containers, in the current version of Amadeus each container is implemented as a directory in the underlying file system, with each cluster in the container stored as a file in the corresponding directory.

Finally, the design assumes that an authentication service exists allowing the receiver of any message to authenticate the sender. It is expected that an authentication service suitable for the needs of Amadeus can be implemented using, for example, the Kerberos authentication service [Steiner et al. 1988].

10.1.2 The Structure of Amadeus

This section presents an overview of the internal architecture of the kernel and the GRT and the functionality of their various sub-components.

10.1.2.1 Kernel Structure. The logical structure of the GRT and of the kernel have already been described in Chap. 9. The roles of the modules making up the kernel are introduced here and described in more detail in later sections. Figure 10.1 shows the main components of the kernel and their sub-components.

The kernel part of the PS is itself composed of a number of distinct modules. The kernel Extent Manager (EM) is responsible for all aspects of extent management including maintaining a database of known extents and their attributes, and also maintaining the mapping from a cluster to the extent to which it belongs. The EM also manages extent activation. The kernel Auditor is responsible for audit data generation for kernel operations.

The kernel part of the VOM is composed of four modules. The kernel Cluster Fault Handler (CFH) is responsible for resolving cluster faults including arranging for clusters to be mapped when necessary and forwarding of invocation requests to the appropriate contexts. The Location Service (LS) is responsible for keeping track of mapped clusters and ensuring that each cluster is mapped into at most one context at any time. The Address Resolution Manager (ARM) is responsible for keeping track of contexts and returning the address of a specified context when necessary. The kernel Context Manager (CM) manages context creation and deletion.

The kernel ES consists of the kernel Load Balancer (LB) which may be used to choose the node at which a faulted cluster is mapped, and the Thread Manager which provides support for concurrency within the kernel.

The kernel SS includes the Storage Manager (SM) which keeps track of which containers are available in the system at any time and also provides the interface between the kernel server and individual storage servers.

The kernel CS provides secure local and remote communication including reliable broadcasting and also includes the Node Manager (NM) which is responsible for keeping track of the nodes in the system.

Finally, the kernel TS supports distributed transaction management.

10.1.2.2 GRT Structure. The main components of the GRT are outlined in Fig. 10.2 and discussed in detail in later sections of this chapter.

The GRT PS includes only the Auditor which is responsible for audit data generation for GRT operations.

As in the kernel, the GRT part of the VOM is made up of a number of different modules. The Object Manager (OM) is responsible for all operations related to the management of objects. The Cluster Manager (ClM) is responsible for cluster creation, mapping and unmapping. On a cluster fault the GRT CFH is responsible for initiating the mapping of the target cluster or the forwarding

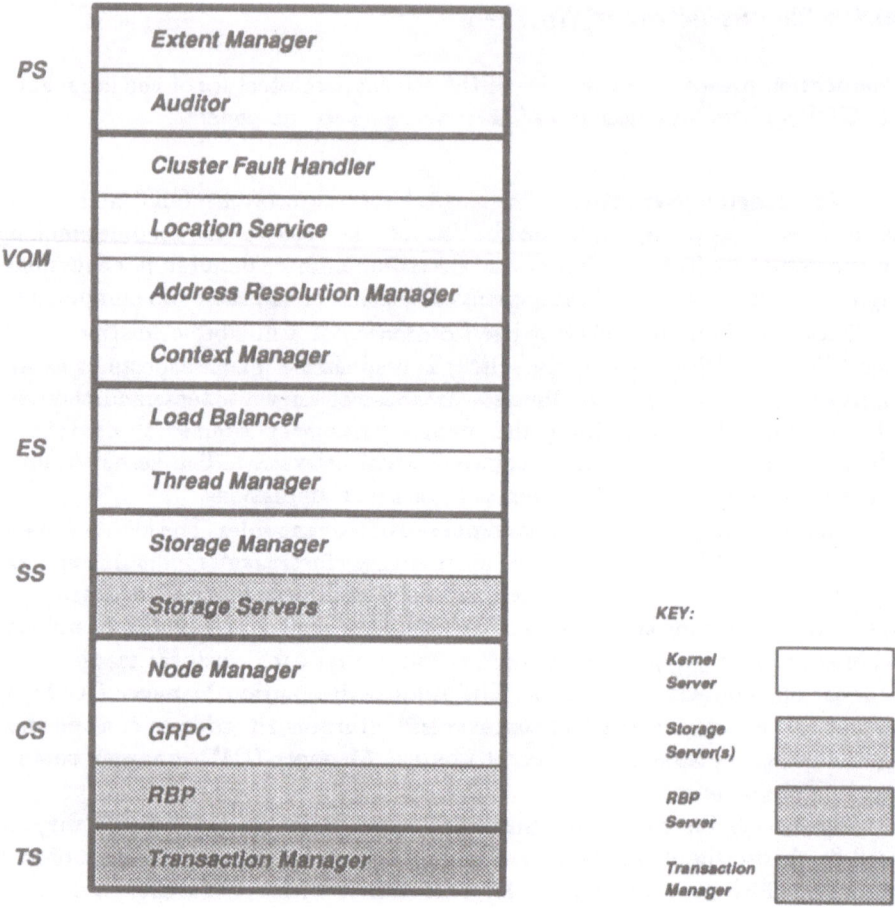

Fig. 10.1. The components of the Amadeus kernel.

of the invocation request (possibly via the kernel CFH) to the target cluster. The GRT CM is responsible for the initialisation and termination of the context.

The GRT ES includes the Activity Manager (AM) which implements jobs and activities and the operations to control these. The AM also implements the cross-context invocation service and some low-level synchronisation facilities. The ES also includes the GRT LB, which may be used to choose the node at which the clusters used by an activity are to be mapped, and the GRT Thread Manager.

The GRT SS provides the interface between the GRT and the storage servers.

The GRT TS is responsible for the synchronisation of accesses to, and recovery of, atomic objects. In particular, the TS encapsulates the RelaX transaction management libraries.

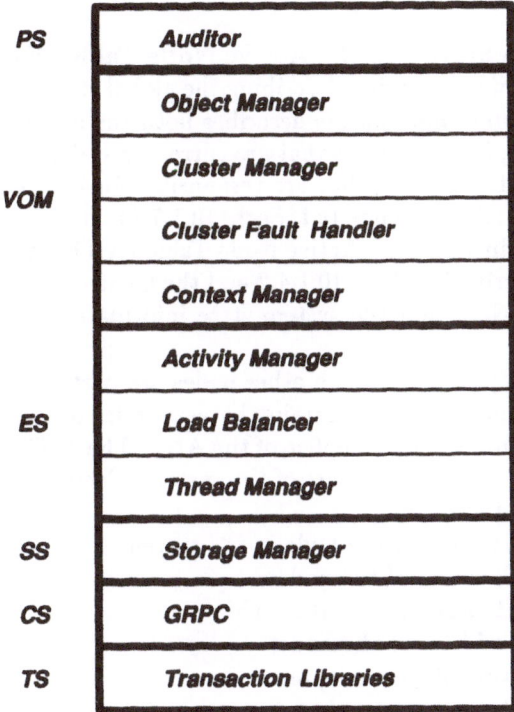

PS	Auditor
	Object Manager
	Cluster Manager
VOM	Cluster Fault Handler
	Context Manager
	Activity Manager
ES	Load Balancer
	Thread Manager
SS	Storage Manager
CS	GRPC
TS	Transaction Libraries

Fig. 10.2. The components of the Amadeus GRT.

Finally, the GRT CS supports secure local and remote communication.

10.1.3 Node Management

An Amadeus *system* consists of a dynamically varying collection of nodes each potentially having a different architecture and running a different version of UNIX. Each node involved in an Amadeus system must run the kernel server. A node *joins* the system when the kernel server is first started on that node. A node *leaves* the system when its kernel server terminates. In general, a node may join or leave the system at any time.

Each node in an Amadeus system is identified by its *node name* which must be unique within that single system. Normally names are assigned statically to nodes by the local (Amadeus) system administrator and the name of the node passed as a command line argument to the kernel when it is started.

Each node also has a network address which is the address used by remote nodes to communicate with the kernel on that node. The form of the network address is known only within the CS and depends on the protocol stack in use in the system.

10.1.3.1 System State and the Active Node Table.

Each node maintains a certain amount of information describing the global state of the Amadeus system. The *system state information* describes both the nodes that are currently part of the system; the containers that are currently available in the system (c.f. Sect. 10.1.4.2) and the nodes that are responsible for controlling the mapping of clusters from each container (c.f. Sect. 10.1.7.1). In particular, the system state information includes the Active Node Table (ANT), described below; the Mount Table, described in Sect. 10.1.4.2 and the Control Node Table, described in Sect. 10.1.7.2. Note that the system state information is fully replicated at each node.

In order to keep track of which other nodes are part of the system and also to maintain information about certain characteristics of those nodes the NMs on each node maintains a local replica of the ANT. The ANT contains one entry for each node that is currently part of the system. Each ANT entry contains:

- the name of the node;
- the current ranking of the node in the system;
- the network address of the node;
- the UNIX (string) name of the node;
- the internet address of the node;
- the architecture of the node, and
- the current load on the node.

The ANT is maintained as a simple one dimensional array indexed by node name.

10.1.3.2 Node Manager Operation.

The kernel NM design relies on the use of totally ordered atomic broadcast and node failure notification mechanisms provided by the RBP. Nodes are ranked according to the order in which they were seen to join the system.

When a kernel is started, its NM takes control to initialise each of the components of the kernel using a configuration file for the node. In particular, this initialisation may include the mounting of some containers at the node (c.f. Sect. 10.1.4.2).

The NM must then advertise the presence of the node and its initial state to the other nodes in the system. In addition, the NM must obtain an up-to-date copy of the system state information.

The joining NM broadcasts a message to advertise its presence to the other nodes, allowing them to update their copies of the system state information appropriately.

The NM on the highest ranked node (if any) is responsible for providing the up-to-date system state to the joining node by broadcasting a reply containing its updated ANT, Mount Table and Control Node Table. Should a failure of the highest ranked node occur after the original message is received but before the reply is sent, the next highest ranked node (if any) takes responsibility for transferring the system state to the joining node.

When a node is about to leave the system the NM broadcasts a message to the other nodes allowing them to update their copy of the system state information including adjusting the rankings of each node.

In addition each node periodically broadcasts a message containing its current values of all the information, such as the load on that node, that is subject to periodic update.

10.1.3.3 Node Management Interface. The NM provides an interface to the other kernel components which allows them to obtain a list of the nodes which are currently active and to obtain information about each active node such as the type of the node and the current load on the node. It is also possible to query whether or not a particular node is currently active. A subset of this interface is also available to applications via the GRT.

10.1.4 The Storage Sub-system

The SS provides facilities for the storage and retrieval of clusters, and for the allocation of system-wide unique identifiers for clusters and objects.

The fundamental requirement that had to be satisfied in the design of the SS was to allow different implementations of containers, and hence cluster storage, to coexist in a single Amadeus system. Implementations making use of the underlying file system, or bypassing the file system and using raw disk, or based on an alternative store such as an existing DBMS are envisaged. In particular, a container can be implemented as:

- a UNIX directory. Each cluster is stored as a file in that directory.
- a raw disk partition. In this case the SS can determine where on disk each cluster is stored. Moreover each cluster can be stored contiguously on disk.
- a large file. As above, except that the container is a single, large file instead of a disk partition; the underlying file system determines the physical location of the file on disk.
- a front end to a storage system such as a DBMS.

The current SS implementation uses the underlying UNIX file system to implement containers and clusters. Another implementation, based on raw disk and supporting replication, which will allow physical cluster and object identifiers[2] to be supported is currently being implemented. This implementation is targeted at applications which, for efficiency, require direct access to objects on disk.

10.1.4.1 Architecture. The SS at any node consists of two major components – the *Storage Manager* (SM) and a collection of *storage servers*. The SM

---

[2]Identifiers which give a hint as to the storage location of the cluster or object on disk.

provides the interface between the SS and its clients. Storage servers implement containers.

The main function of the SM is to hide the implementation of containers, by directing requests to the appropriate, possibly remote, storage server.

Storage servers will be provided for each type (i.e. implementation) of container supported by the SS. At a given node a single storage server handles all requests for local containers of one type.

The SM has components in both the Amadeus kernel and in each GRT at a given node. The functionality of the kernel SM is a superset of that of the GRT SM since the kernel is responsible for initialising the local SS and maintaining data structures such as the node's mount tables (c.f. Fig. 10.3)[3].

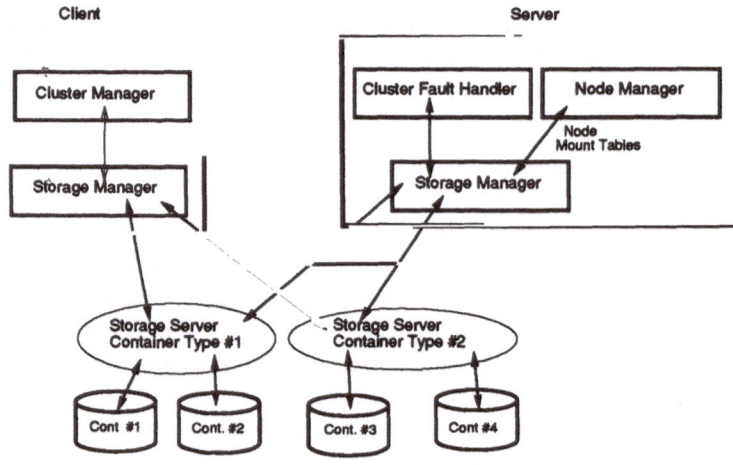

Fig. 10.3. The SS architecture.

A given storage server is local to a single node. However, requests to a storage server may come from both local and remote SMs. It is assumed that all requests received by a storage server can be authenticated.

Each storage server is implemented by a UNIX process. Communication between a SM and a storage server uses the Amadeus CS (c.f. Sect. 10.1.15). Each storage server has a unique network address which is used by both the local SM and all remote SMs to communicate with that server. A storage server is started by the local Amadeus server SM when the first container of the corresponding type is mounted at the node. Each supported container type is identified by a code. The mapping from this code to the text image to use for the corresponding storage server is maintained in a system configuration file.

The Generic Storage Server. The primary function of a storage server is to provide the SM with a suitably high level abstraction of a container. This enables

---

[3]The main clients of the SS are the CFH and NM in the kernel and the CIM in the GRT.

complex container implementations to be used without requiring that the SM be modified whenever a new container implementation is to be added. Each storage server must provide the following services:

- Cluster retrieval and storage;
- Cluster size query;
- Allocation of new cluster and object identifiers;
- Creation of new containers of the appropriate type;
- Mounting and unmounting of containers.

Individual storage servers maintain their own internal state including a list of the containers which they currently have mounted and the information needed to access the disk storage corresponding to each such container.

The Default Storage Server. Although the architecture of the SS allows specialised storage servers to be used, it is expected that a simple implementation based on direct use of the underlying (distributed) UNIX file system is sufficient for the needs of most applications. Moreover, given that the underlying file system provides an authorisation mechanism, it is possible to integrate such a storage server directly into the kernel and the GRT thereby avoiding the overhead of using the CS for communication between the SM and the storage server. The default storage server, which is always present on every node, is implemented in this way.

This implementation can be viewed abstractly as having the storage server existing within the SM (c.f. Fig. 10.4). In practice, this means that if a container implemented using the file system – a *UFS container* – is stored at the node on which the GRT is running, the GRT can access that container directly by making a system call (c.f. Fig. 10.6). If the container is not stored at the node, then the GRT must communicate directly with the remote storage server for the container i.e. the kernel at the node where the container is located (c.f. Fig. 10.7).

10.1.4.2 The Storage Manager and Container Management. The following sections describe the management of containers by the SM.

Supporting Multiple Storage Nodes for a Container. Normally, a container is stored at one node. A replicated container must, of course, be stored at several nodes. Moreover, a container that is stored using a distributed file system, such as AFS or NFS, may appear to be stored at several nodes i.e. at those nodes that have imported the volume storing the container[4]. In order to cater for each of these cases Amadeus admits the possibility that a container may be mounted at several nodes – its *storage nodes* – simultaneously. Such a container is managed by a different storage server at each node at which it is mounted.

---

[4]It may actually be stored at a single node or on several nodes – if the distributed file system supports volume replication.

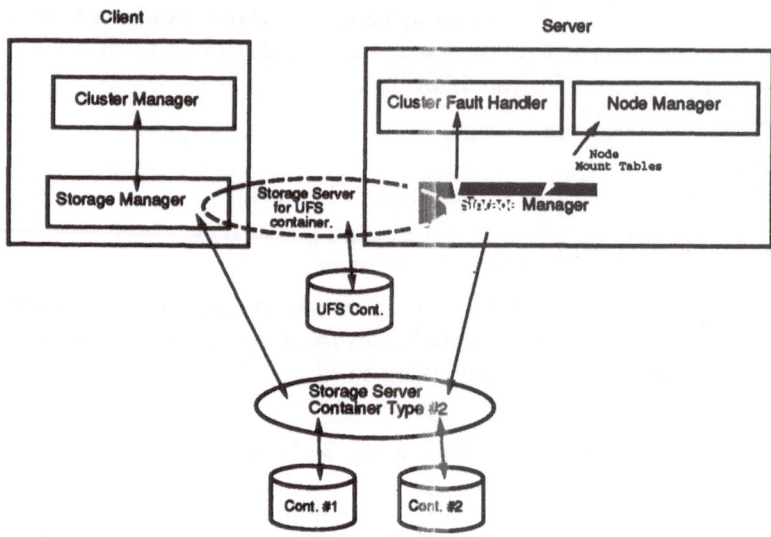

Fig. 10.4. The default storage server.

In the case of a replicated container, each storage server maintains an independent copy of the container. It is the responsibility of each storage server to ensure that its copy of the container is consistent with those of other storage servers.

In the case of a container stored in a distributed file system, only one copy of the container exists, but the underlying file system gives the impression that a copy of the container exists at every node where the file system volume is mounted. Each storage server can treat the container as being stored locally.

Whether or not a particular container can be mounted at several nodes depends on its type. If a given container is of an appropriate type the SM will allow that container to be mounted by more than one node at a time. The system configuration file indicates which container types support multiple mounting.

Data Structures. Whenever the SM receives a request for some container it must determine which storage server is to handle that request. The storage server may be either local, if the node is a storage node for the container, or remote. In any case, the SM at each node must maintain a mapping from a container name to the address(es) of the storage server(s) responsible for that container.

The kernel SM at each node maintains a table – the Local Mount Table (LMT) – which stores, for each container that is currently mounted at the node, the code identifying the type of container and the address of the local storage server which handles requests for that container (c.f. Fig. 10.5).

If the container is implemented by the default storage server the address is empty. In this case the LMT is also used to store the local path-name of the

```
typedef struct {
  ContainerName      lc;            /* container identifier */
  ContainerType      lctype;        /* type of container */
  ContextAddressType server;        /* address of server */
  char               directory[SS_UFS_MaxPath];
} LMTEntry;

typedef struct {
  ContainerName      lc;            /* container identifier */
  ContainerType      lctype;        /* type of container */
  NodeNameType       node;          /* node at which lc is mounted */
  ContextAddressType server;        /* address of server */
} MTEntry;
```

Fig. 10.5. Mount Table Data Structures.

directory actually being used to store the container – this information is used by the default storage server in the local kernel and GRT.

The LMT is shared by the SM components in the kernel and GRT at the node. The LMT is mapped into a shared memory segment created by the kernel SM and attached by each GRT's SM. Only the kernel SM is capable of updating the LMT; all other copies are read-only.

The SM at each node also maintains another table – the Mount Table (MT) – which is similar to the LMT, except that it contains an entry for every container mounted in the system. The MT gives the name(s) of the node(s) at which each container is mounted and the address(es) of the corresponding storage server(s). As in the case of the LMT, the MT is available to be read by the local GRT. The MT is part of the system state information (c.f. Sect. 10.1.3.1) and, as such, is replicated at each node.

Containers are usually mounted at a node at boot time and unmounted when the node leaves the system. Dynamic mounting and unmounting of containers is also supported. It is also possible for a new container to be created (and hence mounted) dynamically. In each case the LMT and MT must be updated and the change to the MT broadcast (atomically) to the other nodes in the system.

SM Initialisation. During node initialisation, the kernel SM is responsible for determining which containers are to be mounted locally and for starting the necessary storage server processes.

Once started, a storage server blocks until it receives a request to mount a container. A mount request gives the storage server all the information it requires to initialise the specified container.

The SM obtains the list of containers to mount from its local mount file and sends requests to the appropriate storage servers to mount each container.

The mount file gives the name and type of each container to be mounted as well as container-type specific information which is passed to the storage server to locate the disk storage for the container.

On system shutdown the SM sends requests to unmount each mounted container to each storage server before requesting the server to shut itself down.

Mounting and Unmounting Containers. Containers are normally mounted on node startup, and are unmounted when the node shuts down. Containers mounted at a given node during startup are described in that node's mount file. Applications may also mount and unmount containers which are not described in the mount file. This will normally apply to movable containers such as floppy or optical disks.

There are four events which involve mounting or unmounting containers, as follows:

1. Node startup.
   All containers described in the node's mount file are mounted locally.
2. Node shutdown.
   All locally mounted containers are unmounted.
3. Container Mount.
   The specified container is mounted locally.
4. Container Unmount.
   The specified container is unmounted.

10.1.4.3 Naming. Each container is known by a system-wide unique name. The SS is also responsible for the allocation of system-wide unique identifiers which are used to name clusters and objects.

An Amadeus unique identifier – UId – is guaranteed to be unique within a single Amadeus system. UIds are not reused. UIds are created by concatenating the name of a container with a generation number which is unique within that container. Note however that the exact structure of a UId is opaque to the other components of Amadeus, so the interface to the SS provides operations to compare UIds and to return the container name and generation number from a given UId.

The next available generation number for each container is stored in the corresponding container.

10.1.4.4 The (Distributed) UNIX File System Implementation. In the current version of Amadeus each container is implemented as a directory, with each cluster that is stored in the container being implemented as a file in that directory. For each container the path-name of the corresponding directory is given in the LMT.

Given that the current implementation assumes an underlying distributed file system it is typical for each node participating in the Amadeus system to mount each container. In this case each container is mounted at every node so that all reads and writes are performed locally.

The UId for a cluster is mapped directly to the path-name for the file in which the cluster is stored. For example, a cluster with a UId having container name equal to 1 and generation number equal to 123 is stored in the file /container_1_path/123.

The next available generation number for each container is stored in a file in the corresponding container directory; this file is only accessible to root.

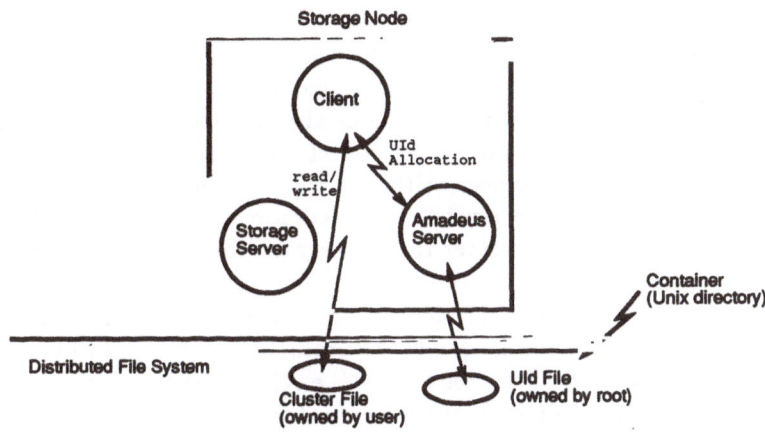

Fig. 10.6. UNIX FS implementation: faulting node is a storage node.

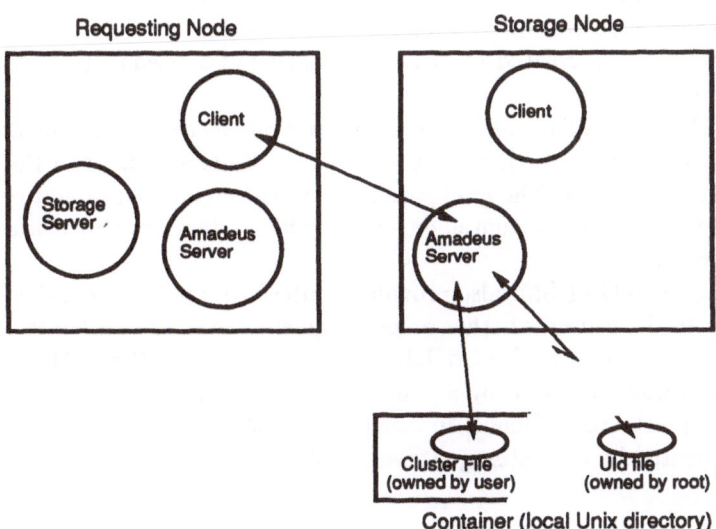

Fig. 10.7. UNIX FS implementation: faulting node is not a storage node.

Security. Since clusters are stored in a UNIX file system they are protected only by the usual UNIX mechanism of access control lists. Each cluster may be read/written by the client which is mapping/unmapping it. Hence each cluster should be both readable and writable by the user who owns the cluster (i.e. the user who owns the extent to which the cluster belongs) to allow mapping and unmapping of the cluster from a client running on behalf of that extent. The GRT storage server creates cluster files with read/write access for the cluster's owner (and, implicitly, the super-user). Even if the owner subsequently changes the protection assigned to the file, only the confidentiality and integrity of that user's own data can be effected if other users, who under Amadeus have no rights to the cluster, are allowed to access or alter the cluster outside of Amadeus. Note however that it is impossible to effect the confidentiality and integrity of data belonging to another user. Although resulting in weaker security, since the file containing the cluster must then be accessible outside of Amadeus, this approach allows the storage server to be integrated into the SM in the kernel and GRT.

Those files storing control information, for example those which are used in the allocation of unique identifiers, must be protected against malicious damage. Hence these files are only accessible to root (i.e., the kernel) on each node. Thus only the storage server running in the kernel is able to allocate unique identifiers.

10.1.4.5 Storage Sub-system Interface. The main interface to the GRT SM is that which is used by the ClM (c.f. Sect. 10.1.11) to read the named cluster into the current context at the specified address. The GRT SM also provides a corresponding routine to write a cluster that is being unmapped. Note that there is no primitive to create a new cluster. As described in Sect. 10.1.11.2, clusters are created in virtual memory and subsequently written to secondary storage.

The GRT SM interface also includes primitives to create, mount and unmount containers. However these routines are essentially wrappers for the corresponding kernel routines. The final parameter to the create and mount routines depends on the type of the container – for the file system implementation it is a path-name.

The kernel and GRT SMs also provide an interface which allows other kernel components to determine whether or not a given container is mounted and if so where. This interface is also available to applications via the GRT.

UIds are always allocated by a storage server. Moreover, allocation of UIds will be a frequent event. Hence, in order to reduce communication overhead, UIds are allocated by each storage server in blocks.

10.1.5 User and Extent Management

The PS at each node is responsible for all aspects of extent management including the creation of new extents and the activation of existing extents. The PS runs in protected mode although it offers an interface to applications via the GRT to, for example, create a new extent.

10.1.5.1 Amadeus Users.
Every registered user on any node that is taking part in an Amadeus system is a legitimate Amadeus user i.e. there is no need for a (UNIX) user to be registered with Amadeus before running an Amadeus application. Note, however, that each user must own an extent before running their first application.

10.1.5.2 Extent Naming.
Each user can have many extents. Each extent is known to its owner by an index number which is allocated by the PS when the extent is created. Extent index numbers are assigned chronologically to extents on a per-user basis.

Within the system each extent is known by a system wide unique name which is formed from the concatenation of the owner's UNIX user identifier and the index number of the extent with respect to its owner.

10.1.5.3 The Extent and Cluster Registers.
An Amadeus system must maintain information about each extent required for extent activation. At run time this information must be accessible to the PSs on each participating node but must otherwise be protected. In the current implementation, the information in the Extent Register is stored as a collection of files in a well-known directory in the underlying distributed file system with one file for each user – the name of the file being the user identifier.

For each extent the following information is maintained:

- the extent name (i.e. the identifier of the extent's owner and the index number of the extent with respect to its owner);
- a list of possible activation nodes for the extent (optional);
- the text image to be used for contexts of the extent, and
- the number of clusters that belong to the extent.

For cluster fault handling the PS also needs to be able to determine, given the name of a cluster, the name of the extent to which that cluster currently belongs. This information in the Cluster Register is also maintained as a collection of files in the underlying distributed file system with a single file holding the mapping information for all the clusters belonging to one container.

10.1.5.4 Extent Creation.
Currently, a request to create an extent can come from only one of two possible sources:

- the mkextent utility;
- an activity running in an existing extent.

Extent creation is handled entirely within the PS at each node since it requires access to the Extent Register. The operation to create an extent takes as parameters the identity of the user on whose behalf the extent is being created, a list of activation nodes and the text image to use for the extent. The name of the new extent is returned.

The only effect of creating a new extent is to make an entry in the Extent Register – initially a new extent contains no clusters and is not active anywhere.

mkextent is an interactive utility provided primarily to allow a new 'Amadeus user' to create his first extent. The **mkextent** utility can only be run at a node where the kernel is already running.

An extent created from an existing extent is owned by the owner of the creating extent. The remaining parameters are obtained from the parameters to the operation to create an extent.

10.1.5.5 Extent Activation. An extent can have contexts at one or more nodes in the system.

A new context can be (but is not necessarily) created for an extent in one of two circumstances:

- as a result of a fault on a cluster belonging to the extent;
- when a user starts an application in the extent.

Invocation Requests. When the kernel CFH (c.f. Sect. 10.1.8) discovers that the target of an invocation request is not mapped, it calls the PS which is responsible for choosing a node at which the cluster can be mapped depending on the activation nodes (if any) specified for the cluster's extent.

The PS must determine the extent for the cluster and obtain the activation nodes for that extent. The PS simply chooses a node at which to map the cluster either from the list of activation nodes for the extent or by load balancing.

Given the node name returned by the PS the kernel CFH will forward the request to that node. When such a forwarded invocation request arrives at a node the local kernel CFH calls the local PS to determine the local context in which the cluster should be mapped and in which the request should be handled if any. The PS checks if a local context for the extent already exists. If not, a new context is created for the extent before the request is forwarded to the appropriate context.

Cluster Mapping Requests. In this case the kernel CFH calls the PS to determine if the target cluster can be mapped into the required context. This is possible only if the context represents the extent to which the cluster belongs.

Starting an Application. An application can be run from the shell by using the interactive utility **launch** which allows a user to specify both an application to run and the extent in which the application is to be started[5]. **launch** also collects any command line parameters to be passed to the application.

---

[5]Recall that currently the only application that can be run in an extent is that corresponding to the text image for the chosen extent.

On receiving a request to start a new application, PS first verifies the requester's right to run the specified application in the specified extent[6]. If valid the request is treated in much the same way as an invocation request. The local PS is used to choose the node at which to start the application. The request is forwarded to the PS at that node which determines the context in which the request should be handled. If an appropriate context already exists then the request is simply forwarded to that context. If no appropriate context already exists, one will be created.

10.1.5.6 The Protection Sub-system Interface. As well as creating a new extent, a user can also delete one of his own existing extents. However destruction of an extent is only permitted if there are no clusters in the extent.

A newly created cluster (c.f. Sect. 10.1.11.2) initially belongs to the extent in which it was created. However, clusters can also be moved between extents belonging to the same owner.

10.1.6 Context Management

An Amadeus system can be viewed as a collection of contexts dispersed throughout a distributed system, each containing a varying collection of clusters. Contexts can be created and deleted on demand as applications are started and invocations are made between contexts on the same or different nodes.

The main design goal was to isolate the higher levels of Amadeus from how contexts were implemented and, in particular, how contexts are addressed and communication between contexts performed.

10.1.6.1 Basics. Contexts are created dynamically by each node as applications are started and cluster faults handled (c.f. Sect. 10.1.5.5).

Once created each context should persist at least until there are no active invocations in the context i.e. there are no activities present in the context. A context may persist longer if it is expected that further invocation requests may arrive in the 'near' future. It is also possible that a context may fail before all the activities that were present have completed, for example, as a result of a node failure.

Each context has a system wide unique name which is formed from the concatenation of the extent and node names. For communication between contexts to proceed each context must have a unique address. The format of the address depends on the inter-context communication mechanism in use and need only be known to the lowest levels of the CS (c.f. Sect. 10.1.15).

The remainder of this section discusses context creation, initialisation, and deletion in detail.

---

[6]Currently only the owner of an extent can start an application in that extent.

10.1.6.2 Context Creation. Contexts are normally created when a new application is started or as a result of a cluster fault. A failed context may also be restarted by the TS if the context contained the youngest committed version of any atomic object at the time of its failure and the object had not been written to secondary storage (c.f. Sect. 10.1.14).

The kernel CM provides a single primitive which can be use both to create a new context and to restart a failed context. Creating a new context basically involves **forking** a new UNIX process and having the new process **exec** the required code having first set the real and effective user identifiers of the new process to be those of the owner of the corresponding extent.

The new context is passed an indication of the circumstances in which it is being created to allow it to initialise itself correctly. In particular, if a new application is being started the mainline is run. If the context is restarting, then the TS takes control to recover the state of the context from its log as described in Sect. 10.1.14. Otherwise, the new context idles until an invocation request is received.

When a new context is created it must register itself with the kernel so that the kernel can begin forwarding requests to it. Note that a failure between the time a context is created by the kernel and the time that the context registers itself must be detected by the CM and propagated to the requester. Thus the CM, having created a new context, waits for that context to register itself (indicating successful initialisation) or for the new UNIX process to die (indicating unsuccessful initialisation). Once the context is registered, and depending on the flag passed as an argument to the process, the mainline may be executed as the initial invocation of a new job.

10.1.6.3 Context Deletion. A context cannot be deleted while there are ongoing invocations present in the context. In order to keep track of when it is safe to delete a context, the GRT CM maintains a reference count for the context. When a context is created, its reference count is initialised to 0. Whenever a thread is created within the context to carry out an invocation either as the result of a job or activity creation, or the arrival of a cross-context invocation in the context, the reference count is incremented. The reference count is decremented as threads terminate. When the reference count reaches zero again, the context is not immediately deleted but rather a timer is set to delay context deletion for some period. If a new invocation request arrives in the context before the timer expires, the timer is cancelled and the request proceeds as normal having incremented the reference count.

When it has been decided to delete a context it is necessary that all mapped clusters be unmapped. Since the kernel cannot unilaterally unmap a cluster for the reasons explained in Sect. 10.1.10.6, it first up-calls the OM to inform it that the context has been terminated. The OM can then tidy up using the normal call to have each cluster unmapped by the CM in turn.

Finally, the kernel CM must be informed that the context is terminating.

10.1.7 Cluster Location

Central to the operation of Amadeus is that only a single image of any cluster may be mapped at any time i.e. a cluster is either mapped in exactly one context or is stored in the SS. The LS is responsible for keeping track of the current location of each mapped cluster. Moreover, the responsibility for ensuring that only a single image of each cluster is mapped rests with the LS. The design of the LS must cater for the possibility that, due to a node crash, a mapped cluster may be *lost* from virtual memory or if not lost[7], may be unavailable while the node at which it was mapped is down.

10.1.7.1 Control Nodes. Since it would be too expensive for each node to keep exact information about the location of every mapped cluster, information about the locations of mapped clusters is partitioned. A single node is assigned the responsibility of maintaining information about the current location of all the clusters from a given container. That node is known as the *control node* for the container. A given node may be the control node for zero, one or more containers. Although not strictly necessary, the control node for a container is always chosen from among the storage nodes for the container. In addition, every node keeps exact information about those clusters which are mapped locally.

The LS at a cluster's control node acts as the central authority in determining whether or not a cluster is mapped, thereby ensuring that a cluster can only be mapped once in virtual memory.

The control node for a cluster represents a single point of failure. If the control node for some container is down then it may not be possible to access clusters from the container even if they are mapped at another node [8]. It will certainly not be possible to map or unmap a cluster from the containers effected, even if it is stored at other nodes. Moreover, the information maintained by the LS must be resilient to node failures.

10.1.7.2 Data Structures. The LS at each node maintains a table – the Control Node Table (CNT) – which gives the name of the control node for each container that is currently mounted. The CNT is part of the system state information (c.f. Sect. 10.1.3.1) and as such is fully replicated at each node.

Each control node maintains a table – the Mapped Cluster Table (MCT) – with one entry for each 'local' cluster that is mapped into virtual memory, giving the name of the node into which the cluster is mapped. The information, maintained in the MCT must survive node failures. Hence, the MCT is backed up on secondary storage and all changes to the MCT forced to disk. Note that, after any node failure, the MCT may not be correct since it may still contain entries for clusters that have been lost from virtual memory as a result of the failure. In this case, the consistency of the MCT is re-established, not when the failed node recovers, but lazily as attempts to access lost clusters are made.

---

[7]For example, because it will be recovered by the TS.
[8]Unless the requester has a valid MCC entry for the cluster.

Finally, each node maintains a table – the Kernel Cluster Table (KCT) – giving, for each cluster that is mapped on the node, the name of the (local) context into which the cluster is mapped. The KCT is lost on a node crash but rebuilt when the node recovers. On a context failure, the KCT is updated when the context is restored. The KCT is therefore always up to date. It is used both to speed the location of a cluster that is mapped locally and to validate the result of an MCT lookup which may be out of date.

10.1.7.3 Locating a Cluster. The kernel CFH at the requesting node calls its local LS whenever a request for an absent cluster is received which may be either an invocation request or a request to map the cluster locally. The type of request is opaque to the LS whose role is to forward the request to the kernel CFH at the node where the target cluster is mapped, if any, or else, to the kernel CFH at the control node for the cluster.

When a cluster is required, the LS at the requesting node attempts to locate the cluster using only local information. If it cannot determine the location of the cluster, then the request is forwarded to the control node for the cluster (as given in the local copy of the CNT) which will have the necessary information to locate the cluster. The operation of the LS is summarised in Fig. 10.8 and Fig. 10.9 for the cases where the target cluster is not already mapped and is already mapped respectively.

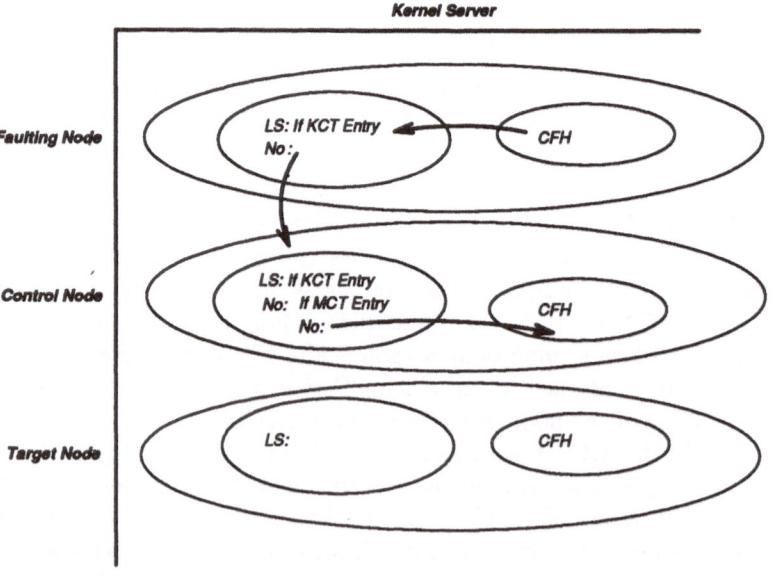

Fig. 10.8. Operation of the LS when cluster is not mapped.

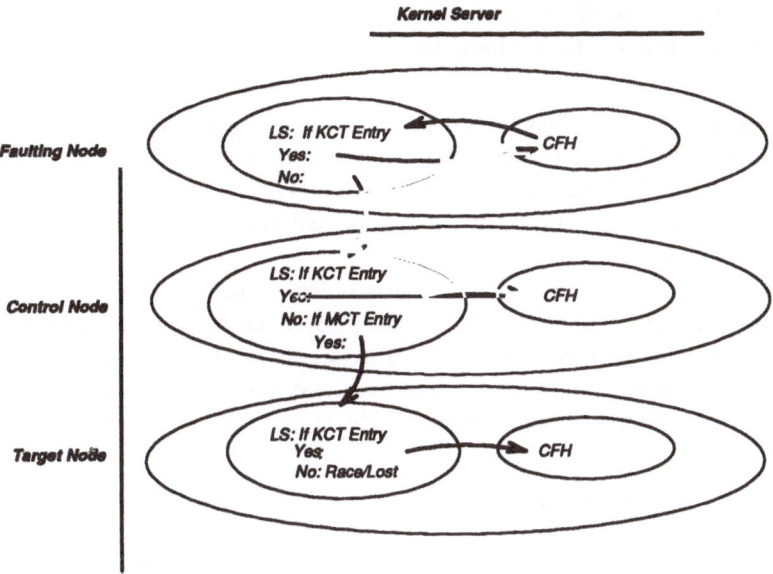

Fig. 10.9. Operation of the LS when cluster is mapped.

The Faulting Node. The LS first searches the KCT to determine if the cluster is mapped into a local context. If so the name of the context is returned immediately to the CFH.

If the cluster is not mapped locally but the node is the control node for the container, the local MCT is searched.

If an MCT entry for the cluster exists then the request is forwarded to the LS at the specified node.

If no MCT entry exists then the cluster is not mapped and the LS returns an appropriate indication to the local CFH.

Alternatively, if the node is not the control node for the required cluster, then the request is forwarded to the LS at the control node.

If a request for a cluster is forwarded to a node (either the control node for the cluster or the node where the cluster is thought to be mapped) which is down, then the request will eventually timeout and an exception be raised in the calling activity.

The Control Node. If a forwarded request is received by the control node for a cluster, the sequence of events is similar to those that take place when the requesting node is also the control node.

The LS first searches the KCT to determine if the cluster is mapped into a local context. If so the local CFH is passed the request together with the name of the context.

If the cluster is not mapped locally the local MCT is searched. If an MCT entry for the cluster exists then the request is forwarded to the LS at the specified node. If no MCT entry exists then the cluster is not mapped and the LS passes the request to the local CFH.

The Mapping Node. When a request for a cluster is received from the control node for the cluster, by the LS at the node thought to be mapping the cluster, the KCT is searched for an entry for the cluster.

If an entry exists, the local CFH is passed the request together with the name of the context.

If no entry exists, then either, due to race conditions, the KCT entry for the cluster has not yet been made or the cluster has been unmapped since the request was forwarded from the control node, or, the cluster has been lost as a result of a previous node failure. In either case the request is returned to the control node which will then determine the status of the cluster.

10.1.8 Cluster Fault Handling

A cluster fault occurs when an attempt to access a cluster that is not mapped into the current context is made. Cluster fault detection is the responsibility of the OM when called to handle an object fault detected by the language-specific run-time.

10.1.8.1 The GRT Cluster Fault Handler. On detecting a cluster fault the OM calls the GRT CFH. The OM may request that an attempted invocation be carried out at some node. The OM passes a description of the attempted invocation to the CFH in a standard form known as a tblock. The tblock header is interpreted by the CFH to obtain the name of the target cluster and other necessary information. The remainder of the tblock is opaque to the CFH but will be passed to the OM in the context in which the cluster is eventually mapped.

Alternatively the OM may request that the cluster be mapped into the current context – assuming that this is allowed by security and that the cluster is not already in use elsewhere.

Data Structures. The GRT CFH maintains a cache – the Mapped Cluster Cache (MCC) – which contains entries for clusters which are not mapped into the context but which have been recently accessed from this context. The MCC entry for a cluster identifies the context in which the cluster is thought to be mapped.

Handling a Cluster Fault in the GRT. For an invocation request, the tblock received is first tagged with the user and extent names, the preferred node for the requesting activity and the address of the context. The CFH then looks up the target cluster in its MCC.

If no MCC entry is found then the request is forwarded to the local kernel CFH. The kernel CFH will locate the context into which the cluster is mapped if any, or else, choose the context into which the cluster should be mapped. If a context other than the requesting context is chosen then the request will be forwarded to the GRT CFH in that context. The invocation will be dispatched to the target object via the OM, the operation carried out and the results returned directly to the requesting context using the context address in the `tblock`. In addition, the identity of the context in which the invocation was carried out is returned with the results and used to update the caller's MCC. The operation of the kernel CFH is discussed in more detail below.

If a MCC entry is found, the request is forwarded directly to the GRT CFH in the specified context where it is passed up to the local OM (c.f. Fig. 10.10).

If the cache entry was valid, the request will be carried out in that context and the results returned to the GRT CFH in the requesting context using the address given in the `tblock`.

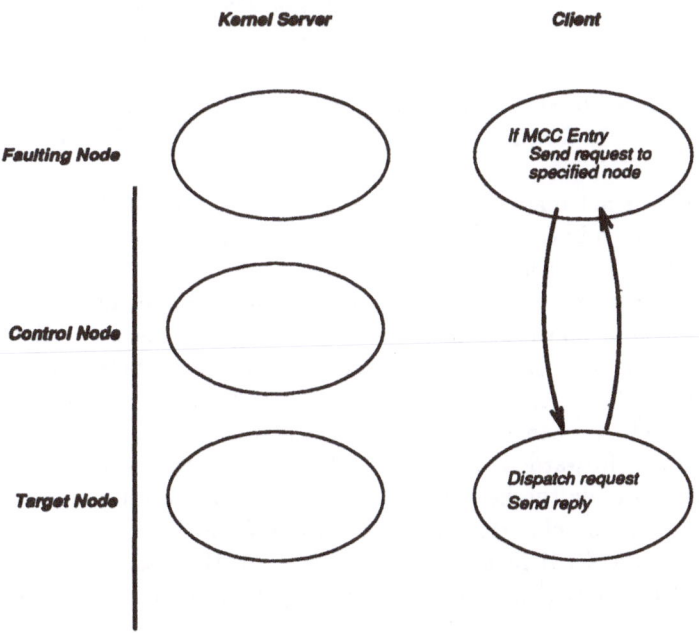

Fig. 10.10. A cluster fault handled within the GRT.

If the cache entry was invalid, the OM in the target context will refuse the request. The local GRT CFH will then treat the request in the same way as an invocation request originating in that context and handle it in the same manner except that the `tblock` will contain the address of the original requesting context so that when the invocation is eventually carried out the results can be sent directly to the caller. In addition, the caller will then be able to update his cache with the address of the context where the invocation was carried out.

When a request to map a cluster is received, it is passed immediately to the kernel CFH without looking for an entry for the cluster in the MCC.

The kernel CFH will locate the context into which the cluster is mapped if any, or else, arrange for the cluster to be mapped into the requesting context if permissible. If the cluster is already mapped the GRT CFH in the requesting context is informed. The operation of the kernel CFH is discussed in more detail below.

10.1.8.2 The Kernel Cluster Fault Handler. The kernel CFH is called by the GRT CFH in one of two circumstances.

- When the GRT CFH receives an invocation request for a cluster for which it has no MCC entry.
- When the GRT CFH receives a request to map a cluster.

Handling a Cluster Fault in the Kernel. In either case the kernel CFH uses the LS to forward the request either to the kernel CFH at the node where the cluster is mapped or, if the cluster is not mapped, to the kernel CFH at the control node for the cluster (c.f. Sect. 10.1.7).

If the cluster is already mapped (c.f. Fig. 10.11), the kernel CFH at the mapping node simply forwards the request to the GRT CFH in the context specified by the LS.

If the cluster is not mapped (c.f. Fig. 10.12), the kernel CFH at the control node must arrange to have the cluster mapped in some context and the request forwarded to the chosen context.

At the control node, the PS is called to determine the node at which to map the cluster depending on the extent to which it belongs and the activation policy for that extent. The local LS is informed where the cluster is being mapped and the request forwarded to that node. If the target node is not a storage node for the cluster, the cluster can be read at the control node and appended to the request before it is forwarded to the kernel CFH at the chosen node.

At the chosen node the kernel CFH calls the PS to determine the context into which to map the cluster. The local LS is informed and the request forwarded to the GRT CFH in the chosen context. In this case the GRT CFH, must call the ClM to map the cluster before dispatching the invocation via the OM.

Once the operation has been carried out, the results are returned directly to the requesting context using the context address from the request. Moreover, the identity of the context in which the request was carried out is also returned to allow an MCC entry for the cluster to be made in the requesting context.

In the case of a request to map a cluster if the cluster is already mapped, the kernel CFH at the mapping node simply returns an error indication to the GRT CFH in the requesting context.

If the cluster is not mapped, the kernel CFH at the control node queries the PS as to whether or not it is permissible to map the cluster into the specified context. If so, the LS is informed where the cluster is being mapped and the

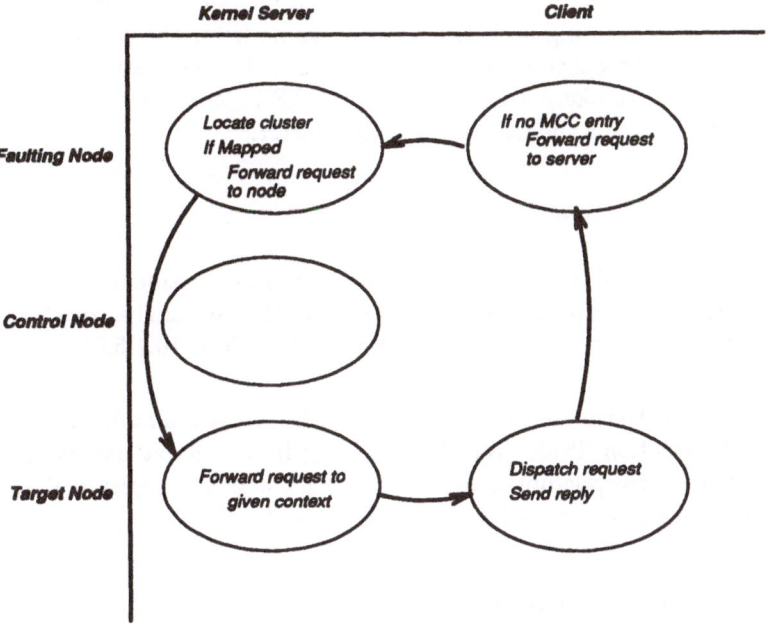

Fig. 10.11. Cluster fault handling when cluster is already mapped.

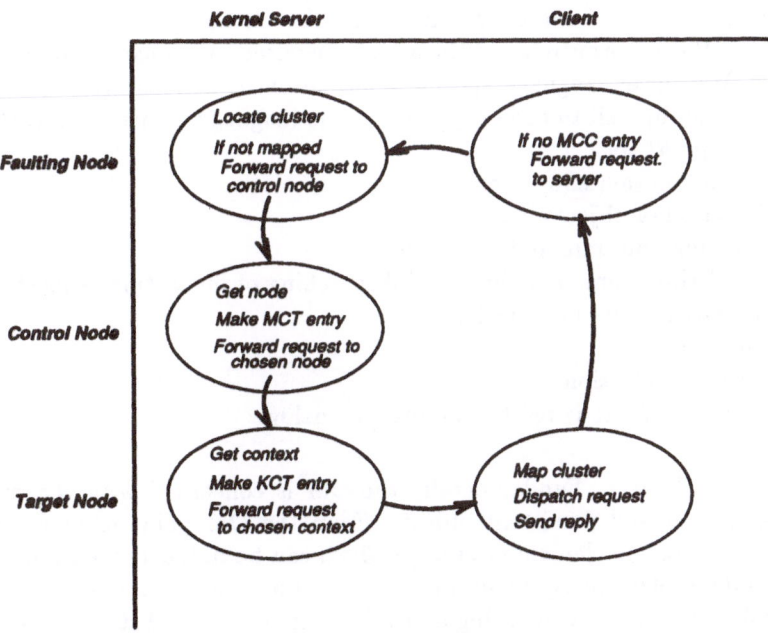

Fig. 10.12. Cluster fault handling when cluster is not mapped.

kernel CFH at the requesting node is informed to proceed with mapping. Optionally, if the requesting node is not a storage node for the cluster the cluster can be read at the control node and returned to the requesting node. At the requesting node, the kernel CFH informs the LS before returning to the GRT CFH which then calls the ClM to map the cluster.

10.1.9 Address Resolution

The main purpose of the ARM is to translate from the name of a local context to its address. To support this function the ARM maintains a register of local contexts which is also used to support the PS (c.f. Sect. 10.1.5.5).

10.1.9.1 Data Structures. At each node the ARM maintains a table – the Address Translation Table (ATT) – mapping from context names to the addresses of the corresponding contexts. The ATT acts as a register of local contexts and contains an entry for each local context.

10.1.10 The Object Manager

This section presents an overview of the functionality of the OM component of Amadeus. The OM provides support for the management of global and persistent objects building on the cluster abstraction supported by the ClM. Rather than putting much of the burden for doing this on the compiler (or programmer), the OM performs most of the actions required in a language independent manner. Whenever language specific information or actions are required, the OM makes an up-call to code supplied for the language. In particular, the OM provides support for:

- object creation and naming;
- detection of objects faults;
- mapping and unmapping of objects;
- marshalling, unmarshalling and dispatching of invocation requests;
- support for atomic objects;
- clustering;
- garbage collection.

Each of these aspects is briefly summarised below.

10.1.10.1 Objects. Fundamentally the OM is concerned with the management of global and persistent objects. From the OM point of view such an object is an opaque element of storage which can be uniquely identified and to which code implementing the interface to the object can be bound dynamically. The OM does not know anything a priori about the internal structure of a particular object nor about the semantics implemented by that object. Information concerning an object required by the OM in order to manage that object must be provided by the language level as described below.

A global or persistent language object – such as, for example, an individual C** or Eiffel** object – must be mapped in a way specific to its programming language, onto an OM object. The most natural mapping is a single OM object for each heap allocated language object. Other mappings are possible. For example, in C**, a language object may be embedded within another language object which is, in turn, mapped onto a single OM object. The term *object* is used as an abbreviation for an OM object, and programming language objects are always qualified as *language objects*.

New global or persistent objects are created by explicitly calling the OM. The OM allocates space for the object (including also space for a header for the object) and returns the address of the object to the language level. When initially created an object is *immature*. Immature objects exist and are known only within the context in which they were created. Objects may become known outside of their context of creation, either because a reference to the object has been passed out of the context, or because the object itself has migrated out of the context. If this happens, the object is *promoted* to being a *mature* object and is given a system wide unique identifier.

An object's header stores information used by the OM to manage the object and to link the object to the code implementing the language specific up-calls required by the OM (c.f. Sect. 10.1.10.7). In normal operation an object's header is transparent to the language level.

10.1.10.2 Object References and Object Fault Detection.

A *stub* is a type of object reference, holding enough information not only to locate the referenced object (i.e. its unique identifier) but also, in the case of a reference to a global object, to create a proxy (see later) for it.

On disk a persistent object is stored with its header being followed immediately by the object's data, possibly containing references to other objects, which is followed by a set of stubs for referenced objects.

The layout of an object's data is controlled by the language level and in general, the space allocated by the language for an object reference is too small to store a full stub. Hence when an object is on disk each reference within an object's data is stored as an offset either to the referenced object if stored in the same cluster, or, in the case of an inter-cluster reference, to a stub for the referenced object. This allows the layout of the object's data to be the same as it would be for a "normal" version of the object.

When two objects are co-located in the same context, the format of references between them is determined by the associated programming language. For example, two co-located C** language objects (in two different OM objects) can use direct memory pointers between them for the duration of their co-residence. The OM, with the aid of language specific support, is responsible for *folding* and *unfolding* stubs to and from language references as necessary. Each object carries representation information at run time which allows, amongst other services, the locations of the object references within it to be found.

When an object is fetched into a context, each of its references is examined in turn. If a reference refers to an object which is located in the same context, it may be replaced by a language reference to that object. Subsequent de-referencing of (and invocation via) that object reference can then use the native language mechanism: for example, two co-located C** objects will then use the usual C++ invocation mechanism, and under these conditions will not use the services of the OM. If, on the contrary, a reference refers to an object which is not (currently) located in the same context, some mechanism to trap attempts to access the absent object through that reference must be used. There are a number of possible approaches to trapping attempted accesses to absent objects. One solution is to require an explicit test for the presence of the referenced object, prior to use of the reference. For efficiency, such explicit testing is usually undesirable. An alternative technique, is to instead represent the referenced object in its absence by a *proxy*. Two different forms of proxy are supported by the OM.

A *G proxy* for an absent global object is essentially an OM object which contains no data but is the same size as the object it represents. The code bound to the proxy, which must be provided by the language level, must implement the same interface as the absent object. G proxies are dynamically created by the OM as required. Such proxies need never be stored, and are invisible to application programmers. A reference to a local proxy is unfolded in the same way as a reference to a co-located object. Further, an invocation via that reference will proceed as indicated above using the language mechanism. The proxy is responsible for reacting to the attempted invocation by calling the OM to handle the *object fault*. If the object represented by the proxy is subsequently mapped into the same context the OM will *overlay* the proxy by its principal – in this way any unfolded (language) references to the proxy or to its internal parts from elsewhere in the context remain valid.

A *P proxy* represents an absent cluster containing a (non-global) persistent object to which a reference has been unfolded. A P proxy is a read-protected area of virtual memory large enough to hold the absent cluster should it be mapped into the context. An unfolded reference to an absent persistent object points at the location in memory where the object will be loaded when the cluster is mapped. An attempt to access an absent persistent object will be caught by the OM as a protection violation resulting in an attempt to map the cluster. When the cluster is mapped the access can then be allowed to proceed as normal.

10.1.10.3 Dispatching and Marshalling.

Dispatching of invocations is performed in a language specific way. In the case of two co-located objects compiled by the same compiler, invocation need not use the services of the OM and so can proceed directly as explained above. For cross-context invocations, each (global) object must be prepared to receive an invocation request in a canonical (Amadeus defined) format and dispatch it in the appropriate language specific way to the appropriate operation or method. Likewise the outcome (if any), including abnormal or exceptional conditions (if any), must be returned and converted into a canonical format. In the case of C** this dispatching mechanism is implemented as an automatically generated additional member function of each class.

Marshalling of invocation frames is the responsibility of both G proxies on the initiating side and of the dispatching mechanism on the recipient side. The OM provides a suite of marshalling routines which allow the language level to marshal the parameters and results of an invocation into the standard message format expected by the kernel including encoding and decoding of individual marshalled values into the canonical format used for transmission between heterogeneous nodes.

10.1.10.4 Atomic Objects. The OM does not distinguish between atomic and non-atomic objects. However it does provide a number of routines which are used by the TS in managing atomic objects. In particular, the OM provides a routine to be up-called by the TS to create a recovery point for an atomic-object when necessary. Recovery points must be known to the OM as they must be visible to the garbage collector. In particular, if a recovery point contains the only reference to an object, that object must be preserved by the garbage collector in case the recovery point is restored as the actual state of an object after a transaction abort. The OM also provides the routines to restore an object from a recovery point in case of transaction abort, delete a recovery point in case of transaction commit and to prepare an object to be written to the log (which requires that an image of the object with all of its references folded be created) during the commit protocol execution.

10.1.10.5 Cluster Management. It is expected that individual objects are rarely required to be remotely usable, and that it is more likely that a number of objects be grouped together as a single unit of distribution.

In practice many applications do not choose to explicitly manage clusters, but rather employ the default mechanisms of the OM. By default, the OM creates new clusters as required, and places each new object into the most recently created cluster, along with other recently created objects.

As well as the default mechanism, the OM provides primitives to explicitly create a new cluster into which subsequent new objects will be placed; and to move an object into the same cluster as another object.

10.1.10.6 Garbage Collection and Cluster Unmapping. The OM currently includes a simple non-incremental mark and sweep garbage collector for immature objects. The roots for the collection are all mature objects within the context and the stacks of all activities executing within the context. Activities within the context are temporarily suspended during garbage collection.

A cluster is naturally unmapped from a context when that context is no longer required. Moreover it is clear that in general, a cluster cannot be unmapped prior to the deletion of the context, unless there are no unfolded references referencing any of the objects within that cluster. To determine if there are unfolded references to an object, the OM must scan the objects in the cluster, and the stacks of all activities executing in the context. This is expensive, and so is coupled with garbage collection of immature objects.

However the OM also provides a primitive to explicitly unmap a cluster from a context. In general, this primitive should be used with care, since for example there may be outstanding invocation frames on the stacks of various activities in the context which have temporary pointer values into the cluster. Nevertheless, an object may be migrated between two machines by explicitly unmapping its cluster at the sending node, and faulting the cluster at the recipient node.

10.1.10.7 Using the Object Manager. In interfacing a programming language to the OM, the OM imposes a number of constraints. First, the OM supplies routines to allocate and deallocate global and persistent objects, which should be used in place of the more usual calls to `malloc` and `free`. The OM also provides a number of routines to, for example, aid marshalling, and to test for the presence of an object or to fault on an absent object.

More importantly, the OM expects that the language-specific run-time supplies a small number of up-call routines which the OM can itself call. These in particular include an up-call to dispatch an incoming invocation request, in the canonical format, to an object; to locate object references within an object; and to prepare an object for use. The latter is used, for example within a C** environment to establish any internal virtual table pointers, or virtual base class pointers, within an object.

Further details concerning the interface between a language-specific run-time and the (OM component of the) GRT can be found in Chap. 11.

10.1.11 Cluster Management

Clusters are the basic unit of storage and mapping supported by Amadeus. Clusters are intended to be used by the OM to store groups of related objects. Other components of Amadeus are not aware of which objects are stored in which clusters.

10.1.11.1 Cluster Structure. Each cluster has a system wide unique name which is an Amadeus unique identifier. A cluster consists of an integral number of pages. Pages of a cluster are mapped contiguously into virtual memory and appear contiguous when stored on secondary storage.

Every cluster has a small fixed size header known to the GRT. The remainder of the cluster data can be used by the OM for storage of objects and any associated management information needed by the OM to locate objects within the cluster.

10.1.11.2 Cluster Creation. Clusters are normally created by the OM in virtual memory. In creating a cluster the OM first allocates a unique identifier for the new cluster by calling the SS. The OM is responsible for allocating space for the cluster in virtual memory and performing any OM specific initialisation. The OM then registers the new cluster with the ClM. The ClM in turn registers the cluster with the LS making the new cluster visible throughout the system.

A new cluster belongs to the extent in which it is created. However, the mapping for a new cluster is not entered into the PS's Cluster Register until the cluster is being unmapped.

10.1.11.3 Cluster Mapping and Unmapping. At any time a cluster can be mapped into at most one context anywhere in the system. Clusters are normally mapped as a result of a cluster fault although there is also a primitive available to explicitly request that a cluster be mapped into the current context (where allowable) (c.f. Sect. 10.1.5.5).

The ClM provides routines to map a cluster into the current context and unmap a cluster from the current context. When mapping a cluster the ClM first determines the size of the cluster by calling the SS and then up-calls to the OM to allocate space for the cluster. The responsibility for all local heap management is assigned to the OM in order to facilitate the implementation of a local garbage collection scheme in the OM. The ClM then reads the cluster from secondary storage into the allocated space and up-calls the OM again in order to allow OM specific initialisation of the cluster.

Clusters are normally expected to be unmapped only when the context into which they are mapped is being deleted (c.f. Sect. 10.1.6.3). However the interface provided by the CM to unmap a cluster is general and can potentially be called at any time. The ClM is called giving it a pointer to the cluster in virtual memory and the size of the cluster. The ClM writes the cluster to secondary storage before up-calling the OM to release the heap space allocated to the cluster.

10.1.12 Job and Activity Management

In this section the management of jobs and activities, including job and activity creation, diffusion, termination and control, is described.

Jobs and activities are intended to be provided as first class objects to application programmers[9]. Hence it is expected that a language level object representing each job or activity exists to which language code is bound so that operations on jobs and activities can be invoked using the usual language calling sequence. The AM then provides a more primitive interface for job and activity management which can be called by the language class code and which operates on the separate distributed representation of the job/activity.

Recall that a job is simply a collection of activities where each activity is essentially a thread of control which may span several contexts on the same and/or different nodes. Each activity in turn consists of one or more *processes*[10]

---

[9]This is a matter for the language designer in the final instance.

[10]These should not be confused with UNIX processes.

where each process is a thread of control executing within a single context. Control within an activity is passed from one context to another by means of cross-context invocations. When a cross-context invocation occurs, the activity's current process is blocked awaiting the results of the invocation and a new process created for the activity in the target context. Thus at any time only one process of an activity may be runnable. The activity's stack is thus distributed over all the processes of the activity with at least one segment of the stack in each context where the activity has an unfinished invocation. An activity can have several processes in the same context if it makes a rebounding call to a context where it already has a (blocked) process. When the activity returns from a cross-context invocation, the process that was created for it in the target context is deallocated.

An activity is said to be *present* in any context where it has at least one incomplete invocation. The activity is said to be *represented* in any context which the activity has visited but at which there are no incomplete invocations. Likewise, a job is said to be *present* at any node where at least one of its activities is present. A job is said to be *represented* at any nodes it has visited but at which the job is not currently present.

10.1.12.1 Naming. Jobs and activities are known by so-called AIds. An AId consists of the concatenation of a UId with a context address. The UId ensures that the AId is globally unique while the context address is used to cache the address of the initial context of the job or activity. The routines to create jobs and activities return AIds for the newly created jobs and activities which can then be used in subsequent GRT calls to exercise control over the job or activity. Typically, the AId would be cached in a language level object.

10.1.12.2 Data Structures. Each job has a descriptor in the job's initial context. The most important pieces of information contained in this descriptor include the job's global state (e.g. running, suspended etc.); a list of all the incomplete activities of the job and the job's so-called 'global lock' which is used to serialise asynchronous operations on the job with activity creations and terminations.

Each activity also has a descriptor in each context in which it is present[11]. The most important information stored in this descriptor includes the AId of the job to which the activity belongs; the activity's local state and a LIFO list of the descriptors of the local processes belonging to the activity.

Each context also contains a hash table – the Activity Manager Table (AMT) – which maps the AId of a job or activity to the address of the corresponding descriptor in the context.

10.1.12.3 Job Creation. Jobs can be created in two different circumstances. The mainline of each application is run as a new job and a running job can

---

[11]And in some contexts in which it is represented.

also create a new job to perform an object invocation asynchronously. In the latter case the parameter block for the invocation to be carried out is passed as a parameter to the AM routine to create a job.

Creating a job only involves allocating a descriptor for the job in the current context with an empty activities-created-list, constructing an AId for the job, making a local AMT entry and creating the initial activity of the job.

In the case of asynchronous job creation, the name for the new job is returned to the caller for use in subsequent job control operations.

10.1.12.4 Activity Creation. Activities are created either explicitly by an application or implicitly as part of job creation. All activities are created as part of the current job and always in the current context.

Creating an activity is similar to creating a new job: a descriptor is allocated and initialised; an AId constructed; an entry made in the context's AMT, and the initial process of the activity created and linked to the new activity. When this process is eventually scheduled it will carry out the target invocation or run the application mainline as appropriate.

Finally, the new activity's name has to be added to its job's list of non-terminated activities. Since the job's list of activities is only maintained in the job's initial context, a message may have to be sent to this context if the activity is being created in any other context. Moreover the activity creation must be synchronised with any asynchronous operations on the job which might be going on in parallel with activity creation. Thus before accessing the job descriptor, the new activity must first acquire the job's global lock, ensuring that no parallel operations are in progress. The activity can then examine the job's global state to determine if any relevant operations have taken place. For example, if the job was explicitly killed during the creation, the activity creation must be aborted or if the job was suspended the activity must be created in the suspended state. If no such operation has taken place the activity is added to the list, so that it will be notified of any further operations on the job, and the global lock released.

10.1.12.5 Activities and Cross-context Invocation. On a cross-context invocation a forwarding pointer – in the activity's current process – is left behind giving the address of the target context, if known by the client (c.f. Sect. 10.1.8). The activity's local state is changed to **remote** and the invocation request message forwarded to the target context. The current process of the activity is then blocked until the reply is received and control within the activity returned to the current context.

On the remote side, the activity may already be represented in the target context and in fact, if the invocation is a rebounding call, it may even be present in the context when the invocation arrives. This is determined by searching the local AMT for an entry for the activity. If the activity is not already represented it is said to *diffuse* to the context and a descriptor is allocated for it and initialised.

In any case, a process is created to carry out the the invocation and is added to the head of the list of processes for the activity in that context. The activity's local state is changed to **active** and the process is scheduled to run.

When the invocation completes, the process will be unlinked from the activity's list and the reply message sent. If the activity has no other processes at the node, then its activity descriptor can be released. However this is not done immediately, in case the activity performs subsequent invocations at the node in quick succession. Instead the descriptor is allowed to time out. When that occurs the AMT entry for the activity is removed and the descriptor deallocated. The next invocation by the activity arriving in the context will cause a new descriptor to be allocated.

10.1.12.6 Activity and Job Termination. An activity terminates when the initial process of the activity exits and thus it always terminates in the activity's initial context. This may happen when the activity's initial invocation completes, when an exception is raised in the activity or when the activity is explicitly killed.

The first step in activity termination is to remove the local AMT entry for the activity prohibiting any further asynchronous operations on the activity. The final step is to inform the owning job about the termination of the activity which may result in a message being sent if the activity was created in a context other than the initial context of its job. The activity is then removed from its job's activities-created-list.

The results of the activity can then be passed back to the creator. For this purpose the kernel up-calls the OM with a pointer to the result block for the activity.

A job terminates when all of the activities belonging to the job have terminated. This is detected during activity termination when the last activity's identifier is removed from the job's list of activities. The job's AMT and descriptor are freed and the results are passed to the OM.

10.1.12.7 Job and Activity Control. Users may invoke operations on jobs or activities. The operations available are: suspend, resume, and kill. Operations on jobs effect all activities belonging to that job.

The execution of all operations on jobs is similar. If the operation is requested from a context other than the job's initial context, the request must first be forwarded to the initial context. Once in the job's initial context, the first step is to acquire the job's global lock. This prevents any activity creation or deletion or other job operations from occurring for the duration of the operation. Next the appropriate operation is performed on each of the activities in the job's list of activities. Then the job's state is modified as necessary to reflect the operation just performed. Finally the lock on the job's list of activities is released.

Operations on activities are more complex since they must locate the activity's current process. This is done using a distributed search algorithm. The idea behind the algorithm is to first find a context where the activity is present and then to follow the activity's forwarding pointers to locate the activity's current context. Since the AId of the activity is available it is always possible to find one context where the activity is present – its initial context. If no forwarding pointer exists for the activity then it is necessary to wait until control within the activity returns to that context before proceeding with the request. When following forwarding pointers, the most recent process belonging to the activity is always used in order to reduce the number of steps taken. Following the forwarding pointers does not guarantee that the activity's current context will be found. It may happen that at the same time that a request is being forwarded, the activity is returning to the source context. In this case the search must be restarted.

The following shows the steps taken when an activity operation request is processed:

- If the activity is present in the current context and if its current process is located here as well, the operation is carried out.
- If the activity is present in the current context but its current process is located elsewhere, the request is forwarded to the context indicated in the forwarding field of the most recently created process of the activity, if any.
- If the activity is not present in the current context, the request is forwarded to the activity's initial context. The address is in the AId.
- If in the activity's initial context and the activity is not present, the search is abandoned. In this case, the activity either never existed or has already terminated.

Once the current process of the activity has been located, the operations proceed as follows:

- **Killing:** Since threads (other than the current thread) cannot be killed (c.f. Sect. 10.1.16), the activity is marked as killed. Later, the activity must check to see if it has been marked as killed, and if so the activity will terminate itself (this is done by causing the activity's current process to terminate with a fatal exception).
- **Suspending:** As for killing, threads (other than the current thread) cannot be suspended (c.f. Sect. 10.1.16). Hence, the activity is marked as suspended. Later the activity will check to see if it has been suspended and if so the activity suspends itself on a semaphore located in the activity's descriptor. (Note the check for suspension must be done after the check for killing.)
- **Resuming:** A suspended activity is resumed by signalling on the semaphore used to suspend the activity.

Finally, there is an operation to put the current activity to sleep for a number of milliseconds.

10.1.12.8 Process Management.

Although a process corresponds to a conventional thread as provided by many other systems, an Amadeus process has more state associated with it and hence the process abstraction is built on an underlying threads package i.e. each process is implemented by a thread.

General FIFO semaphores are the only process synchronisation mechanism provided by the AM for use within the GRT and as a basis for the implementation of other synchronisation mechanisms in the language-specific run-time.

10.1.13 Load Balancing

The advantages of load balancing in any distributed system are well known, e.g. [Jacqmot et al. 1989]. This section looks at how load balancing is incorporated into Amadeus. The conventional technique of load balancing on process creation used in many systems, [Zhou and Ferrari 1987], maps onto load balancing on activity creation in the case of Amadeus. Furthermore it is also possible to perform load balancing at the granularity of an individual cluster fault − i.e. load balancing is used by the PS to choose the node at which to map a cluster provided that this does not conflict with the activation policy for the extent to which the cluster belongs (c.f. Sect. 10.1.5.5.). The justification for this approach is that objects within a cluster exhibit a strong locality of reference and it is likely that the activity will execute within the cluster for a reasonable amount of time before returning to its original cluster or before invoking an operation on another cluster. Long running computations are likely to span multiple clusters each of which will be individually load balanced thus potentially spreading the load of that computation across a number of nodes.

In the current implementation both types (activity and cluster) of load balancing are supported but these are obviously mutually exclusive. When using activity balancing objects being faulted into virtual memory are brought to the activity. When cluster balancing is enabled a placement decision is made on each such fault causing the activity to diffuse if necessary. In either case an activity diffuses to a cluster that is already mapped. It is one of the goals of the current version of Amadeus to experiment with the two types of load balancing to investigate which type is most suitable for our object-oriented applications.

A more in depth discussion of the rationale for this design can be found in [Tangney and O'Toole 1991].

10.1.13.1 Implementation. Load balancing is implemented along standard lines, [Eager et al. 1986], with separate load dissemination, load calculation, location policy and transfer policy layers. In fact, load dissemination is handled by the NM (c.f. Sect. 10.1.3.). Transparent remote execution, often the most troublesome aspect of load balancing, is provided (for free) as an integral feature of the Amadeus environment.

As just outlined, balancing on both activity creation and cluster faulting are supported. It is also possible for the application layer to override the system and explicitly specify (or hint at) the node at which an activity should be created − or an invocation carried out. Finally load balancing can be disabled at system configuration time.

Fundamental to this implementation is the concept of an activity's *preferred node*, i.e. the node at which it will normally execute. If this is not specified by the application at activity creation then it can be chosen by the load balancing module if activity balancing is enabled. Once the preferred node is set all subsequent clusters faulted by the activity are mapped at the preferred node if possible. When cluster balancing is being used a preferred node is not set on activity creation and a separate placement decision is made for each cluster fault. As another alternative the preferred node for an activity can be set explicitly by the application at any time.

Currently load is calculated based on the load average figure returned by UNIX combined with the number of activities on each node. A random element is also used when picking a node in order to avoid swamping and thresholds values are used to avoid going remote when the local node is lightly loaded or the chosen node is already overloaded.

10.1.14 Transaction Management

The TS encapsulates the RelaX transaction management components. RelaX is described in [Schumann et al. 1989] and [Kroeger et al. 1990]. The integration of RelaX and Amadeus is described in detail in [Mock et al. 1992]. In this section a brief overview of transaction management in Amadeus is presented and the interface between the TS and the other components of the system is described.

10.1.14.1 RelaX Transaction Management. In RelaX the active entities in a transaction are known as *participants*. For RelaX, a participant is defined as a thread of control which is confined to a single address space. A transaction may have one or more participants at any time and the set of participants of a given transaction can vary over time. Also in RelaX the units of data accessible within a transaction are known as *resources*.

RelaX supports a model of resources in which each resource has a *committed state* and an *actual state*. The committed state will be updated only within the commit protocol. All accesses to a resource are directed to its actual state, which initially corresponds to the committed state and reflects all modifications to the resource. If a resource is modified within a transaction, a *recovery point* for the resource must be maintained. This recovery point contains enough information to restore the actual state to the before-image of the transaction in case of an abort. Recovery points are value based, but other approaches are not precluded. Note that, as nesting and the use of uncommitted data is allowed, there may be a set of recovery points associated with a resource, i.e. the actual state of the resource is accessible to all active transactions, each saving its individual before-image in a recovery point. In case of a transaction abort the corresponding recovery points are restored.

RelaX is composed of two components, the Transaction Manager and the Generic Transaction Support components. The transaction manager comprises the following components: the recovery graph, the action tree, the commit and abort protocols and the log component, thus subsuming all transaction-specific, resource-independent tasks related to distributed transaction management. The generic transaction support comprises generic recovery and concurrency control supporting resources at a single node. This clear distinction between transaction management and data management corresponds to the X/Open proposal for distributed transaction management [X/Open 1989].

Due to the use of non-strict two-phase locking, dependencies between transactions may arise. The recovery graph is a distributed data structure which on the one hand stores dependencies between transactions and on the other hand keeps track of the nodes visited by a transaction. The recovery graph is consulted during commit/abort protocol execution.

The action tree is a distributed data structure which reflects the nesting structure of transactions and which stores the relationship between transactions and their participants.

The commit protocol is a decentralised agreement protocol that ensures that either all nodes involved in a commit request commit a set of transactions or all these nodes abort the effected transactions. If a node crashes during protocol execution the operational nodes do not have to wait for the faulty node to recover in order to come to a decision that is nevertheless consistent with the view of the crashed node (i.e. a non-blocking protocol). The abort protocol is a decentralised protocol which ensures that an aborted transaction and all of its dependents leave no effect in the distributed system.

The log is a sequence of typed records stored on stable storage with fast sequential access. In the first phase of the commit protocol the effected resources are stably but still revocably stored. Furthermore, the log stores the state of commit requests. The information stored on the log is used during restart. If a faulty node recovers, the log is analysed to select the relevant information.

The generic concurrency control implements non-strict two-phase read/write locking for resources accessed by nested transactions. The generic recovery control manages recovery points of resources. It initiates the creation of a recovery point if necessary and the restoration of a recovery point in case of a transaction abort. Furthermore, during processing of commit requests it determines the correct image of the resource to commit.

10.1.14.2 Amadeus/RelaX Integration. The following sections give an overview of the main issues that had to be addressed in the integration of Amadeus and RelaX.

Resource Management. The resources managed by the TS are individual atomic objects. As for other objects, every atomic object must belong to some cluster. Moreover, a particular cluster can store both atomic and non-atomic objects. In this section, the term 'atomic object' is abbreviated by 'object'.

The SS stores only committed versions of objects. Transactions operate on objects which are mapped into virtual memory. A given object may be accessed by many different transactions while mapped into virtual memory. An object can only be unmapped and written to secondary storage when no transactions are using it. Transaction management is therefore orthogonal to the mapping and unmapping of objects, and in particular, the SS is not involved in committing updates to objects.

Before a mapped object is updated by a transaction, a recovery point is created for the object in virtual memory. If the transaction aborts, the state of the object will be restored to the state given in the recovery point. Before the transaction commits the final state of the object in the transaction is stably saved to prevent its loss in the event of a subsequent failure. For this purpose each context has an associated data log on which a copy of the final state of the object is saved during the prepare phase of the two-phase commit protocol. If the transaction commits, any recovery points for objects modified by the transaction can be discarded. At that point the committed state of the object is still mapped into virtual memory. The copy of the object contained in the SS (if any) is now obsolete but will be updated once the object is unmapped. In the interim, all accesses to the object will be directed to the object mapped into virtual memory. The object may subsequently be modified and changes to it committed by other transactions before being unmapped.

If the node or context in which the object is mapped fails before the object is unmapped, the copy of the object in virtual memory is lost. The up-to-date copy of the object now exists only in the context's log. In this case, even if the node is down, the object, and indeed the cluster to which it belongs, is still considered to be mapped at the node although it will be unavailable until the node recovers (c.f. Sect. 10.1.7).

On a context failure, the context will be restarted and its log used to obtain the youngest committed version of each object that was mapped into the context. Although the unit of transfer between the SS and virtual memory is a cluster, the unit of logging is an object. Hence when recovering a context, the TS must read the clusters, to which the objects found in the log belong, from the SS and overwrite those objects, to which changes have been committed, with the copy of the object obtained from the log. After recovery, the context will therefore contain only those clusters which were present before the crash and which had contained objects to which changes were committed since the cluster was mapped. Other clusters which were present in the context before the crash are lost from virtual memory (c.f. Sect. 10.1.7).

After a node failure, the local TM restarts each context that existed before the crash and that was involved in a transaction.

When a cluster is unmapped from virtual memory, it is necessary to write a record to the log to indicate that the cluster need not be recovered in the context. In addition, in order to reclaim log space and reduce restart time in the case of failure, it is possible to write a copy of a cluster containing only committed updates back to the SS without unmapping the cluster. In this case a record is forced to the log to delimit the extent of log records which must be applied to the cluster after restart.

Participant Management. In Amadeus, each participant corresponds to a process as defined in Sect. 10.1.12.8.

When an activity begins a new transaction, a new process is created for the activity and becomes the initial participant of the transaction. The process which was running when the transaction was created is blocked until the transaction completes. Creating a new process as the initial participant of each transaction allows the state of the activity to be rolled back cleanly in the event of the transaction aborting i.e. simply by deleting all participant processes.

Participants are added to a transaction whenever a new activity is created within the transaction or when any activity involved in a transaction performs a cross-context invocation. Such participants must be registered with the TM at the node where they are created and unregistered as they terminate.

Additionally whenever a participant makes a remote call the TM at both the sending and receiving node must be informed of both the call and the return. A certain amount of control information is also attached by the TM to all remote call and return messages sent within a transaction (c.f. [Schumann et al. 1989]). Moreover, when an activity involved in a transaction performs a cross-context invocation, it cannot return from that call until all processing initiated on behalf of the call has completed. In particular, this means that the activity must wait for all activities created as a result of the call to complete.

Finally, if a cross-context invocation results in a new context joining the transaction, the TM must be informed.

10.1.14.3 The Transaction Sub-system Interface.

The main interface to the TS is that used by a language (via the OM) to manage transactions and, in particular, to make attempts to access atomic objects known to the TS.

The TS uses the services of the OM to make recovery points for individual atomic objects and also to prepare atomic objects for writing to the log.

A number of routines are provided for participant management which are used by the AM to inform the TS when new participants are created and deleted. The TS also provides *synchronisation points* as a means of ensuring that all processing on behalf of a cross-context invocation is complete when the call returns. A synchronisation point is essentially a count of the number of participants which are active on behalf of the call in the target context. Each call results in the creation of a new synchronisation point. When a local participant is created, the count is incremented. When the participant exits the count is decremented. The call cannot return until the count goes to zero.

Finally, the TS provides routines used during remote invocation to inform the TMs at the sending and receiving nodes of the call and the return.

10.1.15 Communications

The CS handles all communication that takes place in an Amadeus system. Depending on the request, one of a number of different possible modes of communication can be used.

- ordered atomic multicast;
- asynchronous notification;
- synchronous request-reply;
- forwarding.

The CS must support each of these forms of communication. Moreover, an important design goal was to make the other components of Amadeus totally independent of the implementation of the CS. For these reasons the high level interface to the CS is cast in terms of the remote requests that can be initiated – i.e. with one routine for each remote request that can be made. Hence, the interface to the CS seen by the kernel and by the GRT is entirely different.

Our intention in defining the interface to the CS in this form was that the CS calls could be implemented using an existing RPC package. Indeed, a prototype version of a CS (excluding atomic multicast) using SunRPC has already been implemented. However, such an implementation is limited by the functionality of the underlying package – for example message forwarding is not typically supported and thus has to be built on top.

For these reasons a message transport service – the Inter-Kernel Message service (IKM) – which provides the various modes of transmission required by Amadeus on top of an underlying unreliable connectionless transport service was implemented.

The IKM provides for the transmission of arbitrary sized messages between clients and kernels in either request-reply or request-only mode. In addition, the IKM supports the forwarding of a message received previously. Finally, the IKM provides the interface to the ordered broadcast service.

The ordered multicast mechanism is provided by RelaX. The protocol used is based on that described in [Chang and Maxemchuk 1984] and is fully described in [Vonthin 1987]. It is not discussed further here.

The other services are supported by a lightweight protocol similar to that used in the V system [Cheriton 1983], but with selective retransmission of partial messages, which is built on top of the unreliable UDP datagram service but which has been designed to be independent of the underlying transport layer.

10.1.15.1 Structure of the Communications Sub-system.
Whether initiated by the kernel or GRT, all remote requests follow a similar path.

The caller (a GRT or kernel component) calls a stub routine for the particular request which it wishes to make. In general, the parameters to this routine depend on the particular request. However all requests take as parameter the address of the callee. Typically this will have been obtained by the caller from the ARM or as a result of a previous request. The role of the stubs is essentially to marshal the parameters of the request into a message, encoding data in a canonical form suitable to support transmission between heterogeneous nodes when required.

In the case of messages including an invocation request i.e. a tblock, the encoding and decoding of the tblock body is the responsibility of the language-specific run-time which is the only component of the system with the type information necessary to interpret user requests. Typically this knowledge is encoded in a language level stub. The `tblock` body is not interpreted by the CS stub routine but is included in the request message as opaque data. The `tblock` header is of course encoded appropriately.

Currently the stubs are hand coded. However an implementation using a standard RPC package could also make use of a stub compiler to generate the stubs from an appropriate IDL description of the interface.

The message is then sent using the underlying message service. Depending on the request the message can be sent synchronously, in which case the caller will be blocked until a reply is received, or asynchronously when no reply is required.

Requests are executed as they arrive in the target process and in parallel with other requests, using threads. On the callee's side, a thread is created for the incoming request and a stub routine for the request is called to decode the message. The appropriate component is then called to carry out the request. If a reply is required it is initiated explicitly by the called component.

10.1.16 Thread Management

Threads are the basic building blocks for processes in the GRT and are used to handle parallel requests in the kernel. Each process is implemented by a single thread. Threads are also used for other Amadeus system functions.

The goal was that various thread packages (including our own implementation) may be used with minimal change to the existing code. For this purpose a generic thread interface has been designed which defines the minimum functionality needed by Amadeus from a threads package.

The most basic operations defined on threads are operations to create a thread and to exit from a thread. When creating a thread, a pointer to a function is used to specify the starting point for the thread. If the thread returns from this function, the thread is terminated. Threads are given priorities which are only taken as hints (i.e. they may be ignored).

Other miscellaneous operations defined are: an operation to put the current thread to sleep for a number of milliseconds, an operation to allow the current thread to give up the processor allowing another thread to run, and an operation to implement a non-blocking select.

There are a number of limitations which result from the thread interface. These are:

- A thread (other than the current thread) cannot be killed. This means that when killing an activity (c.f. Sect. 10.1.12.7) the activity must be marked and later volunteer itself to be killed. This potentially means that an activity might never terminate if it never makes the check to see if it should do so.
- A thread (other than the current thread) cannot be suspended. This introduces similar problems as with killing activities when an activity is suspended.

- The OM garbage collector needs access to the stacks of all the threads in the current context. However not all thread packages allow access to the threads' stacks so some other form of garbage collection is required.

10.2 Other Implementations

10.2.1 CHORUS

The CHORUS implementation of the Comandos virtual machine – CHORUS/COOL v2 – differs from other work in the project in that the implementation was designed, from the outset, to run above the CHORUS nucleus [Rozier et al. 1988] (often referred to as a micro-kernel) as opposed to above a traditional operating system kernel like UNIX.

The main goal of this work was to understand how new generation operating systems, in particular, those based on the object-oriented programming model could be implemented above the CHORUS nucleus. In particular, the goal was to understand the basic set of mechanisms that must be present at the system level to support such operating systems. To do this, requirements from Comandos and ISA [APM 1991], together with experience from the earlier CHORUS/COOL v1 platform, were taken into account in the design of a generic base level. The generic base level is an extension of the existing CHORUS mechanisms which supports all of these requirements. Two of the expected benefits of building at such a low level are worth mentioning:

- The CHORUS Nucleus is designed to support distributed operating systems and thus provides general operating system abstractions suited to distribution, thus, it was not necessary to add distribution support.
- Because it was not built above an existing operating system, the design of the platform is not constrained by the abstractions offered by such an operating system to application builders – which are rarely those that system builders require – nor hampered by its inefficiencies.

To achieve this goal, the kernel level provides a set of distributed mechanisms well suited to supporting the Comandos GRT (c.f. Fig. 10.13) above the CHORUS Nucleus.

It is interesting that the COOL implementation runs alongside the existing UNIX (CHORUS/MiX) system. The COOL system provides an object-oriented programming environment that allows access to the UNIX world. In fact, the COOL implementation uses part of the UNIX system implementation, in particular its file system.

10.2.1.1 The CHORUS System Building Architecture. The CHORUS Nucleus offers a basic set of mechanisms to support operating system development. *Actors* serve as a unit of naming and resource allocation in the system. *Ports* are attached to actors and provide an end point for communication. Ports

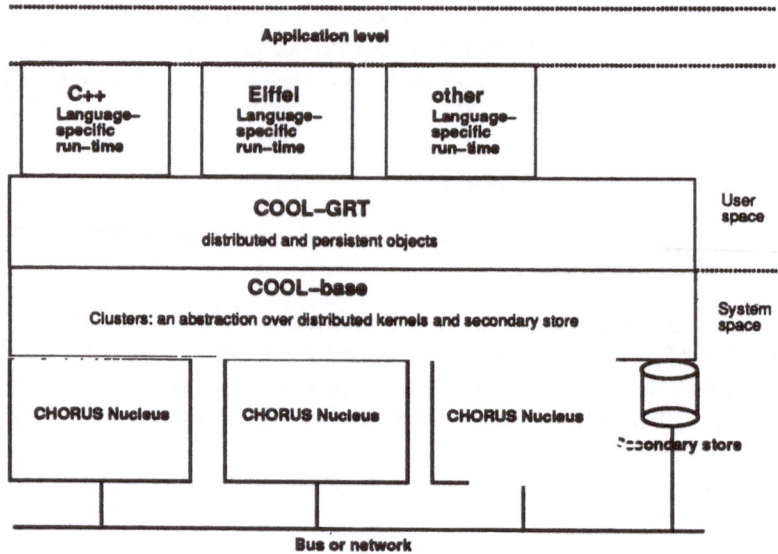

Fig. 10.13. COOL architecture.

are globally named within a set of distributed nodes and the Nucleus is responsible for locating a port and delivering a message to that port. Memory is composed of *regions* attached to actors that can be backed by a secondary storage notion referred to as a *segment*. The relationship between regions and segments is managed by a *mapper*, which is external to the Nucleus. This allows mappers to be system specific – implementing a particular policy for each system. Lastly, *threads* are provided by the Nucleus and can be attached to a particular actor.

Distributed operating systems are built above the nucleus by implementing the functionality of the operating system in a set of independent servers. Each server is a system actor and interacts with other actors to provide a global, distributed operating system interface. For example, CHORUS/MiX V4, a binary compatible implementation of the UNIX SVR4·system is composed of five actors, a process manager that acts as an interface to the system and manages processes, an object manager that implements the file system, a streams manager, an IPC manager for System V IPC and a key manager for distributed file coherency.

10.2.1.2 Extending CHORUS to Support Object-oriented Systems.

Although it has been proved that the basic Nucleus services are well suited to traditional operating systems, even those extended to support transparent distribution, experience with the CHORUS/COOL v1 system had proved that some extensions to these mechanisms were necessary to support object-oriented systems. The COOL-base level incorporates these extensions and provides an extended system interface.

The major extension that the COOL-base level supports is a distributed notion of persistent virtual memory based on a model called the *persistent context space*. The model supports distributed memory through *persistent contexts* and *context spaces*. A persistent context supports data which is guaranteed to persist. A context space is a collection of persistent contexts whose mapped data is maintained in a coherent manner.

The internal structure of a persistent context is based on the notion of *containers* and *clusters* (these are COOL-specific terms and should not be confused with the Comandos terms). A cluster represents a portion of virtual memory supporting one or more GRT level objects. A container is a grouping of clusters such that memory is complete i.e. all direct memory references are resolvable within the container.

Coherency between clusters in a context space is managed by the COOL mapper and uses a distributed, strict coherency mechanism, as described in [Li and Hudak 1989]. Allocation of memory across context spaces uses a global allocation mechanism provided by the COOL-base level.

Clusters are the unit of mapping and unmapping. A cluster, when requested by the GRT level will be located and if necessary mapped into a persistent context. Thus the base level supports a single level store abstraction, providing persistence as required by the Comandos virtual machine, and extends this with an implementation of distributed virtual memory that is suited to object-oriented systems like Comandos.

The base level is implemented as a collection of CHORUS system actors, which, for efficiency reasons, are loaded into the Nucleus address space and accessed via a trap interface. Each COOL-base actor uses the CHORUS IPC mechanism to communicate with other COOL-base actors and to support the distributed management protocols.

10.2.1.3 The COOL Generic Run-time.

The COOL GRT provides the basic set of Comandos virtual machine services (although there is currently no support for the TS and only a lightweight version of the PS) and uses the base level functionality.

The ES is based on the micro-kernel supported threads. Each activity is mapped to a thread, with one thread acting as a virtual processor and possibly supporting multiple Comandos activities. Each activity is uniquely named and managed by a global job management scheme that uses CHORUS IPC to maintain global state.

The GRT uses the cluster abstraction provided by the base level as a place to create and manipulate objects. Thus the COOL version of the Comandos VOM is implemented by both the base level and part of the GRT level. Each cluster comprises two zones, a GRT zone where cluster specific data is held and a user zone where user objects are placed. Clusters are named using a port identifier. Thus for each cluster that exists within a context the GRT creates a port. Communications directed to that cluster are received by the GRT managing that cluster at the port. Objects are named relative to a cluster such that invocation of an object at the GRT interface is mapped into a message sent to the cluster in which that object resides. Since port names are globally unique, a cluster and thus objects managed by the cluster can be moved around the distributed system as required. Hence, the implementation of the Comandos object invocation mechanism is greatly simplified.

As discussed in Chap 3 support for mapping objects into and out of address spaces, using pointer swizzling, based on language-specific information to allow relocation, is provided. The unit of mapping in the COOL implementation is the cluster. Each cluster, comprising multiple virtual memory regions, is mapped by an equivalent number of storage segments. When a cluster is mapped to or from store, the base level reads or writes regions using the COOL mapper. This operation can be likened to a paged virtual memory system where pages of data are similar to regions. The COOL mapper is responsible for managing both the consistency of the data across contexts and the consistency of the data on secondary store. Thus, the COOL mapper (or mappers) collaborate to provide the SS. This is actually based on the UNIX file system and uses files to hold segments.

10.2.1.4 Conclusion.
The CHORUS implementation of the Comandos architecture was not designed to provide yet another implementation of the same interface over UNIX, but to explore the use of the CHORUS micro-kernel as support for a system-level implementation of Comandos. In all cases the basic micro-kernel mechanisms have been used to support global management schemes that are scalable. In general, the basic system model, and mechanisms that CHORUS supports are adequate to support a system such as Comandos. However, the virtual memory system has been greatly extended to support objects in a distributed environment allowing increased flexibility and performance to be gained.

The COOL programming environment consists of a tool (COOLPP) that is capable of generating multiple preprocessors, and a COOL++ preprocessor that implements the C++ language-specific run-time.

The system has been validated using the Comandos pilot application, CIDRE. A fully functional version of CIDRE, written in C++ currently runs on a network of Intel 386 machines, hosting CHORUS/MiX and the COOL implementation of the Comandos virtual machine.

10.2.2 Mach

The Mach micro-kernel [Accetta et al. 1986, Golub et al. 1990] was developed at Carnegie Mellon University, as a new foundation for operating systems. It provides extensible memory management, threads, and an extensive IPC facility.

In versions 2.5 and earlier, Mach was combined with UNIX to deliver a complete operating system environment; the architecture of OSF/1 is similar to Mach 2.5. Version 3, however, provides Mach as a pure kernel, with no other operating system functionality in kernel space. Particular operating system environments are provided by means of user space servers. To date, servers have been prototyped for BSD, OSF/1, SVR4, Sprite, and DOS.

Although it is a goal of the Mach kernel to minimise abstractions provided by the kernel, it is not a goal to be minimal in the semantics associated with those abstractions. As such, each of the abstractions provided has a rich set of associated semantics. Although this makes it difficult to identify key areas, the main kernel abstractions are considered to be the following:

- Task – the unit of resource allocation encompassing address space and port rights.
- Thread – the unit of CPU utilisation.
- Port – communication channel, accessible only via send/receive capabilities (rights).
- Message – collection of data objects.
- Memory object – internal unit of memory management

10.2.2.1 Goals of the Mach Implementation of Comandos. The micro-kernel approach allows other servers to be developed, as well as those implementing the semantics of an operating system. However, until recently, there has been very little work on implementing servers over Mach, other than those implementing different operating system personalities. The basic mechanisms offered by Mach can be matched closely to the abstractions of the Comandos virtual machine, and this provides the motivation for implementing Comandos over Mach, with two major objectives:

- To evaluate the benefits of the micro-kernel technology for the support of a distributed object-oriented operating system such as the Comandos virtual machine;
- To investigate the suitability of Mach for application servers other than those emulating operating system personalities, with particular emphasis on performance evaluation.

Within the Comandos project, two approaches have been explored: adaptation of existing UNIX implementations to use the Mach mechanisms (this approach has been followed both in adapting Guide-1 to run over Mach 2.5 [Boyer et al. 1991] and in adapting Amadeus and IK to run over Mach 3.0; this approach is described in Sect. 10.2.2.2 below. A more fundamental approach involves a major redesign based on the exploitation of the Mach 3.0 capabilities, and this approach has been adopted for the Guide-2 implementation, which is described in Sect. 10.2.2.3.

10.2.2.2 Adaptations of Existing Comandos Implementations. These adaptations implemented only a subset of the Comandos virtual machine, and were carried out essentially as feasibility studies, to test the ideas of mapping Comandos abstractions onto Mach ones. For example:

- the use of Mach tasks for Comandos jobs;
- the use of Mach threads for Comandos activities;

- the use of Mach ports as object references.

Both the IK and Amadeus adaptations to Mach 3.0 continue to use UNIX functionality in addition to the Mach mechanisms. This is provided by a user-level UNIX server (work has been done using both the BSD UNIX server, developed by Carnegie Mellon University, and the OSF/1 server, developed by the OSF Research Institute).

The modifications to Amadeus in adapting it to run over Mach 3.0 included:

- the use of Mach Cthreads to replace the Amadeus non-preemptive light-weight process package based on the interval timer;
- the use of the Mach network shared memory server for shared information within one host (UNIX Amadeus uses System V shared memory);
- UNIX Amadeus uses NFS for the SS; the Mach version uses either AFS or the Mach Remote File System;

The current version continues to use UDP datagrams as the basis of the IKM protocol, and has not been modified to use Mach IPC.

In MachIK, the version of IK adapted for Mach 3.0, a port is associated with each distributed object, and send rights are used as references to these objects. Using ports as distributed object references has several advantages:

- Location transparency – a message can be sent to a port in a location transparent way. This built-in Mach feature provides a cheap way to implement location transparent invocation.
- Port migration – receive rights can be moved between tasks. When migrating an object the receive right is moved to the destination context; the other contexts can continue to invoke the object unaware of its movement. However, the kernel does not yet properly support the migration of receive rights.
- No more senders notification – the programmer can request a notification when the last send right to one of his receive rights dies. This basic mechanism was used to implement garbage collection for distributed objects.
- Protection by capabilities – access to objects is protected by the capability mechanism associated with Mach ports.
- Port death notifications – if requested, a task can receive notification whenever one of the rights in the port name space dies. This mechanism is useful in detecting child death and orphans in remote invocations.

Lazy evaluation techniques are used to reduce the overhead associated with distributed objects. A port is only allocated when a reference to the related object is exported.

The current implementation does not exploit the user level memory management mechanisms provided by Mach which offer interesting possibilities such as the ability to share objects using distributed memory.

10.2.2.3 Native Implementation of Comandos on top of Mach 3.0.
This section describes the principles of Guide-2, a native implementation of the Comandos system on top of the Mach 3.0 micro-kernel.

As for Amadeus and MachIK, jobs and activities are mapped onto Mach tasks and threads. More precisely, any context within a job is represented by a Mach task. This scheme provides isolation of context address spaces. Consequently, a job is a collection of Mach tasks, one per context.

A major feature of Guide-2 is the extensive use of memory management facilities offered by Mach 3.0, i.e. *external pagers*. External pagers allow the simultaneous implementation of several strategies for sharing objects over a network: a single image for an object or multiple copies of an object with different consistency policies. The main characteristics of the Guide-2 VOM are summarised below; details of the design can be found in [Boyer 1991].

- A cluster is represented by a Mach memory segment which is handled by a specific external pager. Class objects (i.e. methods code) are shared using a "multiple image" policy while data objects are shared using the "single image" policy.
- Contexts are represented by Mach tasks, and a Mach port is associated with each context. This allows:
  - high-level protection, as port identifiers are unforgeable, and thus it is not possible to access any object within a context without permission ("permission" here being assimilated to the port identifier).
  - migration of contexts, as ports are themselves subject to migration. This facility is used to support load balancing.
  - handling of node failures, as event notification on ports allows the detection of abnormal termination of jobs and activities.

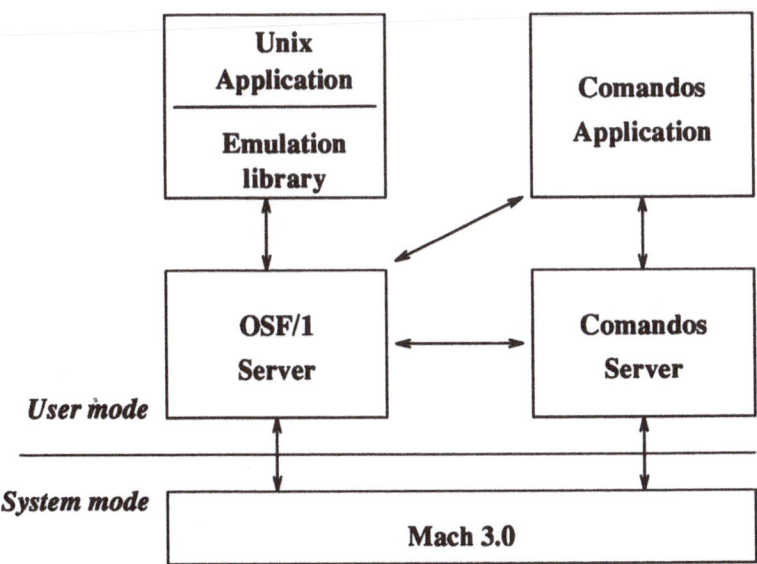

Fig. 10.14. Guide-2 architecture.

Guide-2 is implemented on a network of i486-based Zenith machines, running OSF/1 MK. The general architecture is depicted in Fig 10.14. On top of Mach 3.0 two servers coexist: the OSF/1 single server which implements the UNIX environment, and the Comandos server which implements the Comandos virtual machine. The Comandos server, as well as Comandos applications, can reuse all of the services provided by the UNIX environment. In the current version only the Comandos language is supported by the Comandos server.

11. Interfacing a Language to the Virtual Machine

This chapter describes the implementation of Eiffel**, the extended version of the Eiffel programming language supported by Amadeus. Eiffel** provides support for distribution, persistence, concurrency and transactions. All objects in an Eiffel** application are potentially global and persistent, while concurrency and transactions are available through the use of library classes. See Chap. 4 for further details.

The implementation of Eiffel** required no changes to the Eiffel programming language – persistence and distribution are transparent to the programmer. Moreover only minimal changes and extensions to the Eiffel run-time (ERT) were necessary. No changes have been made to the Eiffel compiler. This has been made possible by the extensive run time type information provided by Eiffel, which enables all objects to be treated in a uniform manner.

The type information provided by the ERT means that there is no need to generate different up-calls for each class. All objects in the system use the same up-call code. Preprocessing is necessary to generate proxy functions for each of the exported functions in a class in order to support remote access to instances of the class. Preprocessing is also necessary to generate the code for each class which is necessary to support atomic instances of the class and also to implement transaction creation and asynchronous invocation of objects.

The next section describes those details of the VMI (the interface between the GRT and a language-specific run-time) which are necessary to understand the remainder of this chapter. The following section describes the ERT. The implementation of persistence, distribution, concurrency and transaction support are all dealt with in turn in subsequent sections.

11.1 The Generic Run-time

Comandos objects can be distributed and persistent. An object mapped on a given node may be referenced by an object in a context on another node; in this case this reference will actually refer to a *proxy* for the object. Invoking on this proxy will result in an RPC on the real object if the object cannot be mapped.

A Comandos object consists of a header and space for language objects. Contained in the header is a stub for the object. This consists of the global name of the object, the identifier of the object's cluster and information to allow the creation of a proxy for the object. Also contained in the header is the *up-call* structure which is used by the GRT to obtain language-specific information about the language object such as the number of pointers in the object and their locations.

A GRT up-call structure is stored in another GRT data structure called a *class descriptor*. There is a class descriptor for every class in the application. This descriptor also contains the class name, the size of instances of the class and a class identifier (cid). A class descriptor is embedded in its own GRT object, and the creation of a class descriptor object for each class takes place in **regclasses**, a function that is called by the GRT as part of its initialisation, before the application mainline is called. The class descriptor is used to initialise the up-call structure in the GRT header of an object when the object is created.

11.1.1 Down-calls

This section describes some of the down-calls available to a language to enable it to interact with the underlying platform.

- **grt_create()** – This is used to create a GRT object. The language pre-processor inserts this call whenever an object is created in the language. The GRT allocates space for the GRT header and the language object, initialises some of the fields in the GRT header and returns a pointer to the uninitialised language object as a result back to the language-specific run-time.
- **grt_resolve()** – A check to see if the given object is mapped locally.
- **grt_promote()** – A down-call to promote the given GRT object. This involves assigning a global name to the object.
- **grt_make_atomic()** – A down-call to promote an object from being non-atomic to being atomic.

11.1.2 Up-calls

Each GRT object has a set of up-calls which can be generated by the language preprocessor and are invoked by the GRT through the up-call structure in the GRT header. The up-calls required are as follows:

- **create()** – Invoked when an object is created. Initialises the language-specific bindings for the object (e.g. setting up of the function table).
- **activate()** – Invoked when an object is being made active, i.e. going from being a proxy object to being the real object. It performs this transformation by binding the real class code to the object.
- **deactivate()** – Invoked when an object is being made inactive. It binds the proxy class code to the object.

- `nextptr()` – Returns a pointer to the nth pointer in the object. Invoked when the object is being mapped and unmapped so the GRT can unfold and fold its pointers.

- `norefs()` – Returns the number of pointers in the object. Invoked when the GRT is allocating space for the object in its cluster.

- `onuse()` – Same function as the `create` up-call. Invoked as the final step in making an object active.

- `dispatch()` – Invoked when an incoming RPC for the object is received. This up-call invokes the object specific `dispatch` function (generated by the language preprocessor) which unbundles the parameters and invokes the target operation.

- `make_atomic()` – Binds the atomic code to the object. Up-called by the GRT as part of the process of making an object atomic, a process initiated by the `make_atomic` down-call.

The up-calls `create`, `onuse`, `nextptr`, `norefs`, `dispatch` and `make_atomic` must be provided by each global and persistent object, while `activate` and `onuse` are required for each proxy.

11.2 The Eiffel Run-time

The ERT provides the execution environment for Eiffel applications. Since multiple inheritance and polymorphism are key features of Eiffel, the run time mechanism for locating a routine when it is invoked is sufficiently generic to be able to handle each of these cases and hence incurs a small penalty over a standard procedure call. Genericity is also a key feature of Eiffel, and the ERT implements genericity with no code duplication. Refer to [Meyer 1989a] for a full description of the Eiffel language.

Eiffel provides a facility for automatic compilation management called **es** which is responsible for compiling and linking all the classes in an application. The compiler uses C as an intermediate language and the ERT is written in C. The execution sequence of an Eiffel application starts when the `Create` routine of a specified *root* object is invoked, and ends when the `Create` routine completes.

11.2.1 Types and Objects

Eiffel is a strongly typed language. Every *entity* is declared to be of a certain type. An entity can be an instance of a *class type* or an instance of an *expanded type*. The run time value of an entity of a class type is a pointer to an object of that class. The run time value of an entity of an expanded type is an actual object, rather than a reference to an object. An entity of an expanded type can be of one of the simple types, (`INTEGER`, `REAL`, `CHARACTER`, `DOUBLE`, `BITS` or `BOOLEAN`) or it can be an expanded (i.e. in-line) instance of a class type. All objects, except those declared to be of simple types, contain information used by the ERT which is transparent to the Eiffel programmer. Contained in this information is a number, known as the *Dynamic Type* (DT) of the object, which is the same in all objects of a given class. The DT, along with other information, is stored in a header at the start of each object. The use of the DT will be described in the next section on the ERT data structures for object management.

11.2.2 Object Layout

Figure 11.1 shows a snap-shot of an Eiffel object during system execution. Note that there are two fields in the header, the info field, which contains the DT of the object, and the link field, which points to the last object allocated by the ERT. The link field is used by the Eiffel garbage collector to keep track of objects. In Eiffel, an object reference always points to the info field of the object being referenced, or is void. The info field bits are used by the ERT for the following purposes:

- bits[0..19] The object's DT, an integer common to all instances of the same class. If the object is a special object, it will give the number of fields in the data.
- bits[20] Expanded flag. This bit is set if the object is an expanded object.
- bits[21] Invariant flag. Set if there is a class invariant defined.
- bits[22] Mark flag. Used by Eiffel components such as the garbage collector and STORABLE (an Eiffel class that provides persistence) to mark objects when traversing an object tree.
- bits[23] Special object flag. Set if the object is a special object.
- bits[24..27] Generic bits. Bit 27 determines if the object's class is a generic type. In a special object, bit 27 indicates whether or not the special contains in-line data or is made up of references to other objects.
- bits[28..31] These bits are used by the ERT garbage collector.

The instance data consists of a number of fields called *datums*. A single datum can be a reference to another object, in which case it will contain a virtual memory address, or can contain an INTEGER, REAL, BOOLEAN or CHARACTER. A number of datums can go to make up an expanded object or a value of type DOUBLE or BITS. If the expanded object is an instance of a class type, its ERT header will appear in the instance data of the enclosing object. A DOUBLE occupies 2 datums, while an instance of BITS M (bit string of M bits) occupies (M div number of bits in a datum) + 1 datums. If a class B inherits data from a class A, then instances of B will be structured so that the ERT header will come first, then the data inherited from A, followed by the data for B.

The ERT provides functions and macros with which the programmer can obtain information about an object, given a reference to the object. These functions and macros interrogate the info field of the object, and the ERT data structures for the object's class. For instance, it is possible to get the DT of an object, determine if it is in-line, get the name of its class, get the number of

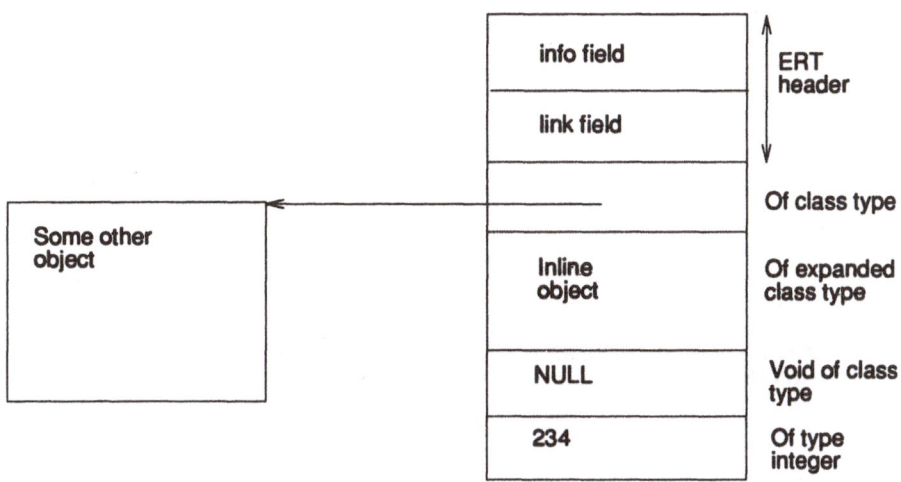

Fig. 11.1. An Eiffel object.

fields in the object, get the type of a field, and get the names of the fields and methods of the object given a reference to the object.

The ERT also provides so-called *special objects*, which are used to implement classes such as STRING and ARRAY, and are basically blocks of memory used to hold the string's characters or the array's elements. Figure 11.2 show a snapshot of an object of type ARRAY[INTEGER]. The array object has fields for the upper and lower bounds, as well as a pointer to the array elements, contained in a special object. The special object consists of fields for each of the elements in the array. The generic bit in the special object's info field is not set which indicates that its data fields are not object references. Because the special object is allocated immediately after the array object, its link field points to the array object. This example shows how Eiffel implements genericity through the use of special objects, as special objects can contain objects of any type. Special objects are transparent to the programmer and are always associated with another object such as a STRING or an ARRAY.

11.2.3 ERT Data Structures for a Class

Figure 11.3 shows the data structures that are set up for each class in an Eiffel application on ERT initialisation. Given the DT of the object a pointer refers to, the following information about the object can be obtained:

- Class_names[DT] – The name of the object's class.
- Object_size[DT] – The number of fields in the object.
- Num_routines[DT] – The number of methods in the class.
- Routines[DT] – Gives a pointer to a function table for the class routines. Invoking on an object always results in an indirection through this table.

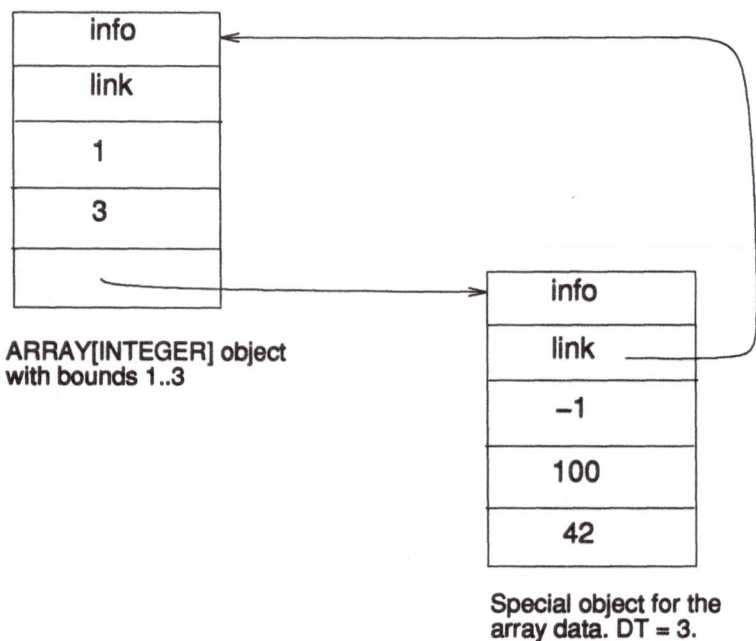

Fig. 11.2. A special object used to implement an Eiffel array.

- Routine_names[DT] – The names of the object's methods.
- Attributes[DT] – The types of the attributes of the object's data, according to the following type-code:
    - greater than or equal 0 : object reference
    - −1 : integer
    - −2 : real
    - −3 : packed booleans
    - −4 : character
    - −9 : generic
    - −340 : expanded type
    - less than −350 : bits M

This code uses positive numbers for attributes of class types (i.e. where the attribute is a reference to an object) giving the DT of the class, and negative numbers for in-line objects. Note that in the case of attributes of generic and expanded types, it is necessary to look in the info field of the actual object to determine that attribute's DT. The entry for an entity declared to be of BITS M will be set such that − (Attributes[DT][i] − 350) gives the number of datums taken up by the entity. For example, an entity that is declared to be of BITS 256 will have an entry equal to −350 + (256 div bits_in_a_datum) + 1. If bits_in_a_datum is 32, then this will be −342.

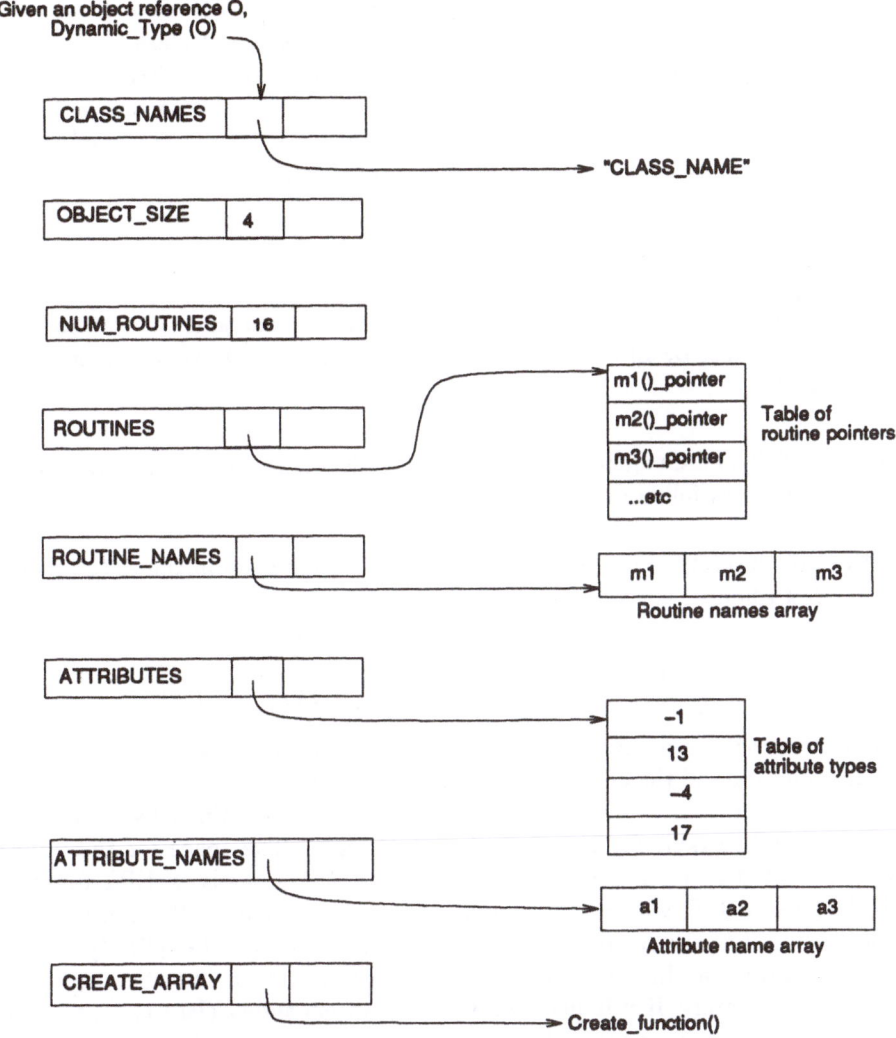

Fig. 11.3. ERT data structures.

- **Attr_names[DT]** – The names of the object's attributes.
- **Create_Array[DT]** – A pointer to the **Create** function for the class.

All classes in the application have entries in these tables. The range of DT goes from 0 to **num_classes** − 1, where **num_classes** is the number of classes in the application. The Eiffel code that the programmer writes for a class compiles into C code with functions for all the methods of the class, plus initialisation functions for the entries in the ERT data structures, shown in Fig. 11.3, for the class. Eiffel compilation also generates a C mainline, which invokes the initialisation functions for each class to initialise the ERT data structures, before invoking the **Create** function of the application's root class.

To summarise, C programmers might like to think of an Eiffel object as a **struct** containing the data for the object, and a function table for the methods, where, to invoke an object's method, the address of the struct is passed to the function as well as the parameters for the invocation.

11.2.4 Object Creation, Access and Invocation

This section describes how object creation, data access and invocation take place at run time by illustrating the run time sequence of events using C-like pseudo-code.

11.2.4.1 Object Creation. At the language level, an Eiffel object is created and initialised as follows :

```
x.Create(args);
```

At the ERT level, the following steps are taken to create and initialise the object to which **x** refers:

```
DTx = Attributes[DT(Current)][i];
DCurrent[i] = Allocate(DTx);
(*Create_Array[DTx])(DCurrent[i], args);
```

where **Current** is a pointer to the current object and **DCurrent** is a pointer to the instance data of the current object. The object reference **x** is located at field **i** in the current object's instance data and its DT is obtained by looking up the **Attributes** table for the current object's class. The space for the object is then created by passing this DT to **Allocate**. **Allocate** is an ERT function which, given a DT, will return a pointer to an initialised ERT header for the object, as well as the required memory space for the data, all explicitly zeroed. The invocation of the object's **Create** function will then initialise this data space appropriately. If **x** is declared to be of an expanded class type, there is no need to call **Allocate**, as the space has already been allocated when the current object was created. The header is marked as being expanded, and the **create** function is invoked. Special objects are allocated using a function called **spAllocate** which is given the number of datums required for the special object rather than the DT.

11.2.4.2 Object Access. At the language level, the data members of an Eiffel object are accessed as:

```
x.y;
```

At the ERT level, this is implemented as follows:

```
DCurrent[i][Access(DCurrent[i]) + os];
```

where **DCurrent** is a pointer to the instance data of the current object. **DCurrent[i]** is the run time value of **x**, field **i** in the instance data of the current object. This is a pointer to the object to which **x** refers. The data member **y** in **x** is located at an offset **os** from the start of the instance data for **x**. **Access** is an ERT function which, given a pointer to an object, returns a pointer to that object's instance data. Add **os** to **Access(DCurrent[i])** to obtain the location of **y** in the instance data of **x**. Both **i** and **os** are generated at compile time. If **x** is an expanded object, the access is implemented as follows :

```
*(Access(DCurrent + i) + os);
```

i.e. get a pointer to the instance data of the expanded object **x**, **Access(DCurrent[i])**, get a pointer to the feature y in x, **Access(DCurrent[i]) + os**, and de-reference it.

11.2.4.3 Object Invocation.
At the language level, a method of an Eiffel function is invoked as follows :

```
x.y(args);
```

At the ERT level, this becomes:

```
(*Routines[DT(DCurrent[i])][os])(DCurrent[i], args);
```

where **DCurrent** is a pointer to the current object's instance data and **i** is the offset of **x** in the current object's instance data. **Routines[DT(DCurrent[i])]** yields a pointer to the routines table for **x**'s class. A pointer to the routine **y** is located at some index **os** within this table. The routine is invoked by indirecting through the routines table, passing it a reference to **x** as well as the actual arguments.

11.2.5 Functionality Provided by the ERT

The ERT provides functionality which, at the C code level, allows all Eiffel objects to be treated in a uniform manner. This has implications for the implementation of both persistent and distributed objects, which will become apparent later. This section presents a list of some of the important functions provided by the ERT which are used in implementing both persistence and distribution. (In the following function headers, o is a reference to an Eiffel object).

- **boolean is_special(void* o);** Return TRUE if o is a special object.
- **int c_dynamic_type(void* o);** Get the DT of o.
- **int c_size(void* o);** Get size (in bytes) of o.
- **int c_fd_nb(void* o);** Return the number of datums in o.
- **int c_lfd_nb(void* o);** Return the number of logical entities in o.
- **int num_classes;** Constant giving the number of classes in the system.
- **void* c_field(int i, void* o);** Return pointer to field i of o.
- **boolean c_f2_expanded(int i, void* o);** Return TRUE if field i of o is an expanded object.
- **int c_field_type(void* o, int i);** Get the type-code of field i of the given object.
- **boolean field_pointer(void* o, int i);** Return TRUE if field i of o is of a class type.

11.3 Persistence

This section discusses the implementation of persistence in Eiffel**. To use the support provided by the platform, all Eiffel** objects are created as GRT objects. Each ERT object includes a GRT header. Two matters must be addressed in implementing persistence; providing the necessary up-calls for Eiffel** objects and supporting object creation so that when an object is created, it has an initialised GRT header as well as an ERT header.

11.3.1 Interfacing the ERT and GRT

Figure 11.4 shows persistent Eiffel** object creation. The up-call object is the means of providing the GRT with language-specific information about the object. For example the GRT can invoke an object's up-call functions to determine the number of references in the object's instance data and obtain each of these references in a cyclical fashion via the up-call functions **norefs** and **nextptr** respectively.

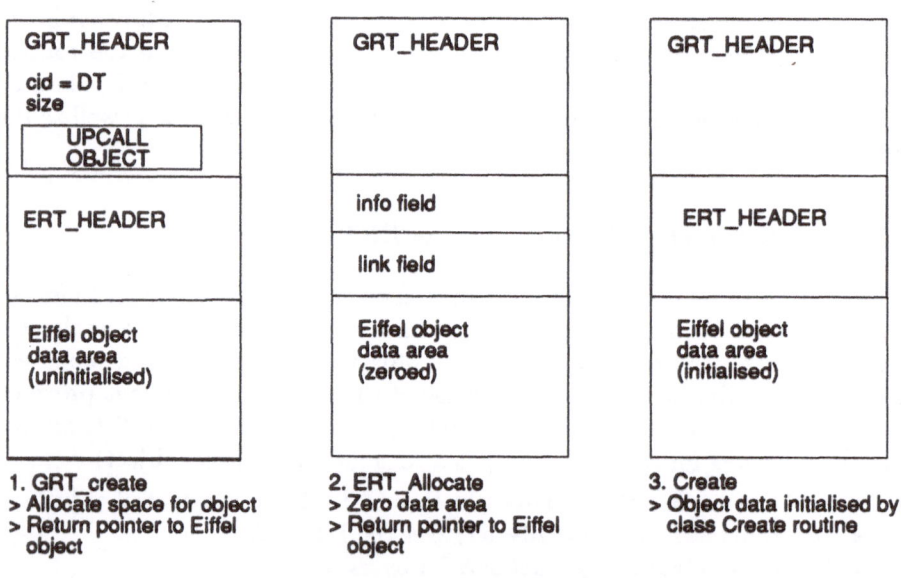

Fig. 11.4. Persistent object creation.

With the support provided by the ERT it has been possible to write generic, class independent up-calls, the idea being that all objects in the application use the same generic up-call code. The **nextptr** and **norefs** functions of the generic up-call object make use of ERT functionality. All the other up-call functions take default actions.

In Eiffel** the GRT is made aware of the number of classes in the system, and, during **regclasses**, can make up-calls to get a class name and size, given

a DT in the range 0..num_classes − 1, in order to facilitate registering of a
class descriptor for this class as part of GRT initialisation. The class identifier
for a class descriptor is set to be the DT of the class as assigned by the ERT.

The following functions have been defined as a layer between the ERT and
GRT and are used by the up-calls from the GRT to the ERT:

- int sp_nfields(void* e) – Get the number of fields in a special object.

  ```
  int sp_nfields(void* e)
   if is_special(e)
     return c_dynamic_type(e);
   else
     return -1;
  ```

- char* ert_class_name(void* e) – Get the name of an object's class.
  Note that special objects do not have any entry in the Class_names array;
  their DT is really the number of fields in the object.

  ```
  char* ert_class_name(void* e)
   if is_special(e)
     return "special";
   else
     return Class_names[c_dynamic_type(e)];
  ```

- void ert_set_DT(void *e, int newDT) – Set the DT of a given object.

  ```
  void ert_set_DT (void *e, int newDT)
   e->info = e->info + newDT
  ```

- int ert_DT_by_name(char* name) – Get the DT of a given class.

  ```
  int ert_DT_by_name(char* name)
   for each DT in 0..num_classes - 1
     if Class_names[DT] == name
       return DT;
   return -1;
  ```

- char* ert_name_by_DT(int DT) – Get name of class with given DT.

  ```
  char* ert_name_by_DT(int DT)
   return Class_names[DT];
  ```

- int ert_size_by_DT(int DT) – Determine the physical size of objects
  with the given DT when they are created.

  ```
  int ert_size_by_DT(int DT)
   return Object_size[DT]*bytes_in_datum
                        + bytes_in_ert_header;
  ```

- int ert_spnorefs(void* e) – Determine number of references in a special object. In a special object the generic bit means that the object consists of references to other objects or consists of in-line expanded data.

  ```
  int ert_spnorefs(void* e)
   if generic bit set in e->info
     return  sp_nfields(e);
   else
     return 0;
  ```

- **void* ert_spnextptr(int n, void* e)** – Returns a pointer to the nth reference of a special object. If the special object does contain references and **n** is less than the number of fields in the object, it suffices to return a reference to the nth field of the object.

```
void* ert_spnextptr(int n, void* e)
  if (generic bit set in e->info)
              AND (n < sp_nfields(e))
    return address of field n of e;
  else
    return NULL;
  end
```

- **int ert_norefs(void* e)** – Returns the number of references in an Eiffel object. Check first if the object is a special object. If not, go through each field of the object. If that field is a reference then increment the **norefs** count, else if it is an expanded object, increment **norefs** by the number of references contained within the field.

```
int ert_norefs(void* e)
  set norefs to 0;
  if is_special(e)
    return ert_spnorefs(e);
  else
    for each field i in e
      if c_f2_expanded(i, e)
        norefs += number of references in c_field(i, e);
      else
        if field_pointer (i, e)
          norefs++;
        end
      end
    return norefs;
  end
```

- **void* ert_nextptr(int n, void* e)** – Return a reference to the nth object pointer in an object. This includes a check for **e** being a special object. It also includes checking expanded objects for the nth reference. A counter, **ref_count**, is kept of the number of references encountered as the fields of the object are checked in turn. If a field is an expanded object, then a check is made to see if the nth reference is in here so the n $-$ **ref_count** reference in this field is obtained. If this returns **NULL**, **ref_count** is updated by the number of references within this expanded object. When a field reference is encountered, a check is made to see if this is reference number n. If so, that field's address can be returned, else **ref_count** can be incremented and the search continues.

```
    void* ert_nextptr(int n, void* e)
     set ref_count to 0; /* Number of references so far */
     if is_special(e)
       return ert_spnextptr(n,e);
     else
       for each field i in e
         if c_f2_expanded(i, e)
           if nextptr = ert_nextptr(n-ref_count, c_field(i,e))
             return nextptr;
           else
             ref_count += ert_norefs(c_field(i,e));
           end
         else
           if field_pointer(i,e) AND n == ref_count
             return address of c_field(i,e);
           else
             ref_count++;
           end
         end
       end
     end
     return NULL;
```

Given these functions, it is relatively straightforward to define generic up-call functions and a generic **regclasses** function. Here are the up-calls of the generic up-call structure that are necessary to implement persistence: (note: **data()** returns a pointer to the Eiffel** object embedded in the GRT object)

- void *nextptr(int n) {return ert_nextptr(n, data());}

  Return reference to the nth pointer in the objects instance data.

- int norefs() {return ert_norefs(data());}

  Return number of references in the objects instance data.

The generic **regclasses** code is presented below:

```
void regclasses() {
  upcall_structure UC; /* Instance of generic up-call class */
  class_descriptor CD; /* Another GRT data structure  */

  CD.upcall = UC;
  for DTindex in 0 to num_classes -1 {
    CD.class_name = ert_name_by_DT(DTindex);
    CD.size = ert_size_by_DT(DTindex);
    CD.cid = DTindex; Register(CD);
  }
  /* Register a class descriptor for the SPECIAL class */
  CD.class_name = "special";
  CD.size = 0; CD.cid = -1;
  Register(CD);
}
```

Every Eiffel** application can use this `regclasses`. The only attributes that have to be different in each class descriptor object are the class name, the instance size and the cid.

11.3.2 Down-calls

The functionality provided by the ERT means that no code generation is necessary for registering class descriptors for each class. A generic `regclasses` can be applied to all applications. It takes every DT in the system, 0..num_classes − 1, and for each one registers a class descriptor object with the GRT. It is necessary to insert the name of the class and the size of objects of the class in the class descriptor. The cid of each class descriptor is set to the DT of the class. It also initialises each class descriptor with the same up-call object, so that all objects of all classes will share the same up-call table. This policy of registering class descriptors with the GRT for all Eiffel classes in the system means that all Eiffel objects are potentially persistent. Special objects, which have no entries in the ERT data structures of Fig. 11.3, are registered by the GRT with a DT of −1, and a name of "special". Their size, which varies, is set to 0 in the class descriptor. When the ERT is allocating a special, it passes in the size rather than the DT, and the GRT can set the correct size in the GRT header using this value.

During creation of a persistent object, the ERT's `Allocate` function makes use of the following down-call:

    void* persis_create(int sz, int DT, char* class_name);

when allocating memory for the object, instead of using `malloc`. This function will return a pointer to a memory chunk of `sz` bytes with a GRT header above it, i.e. a pointer to the data area of a GRT object. So, `Allocate` initialises the ERT header as before, zeroes the data area and returns a pointer to the newly allocated object, which now has a GRT header. The function `persis_create` down-calls a GRT create function to allocate and initialise the GRT header and data area. Figure 11.4 shows how a persistent object is allocated and initialised.

In Eiffel, persistence is available to the programmer via the STORABLE and ENVIRONMENT library classes, which allow the conservation of objects in secondary storage. In Eiffel** class STORABLE has been altered to use the GRT down-calls to do the storing and retrieving, thus rendering the GRT transparent to an application that uses STORABLE. It is important also to note that this has been done only for name storage. STORABLE in Eiffel** still permits persistence through file descriptor and FILE storage, but this is unchanged from Eiffel.

11.3.3 Problems in the Implementation of Persistence

The problems outlined in this section were encountered during the implementation of persistence, but are common to the implementation of Eiffel** in general.

11.3.3.1 GRT and ERT Initialisation. An application can be thought of as having two stages; GRT initialisation and application mainline. The former is invisible to application programmers, who would view their programs as having only the latter stage. Note that `regclasses` is called as part of GRT initialisation. This causes a problem with an Eiffel** application, where ERT initialisation, i.e. the setting up of all the structures described in Fig. 11.3 for each class, is called in the application mainline stage. The generic `regclasses` which Eiffel** uses cannot be called until all the ERT information on the classes is available, so `regclasses` is called after ERT initialisation, as part of the Eiffel mainline. This means an interleaving of the two stages, GRT initialisation and application mainline.

11.3.3.2 Signals. The ERT installs signal handlers to deal with exceptions. For instance, to deal with segmentation violation, the signal handler will print a diagnostic attempting to show where the crash occurred, which could be, for example, an attempt to use an uninitialised pointer. The installation of these handlers is done at ERT initialisation. However, in an Eiffel** program, the GRT will have, as part of GRT initialisation, installed its own signal handlers. Thus, the ERT handlers will overwrite those of the GRT. This is because, at the present time, the GRT allows only one handler per signal. The ideal solution is to change the GRT to allow several handlers for a signal. The GRT would then have to be able to determine which handler to invoke, i.e. be aware of what is causing the signal, the ERT or the GRT. A good illustration of this is the case of `SIGALRM`, which the GRT uses to schedule threads. The ERT installs a handler for this which treats it like a segmentation violation, in that it will attempt to print a diagnostic and abort the program. Whenever a thread is scheduled, the program will be aborted. The temporary solution is to prevent the ERT from installing handlers for those signals that the GRT handles. The ideal solution is to allow the ERT install handlers for these signals, and the kernel will be able to determine which handler to call.

11.3.3.3 Special Objects and Heterogeneity. Figure 11.2 shows how special objects are used to implement an array object. The ERT uses a function `spAllocate(size)` to allocate special objects, which, unlike `Allocate` which is given the DT of the desired object, is passed the size required. This function has to be changed to put a GRT header on top of the object returned in order for it to persist. It invokes `persis_create` in order to do so, passing it the size. The cid in the special's GRT header is set to -1. Whereas the ERT keeps no data structures for special objects, the GRT registers a class descriptor for them and they must have a GRT class identifier and a global identifier in order to persist.

Another potential problem with special objects is that while it can be determined whether they contain expanded objects or references, if they contain expanded objects and these are instances of objects that carry no run time information (e.g. `INTEGER`) it is not possible to determine the type of the object. This would have serious implications for heterogeneity. For transferring and storing an object such as an array of integers on a heterogeneous network, it is necessary to convert it to a machine-independent form. To do so, one must be able to determine the types of its constituent parts. This is not currently supported in Eiffel**.

11.3.3.4 Garbage Collection. Eiffel links all the objects created in a linked list via the `link` field that exists in every object's header (c.f. Fig. 11.1). An application must be compiled with Eiffel garbage collection turned off (which is the Eiffel default). The `link` is not used and is ignored. At the moment, Eiffel garbage collection is disabled in Eiffel** making the `link` field redundant.

11.3.4 Compilation

To make use of all the GRT facilities, the Eiffel** programmer must use the SYSTEM class, an Eiffel class which is basically an interface to the GRT down-calls. An Eiffel** program must first generate a C package which consists of C code for all the classes in the system and C code for the ERT. This is necessary because ERT files must be altered in order to interface to Amadeus. The `makefile` produced is also edited to compile and link with Amadeus.

11.4 Distribution

This section discusses the implementation of distribution in Eiffel**. The approach adopted for distribution is similar to that for persistence in that an Eiffel** object can be *potentially* distributed. Distribution is transparent to the programmer. This requires generating a proxy routine for each exported routine in the class definition, as well as generating a `dispatch` routine for each class to handle incoming operations that have been initiated remotely. This means, however, that it is not possible to access the exported data attributes of an object remotely. Access to a remote object can only be through its exported routines.

11.4.1 Calling Mechanism

For each class a routines table for its proxy routines is set up that mirrors the true routines table of the class. A proxy function attempts to map in the real object or, if this is unsuccessful, to pack the parameters into a transmission block and perform a RPC. In this case the corresponding function will be invoked on the real object remotely, via the real object's `dispatch` routine. The routines table of Fig. 11.3 is expanded to include entries for the proxy code of all the classes in the system. The DT of the proxy code for a class C can be obtained

by the simple rule : DT_proxy = DT_C + num_classes. This gives the index for
the proxy code for the class C in the routines table.

When an object is already mapped into another context, attempting to map
the object into a different context will result in a *proxy* object being created.
The proxy object is the same size as the real object, but its data space is
uninitialised, resulting in some memory wastage but making it very easy to
overlay the proxy should the real object it represents become available to be
mapped in. The DT of the proxy object is equal to the DT of the true object
plus the number of classes in the system ensuring that invocation on the proxy
object will result in indirection through the proxy function table, as shown in
Fig. 11.5.

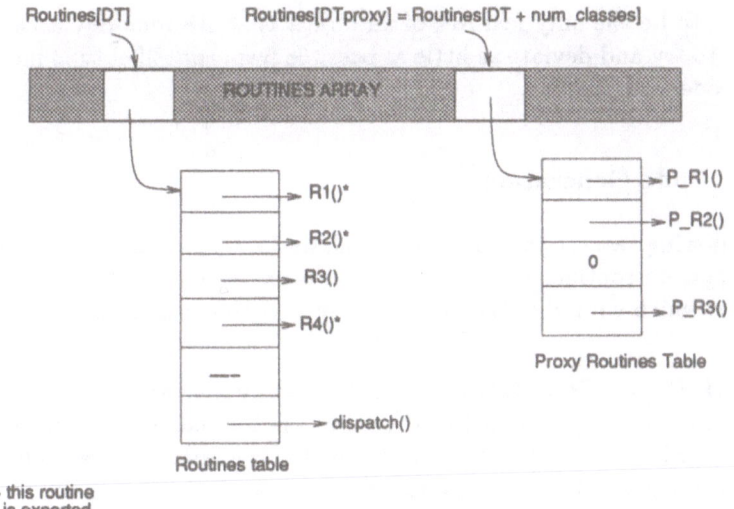

Fig. 11.5. Routines array.

Thus, the call:

$$x.func\ (args);$$

at the Eiffel** level becomes:

        (*Routines[Dynamic_type(x)][os])(x, args); ==
        (*Routines[DT + num_classes][os])(x, args);

at the ERT level.

This will result in the proxy function packing **args** into a transmission
block and performing an RPC. In the remote context, where the true object is
mapped, the GRT will up-call the true object's **dispatch** up-call, giving it the
transmission block which contains the parameters and indicates which function
to invoke. This in turn calls the **dispatch** routine which has been added to the
class's routines table, which finally invokes the specified routine on the object.
Then, possible return data is packed into a transmission block which is returned
to the calling context.

During routine calls between objects in different contexts, parameters are passed by reference, except for instances of the basic types which are passed by value. When passing an object reference, a *stub* for the object is passed in the transmission block (resulting in the object being promoted if not already so) enabling the remote object which is being invoked to access it. The lack of pointer variables in Eiffel, as well as its reference semantics, enable the passing of arbitrarily large objects between contexts by simply passing the stub for the object in all cases.

A draw-back of distribution is that remote access to an Eiffel** object can only be through its exported routines; direct access to its exported data items is not possible as the data-space of the proxy is uninitialised. This makes the Eiffel** type model weaker than the Eiffel type model in allowing just exported routines to be the only features of an object that are remotely accessible; it is an aim to try and deviate as little as possible from the Eiffel type model for the type model of Eiffel**.

11.4.2 Code Generation

The following two sections present templates for generating proxy routines and the dispatch routine. At the ERT level, parameters are treated in a uniform manner, which simplifies the generation of this code a great deal.

11.4.2.1 Proxy Code Generation. The proxy routine for each exported routine of a class C is positioned at the same offset in the proxy routines table as the routine it remotely invokes is positioned in the real routines table. All proxy routines are generated from the following proxy routine template:

```
<return_type> CLASSNAME_FUNCNAME_pr(void* current <arg_list>) {
<return_decl>
const int opid = ert_rout_index(current, FUNCNAME);
aon_oo *_t = ((aon_oo *)current)->object();

if (!amadeus.resolve(_t)) {
  Eiffel_aon_marshal aon_m(_t, opid, <arg_size>, <no_stubs>);
  <push_list>
  if (aon_m.rpc()) {
    <pop>
    return <return_id>;
  }
}
return (*Routines[ert_dynamic_type(current)][opid])
                              (current <arg_names>);
}
```

```
<return_type> -> datum | void

<arg_list>      -> nil
                -> ,datum IDENTIFIER <arg_list>

<return_decl> -> nil
                -> datum RETURN_NAME

<arg_size>      -> size_of(datum) * no. of ids. in <arg_list>
                    + size_of(datum) iff <return_decl> not nil

<no_stubs>      -> no. of object ids. in <arg_list>
                    + 1 iff <return_decl> not nil

<push_list>     -> nil
                -> aon_m.push(IDENTIFIER); <push_list>

<pop>           -> nil
                -> aon_m.nargs_reset();
                        RETURN_NAME = aon_m.pop();

<return_id>     -> nil
                -> RETURN_NAME

<arg_names>     -> nil
                -> <id_list>

<id_list>       -> IDENTIFIER
                -> <id_list>,IDENTIFIER
```

For each exported routine F in class definition C there will be a proxy function F_C_pr. The basic mechanism is that if the object cannot be mapped, the parameters plus the stub of the proxy (which will be identical to the stub of the real object, and enables the GRT at the remote node to locate the object) and the operation identifier (opid) are all packaged and a RPC is performed to the remote context where the true object is located. On completion of the RPC call, return data (if any) is popped and returned to the caller.

Parameters are treated in a uniform fashion. A check is made to see if the parameter being pushed is a reference to an object, and if so a stub for the object is pushed and a flag is set to indicate that this parameter is an object reference. When popping of parameters is taking place at the remote node, the dispatch routine will be able to distinguish between parameters that are object references and parameters that are instances of basic types.

11.4.2.2 Dispatch Code Generation. Each class's routines table must be augmented with a dispatch routine which is responsible for performing incoming remote invocations.

```
aon_tblock *CLASSNAME_dispatch(aon_tblock* b, void* current) {
 Eiffel_aon_marshal aon_m(((aon_oo*) current)->object(),b);
 int DT = ert_dynamic_type (current);
 switch(aon_m.which()) { <cases>
                         default:; }
 return b;
}
```

```
<cases>        -> <case_i><more_cases>

<more_cases>   -> <cases>
               -> nil

<case_i>       -> case <i>: { aon_UNLOCK 1;
                  <return_decl> <param_decl>
                  <pop_list> <func_call> <push>
                  } break;

<i>            -> no. in range 0..ert_routine_count(current)-1

<return_decl>  -> nil
               -> datum RETURN_NAME;

<param_decl>   -> nil
               -> datum <id_list>

<pop_list>     -> nil
               -> IDENTIFIER = aon_m.pop(); <pop_list>

<func_call>    -> <func_assign><func_call>

<func_assign>  -> nil
               -> RETURN_NAME =

<func_call>    -> (*Routines[DT][<i>])(current, <arg_names>)

<push>         -> nil // => <return_decl> & <func_assign> = nil
               -> aon_m.reset();
                  aon_m.nargs_reset();
                  aon_m.push(RETURN_NAME);
```

This code generation is implemented using the UNIX Yacc and Lex compiler development tools.

11.4.3 Up-calls for Distribution

Now that distribution has been discussed, the remainder of the generic up-call object definition can be presented as well as the up-call object definition for each proxy class. As stated before, all objects in the system contain the same up-call code. All proxy objects contain the same proxy up-call code.

The up-call object functions are as follows (note that `object()` returns a pointer to a GRT object, while `data()` returns a pointer to an Eiffel** object):

- `void deactivate() {object()->cid += num_classes;}`
  Switch cid in GRT header to be that of the proxy code.

- `void onuse() {ert_set_DT(data(),object()->cid);}`
  Set DT of the object to be cid in GRT header.

- ```
  aon_tblock *dispatch(aon_tblock *t) {
    return ((*Routines[ert_dynamic_type(data())]
                   [ert_routine_count(data())])(b, data())));
  }
  ```
  Up-call the object's dispatch routine.

The proxy up-call object functions are:

- `void activate() {object()->cid -= num_classes;}`
  Switch cid in GRT header to be that of the true code.

- `void onuse() {ert_set_DT(data(), object()->cid);}`
  Set DT of the object to be cid in GRT header.

Note that `activate` is called when the object is being mapped in, while `onuse` is called after an attempt to map the object in; this has resulted in a proxy being created, so the DT in the ERT header must be set to that of the proxy code, ensuring that subsequent invocations on this object will result in an indirection through the proxy routines table.

To support distribution, a class descriptor object for the proxy code as well as a class descriptor for the actual class must be registered with the GRT. The following is pseudo-code for the `regproxies` function, called as part of `regclasses` to register class descriptor objects for the proxy code of each class:

```
void regproxies() {
proxy_upcall_structure PUC;
class_descriptor       CD;

CD.upcall = PUC;

for (DTindex in 0 to num_classes -1) {
  CD.class_name = ert_name_by_DT(DTindex) + "proxy";
  CD.size = ert_size_by_DT (DTindex);
  CD.cid = DTindex + num_classes;
  Register (CD);
}
}
```
```

11.4.4 Problems in Distribution

This section outlines some problems related to heterogeneity and dynamic linking which arose in the implementation of distribution.

The treatment of parameters at the ERT level means it is impossible to distinguish between basic type instances, i.e. if a given datum is an INTEGER or a FLOAT or a CHARACTER. This has serious implications for heterogeneity, whereby it is necessary to determine the type of the given datum in order to package it for transferring between heterogeneous nodes. An up-call mechanism to determine the type of a given datum, if it is not an object reference, would be necessary in order to support heterogeneity.

The current scheme for the dynamic typing of proxy code depends on there being a fixed number of classes in the application at compile time. This scheme would be inconsistent if dynamic linking were introduced, whereby classes are linked in during execution of the program, rather than all being linked together at compile time which is currently what happens with Eiffel and Eiffel**.

11.5 Concurrency

This section discusses the implementation of concurrency in Eiffel**. The Eiffel** programmer's interface to concurrency is through class interfaces. To exploit concurrency in Eiffel** an object must use an instance of one of the concurrent classes (ACTIVITY or JOB) or inherit from them. The ACTIVITY and JOB interfaces provide for asynchronous invocation on an object and allow suspension/termination/resumption of the invocation as well as testing for invocation termination and recovery of invocation results.

11.5.1 Implementation

The following segment of code shows how an ACTIVITY instance is used to perform an asynchronous invocation on an object.

```
act : ACTIVITY;
    -- Somewhere in the code of some class
    -- a reference to an ACTIVITY object

act.Create(obj, "op1", 1, 2, A_ref);
    -- Create activity to do invocation:
    -- invoke routine "op1" of object obj

i := act.wait_int;
    -- Wait for the result
```

The invocation is initiated by calling the Create function of the ACTIVITY object. As arguments to the ACTIVITY's Create it must be able to take a reference to the object upon which the invocation is taking place, the name of the method that is being invoked and then the parameters for the invocation.

One complication in Eiffel** is the lack of variable sized parameter lists, and obviously the Create function of the concurrent classes must be able to take a variable number of parameters. The Eiffel** preprocessor captures all occurrences of ACTIVITY creation in an Eiffel** file and replaces the variable parameter list in the ACTIVITY Create call with an argument object reference. The argument object will be declared immediately after the ACTIVITY declaration, and code is produced to push each of the parameters onto the argument object. After preprocessing, the above code will look like :

```
act : ACTIVITY;

arg : ARG_OBJ;
    -- Create an object to store the parameters
    -- to an asynchronous object invocation

arg.PushINTEGER(1);
arg.PushINTEGER(2);
arg.PushOBJECT(A_ref);
    -- Insert parameters into argument object

act.Create(obj, "op1", arg);
        -- Variable sized argument list stored in arg
```

This is simply a translation from incorrect Eiffel code to Eiffel code that will be acceptable to the Eiffel compiler.

11.6 Transactions

This section describes the implementation of the transactional facility in Eiffel**.

Like persistence and distribution, the approach taken for transactions is that all objects in an Eiffel** system are potentially atomic. An object can be promoted to being atomic at any time.

```
make_atomic (i);
    -- Make it atomic by making a down-call to the GRT
    -- This make_atomic routine is inherited from class
    -- AMADEUS which is the Eiffel** interface to the GRT.
```

As in the case of distribution, the Eiffel** preprocessor generates an atomic routine for every exported routine in a class's definition, and sets up a routine table for these atomic routines. This table will be accessed at run time by a DT for the atomic code. Making an object atomic involves switching its DT to the DT for the atomic code, so subsequent invocations will indirect through the atomic routines table.

When an invocation is made on an atomic object, the atomic routine locates the actual routine (by calculating the true DT), invokes it and returns results to the caller.

Because accesses to atomic objects are trapped through functions, a similar restriction to distribution applies in that access to an atomic object should only be through its exported routines. So atomic objects should only be accessed through their class's exported routines.

Distribution and transactions imply that a class will have three DTs, one for accessing the class methods (i.e. the real DT as assigned by the ERT), one for the proxy code and one for the atomic code. The DT of the atomic code can be obtained by the following simple rule: DT_atomic_code = DT + 2 * num_classes. The consequence of this is that in the Eiffel** run-time, the Routines table is three times as big as the equivalent one for Eiffel, due to the fact that each class in Eiffel** has proxy code to support distribution and atomic code to support transactions.

The generic up-call object definition includes the following function:

    void make_atomic{ert_set_DT(data(),object()->cid+num_classes*2;}

which is up-called by the GRT as part of the make_atomic down-call. It sets the DT of the object to the DT for the atomic code to ensure that further invocations on the object will indirect through the atomic routines table.

The Eiffel** programmer's interface to using transactions is through the TRANSACTION class interface. The transaction interface is synchronous, but in other respects it is similar to the job and activity interface, especially with regards to creating a transaction to perform an invocation on an object.

The means of starting a transaction on an object is identical to that for starting an activity on the object, and the same complication exists as with the ACTIVITY class interface with the need to be able to pass variable sized parameter lists to the transaction's Create feature. Transaction creations are caught by the preprocessor and filtered out in the same way ACTIVITY and JOB creations are.

The TRANSACTION_OPTIONS class provides programmers with an interface enabling them to alter the transaction state and thus control the way the transaction behaves.

11.7 Conclusion

Eiffel** provides an object-oriented, persistent, distributed, concurrent and transactional programming language environment with Eiffel as the programming language model. Eiffel** was intended to support all the features of the underlying environment without altering or compromising the Eiffel programming language and model. The extent of information provided by the ERT has enabled this goal to be achieved with minimum violation of the given constraint (c.f. Sects 5.1 and 7). It has been possible to implement Eiffel** without making changes to the Eiffel compiler or language, and with only minimal changes to the ERT.

Existing Eiffel programs and software components can be taken and used in the Eiffel∗∗ environment without any alteration, a feature that is consistent with Eiffel's philosophy of software reusability and modularity. The mechanisms of persistence, distribution, concurrency and transactions are all transparent to the Eiffel∗∗ programmer. The programmer can interact with the underlying environment using supplied classes. The programming model of Eiffel∗∗ remains faithful to that of Eiffel, with the exception of the restriction of non-data access for remote and atomic objects.

12. Conclusions

This book provided a general presentation of the Comandos distributed application platform. The first part focused on the description of the functionality provided by the platform, design choices and innovative aspects. The second part gave an overview of the implementation of the platform.

This last chapter summarises the main benefits expected from the use of the Comandos platform and outlines some of the achievements of the Comandos project both from the industrial and academic points of view.

12.1 The Challenge of Distributed Computing and the Promise of the Comandos Technology

Networking is undergoing tremendous changes. The emergence of LANs stimulated the development of distributed applications as connection to a network became easy and inexpensive. The speed and availability of network technologies have increased and continue to improve. As a result, distributed applications with similar distribution requirements have evolved in many application domains such as computer aided design, office and business systems, concurrent engineering and software engineering. In fact, most real world applications are distributed by nature. Only the limited capabilities of networked systems have, up to now, restricted users to centralised systems.

The distributed systems sector is growing faster than most other sectors of the computer industry. The market is forecast to be 9 BECUs in Europe by 1995, 80% of which will be for software and services.

Computer users require a communications environment that will allow information to flow from wherever it is stored to wherever it is needed, without unnecessarily exposing the complexity of the network to the end user, the system manager, or the application developer. To encourage and support the development of distributed applications, various computing models and architectures have been proposed over the last few years, for example, the OSF's DCE. This architectural framework (as well as the earlier OSI standards) represent a major step in the evolution of distributed systems, as it allows inter-operability across heterogeneous environments.

Today the lack of an integrated, high-level set of development tools for use in a distributed heterogeneous environment prohibits full exploitation of this emerging technology. This is because current distributed environments (including DCE) are very complex to use for application programming. On the other hand, existing software engineering methodologies and tools do not fulfill the specific requirements of distribution, and the development of distributed applications is still a difficult and cost intensive task. Therefore, providing a rich development environment, encompassing a wide variety of heterogeneous platforms, is a major challenge that the industry faces.

The overall objective of the Comandos project was to specify and construct an integrated platform for programming and operating multi-vendor distributed systems. This platform is targeted at application programmers and system integrators, and aims to reduce the overall cost of the development, maintenance, and evolution of large distributed applications. The Comandos platform allows both the development of new applications, and the reuse of existing (UNIX-oriented) applications.

12.2 Benefits of the Comandos Technology

The Comandos technology has been in use for several years in different real-world environments both inside and outside of the consortium. This experience, as well as the lessons drawn from the study of the state of the art, has shown the main benefits expected from the use of the Comandos technology for the development of new distributed applications. In the context of Comandos "new applications" apply both to newly designed applications and existing centralised applications which are redesigned for a distributed environment.

This section outlines these benefits both from the application developer and end-user points of view.

12.2.1 Main Benefits for the Application Developer

The primary objective of the Comandos technology is to reduce the cost of the development and maintenance of distributed applications. This is achieved by providing the application developer with:

- a rich computational model, which goes far beyond the classical client-server model, and which encompasses both data modelling and distributed computations;
- distribution transparency;
- persistence, which frees the application developer from explicitly saving and loading long-lived data;
- management of complex objects;
- separation between mechanisms and policies, which allows a given Comandos configuration to be tailored to specific application requirements;
- linguistic support, and associated development tools, which together allow the rapid and safe development of reusable distributed application components;

- inter-operability with UNIX applications, which protects customer's investments when using this new advanced environment.

In addition, application developers can take advantage of the numerous and well-known benefits provided by the object-oriented approach which has been followed by Comandos.

12.2.2 Main Benefits for the End-user

Although the Comandos project was initially targeted at office and business systems, the experience drawn so far has convinced us that the Comandos technology is also valuable as a basis for integrated information systems in such other application domains as computer aided design and software engineering.

The features provided by the Comandos technology are especially suited for CSCW applications, which involve the management of complex shared data structures (of variable granularity) by cooperating users. These benefits have been illustrated by several large-scale groupware applications developed in the framework of the project.

12.3 Industrial Achievements

A strategic result of the Comandos project was the demonstration of working prototypes of the Comandos platform, thus proving its feasibility on a number of underlying host environments. The prototype platform is now used in many companies and research institutes throughout Europe.

The Comandos technology has been submitted to several requests for technology issued by the Open Software foundation and the Object Management Group. This served to publicise the work of the project and facilitated the export of the Comandos technology on a world-wide basis.

The Comandos project has contributed to the competitiveness of European industry both by the use of Comandos results and also by the provision of highly trained employees in distributed systems. Many of the companies are using the results from Comandos either in future products or are marketing individual results as stand alone products.

Bull is using results of Comandos to enhance their Distributed Computing Model with an object-oriented platform and development environment. In addition, the Distributed Directory Service (c.f. Chap. 7) developed in Comandos is being used directly to provide a building block for their Integrated System Management facilities.

To offer its customers comprehensive solutions and products combining hardware as well as software, Siemens Corporate Research has an important task in observing new trends and technology in diverse subjects. Secure distributed systems will play an important role in many segments of Siemens market. Siemens Corporate Research obtained much experience and competence in the areas of distributed systems, object-oriented programming and security by working in the Comandos project and thus are better able to transfer this technology to the product divisions of Siemens. In addition to this general result Comandos has enabled Siemens to develop three major tools: The Distributed Directory Service has been adapted for use by the Automation Systems division. The Protocol Data Analysis Tool is now ready for testing in a real application environment and there is significant interest in bringing it to the market. A prototype of the Comprehensive Risk Management Tool will be used in further research projects and is receiving strong interest from several of the company's product divisions.

Chorus Systèmes's work within the Comandos project has had two distinct effects: The first has been the influence on its core technology, the CHORUS micro-kernel and the distributed UNIX system called MiX. In particular, techniques developed for the Comandos kernel have directly influenced aspects of the current micro-kernel design. Further, the services provided by the COOL implementation of the Comandos architecture are being evaluated as a means of improving the structure of the multi-server MiX implementation. Secondly, Chorus Systèmes is committed to commercialising the COOL platform as an application environment running alongside the MiX system. An initial version of this platform is already in beta release and products are planned for 1993.

SEPT, along with other French partners are using their results in the French national project AMBIANCE, which is entirely funded by the French PTT. The basis of AMBIANCE will be a distributed object system for use in the telecommunications area, which will be used by pilot clients in 1993.

Industrial activities are conducted in the Computer Integrated Business (CIB) framework of Fraunhofer-IAO and Universitaet Stuttgart (IAT). IAT have provided consultation to user organisations in the field of distributed, open systems. Consulting activities included the transfer of Comandos concepts and software components. Various contacts to manufacturers in the information technology sector have been established. Further joint development of the Comandos management tools developed by Fraunhofer has started and will be continued.

IONA Technologies Ltd is a new company founded in March 1991 by key members from the Distributed Systems Group, Trinity College Dublin. This has become possible through their participation in Comandos. IONA Technologies is a "technology retailer" and is bringing a commercial and industrial strength distributed, object-based platform to the market. This platform will be CORBA compliant.

The principal benefit of the Comandos project for the OSF Research Institute has been to provide information on the use of the Mach micro-kernel technology for the construction of an object-oriented platform for distributed applications. Until recently, very little experience had been available concerning the use of Mach other than as an infrastructure for operating system servers. The Comandos project has provided an opportunity to test the technology in circumstances where the Mach mechanisms such as virtual memory management and IPC are exercised in a different way from that of an operating system server. In addition, experiments have been carried out with servers which use Mach services directly, as well as using (UNIX) operating system services. Finally, an evaluation has been made of some of the performance benefits of building such platforms directly over the Mach micro-kernel, rather than over a traditional monolithic operating system, which provides less direct access to the basic services required by the Comandos kernel.

12.4 Research Achievements

The Comandos project has integrated operating system, programming language and database technologies in order to provide an integrated platform for distributed applications. The object paradigm was used in all aspects of the project from application construction to the units of storage.

Comandos has contributed to the state of the art in (distributed) operating systems, programming languages, data management, and security and administration tools. This claim is supported by the large number of Ph.D and Masters theses and published papers originating from the project (c.f. App. E). Specific achievements include:

- the definition of a conceptual model of, and an architecture for, an integrated applications support environment supporting the construction of distributed, persistent object-oriented applications;
- a demonstration that the construction of such an environment is feasible both on UNIX systems and using micro-kernel technology;
- the implementation of a Generic Run-time system which facilitates the use of existing and new object-oriented languages, for the development of distributed and persistent applications, without requiring each language to adopt a common object model or invocation mechanism;
- the implementation of a new language specifically aimed at the construction of distributed applications involving shared persistent data;
- the definition and implementation of a novel object-oriented data model including binary relations as collections;
- the definition of a canonical type model suitable for capturing the type models of object-oriented programming languages and the implementation of a type manager supporting cross-language invocation.
- the implementation and integration of a collection of sophisticated tools for distributed application development and system administration.

Appendix

Appendix

A. Example Programs

As an example of the use of the programming languages supported by the Comandos platform this section presents an example distributed application programmed using each of the supported languages – C++, Eiffel and Guide.

The example itself is based on a distributed mail system. This choice was dictated by the following considerations:

- the example should illustrate the major features of the Comandos model - transparent distribution, persistence and atomicity;
- the example should be based on a realistic application with which most readers will be familiar;
- the example should be simple enough to keep the programs small allowing (most of) the source code to be given.

The choice of a single application example allows us to illustrate the similarities and the differences between the supported languages. The example should not, however, be construed as a real life illustration of the application domain. Such a case study has already been described in Chap. 8. Moreover the application does not illustrate the full functionality of the Comandos platform. In particular, concurrency and security are not addressed.

A.1 Specification of the SimpleMail Application

The application provides a mail service to a set of users on a network of computers. The following functions are provided for each user registered with the service:

- transmission of mail to other registered users;
- reception of mail from other registered users.

The set of users is assumed to be fixed (no addition or deletion of users is provided).

The following requirements were imposed on the mailing system:

- Transparency: a user may use any machine; messages may be stored on any machine; distribution should be completely invisible to users.
- Flexibility: the mailing system should support different naming schemes and different message formats.

In order to meet these requirements, the SimpleMail application is designed as a set of objects (c.f. Fig. A.1) relying on the underlying system to support transparent distribution and persistence. The following classes of objects are defined.

- **Message** objects implement messages. There is one object per message (messages sent to multiple destinations need not be duplicated). **Message** objects are both remotely accessible and potentially persistent.
- **Mailbox** objects are collections of (references to) messages. There is one **Mailbox** object per registered user. Again **Mailbox** objects are remotely accessible and potentially persistent.
- **Mail_Directory** objects provide the association between user names and mailboxes. There is actually a single object of this class in the application. The **Mail_Directory** object is remotely accessible and persistent.
- **Mailer** objects provide the interface to the mail services for active users. There is one **Mailer** object per active user. **Mailer** objects are remotely accessible but need not be persistent - a new **Mailer** object can be created for each user session.

In addition a number of library and other classes are used in the application.

The **Mail_Directory** class provides at least the following methods:

- a constructor – called on object creation; initialises an empty directory;
- **add_item(name:string,value:any)** – inserts a (name,value) pair into the directory;
- **get_value(name):any** – returns the value associated with the given name (or nil);
- **remove_item(name)** – removes a (name,value) pair, if present.

The **Mail_Directory** class may be derived from an existing **Directory** class, if available, or make use of an existing name service.

In order to illustrate the flexibility provided by inheritance, a generic **Text** class is assumed to be available, with the following methods:

- a constructor – called on object creation; initialises an empty text;
- **edit** – calls an interactive text editor;
- **display** – displays the text.

Class **Message** may then be defined as a subclass of **Text** and additional methods defined where necessary.

Class **Mailbox** has at least three methods:

- a constructor – called on object creation; initialises an empty mailbox;
- **insert(ref)** – inserts a (reference to a) message in the mailbox;
- **remove(ref)** – removes a (reference to a) message from the mailbox.

The relationships between the objects that make up the SimpleMail application are illustrated in Fig. A.1.

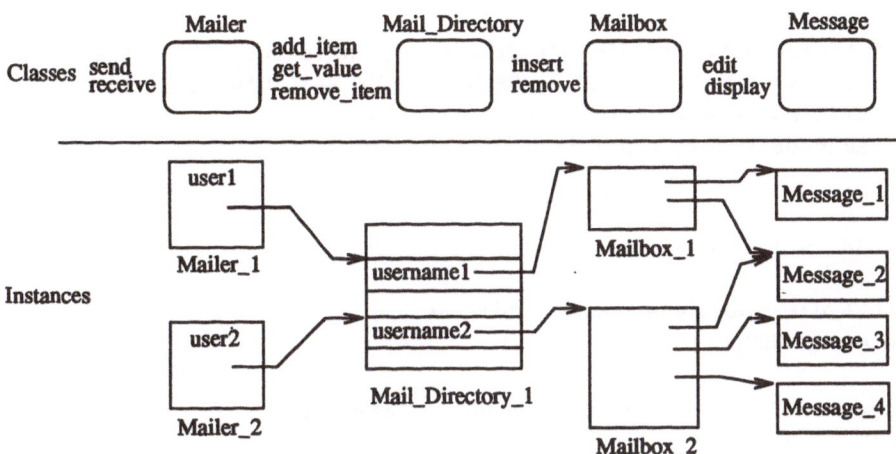

Fig. A.1. The SimpleMail application.

A.2 C++

Note that support for fault tolerance in the C** mail application is provided by use of atomic objects and transactions. All the persistent state maintained by the application is held by atomic objects. Thus all instances of the classes **Mail_Directory, MailBox**, and **Message** used by the application are atomic objects. All the operations that modify these atomic objects must be run in transactions. In fact, the operations chosen to be run in transactions correspond to the operations available to users of the application. Thus, the operations **send**, receive, list_mail, and remove_mail from class **Mailer** all run as transactions. Each time the application is run, a list of registered users it output. This operation is not run in a transaction since it is a read-only operation.

A.2.1 Application Mainline

```
#include "mailer.h"
#include "transaction.h"

int main() {

  Mail_Directory *mail_dir ;    // Mail directory object
  Mailer *my_mailer ;           // User interface to mail service
  Output *o ;
  char name[20] ;
  int i ;
  char ch ;
```

```
if (amadeus.reset()) {  // Create mail directory first time run
  cout << " MAIL SYSTEM -- CREATING NEW MAIL DIRECTORY \n" ;
  mail_dir = new {ATOMIC} Mail_Directory () ;
  amadeus.record ("dir.ns", mail_dir) ;
}

cout << " MAIL SYSTEM \n" ;

mail_dir = amadeus.lookup ("dir.ns") ;
o = new Output () ;

cout << "\nPlease enter your user name>>" ;
cin >> name ;

my_mailer = new Mailer (name, mail_dir) ;

transaction T;

while (1) {
 cout << " \n **** MAILING SERVICE **** \n" ;
 cout << " \n List of registered users \n" ;
 mail_dir->list_users (o) ;
 cout << " USER : " << name << "\n" ;
 cout << " Mailing Commands : \n" ;
 cout << " S) Send mail \t\t R) Remove mail \n" ;
 cout << " D) Show mail \t\t L) List all mail headers\n" ;
 cout << " C) Clear screen \t X) Exit\n" ;
 cout << " Enter Choice >> " ;
 cin >> ch ;


 switch (ch) {
  case 'S' :
       cout << " \n *** Send Mail ***\n" ;
       // perform my_mailer->send() in a transaction
       T.begin(my_mailer, Send_ID);
       if (T.bad()) cout << "Failed to send mail\n";
       break ;
  case 'D' :
       cout << "\n *** Display a Mail ***\n" ;
       // perform my_mailer->receive() in a transaction
       T.begin(my_mailer, Receive_ID);
       if (T.bad()) cout << "Failed to display mail\n";
       break ;
```

```
    case 'R' :
        cout << "\n *** Remove a Mail ***\n" ;
        // perform my_mailer->remove_mail() in a transaction
        T.begin(my_mailer, RemoveMail_ID);
        if (T.bad()) cout << "Failed to remove mail\n";
        break ;
    case 'L' :
        cout << "\n *** List Mailbox headers ***\n" ;
        // perform my_mailer->list_mail() in a transaction
        T.begin(my_mailer, ListMail_ID);
        if (T.bad()) cout << "Failed to list mail\n";
        break ;
    case 'X' :
        cout << "...EXITING\n" ;
        amadeus.exit () ;
    case 'C' :
        system ("clear") ;    // Use UNIX command to clear screen
        break ;
    default :
        cout << "???\n" ;
  }
 }
 cout << "...BYE\n" ;
}
```

A.2.2 Class Mailer

```
#ifndef mailer_h
#define mailer_h

#include "mail_directory.h"
#include <time.h>
#include <stream.h>

// Mailer class. Provides the interface to the mail system for
// active users. There is a Mailer object created for each user
// when they run the application.

class Mailer {
 private :
  Mail_Directory *dir ;     // System-wide mail directory.
  Mailbox *my_box ;         // User's mailbox.
  char my_name[NAME_LEN] ;  // User's mail name.
  Output *o ;
```

```
char **get_mail_list (int num) const;
    // Read and return a list of 'num' mail names.
    // --Used by send().

void post_to_list (char **list, Message *mail) ;
    // Post given message to each name in given list.

public :
Mailer (char *name, Mail_Directory *d) ;
    // Look up the mail directory, get mapping for
    // my mailbox. If one does not exist, create it.

// The next 5 operations are used to create transactions
// (the _IDs must match the operations' identifiers)

global void create(const char *name, Mail_Directory *d);
    // invoked as a transaction from the constructor
#define Create_ID        0

global void send ();
#define Send_ID          1
    // Create a new message. For each destination and cc,
    // find mailbox using mail directory and insert message
    // into mailbox.

global void receive ();
#define Receive_ID       2
    // Display a mail message.

global void list_mail ();
#define ListMail_ID      3
    // List all the mail headers in the users mailbox.

global void remove_mail ();
#define RemoveMail_ID    4
    // Remove a mail message from the users mailbox.
} ;
#endif
```

```
#include "mailer.h"
#include "transaction.h"

void error (char *s, char *t) {
 cout << "ERROR " << s << " " << t << "\n" ;
}

Mailer::Mailer (char* name, Mail_Directory *d) {
 // Mailer : constructor
 // calls the create operation in a transaction

 transaction T(this, Create_ID, ArgList + name + d);
 if (T.bad()) cout << "Failed to create mailer\n";
}

void Mailer::create (const char* name, Mail_Directory *d) {
 // Get users mailbox from mail directory. If one does not exist,
 // register a new mailbox for this user with the mail directory.

 dir = d ;
 if ((my_box = dir->get_value (name)) == (Mailbox *)0) {
    cout << "Inserting Mailbox for " << name << "\n" ;
    my_box = new Mailbox();
    // each mailbox should be an atomic object
    amadeus.create_atomic(my_box);
    dir->add_item (name, my_box) ;
 }
 strcpy (my_name, name) ;
 o = new Output () ;
}

char **Mailer::get_mail_list (int num) const {
 // Private function to read and return a list of mail names.

 char **mail_names = (char **)malloc (MAX_DESTS) ;

 for (int i = 0; i < num ; i++) {
     cout << " Enter mail name " << i+1 << "  >> " ;
     mail_names[i] = new char[12] ;
     cin >> mail_names[i] ;
 }
 mail_names[i] = (char *) NULL ;
 return mail_names ;
}
```

```
void Mailer::post_to_list (char **list, Message *mail) {
 // Private function to post to each name in the given list.

 Mailbox *target ;

 for (int i = 0; list[i] ; i++) {
  if ((target = dir->get_value (list[i])) == NULL)
     error(list[i], " -- no such user; no mail sent") ;
  else
     target->insert (mail) ;
  delete list[i] ;
 }
}

void Mailer::send ()  {
 // Format and dispatch a mail message.

 char sender[NAME_LEN], **destinations, **ccs ;
                   // Data for creating messages.
 int  no_dests, no_ccs, i ;
 Message *m ;
 Mailbox *target ;

 cout << " Enter number of destinations >> " ;
 cin >> no_dests ;
 cout << " Enter number of carbon copies >> " ;
 cin >> no_ccs ;

 destinations = get_mail_list (no_dests) ;
 ccs = get_mail_list (no_ccs) ;

 m = new Message(destinations, no_dests, ccs, no_ccs,
                                 my_name, dir->get_id()) ;
 // each message is an atomic object
 amadeus.create_atomic(m);

 post_to_list (destinations, m) ;
 post_to_list (ccs, m) ;
}

void Mailer::list_mail () {
 my_box->list(o) ;
}
```

```
void Mailer::receive () {
 int id ;

 cout << " Enter message id ::" ;
 cin >> id ;
 my_box->read_msg (id, o) ;
}

void Mailer::remove_mail () {
 int id ;

 cout << " Enter message id ::" ;
 cin >> id ;
 cout << "Mail number " << id  ;
 cout << (my_box->remove (id) ? " removed\n" : " not found\n") ;
}
```

A.2.3 Class Mail_Directory

The following version of class Mail_Directory makes use of the Amadeus lookup and record operations to actually maintain the relationship between the names of users and their mailboxes.

Mail_Directory is also responsible for the allocation of unique identifiers for mail messages which can be used by users of the program to refer to individual messages.

```
#ifndef mail_directory_h
#define mail_directory_h

#include "mailbox.h"
#include "pint.h"

// Mail directory class.
// Maintains association between user name and mailbox.

permclass Mail_Directory {
   int users ;        // Keeps track of current number
                      // of users in the system.
   pint *glob_id ;  // For generating message ids.
   char names[MAX_USERS][NAME_LEN];  // User names.

 public :
   Mail_Directory () ; // Initialise private data.
```

```
  global void add_item (const char *name, Mailbox *value) ;
        // Create and register mailbox for 'name',
        // increment users

  global Mailbox *get_value (const char *name) const;
        // Return mailbox associated with 'name',
        // NULL if there is none registered

  global int remove_item (const char *name) ;
        // removes value associated with 'name'.

  global void list_users (Output *o) const;
        // List all names in 'names' array

  global int get_id () { return (*glob_id)++ ; }
        // Return unique id
} ;

#endif
#include "mail_directory.h"

Mail_Directory::Mail_Directory() {
 glob_id = new {ATOMIC} pint(1) ;
 users = 0 ;
}

void Mail_Directory::add_item(const char *name, Mailbox *value) {
 // Check first that adding a new item does not excced the
 // maximum number of names or that the given name is not
 // already recorded.
 if (users+1 == MAX_USERS) {
    cout << "No more users possible\n" ;
    return ;
 }

 for (int i = 0; i < users; i++)
    if (strcmp(name, names[i]) == 0)
      return ;

 strcpy(names[users], name) ;
 amadeus.record(names[users++], value) ;
}
```

```
Mailbox *Mail_Directory::get_value(const char *name) const {
// Return the value associated with the given name, returning
// NULL if a value for this name is not found.

 for (int i = 0; i < users; i++)
    if (strcmp(name, names[i]) == 0)
      return amadeus.lookup(names[i]) ;
 return (Mailbox *) NULL ;
}

int Mail_Directory::remove_item(const char *name) {
// When given name is found, copy down all higher placed names,
// decrment the no. of active users and return 1 to indicate
// successful removal.

 for (int i = 0; i < users; i++)
    if (strcmp(name, names[i]) == 0) {
      while (i < users - 1)  {
         strcpy(names[i], names[i+1]) ;
         i++ ;
      }
      users-- ;
      return 1 ;
    }
 return 0 ;
}

void Mail_Directory::list_users(Output *o) const {
// Use given output object to list all registered names.

 o->PrintString("\nRegistered mail users\n") ;
 for (int i = 0; i < users; i++) {
    o->PrintString(names[i]) ;
    o->PrintString("\n") ;
 }
}
```

A.2.4 Class Mailbox

```
#ifndef mailbox_h
#define mailbox_h

#include "message.h"
#define MAX_MSGS 40

// User's mailbox object.
// Holds lists of references to read and unread messages.

permclass Mailbox {
 private :
  Message *unread_messages[MAX_MSGS] ;
     // Array of unread messages.
  Message *read_messages[MAX_MSGS] ;
     // Array of read messages.
  void move_message(int i) ;
     // Move message at index i in unread list to read list.
 public :
  Mailbox() ;

  global int insert (Message *message) ;
     // Add message to unread list

  global int read_msg (int id, Output *o);
     // Display message with given id
     // If message on unread list, move it to read list

  global int remove (int id) ;
     // Remove message with the given id

  global void list (Output *o) const;
     // For each message on read and unread lists,
     // call the display_header method.
} ;
#endif

#include "mailbox.h"

Mailbox::Mailbox() {
 // Mailbox Constructor : Initialise all message slots to NULL.

 for (int i = 0 ;i < MAX_MSGS; i++)
  unread_messages[i] = read_messages[i] = NULL ;
}
```

```
int Mailbox::insert(Message *message) {
// Find an unused slot in the unread message list and insert
// the given message here.

 for (int i = 0; i < MAX_MSGS; i++)
  if (unread_messages[i] == NULL) {
       unread_messages[i] = message ;
       return 1 ;
  }
 return 0 ;
}

void Mailbox::move_message(int i) {
// Move message at given index in the unread messages list
// to an unused place in the read messages list.

 for (int j = 0; j < MAX_MSGS; j++)
  if (read_messages[j] == NULL) {
       read_messages[j] = unread_messages[i] ;
       unread_messages[i] = NULL ;
  }
}

int Mailbox::read_msg(int id, Output *o) {
// Search both message lists for the message with the given id,
// and use the given output object to display it if it is found.

 for (int i = 0; i < MAX_MSGS; i++) {
  if (unread_messages[i] && unread_messages[i]->get_id() == id) {
     unread_messages[i]->display(o) ;
     move_message(i) ;
     return 1 ;
  }
  if (read_messages[i] && read_messages[i]->get_id() == id) {
     read_messages[i]->display(o) ;
     return 1 ;
  }
 }
 return 0 ;
}
```

```
int Mailbox::remove(int id) {
// Search both message lists for the message with the given id,
// and annul its slot when and if the message is found.

 for (int i = 0; i < MAX_MSGS; i++) {
  if (unread_messages[i] && unread_messages[i]->get_id() == id) {
    unread_messages[i] = NULL ;
    return 1 ;
  }
  if (read_messages[i] && read_messages[i]->get_id()== id) {
    read_messages[i] = NULL ;
    return 1 ;
  }
 }
 return 0
}


void Mailbox::list(Output *o) const {
// Use given output object to display every message header.

 for (int i = 0; i < MAX_MSGS; i++) {
  if (unread_messages[i])
    unread_messages[i]->display_header(o) ;
  if (read_messages[i])
    read_messages[i]->display_header(o) ;
 }
}
```

A.2.5 Class Message

```
#ifndef message_h
#define message_h

#include "objs.h"
#define MAX_USERS 8
#define MAX_DESTS MAX_USERS
#define DEST_LEN 16
#define MAX_CC MAX_USERS -1
#define NAME_LEN DEST_LEN
```

```
// Message class. includes destination and cc list, sender,
// id and timestamp as well as a text object.

permclass Message : public Text {
 private :
  char destinations[MAX_DESTS][DEST_LEN] ;
  char cc[MAX_CC][DEST_LEN] ;
  char sender[NAME_LEN] ;
  int timestamp ;
  int message_id ;
  int no_dests, no_ccs ;

 public :
  Message (char *dests[],
           int num_dests,
           char *ccs[],
           int num_ccs,
           char* sndr,
           int id) ;
      // Initialise header data with given message data
      // and edit inherited text object.

  global int display (Output *o) const;
      // Display header data and text using given output object.

  global void set_id (int id) ;
      // Set message_id to given id

  global int get_id () const;
      // Return message_id.

  global int display_header (Output *o) const;
      // Display header data using given output object.
} ;

#endif
```

```
#include "message.h"

Message::Message (char *dests[], int num_dests,
                  char *ccs[], int num_ccs,
                  char* sndr, int id) : Text(id) {
 int i ;
 for (i = 0; i < num_dests; i++)
   strcpy (destinations[i], dests[i]) ;
 for (i = 0; i < num_ccs; i++)
   strcpy (cc[i], ccs[i]) ;
 strcpy (sender, sndr) ;
 message_id = id ;
 no_dests = num_dests ;
 no_ccs = num_ccs ;
 edit () ;
}

void Message::set_id (int id) {
 message_id = id ;
}

int Message::get_id () const {
 return message_id  ;
}

int Message::display_header (Output *o) const {
 int i ;
 o->PrintString("\nTo: ") ;
 for (i = 0; i < no_dests; i++) {
   o->PrintString (destinations[i]) ;
   o->PrintString(", ") ;
 }
 o->PrintString("\ncc: ") ;
 for (i = 0; i < no_ccs; i++) {
   o->PrintString (cc[i]) ;
   o->PrintString(", ") ;
 }
 o->PrintString ("\nFrom : ") ;
 o->PrintString (sender) ;
 o->PrintString ("\nTime : ") ;
 o->PrintInt (timestamp) ;
 o->PrintString ("\nMessage Id: ") ;
 o->PrintInt (message_id) ;
 o->PrintString ("\n-----\n") ;
}
```

```
int Message::display (Output *o) const {
 display_header (o) ;
 Text::display (o) ;
 return 1 ;
}
```

A.2.6 Utility and Library Classes

A number of library classes – Output, pint and Text – are used by the application. Only class Text is given in full here. The main point of interest is the use of a standard UNIX editor – vi – to edit the contents of an instance of Text.

```
#ifndef text_h
#define text_h

#include <stream.h>
#define MAXLEN 256
#include <amadeus.h>

// Text class. A Text object is used as the body of a message.

class Text {
 private :
  char filename [MAXLEN] ;

 public  :
  Text (char* buffer) ;
      // set filename to given string.

  Text (int file_id) ;
      // set filename to given integer.

  int edit () const;
      // Invoke vi editor on filename.

  int display (Output *o) const;
      // display contents of filename.
} ;
#endif
```

```
#include "text.h"

Text::Text (char* buffer) {
 strcpy (filename, buffer) ;
}

Text::Text (int file_id) {
 sprintf (filename, "%d", file_id) ;
}

int Text::edit () const {
 char vi_file[20] ;
 sprintf (vi_file, "vi %s", filename) ;
 system (vi_file) ;
 return 1 ;
}

int Text::display (Output *o) const {
 o->PrintFile (filename) ;
 return 1 ;
}
```

A.3 Eiffel

A.3.1 Application Mainline

```
class ROOT
 -- Root class for the mail system

inherit
 AMADEUS

feature

 m : MAILER ;             -- User interface to mail system
 mail_dir : MAIL_DIRECTORY ;
 user_name : STRING ; -- User name

 Create is
  do
   if reset = 1
    then
     io.putstring ("CREATING NEW MAIL DIRECTORY\n") ;
     mail_dir.Create ;
     record ("dir.ns", mail_dir)
    else
     mail_dir ?= lookup ("dir.ns") ;
     io.putstring (" *** Mail Service *** \n\n") ;
     io.putstring (" Please Enter your name >> ") ;
     io.readline ;
     user_name.Create (io.laststring.count) ;
     user_name.set (io.laststring, 1, io.laststring.count) ;
     m.Create (user_name, mail_dir) ;
     interact
   end ;
  end ;
```

```
 interact is
  local
   stop : BOOLEAN   ;
   request : CHARACTER
  do
   from
    stop := false
   until
    stop
   loop
    io.putstring ("USER : ") ;
    io.putstring (user_name) ;
    io.putstring(" \n Enter next command (one character) \n");
    io.putstring(" E) for enter message \n") ;
    io.putstring(" R) to Read a message \n") ;
    io.putstring(" L) to List messages \n") ;
    io.putstring(" D) to delete a message \n") ;
    io.putstring(" Q) for Quit >> ") ;
    io.input.readchar ;
    request := io.input.lastchar;
    io.input.readchar ;
    inspect request
     when 'E', 'e' then
      io.putstring ("\n\n Post Message \n") ;
      m.send
     when 'L', 'l' then
      io.putstring ("\n\n ** Scan Mail ** \n\n") ;
      m.list_mail
     when 'D', 'd' then
      io.putstring ("\n\n ** Remove Mail ** \n\n") ;
      m.remove_mail
     when 'R', 'r' then
      io.putstring ("\n\n ** Read Mail ** \n\n") ;
      m.receive
     when 'Q', 'q' then
      stop := true
     else
      io.putstring("??? \n") ;
    end ;
    io.putstring ("\n\n") ;
   end
  end ;

end ; -- class ROOT
```

A.3.2 Class Mailer

```
class MAILER export send, receive, list_mail, remove_mail
 -- class Mailer, implements user interface to the mail system

feature

 my_box : MAILBOX ;        -- User's mailbox
 dir : MAIL_DIRECTORY ;    -- System-wide mail directory
 my_name : STRING ;        -- User's name

 Create (n : STRING ; d : MAIL_DIRECTORY) is
  -- Register user's name and get mailbox from mailing directory
  -- If no mailbox exists for user, register one.
  do
   my_name := n ;
   dir := d ;
   my_box ?= dir.get_value (my_name) ;
   if my_box.Void
    then
     io.putstring ("Inserting Mailbox for ") ;
     io.putstring (my_name) ;
     io.putstring ("\n") ;
     my_box.Create ;
     dir.add_item (my_name, my_box)
    end ;
  end ;

 send  is
  -- Compose and dispatch a message object
  local
   dests, ccs : MAIL_LIST ;
   m : MESSAGE ;
  do
   dests.Create ; ccs.Create ;
   io.putstring ("To: ") ; dests.enter ;
   io.putstring ("cc: ") ; ccs.enter ;
   m.Create (dests, ccs, my_name, dir.get_id) ;
   io.putstring ("Posting to ") ;
   dests.display ;
   send_to_mail_list (dests, m) ;
   io.putstring ("Posting to ") ;
   ccs.display ;
   send_to_mail_list (ccs, m)
  end ;
```

```
send_to_mail_list (dsts : MAIL_LIST ; m : MESSAGE) is
 -- For each address in given mail list,
 -- insert given message in it's mailbox
 local
  t : STRING ;
  b : MAILBOX
 do
  from
   t := dsts.next_string
  until
   t.equal ("")
  loop
   b ?= dir.get_value (t) ;
   if b.Void
   then
    io.putstring (t) ;
    io.putstring (" -- Not a registered mail service user\n")
   else
    b.insert (m)
   end ;
   t := dsts.next_string
  end ;
 end ;

receive is
 local
  id : INTEGER
 do
  io.putstring (" Enter message id >>") ;
  io.readint ;
  my_box.read_msg (io.lastint)
 end ;

remove_mail is
 do
  io.putstring (" Enter message id >>") ;
  io.readint ;
  if my_box.remove (io.lastint) = TRUE
   then
    io.putstring ("Message successfully removed\n")
   else
    io.putstring ("Message with given id not in mailbox\n")
   end ;
 end   ;
```

```
list_mail is
 do
  my_box.list
 end ;


end ; -- class MAILER
```

A.3.3 Class Mail_Directory

```
class MAIL_DIRECTORY export list_users, get_id,
                             add_item, get_value
 -- MAIL_DIRECTORY class, provides association between user
 -- name and mailboxes using AMADEUS run-time operations

inherit
 AMADEUS

feature

 items : LINKED_LIST[STRING] ;   -- User names
 nb_elements : INTEGER ;          -- No. of elements registered
 id_gen : PINT ;                  -- For message identifiers

 Create is
  do
   items.Create ;
   items.start ;
   nb_elements := 0 ;
   id_gen.Create (0)
  end ;

 add_item (item_name : STRING ; value : ANY) is
  -- Enter item_name in user names list and
  -- register value with Amadeus environment
  do
   items.put_right (item_name) ;
   record (item_name, value) ;
   nb_elements := nb_elements + 1
  end ;

 get_value (item_name : STRING) : ANY is
  do
   Result := lookup (item_name)
  end ;
```

```
contains (item_name : STRING) : BOOLEAN is
 -- Determine whether or not given name is registered
 do
  items.search_equal (item_name) ;
  if not items.off
   then
    Result := TRUE
   else
    Result := FALSE
   end ;
  items.start
 end ;


remove_item (item_name : STRING) : BOOLEAN is
 -- Remove given name from directory names list
 do
  items.search_equal (item_name) ;
  if not items.off
   then
    items.remove ;
    nb_elements := nb_elements - 1 ;
    Result := TRUE
   else
    Result := FALSE
   end ;
  items.start
 end ;


list_users is
 -- Display names of all registered users
 local
  t : LINKED_LIST[STRING]
 do
  from
   t := items ;
   t.start
  until
   t.offright
  loop
   io.putstring (t.item) ;
   io.putstring ("\n") ;
   t.forth
  end ;
 end ;
```

```
get_id : INTEGER is
 -- Return a new, unique id
 do
  Result := id_gen.inc
 end ;


invariant
 nb_elements >= 0


end ;   -- class MAIL_DIRECTORY
```

A.3.4 Class Mailbox

```
class MAILBOX export insert, read_msg, remove, list
 -- class Mailbox, implements user's mailbox as a list
 -- of unread messages and a list of read messages


feature

 unread_messages, read_messages : MESSAGE_LIST ;

 Create is
  do
   unread_messages.Create ;
   read_messages.Create ;
  end ;

 insert (m : MESSAGE) is
  -- Put mesasge in list of unread messages
  do
   unread_messages.insert_msg (m)
  end ;

 remove (i : INTEGER) : BOOLEAN is
  -- Remove message with given id from read messages list
  do
   Result := read_messages.remove_msg (i)
  end ;

 list is
  do
   unread_messages.list_msgs ;
   read_messages.list_msgs
  end ;
```

```
read_msg (i : INTEGER) is
 -- display header and text of message with given id
 local
  msg : MESSAGE
 do
  msg := unread_messages.get_msg (i) ;
  if msg.Void
   then
    msg := read_messages.get_msg (i) ;
    if msg.Void
     then
      io.putint (i) ;
      io.putstring (" -- No such message\n")
     else
      msg.display
     end ;
   else
    msg.display ;
    read_messages.insert_msg (msg) ;
    unread_messages.remove_msg (i)
   end ;
 end ;

end ; -- class MAILBOX
```

A.3.5 Class Message

```
class MESSAGE export display, get_id, display_header
 -- class Message, message consists of message header and text

inherit
 TEXT rename Create as text_create, display as text_display ;
 BASIC_ROUT

feature

 message_id : INTEGER ;              -- Unique within mailbox
 destinations, carbon_copies : MAIL_LIST ;
 sender : STRING ;                   -- Sender of this message
```

```
Create (dests, cc : MAIL_LIST ;
        poster : STRING ; id : INTEGER) is
 -- Initialise message header and text
 do
  sender.Create (poster.count) ;
  sender.set (poster, 1, poster.count) ;
  destinations := dests ;
  carbon_copies := cc ;
  message_id := id ;
  text_create (to_string (id)) ;
  edit
 end ;

get_id : INTEGER is
 do
  Result := message_id
 end ;

display_header is
 do
  io.putstring ("To: ") ;
  destinations.display ;
  io.putstring ("Cc: ") ;
  carbon_copies.display ;
  io.putstring ("From: ") ;
  io.putstring (sender) ;
  io.putstring ("\nMessage ID: ") ;
  io.putint (message_id) ;
  io.putstring ("\n-----------------\n")
 end ;

display is
 do
  display_header ;
  text_display
 end ;

end ; --class MESSAGE
```

A.3.6 Utility and Library Classes

A number of library and utility classes are used by the application including
AMADEUS, PINT, BASIC_ROUT, TEXT, MESSAGE_LIST and MAIL_LIST. The latter
three classes are given below.

```
class TEXT export edit, display, newname, remove
 -- Text class, implements text as a string that can be
 -- overwritten and displayed

feature

 file_name : STRING ;
 command   : STRING ;

 Create (n : STRING) is
  -- Set file name and initialise command string
  -- to be used to perform operations on the file
  do
   file_name.Create (n.count) ;
   file_name.set (n, 1, n.count) ;
   command.Create (n.count + 4) ;
   command.set (n, 1, n.count)
  end ;

 edit is
  -- Invoke VI editor on file
  external
   system language "C"
  do
   command.prepend ("vi ") ;
   system (command.to_c) ;
   command.set (file_name, 1, file_name.count)
  end ;

 display is
  -- Use UNIX cat utility to display text file
  external
   system language "C"
  do
   command.prepend ("cat ") ;
   system (command.to_c) ;
   command.set (file_name, 1, file_name.count)
  end ;

 newname (new_name : STRING) is
  -- Accept a new file name
  do
   file_name.set (new_name, 1, new_name.count) ;
   command.set (new_name, 1, new_name.count)
  end ;
```

```
remove is
 -- Remove file associated with current file name
 external
  unlink language "C"
 do
  unlink (file_name.to_c)
 end ;

end ;  -- class TEXT

class MESSAGE_LIST export get_msg, remove_msg,
                         insert_msg, list_msgs
 -- Class MESSAGE_LIST implements a group of messages with
 -- operations to get, remove message by message id., and insert
 -- message as an array of messages

feature

 messages : ARRAY[MESSAGE] ;
 curr_range : INTEGER ;   -- Where to put the next message

 get_index (i : INTEGER) : INTEGER is
  -- routine to get the index in the array of the
  -- message with the given id
  local
   count : INTEGER
  do
   from
    count := 1 ;
   until
    count = curr_range or messages.item(count).get_id = i
   loop
    count := count + 1
   end ;
   Result := count
  end ;

 Create is
  do
   messages.Create (1, 25) ;
   curr_range := 1 ;
  end ;
```

```
insert_msg (m : MESSAGE) is
 -- Enter given message into message array
 do
  if curr_range = messages.upper
   then
     messages.resize (messages.lower, messages.upper + 5)
   end ;
  messages.put (m, curr_range) ;
  curr_range := curr_range + 1
 end ;


get_msg (i : INTEGER) : MESSAGE is
 -- Return message with given id
 local
  ind : INTEGER
 do
  ind := get_index (i) ;
  if ind < curr_range
   then
    Result := messages.item (ind)
   end ;
 end ;


remove_msg (i : INTEGER) : BOOLEAN is
 -- Remove message with given id
 local
  ind : INTEGER
 do
  ind := get_index (i) ;
  if ind < curr_range
   then
    -- Message at index 'count' is message to be removed
    from
    until
     ind = curr_range
    loop
     messages.put (messages.item (ind+1), ind) ;
     ind := ind + 1
    end ;
    curr_range := curr_range - 1 ;
    Result := TRUE
   else
    Result := FALSE
   end ;
 end ;
```

```
    list_msgs is
     local
      ind : INTEGER
     do
      from
       ind := 1 ;
      until
       ind = curr_range
      loop
       messages.item (ind).display_header ;
       ind := ind + 1
      end ;
     end ;

end ; -- class MESSAGE_LIST


class  MAIL_LIST export enter, display, next_string
 -- class MAIL_LIST, implementing list of mail addresses as
 -- a linked list of strings that can be entered, iterated
 -- through and displayed

feature

 names : LINKED_LIST[STRING] ;
 null_string : STRING is "" ;

 Create is
  do
   names.Create
  end ;

 next_string : STRING is
  -- Return string at cursor position and move cursor on
  -- If at end of list, reset cursor and return Null
  do
   if names.offright
    then
     names.start ;
     Result := null_string
    else
     Result := names.item
     names.forth
    end ;
   end ;
```

```
enter  is
 -- Read and enter strings until CR is entered
 local
  tmp : STRING ;
 do
  names.start  ;
  from
   io.readline
  until
   io.laststring.equal(null_string)
  loop
   tmp.Create (io.laststring.count) ;
   tmp.set (io.laststring, 1, io.laststring.count) ;
   names.put_right (tmp) ;
   io.readline
  end ;
  names.start
 end ;

 display  is
 -- write each string in the list to standard output
 do
  names.mark ;
  from
   names.start
  until
   names.offright
  loop
   io.putstring (names.item) ;
   io.putstring (" ") ;
   names.forth
  end ;
  io.putstring ("\n") ;
  names.return
 end ;

end ; -- class MAIL_LIST
```

A.4 Guide

A.4.1 Class Mailer

```
TYPE Mailer IS

 METHOD initOnNew; SIGNALS Error;
 // called at object creation
 // initialises the mailer for the user

 METHOD send (IN text : REF Text, users: List OF Username);
   SIGNALS Error_Insert;
 // send the text to the users

 METHOD receive : List OF REF Message;
 // returns the messages received and not read

END Mailer.

CLASS Mailer IMPLEMENTS Mailer IS

 maildir : REF Mail_Directory;

 METHOD initOnNew; SIGNALS Error;
 user : Username;
 BEGIN
  maildir := ASSERTYPE ( catal.Search ("mbox_dir") );
  user := my_domain.owner;
  maildir.subscribe ( user );
  EXCEPT
   Unknow: RAISE Error;
  END;
 END;

 METHOD receive : List OF REF Messages;
 BEGIN
  RETURN maildir.get_value(my_domain.owner).read;
 END;
```

```
METHOD send (IN text : REF Text, users: List OF Username);
  SIGNALS Error_Insert;
msg : REF Message;
mbox : REF Mailbox;
user : Username;
BEGIN
 msg := Message.New;
 msg.made (text, users);
 user := users.First;
 WHILE user # NIL
 DO
   mbox := maildir.get_value (user);
   mbox.Insert (msg);
   user := users.Next;
 END;
 EXCEPT
  Unknow: RAISE Error_Insert;
END;

END Mailer.
```

A.4.2 Class Mail_Directory

```
TYPE Mail_Directory SUBTYPE OF Directory OF REF Mailbox IS

 METHOD subscribe ( IN name : Username );
 METHOD unsubscribe ( IN name : Username ); SIGNALS Unknow;

END Mail_Directory.

CLASS Mail_Directory SUBCLASS OF Directory OF REF Mailbox
  IMPLEMENTS Mail_Directory

 METHOD subscribe ( IN name : Username );
 BEGIN
  IF SELF.get_value ( name ) = NIL
  THEN
   SELF.add_item ( name, Mailbox.New );
  END;
  EXCEPT
   Exist : ; // bizarre
  END;
 END;
```

```
METHOD unsubscribe ( IN name : Username ); SIGNALS Unknow;
BEGIN
 list.remove_item ( name );
 EXCEPT
  Unknow : RAISE Unknow;
 END;
END;


CONTROL
 READER (get_value), WRITER (subscribe, unsubscribe);

END Mail_Directory.
```

A.4.3 Class Mailbox

```
TYPE Mailbox SUBCLASS OF Text IS

 METHOD initOnNew;
 // called at object creation - initialises an empty mailbox

 METHOD insert (msg : REF Message); SIGNALS Full
 // inserts a reference to a message in the mailbox

 METHOD remove (msg : REF Message); SIGNALS Unknow;
 // removes a reference to a message from the mailbox

 METHOD read : List OF REF Messages;
 // returns the unread message

 METHOD read (IN i : Integer) : Messages;
 // returns message number i

END Mailbox.

CLASS Mailbox IMPLEMENTS Mailbox IS

 list : List OF REF Message;
 last : Integer = 0;

 METHOD initOnNew;
 BEGIN
  list := List.New;
 END;
```

```
METHOD insert (msg : REF Message); SIGNALS Full;
BEGIN
 list.Last;
 list.Append (msg);
 EXCEPT
  Full : RAISE Full;
 END;
END;


METHOD remove (msg : REF Message); SIGNALS Unknow;
tmp : REF Message;
BEGIN
 tmp := list.First;
 WHILE tmp # NIL
 DO
  IF tmp = msg
  THEN
   list.Delete;
   RETURN;
  ELSE
   tmp := list.Next;
  END;
 END;
 RAISE Unknow;
END;


METHOD read : List OF REF Messages;
tmp : List OF REF Messages;
msg : REF Message;
BEGIN
 IF last > list..Nbitem
 THEN
  tmp := List.New;
  msg := list.Go(last).Next;
  WHILE msg # NIL
  DO
   tmp.Insert(msg);
   last := last+1;
   tmp := list.Next;
  END;
 ELSE
  RETURN NIL;
 END;
END;
```

```
METHOD read (IN i : Integer) : Messages;
BEGIN
 IF i <= list.Nbitem
 THEN
  RETURN list.Go(i);
 ELSE
  RETURN NIL;
 END;
END;


CONTROL
 READER (read), WRITER (insert, remove);

END Mailbox.
```

A.4.4 Class Message

```
TYPE Message SUBTYPE OF Text IS

 METHOD made (IN txt : REF Text ; users : List OF Username);
 // makes a message with the given text

END Message.
```

```
CLASS Message IMPLEMENTS Message IS

 from : Username;
 to : List OF Username;
 contents : REF Text;

 METHOD made (IN txt : REF Text ; users : List OF Username);
 BEGIN
  contents := txt;
  from := my_domain.owner;
  to := users;
 END;

 METHOD edit;
 BEGIN
  // edit the message
  ...
  // edit the text using an interactive text editor
  contents.edit;
 END;
```

```
METHOD display;
BEGIN
 // display the message
 ...
 // display the text
 contents.display
END;

CONTROL
 READER (display), WRITER (made, edit);

END Message.
```

A.4.5 Utility and Library Classes

```
// Type definition
SYNONYM Username = STRING[40];

// Comandos library
// Some pre-defined types and classes are reused

// Next is a partial description of a generic type Collection
TYPE CONSTRUCTOR Collection OF [typ_elt : REF Top] IS

 METHOD init;
 // initialise an instance
 METHOD insert(IN elt: typ_elt);
 // inserts an item (no effect if item already in collection)
 METHOD remove(IN elt: typ_elt); SIGNALS not_here;
 // removes the item
 METHOD is_in(IN elt: typ_elt): Boolean;
 // returns TRUE if the item is in the Collection
 METHOD size:Integer;
 // returns the size of the collection
 METHOD select(IN p: Predicate): REF Collection OF [typ_elt];
 // returns the sub-collection selected by the predicate passed
 // as a method's parameter
 // a predicate is a boolean expression which can only combine
 // visible variable of the Collection basic type
 METHOD select_one(IN p: Predicate): typ_elt;
 // selects one document with this predicate

 //... other methods exist in type Collection

END Collection.
```

```
// This is a partial description of a generic type List
TYPE CONSTRUCTOR List OF [ T ] IS

 METHOD First;
 // puts current pointer on first item of list
 METHOD First : T;
 // puts current pointer on first item of list, and returns it
 METHOD Next;
 // puts current pointer on next item of list
 METHOD Next : T;
 // puts current pointer on next item of list, and returns it
 METHOD Current : T;
 // returns current item of list
 METHOD Previous;
 // puts current pointer on previous item of list
 METHOD Previous: T;
 // puts current pointer on previous item of list, and returns it
 METHOD Go (IN i : Integer);
 // puts current pointer on ith item of list
 METHOD Go (IN i : Integer) : T;
 // puts current pointer on ith item of list, and returns it
 METHOD Last;
 // puts current pointer on last item of list
 METHOD Last : T;
 // puts current pointer on last item of list, and returns it
 METHOD NbItems : Integer;
 // returns number of items which are present in list
 METHOD Insert (IN o : T);
 // inserts an item before current one
 METHOD Appends (IN o : T);
 // inserts an item after current one
 METHOD Delete;
 // deletes current item
 METHOD Delete : T;
 // deletes current item of list, and returns it
 METHOD Delete(IN i : Integer);
 // deletes item given in parameter
 METHOD Concat(IN l : REF List OF T);
 // concats a parameter list

END List.
```

```
// Application library

// The generic type Item has two visible variables
//        a name
//        a value
// and has for methods implicitly declared :
//        put and get a name or a value
TYPE CONSTRUCTOR Item OF [T] IS
 name : Username;
 value : T
END Item.

// The generic class Item has two variables (defined in a
// type Item) and the method's code is generates by the
// Guide compiler
CLASS CONSTRUCTOR Item OF [T] IS
END Item.

TYPE CONSTRUCTOR Directory OF [ T ] IS

 METHOD initOnNew;
 // called at object creation - initialises an empty directory

 METHOD add_item (name : String, value : T); SIGNALS Exist;
 // inserts a (name,value) pair

 METHOD get_value (name) : T;
 // returns the value associated to a name (or nil)

 METHOD remove_item (name); SIGNALS Unknow;
 // removes a (name, value) pair, if present

END Directory.

CLASS CONSTRUCTOR Directory OF [ T ] IMPLEMENTS Directory IS

 list : REF Collection OF REF Item OF T;

 METHOD initOnNew;
 BEGIN
  list := Collection.New;
 END;
```

```
METHOD add_item (name : String, value : T); SIGNALS Exist;
tmp : REF Item;
BEGIN
 // if not exist, insert it
 IF list.select_one ( name = [name] ) = NIL
 THEN
  tmp := tmp.New;
  tmp.name = name;
  tmp.value = value;
  list.insert ( tmp );
 ELSE
  RAISE Exist;
 END;
END;

METHOD get_value (name) : T;
BEGIN
 RETURN list.select_one ( name = [name] )
END;

METHOD remove_item (name); SIGNALS Unknow;
BEGIN
 list.remove (name);
 EXCEPT:
  not_here: RAISE Unknow;
END;

CONTROL
 READER ( get_value ) , WRITER ( add_item, remove_item );

END Directory.

TYPE Text IS

 METHOD initOnNew;
 // called at object creation - initialises an empty text

 METHOD edit;
 // calls an interactive text editor

 METHOD display;
 // displays the text

END Text.
```

```
CLASS Text IMPLEMENTS Text IS

 contents : ...

 METHOD initOnNew;
 BEGIN
 ...
 END;

 METHOD edit;
 BEGIN
 ...
 END;

 METHOD display;
 BEGIN
 ...
 END;

 CONTROL
  READER (display), WRITER(edit);

END Text.
```

B. Available Software

1. The Amadeus platform (Green release).
   - **Description**: The reference implementation of the Comandos platform supporting distribution, persistence, concurrency and transactions in a heterogeneous environment. The reliable broadcast protocol and RelaX transaction manager are used to provide transaction support. Applications can be written using extended C++ or Eiffel. The release includes numerous demonstration applications and full documentation.
   - **Environment**: SunOS 4.x on Sun-3 and SPARCstation; ULTRIX 4.x on DECstation 2100/3100/5100 and Mach 3.0 with BSD single server on PCs.
   - **Licencing conditions**: Licence available to academic and industrial researchers for experimentation and evaluation. Eiffel V2.3 licence required for Eiffel support.
   - **Contact point**:
     Vinny Cahill
     Trinity College Dublin
     Dept. of Computer Science,
     Dublin 2, Ireland
     Phone: +353 (1) 702 1795, Fax: +353 (1) 677 2204
     Email: amadeus@dsg.cs.tcd.ie

2. GUIDE (v1.6).
   - **Description**: Comandos system on top of UNIX together with Comandos language compiler and development tools (including a debugger and simple Type Manager). Includes basic system services, support for the X Window System and OSF/Motif, and provides access to (and from) UNIX applications. The release also includes the following applications: a Distributed Directory Service (which provides a subset of X.511 services); the GRIFFON editor which provides cooperative editing of structured documents; a distributed mail system and other demonstration applications.
   - **Environment**: Bull DPX/2 running BOS 2.x; Sun-3 and Sun-4 running SunOS 4.x and DECstation 3100/5100 running ULTRIX 4.x.
   - **Licencing conditions**: For experimentation and evaluation only (copyright). UNIX and OSF/Motif licences required.

- Contact point:
  Roland Balter
  Bull-IMAG
  2 rue Vignate, F-38610 Gieres, France
  Phone: +33 76 54 49 12, Fax: +33 76 54 76 15
  Email: balter@imag.fr

3. GUIDE (v2).
   - **Description**: Comandos system on top of Mach 3.0 together with Comandos language compiler and development tools (Debugger, etc.). Includes basic system services and support for the X Window System and OSF/Motif. Provides access to (and from) UNIX applications. and supports GRIFFON which provides cooperative editing of structured documents.
   - **Environment**: Bull-Zenith i386/486 running OSF/1-MK.
   - **Licencing conditions**: For experimentation and evaluation. Requires UNIX, OSF/1 MK and OSF/Motif licences.
   - **Contact point**:
     Sacha Krakowiak
     (For address see 2. above)
     Email: krakowia@imag.fr

4. The IK Platform.
   - **Description**: Supports fine-grained objects in an heterogeneous host environment. The platform offers an extended C++ as programming language, distribution, persistence, concurrency, garbage collection, dynamic linking, and a programming environment composed of a browser, inspector and the ET++ library.
   - **Environment**: SunOS on Sun-3 and Sun-4; Mach 2.6 and 3.0 on PCs.
   - **Licencing conditions**: Publicly available.
   - **Contact point**:
     Pedro Sousa
     INESC
     Rua Alves Redol 9-6, P-1000 Lisbon, Portugal
     Phone: +351 (1) 3100 287 or +351 (1) 3100 000 Ext. 287
     Fax: +351 (1) 52 58 43
     Email: ik-staff@sabrina.inesc.pt

5. The Secure Transmission System.
   - **Description**: A secure communication package providing mechanisms to protect transmitted data against replication, modification and elimination. The Secure Transmission System preserves the confidentiality, the integrity and the availabilty of the protected data and provides mechanisms for authentication.
   - **Environment**: SunOS on Sun-3 and Sun-4.
   - **Licencing conditions**: Academic Use Only. Kerberos licence required.

- Contact point:
  Manel Medina
  Universitat Politecnica de Catalunya
  Dept. Arquitectura de Computadors
  Barcelona, Spain
  Phone: +34 (3) 4016984, Fax: +34 (3) 4017055
  Email: medina@ac.upc.es

6. COOL (v2).
   - Description: Implementation of the Comandos platform on top of the CHORUS micro-kernel. Supports distribution, persistence, concurrency and provides a C++ pre-compiler.
   - Environment: CHORUS/MiX on PC compatible machines.
   - Licencing conditions: Available for experimentation and evaluation. CHORUS/MiX V.3.2 licence required.
   - Contact point:
     Didier Irlande
     Chorus Systemes
     6 avenue Gustave Eiffel,
     F-78182 Saint-Quentin-en-Yvelines Cedex, France
     Phone: +33 (1) 30 64 82 00, Fax: +33 (1) 30 57 00 66
     Email: di@chorus.fr

7. The Reliable Broadcast Protocol.
   - Description: A reliable broadcast service for UNIX/Ethernet environments. Includes node failure detection and indication.
   - Environment: UNIX systems providing C.
   - Licencing conditions: Licence available to academic and industrial researchers for experimentation and evaluation.
   - Contact point:
     Dr. Reinhold Kroeger
     GMD (German National Research Centre for Computer Science)
     P.O. Box 1316, 5205 Sankt Augustin 1, Germany
     Phone: +49 (2241) 142 322, Fax: +49 (2241) 142 105
     Email: kroeger@gmdzi.gmd.de

8. The RelaX Transaction Manager.
   - Description: Extensible Transaction Manager. Provides distributed, generalised transaction functionality in an X/Open XA-Interface conformant manner.
   - Environment: UNIX systems providing C and C++.
   - Licencing conditions: Licence available to academic and industrial researchers for experimentation and evaluation.
   - Contact point:
     Dr. Reinhold Kroeger
     (For address see 7. above)

9. The ODMS Portable Toolkit.
    - **Description**: Class library which implements the BROOM data model. The library supports the management of potentially large inter-related collections of persistent objects.
    - **Environment**: C++.
    - **Licencing conditions**: Unspecified.
    - **Contact point**:
        Dr. David J. Harper
        Dept. of Computing Science
        University of Glasgow,
        17 Lilybank Gardens, Glasgow G12 8Q2, Scotland
        Phone: +44 (41) 339 8855, Fax: +44 (41) 330 4913
        Email: djh@dcs.glasgow.ac.uk
10. The Bidirectional Communication Service.
    - **Description**: Inter-process communication between hosts.
    - **Environment**: Sun-3/50, Sun-3/60 and SPARCstation providing C, C++ and SunRPC.
    - **Licencing conditions**: Unspecified.
    - **Contact point**:
        Helmut Meitner
        Fraunhofer-Institut für Arbeitswirtschaft und Organisation
        Nobelstrasse 12c, 7000 Stuttgart 80, Germany
        Phone: +49 (711) 970 2343, Fax: +49 (711) 970 2300
        Email: meitner@iao.fhg.de
11. The System Observation Facility.
    - **Description**: Collection of measurement data in distributed systems.
    - **Environment**: Sun-3/50, Sun-3/60, SPARCstation and IBM PS/2 (partly) providing C, C++, the bidirectional communication service and NFS.
    - **Licencing conditions**: Unspecified.
    - **Contact point**:
        Helmut Meitner
        (For address see 10. above)
12. The System Control Facility.
    - **Description**: Execution of control activities in distributed systems.
    - **Environment**: Sun-3/50, Sun-3/60, SPARCstation and IBM RS6000 providing C and sh.
    - **Licencing conditions**: Unspecified.
    - **Contact point**:
        Helmut Meitner
        (For address see 10. above)

13. The User and Host Administration Tool.
    - **Description**: Analysis of user activities, host usage and workload.
    - **Environment**: Sun-3/50, Sun-3/60 and SPARCstation providing C++, InterViews 2.6 and X11R4.
    - **Licencing conditions**: Unspecified.
    - **Contact point**:
        Helmut Meitner
        (For address see 10. above)

14. The Distributed Information System Designer.
    - **Description**: Organisational design, business process simulation, generation of software requirements.
    - **Environment**: Sun-3/50, Sun-3/60 and SPARCstation providing C and C++, InterViews 2.6, X11R4 and Oracle.
    - **Licencing conditions**: Unspecified.
    - **Contact point**:
        Helmut Meitner
        (For address see 10. above)

15. The Risk Management Tool.
    - **Description**: Analysis of dependability aspects.
    - **Environment**: Sun-3/50, Sun-3/60 and SPARCstation providing C++, InterViews 2.6 and X11R4.
    - **Licencing conditions**: Unspecified.
    - **Contact point**:
        Helmut Meitner
        (For address see 10. above)

16. The Audit Analysis Tool (AAT).
    - **Description**: Configurable audit data analyzer with comfortable OSF/Motif interface. Very complex search rules may be defined at run time. Analyzes audit data produced by Amadeus.
    - **Environment**: SPARCstation, providing ANSI C, X11R4, OSF/Motif 1.1 and Amadeus.
    - **Licencing conditions**: Unspecified.
    - **Contact point**:
        Cornelia Persy
        Siemens AG ZFE ST SN 53
        Otto-Hahn-Ring 6, 8000 München 83, Germany
        Phone: +49 (89) 636 46499, Fax: +49 (89) 636 44424
        Email: persy@aying.zfe.siemens.de

17. The Distributed Directory Service (DDS).
    - **Description**: CCITT X.500 Name Server with Modify, Read and Search services and supporting convenient schema management facilitating the management of user specific object classes and class relations. A graphical DUA interface is implemented using the X Window System and OSF/Motif.

- **Environment**: SPARCstation providing C++, X11.4, OSF/Motif 1.1 and Amadeus.
- **Licencing conditions**: Unspecified.
- **Contact point**:
    Cornelia Persy
    (For address see 16. above)

18. The Comprehensive Risk Management Tool.
    - **Description**: Demonstrator of a Security Control Centre for distributed systems providing OSF/Motif interface. Collects sensor and audit data and combines them based on mathematical and logical data providing risk assessment and suggestions for safeguards.
    - **Environment**: SPARCstation providing ANSI C, X11R4, OSF/Motif 1.1, Amadeus and PDAT.
    - **Licencing conditions**: Unspecified.
    - **Contact point**:
        Cornelia Persy
        (For address see 16. above)

19. CIDRE.
    - **Description**: The CIDRE groupware application provides intelligent circulation of distributed folders within an enterprise.
    - **Environment**: Guide (v1.6) on Bull DPX/2 running BOS 2.x, Sun-3 and Sun-4 running SunOS 4.x and DECstation 3100/5100 running ULTRIX 4.x or CHORUS/COOL v2 on PC compatible machines running CHORUS/MiX.
    - **Licencing conditions**: Contact address below for licencing conditions.
    - **Contact point**:
        Jean-Marc Deshayes
        SEPT
        42 rue des Coutures, F-14066 Caen, France
        Phone: +33 31 75 91 43, Fax: +33 31 75 06 31
        Email: deshayes@sept.fr

C. Comandos Glossary

This appendix summarises the terminology used in the project. Normal font is used for an explanation of each term, *while small font is used to provide a more formal definition.*

activity: The sequential activation of one or more objects in one or more contexts, possibly on different nodes.

atomic object: Atomic objects are those objects for which transactional properties are guaranteed.

cell: The basic organisational and administrative component within an enterprise.

class: A concrete realisation of a particular type, i.e. the state template and associated methods. A class can be instantiated to create multiple objects.

cluster: A set of objects which are grouped together so as to improve the efficiency of retrieval from (and storage to) a container.

collection: A logical grouping of objects which reflects a semantic category in the application domain.

More rigourously a collection may be a grouping of values rather than just a grouping of objects. Further, a collection may be unary or binary depending on whether its elements are atomic or pair values respectively.

conformance: A means to identify type relationships.

More rigourously, conformance is a relation over types defined by logical implication: a type X conforms to a type Y if any value which satisfies type X also satisfies type Y.

container: A (secondary) storage unit that provides a repository for objects.

context: A dynamically varying collection of objects co-located at the same node. A context is an abstraction of a virtual address space.

extension: The set of objects of a given type.

More rigorously, the set of objects which satisfy a type (c.f. also "collection").

extent: A set of objects which are mutually trusted. An implementation of the Comandos architecture may, as a result, not protect the objects of an extent from one another.

global name: A system wide unique identifier which is both immutable, and fixed sized. It unambiguously identifies an object, thus designating a unique object in time and space.

inheritance: A mechanism used to construct a class by incremental refinement of at least one other class.

instance: An object created by instantiating a class.

interface: The abstract characteristics of an object which are visible at the object's boundary. An interface describes a set of potential requests in which an object can meaningfully participate.

job: A set of one or more activities sharing one or more contexts. A job represents parallel processing of objects in a collection of (one or more) contexts.

language name: A name which is specific to an associated programming language execution environment. Typically a language name is a 32 bit direct pointer, or an index into a table.

multiple inheritance: The use of inheritance to construct a class by incremental refinement of more than one other class.

name: A value which identifies an object, although possibly ambiguously: unlike a global name, an object name may denote different objects at different times and at different points in space. See also symbolic name and language name.

node: One or more processors which share some primary memory.

object: An object is an instance of a class.

More rigorously, an object is an encapsulation of state and a set of operations which embody an abstraction characterised by an interface.

operation: An identified service which can be requested. An operation has an associated signature.

persistence: A judgement that an entity remains the same entity at different times and at different points in space.

persistent object: An object having a known global name. An implementation of the Comandos architecture may provide support for persistent objects by ensuring that the system maintains all objects whose global names are directly or indirectly known to it via some designated "root" objects.

reference: A synonym for global name.

signature: A description of an operation which may restrict the possible actual parameter values that are meaningful in requests which name that operation. A request whose actual parameters do not satisfy the signature associated with the request is meaningless.

state: The information about the history of previous requests needed to explain the behaviour of future requests.

sub-type: A type derived from a super-type.

super-type: A type from which at least one other type is derived by refinement.

symbolic name: A high level oriented name, used by applications and end users.

type: An interface exported by an object describing some (i.e. not necessarily all) of the operations supported by that object.

More rigorously, a type is a predicate – i.e. a boolean assertion – defined over values, and which can be used in a signature to restrict a possible parameter or characterise a possible result.

value: Any entity which can be a possible actual parameter in a request. Values which identify objects are called object names. Values which identify other entities are called literals.

D. Abbreviations

ACL Access Control List
AFS Andrew File System
AM Activity Manager
AMT Activity Manager Table
ANT Active Node Table
ARM Address Resolution Manager
ATT Address Translation Table
AuM Authentication Module
BA Business Activity
BP Business Process
BROOM Binary Relational Object-Oriented Model
CFH Cluster Fault Handler
CIDRE Circulation Intelligente de Dossiers REpartis
ClM Cluster Manager
CM Context Manager
CNT Control Node Table
CORBA Common Object Request Broker Architecture
CRM Comprehensive Risk Management
CS Communication Sub-system
CSCW Computer Supported Cooperative Working
CU Control Unit
DAP Directory Access Protocol
DCE Distributed Computing Environment
BCS Bidirectional Communication Service
DDS Distributed Directory Service
DIT Directory Information Tree
DME Distributed Management Environment
DN Distinguished Name
DISDES Distributed Information System Designer
DML Data Manipulation Sub-Language
DSA Directory System Agent
DSDL Data and Storage Definition Language
DSP Directory System Protocol
DT Dynamic Type
DUA Directory User Agent

ERT Eiffel Run-Time
ES Execution Sub-system
EU Evaluation Unit
GRT Generic Run-Time
GRPC Generic Remote Procedure Call Interface
ICN Information Control Net.
IDL Interface Definition Language
IKM Inter-Kernel Message service
INGRID Interactive Graphical Interface Designer
IPC Inter-Process Communication
IT Information Technology
KCT Kernel Cluster Table
LAN Local Area Network
LB Load Balancer
LMT Local Mount Table
LS Location Service
MCC Mapped Cluster Cache
MCT Mapped Cluster Table
MT Mount Table
NCS Network Computing System
NFS Network File System
NM Node Manager
ODMS Object Data Management Service
ODP Open Distributed Processing
OM Object Manager
OMA Object Management Architecture
OMG Object Management Group
ORB Object Request Broker
OSF Open Software Foundation
OSI Open Systems Interconnection
PCTE Portable Common Tool Environment
PDAT Protocol Data Analysis Tool
PS Protection Sub-system
RBP Reliable Broadcast Protocol
RLI Representation Level Inter-operability
RiskMa Risk Management Tool
RPC Remote Procedure Call
SC Security Context
SCC System Control Centre
SCF System Control Facility
SCMM Security Context Management Module
SecCC Security Control Centre
SLI Specification Level Inter-operability
SM Storage Manager
SOC System Observation Centre

SOF System Observation Facility
SPM Secure Protocol Module
SS Storage Sub-system
STIM Security Transport Interface Module
STPDU Secure Transport Protocol Data Unit
STS Secure Transfer Service
TM Transaction Manager
TPDU Transport Protocol Data Unit
TpM Type Manager
TS Transaction Sub-system
UDP Internet User Datagram Protocol
UI UNIX International
UsrAdm User and Host Administration Tool
VMI Virtual Machine Interface
VOM Virtual Object Memory
WAN Wide Area Network
XOM X/OPEN Object Management Layer

E. Comandos Publications

E.1 Papers and Reports

[1] Alves Marques, J. and Guedes, P. Extending the Operating System to Support an Object-Oriented Environment. In Meyrowitz, N. (Ed.): *OOPSLA (Object-Oriented Programming: Systems, Languages and Applications) '89 Conference Proceedings*, SIGPLAN Notices, 24(10):113–122, 1989.

[2] Alves Marques, J., Balter, R., Cahill, V., Guedes, P., Harris, N., Horn, C., Krakowiak, S., Kramer, A., Slattery, J. and Vandome, G. Implementing the Comandos Architecture. In *ESPRIT '88: Putting the Technology to Use*, Elsevier Science Publishers, Amsterdam, 1988. pp. 1140–1157.

[3] Amaral, P., Jacquemot, C. and Lea, R. Implementing a Modular Object-Oriented Distributed Operating System on Top of CHORUS. In *Proceedings of the OPENFORUM '92 Technical Conference: Distributed Computing Practice and Experience*, Utrecht, The Netherlands, 1992. EurOpen/UniForum, London, 1992. pp. 193–203.

[4] Amaral, P., Lea, R. and Jacquemot, C. A Model for Persistent Shared Memory Addressing in Distributed Systems. In Cabrera, L.-F. and Jul, E. (Eds.): *Proceedings of the 2nd International Workshop on Object-Orientation in Operating Systems*, Dourdan, France, September 1992. IEEE, Los Alamitos, 1992. pp. 2–12.

[5] Baker, S. *System Issues in Persistent Programming and OODBMS Integration.* PhD thesis, Department of Computer Science, Trinity College Dublin, July 1992.

[6] Balter, R. Construction and Management of Distributed Office Systems – Achievements and Future Trends. In *Proceedings of the 1989 ESPRIT Conference*, Brussels, Belgium, 1989. Kluwer Academic Publishers, Dordrecht, 1989. pp. 47–58.

[7] Balter, R., Banâtre, J.-P. and Krakowiak S. *Construction des Systèmes d'Exploitation Réparties.* INRIA, Rocquencourt, 1991.

[8] Balter, R., Bernadat, J., Decouchant, D., Duda, A., Freyssinet, A., Krakowiak, S., Meysembourg, M., Le Dot, P., Nguyen Van, H., Paire, E., Riveill, M., Roisin, C., Rousset de Pina, X., Scioville, R. and Vandome, G. Architecture and Implementation of Guide, an Object-Oriented Distributed Operating System. *Computing Systems*, 4(1):31–67, 1991.

[9] Balter, R., Decouchant, D., Duda, A., Freyssinet, A., Krakowiak, S., Mey-sembourg, M., Riveill, M., Roisin, C., Rousset de Pina, X., Scioville, R. and Vandome, G. Experience with Object-Based Distributed Computation in the Guide Operating System. In *Proceedings of the 2ⁿᵈ Workshop on Workstation Operating Systems*, Asilomar, CA, USA, 1989. IEEE, Los Alamitos, 1989. pp. 16–19.

[10] Beguin, A., Bourdon, F., Deshayes, J.-M., Greard, M., Tourrade, D. and Touzeau, P. CIDRE, Intelligent Circulation of Distributed Folders. In *Proceedings of the 5ᵗʰ International Workshop on Telematics*, Denver, Colorado, USA, 1989. IEEE, Los Alamitos, 1989.

[11] Blair, G.S. and Lea, R. The Impact of Distribution on the Object-Oriented Approach to Software Development. *IEE Software Engineering Journal*, 7(2):130–139, 1992.

[12] Blott, S.M., Harper, D.J., and Norrie, M.C. Active Queries – a Lazy Approach to Query Evaluation in Object-Oriented Databases. In Yesha, Y. (Ed.): *Proceedings of the 1ˢᵗ International Conference on Information and Knowledge Management*, Baltimore, Maryland, USA, 1992. ISMM, 1992. pp. 576–583.

[13] Blott, S.M., Norrie, M.C., Harper, D.J. and Walker, A.D.M. Detecting Semantic Violations in Generalised Classification Structures. Technical Report DB-92-3, Department of Computing Science, University of Glasgow, 1992.

[14] Boyer, F. A Casual Distributed Shared Memory based on External Pagers. In *Proceedings of the USENIX Mach Symposium*, Monterey, CA, USA, 1991. USENIX, Berkeley, 1991. pp. 41–57.

[15] Boyer, F., Cayuela, J., Chevalier, P.Y., Freyssinet, A. and Hagimont, D. Supporting an Object-Oriented Distributed System: Experience with UNIX, CHORUS and Mach. In *Proceedings of the 2ⁿᵈ Symposium on Experiences with Distributed and Multiprocessor Systems*, Atlanta, GA, USA, 1991. USENIX, Berkeley, 1991. pp. 283–300.

[16] Bullinger, H., Reim, F. and Rothkopf, B. Verteilte Informationssysteme fuer das Produktionsmanagement. *CIM Management*, 8(1):4–9, 1992.

[17] Cahill, V. OISIN: The Design of a Distributed Object-Oriented Kernel for Comandos. Master's thesis, Department of Computer Science, Trinity College Dublin, March 1988.

[18] Cahill, V. and Kramer, A. OISIN: Operating System Support for Objects in a Distributed Environment. *IEEE Technical Committee on Operating Systems Newsletter*, 5(1):4–8, 1991.

[19] Cahill, V., Baker, S., Tangney, B., Horn, C. and Harris, N. On Object-Orientation as a Paradigm for General Purpose Distributed Operating Systems. In *Proceedings of the 5ᵗʰ SIGOPS European Workshop*, Le Mont Saint-Michel, France, 1992. IRISA/INRIA, Rennes, 1992.

[20] Cahill, V., Horn, C. and Starovic, G. Towards Generic Support for Distributed Information Systems. In Cabrera, L.-F., Russo, V. and Shapiro, M. (Eds.): *Proceedings of the International Workshop on Object-*

Orientation in Operating Systems, Palo Alto, CA, USA, 1991. IEEE, Los Alamitos, 1991. pp. 104–107.

[21] Cahill, V., Horn, C., Starovic, G., Lea, R. and Sousa, P. Supporting Object-Oriented Languages on the Comandos Platform. In *Proceedings of the 1991 ESPRIT Conference*, Brussels, Belgium, 1991. Commission of the European Communities, Luxembourg, 1991. pp. 427–438.

[22] Cahill, V., Taylor, P., Starovic, G., Tangney, B. and O'Grady, D. Supporting the Amadeus Platform on UNIX. Technical Report TCD-CS-92-25, Department of Computer Science, Trinity College Dublin, July 1992.

[23] Chevalier, P.Y. A Replicated Object Server for a Distributed Object-Oriented System. In *Proceedings of the 11th Symposium on Reliable Distributed Systems*, Houston, TX, USA, 1992. IEEE, Los Alamitos, 1992. pp. 4–11.

[24] Chevalier, P.Y., Hagimont, D., Krakowiak, S. and Rousset de Pina, X. System Support for Shared Objects. In *Proceedings of the 5th SIGOPS European Workshop*, Le Mont-Saint-Michel, France, 1992. IRISA/INRIA, Rennes, 1992.

[25] Cooper, R.L. Comandos – A Distributed Heterogeneous Platform for Data Intensive Applications. *Journal of Control Systems and Machines*, 9, 1991.

[26] Crane, S. Recovery from Failure in an Object-Oriented Distributed System. Master's thesis, Department of Computer Science, Trinity College Dublin, 1990.

[27] Crane, S. and Tangney, B. Failure and Recovery in an Object-Oriented Distributed System. Technical Report TCD-CS-91-02, Department of Computer Science, Trinity College Dublin, February 1991.

[28] Daly, D., Cahill, V. and Horn, C. UNIX and Object-Oriented Distributed Systems. In *Proceedings of the EUUG Autumn Conference*, Vienna, Austria, 1989. EUUG, Buntingford, 1989.

[29] Decouchant, D. *Partage et Migration de l'Information dans un Système Réparti à Objets*. PhD thesis, Université Joseph Fourier (Grenoble), 1987.

[30] Decouchant, D. A Distributed Object Manager for the Smalltalk-80 System. In Kim, W. and Lochovsky, F.H. (Eds.): *Object-Oriented Concepts, Applications and Databases*, Addison-Wesley, New York, 1989. pp. 487–520.

[31] Decouchant, D. and Duda, A. Remote Execution and Communication in Guide, a Distributed Object-Oriented system. In *Proceedings of the Workshop on Experimental Distributed Systems*, Huntsville, AL, USA, 1990. IEEE, Los Alamitos, 1990.

[32] Decouchant, D., Duda, A., Freyssinet, A., Riveill, M., Rousset de Pina, X., Scioville, R. and Vandome, G. Guide: An Implementation of the Comandos Object-Oriented Architecture on UNIX. In *Proceedings of the EUUG Autumn Conference*, Lisbon, Portugal, 1988. EUUG, Buntingford, 1988. pp. 181–193.

[33] Decouchant, D., Finn, E., Harris, N., Horn, C., Krakowiak, S. and Riveill, M. Experience with Implementing and Using an Object-Oriented Distributed System. In *Proceedings of the Workshop on Experiences with Distributed and Multiprocessor Systems*, Fort Lauderdale, FL, USA, 1989. USENIX, Berkeley, 1989. pp. 301–310.

[34] Decouchant, D., Krakowiak, S., Meysembourg, M., Riveill, M. and Rousset de Pina, X. A Synchronization Mechanism for Typed Objects in a Distributed System. In Agua, G., Wegner, P. and Yonezawa, A. (Eds.): *Proceedings of the Workshop on Object-Oriented Concurrent Programming*, SIGPLAN Notices, 24(4):105–108, 1989.

[35] Decouchant, D., Le Dot, P., Riveill, M., Roisin, C. and Rousset de Pina, X. A Synchronization Mechanism for Typed Objects in a Distributed System. In *Proceedings of the 11th International Conference on Distributed Computing Systems*, Arlington, TX, USA, 1991. IEEE, Los Alamitos, 1991. pp. 152–159.

[36] Decouchant, D., Normand, V. and Vandome, G. Application Design using the Comandos Distributed Object-Oriented System. In Bullinger, H.J. (Ed.): *Proceedings of the 4th International Conference on Human-Computer Interaction*, Stuttgart, Germany, 1991. Elsevier Science Publishers, Amsterdam, 1991. pp. 359–363.

[37] Decouchant, D., Paire, E. and Riveill, M. Efficient Implementation of Low-level Synchronization Primitives in the UNIX-based Guide Kernel. In *Proceedings of the EUUG Autumn Conference*, Vienna, Austria, 1989. EUUG, Buntingford, 1989. pp. 283–289.

[38] Deshayes, J.-M., Abrossimov, V. and Lea, R. The CIDRE Distributed Object System Based on CHORUS. In *Proceedings of TOOLS (Technology of Object-Oriented Languages and Systems) Europe '89*, Paris, France, 1989. SOL, Paris, 1989. pp. 521–529.

[39] Deshayes, J.-M. and Merciol, F. Objectif : Objets. *Interfaces*, 103/104:42–45, 1991.

[40] Distributed Systems Group. Amadeus Installation and Maintainence Guide (Amadeus v2.0). Technical Report TCD-CS-92-02, Department of Computer Science, Trinity College Dublin, February 1992.

[41] Distributed Systems Group. C** Programmer's Guide (Amadeus v2.0). Technical Report TCD-CS-92-03, Department of Computer Science, Trinity College Dublin, February 1992.

[42] Distributed Systems Group. Overview of the Amadeus Project (Amadeus v2.0). Technical Report TCD-CS-92-01, Department of Computer Science, Trinity College Dublin, February 1992.

[43] El-Habbash, A., Grimson, J. and Horn, C. Towards an Efficient Management of Objects in a Distributed Environment. In Agrawal, R. and Bell, D. (Eds.): *Proceedings of the 2nd International Symposium on Databases in Parallel and Distributed Systems*, Dublin, Ireland, 1990. IEEE, Los Alamitos, 1990. pp. 181–190.

[44] El-Habbash, A., Harris, N.R., and Baker, S. Supporting Automated Management in Distributed Persistent Object Classes. In Sadanandan, P. and Vijayaraman, T.M. (Eds.): *COMAD '91 - Advances in Data Management*, Tata McGraw Hill, New Delhi, 1991. pp. 347–359.

[45] Exertier, F. *Extension Orientée Objet d'un SGBD Relationel.* PhD thesis, Université Joseph Fourier (Grenoble), 1991.

[46] Ferreira, P. Reclaiming Storage in an Object-Oriented Platform Supporting Extended C++ and Objective-C Applications. In Cabrera, L.-F., Russo, V. and Shapiro, M. (Eds.): *Proceedings of the International Workshop on Object-Orientation in Operating Systems*, Palo Alto, CA, USA, 1991. IEEE, Los Alamitos, 1991. pp. 100–102.

[47] Ferreira, P., Sequeira, M., Zúquete, A., Matos, D., Lopes, C. and Sousa, P. IK 1.0 EC++ User's Manual. Technical Report COMANDOS-INESC-TR-0021, INESC, 1991.

[48] Fichtner, J. Risk Management fuer IT-Systeme – Uebersicht ueber vorhandene Methoden und Werkzeuge. In Lippold, H. and Schmitz, P. (Eds.): *Sicherheit in netzgestuetzten Informationssytemen*, Vieweg, Braunschweig, 1992. pp. 309–329.

[49] Fichtner, J. and Persy, C. Concept of a Security Control Center. In Frey, H.H. (Ed.): *Safety of Computer Control Systems 1992 (SAFECOMP '92): Computer Systems in Safety-Critical Applications*, Zurich, Switzerland, 1992. Pergamon Press, Oxford, 1992. pp. 267–271.

[50] Finn, E. The Implementation of Virtual Memory for a Distribtued Operating System. Master's thesis, Department of Computer Science, Trinity College Dublin, February 1990.

[51] Freyssinet, A. *Conception et Réalisation d'un Système Réparti à Objets.* PhD thesis, Université Joseph Fourier (Grenoble), 1991.

[52] Freyssinet, A., Krakowiak, S., and Lacourte, S. A Generic Object-Oriented Virtual Machine. In Cabrera, L.-F., Russo, V. and Shapiro, M. (Eds.): *Proceedings of the International Workshop on Object-Orientation in Operating Systems*, Palo Alto, CA, USA, October 1991. IEEE, Los Alamitos, 1991. pp. 73–77.

[53] Glasgow Comandos ODMS Group. The Comandos ODMS Portable Toolkit. Technical Report DB-92-4, Department of Computing Science, University of Glasgow, 1992.

[54] Guedes, P. and Alves Marques, J. Operating System Support for an Object-Oriented Environment. In *Proceedings of the 2nd Workshop on Workstation Operating Systems*, Asilomar, CA, USA, 1989. IEEE, Los Alamitos, 1989. pp. 37–42.

[55] Hagimont, D., Krakowiak, S. and Rousset de Pina, X. Protection in an Object-Oriented Distributed Virtual Machine. In Cabrera, L.-F. and Jul, E. (Eds.): *Proceedings of the 2nd International Workshop on Object-Orientation in Operating Systems*, Dourdan, France, September 1992. IEEE, Los Alamitos, 1992. pp. 273–277.

[56] Harper, D.J. and Norrie, M.C. Data Management for Object-Oriented Systems. In Jackson, M.S. and Robinson, A.F. (Eds.): *Aspects of Databases*, Butterworth-Heinemann, Oxford, 1991. pp. 69–72.

[57] Harper, D.J. and Norrie, M.C. (Eds.). The Glasgow Collection of Comandos Papers. Technical Report CSC/91/R16, Department of Computing Science, University of Glasgow, 1991.

[58] Harper, D.J., Norrie, M.C. and Walker, A.D.M. Bulk Types for Data Modelling in Persistent Object Systems. *Journal of Control Systems and Machines*, 9, 1991.

[59] Hofstetter, I. and Roos, A. Leistungsbeobachtung und Systemmodifikation in einem Netzwerk von Arbeitsstationen. *SUGinfo*, 2:4–9, 1990.

[60] Horn, C. and Cahill, V. Supporting Distributed Applications in the Amadeus Environment. *Computer Communications*, 14(6):358–365, 1991.

[61] Horn, C. and Krakowiak, S. Object-Oriented Architecture For Distributed Office Systems. In *ESPRIT '87: Achievements and Impact*, Elsevier Science Publishers, Amsterdam, 1987. pp. 1490–1500.

[62] Horn, C., Ness, A. and Reim, F. Construction and Management of Distributed Office Systems. In Bullinger, H.-J., Protonotarios, E.N., Bouwhuis, D. and Reim, F. (Eds.): *EURINFO '88: First European Conference on Information Technology for Organisational Systems*, Athens, Greece, 1988. Elsevier Science Publishers, Amsterdam, 1988. pp. 378–385.

[63] Jamrozik, H., Santana, M. and Roisin, C. A Graphical Debugger for Object-Oriented Distributed Programs. In Meyer, B., Korson, T. and Vaishnavi, V. (Eds.): *TOOLS 5 (Technology of Object-Oriented Languages and Systems)*, TOOLS Conference Series, Prentice-Hall, 1991. pp. 117–128.

[64] Krakowiak, S., Meysembourg, M., Nguyen Van, H., Riveill, M., Roisin, C. and Rousset de Pina, X. Design and Implementation of an Object-Oriented, Strongly Typed Language for Distributed Applications. *Journal of Object-Oriented Programming*, 3(3):11–22, 1990.

[65] Kramer, A. The Design and Implementation of the OISIN Runtime. Master's thesis, Department of Computer Science, Trinity College Dublin, September 1989.

[66] Kroeger, R., Mock, M. and Schumann, R. The RelaX Architecture – Overview and Interfaces. GMD-Studie. To appear 1993.

[67] Kroeger, R., Mock, M. and Schumann, R. The RelaX Transactional Object Management System. In Rosenberg, J. and Leslie Keedy J. (Eds.): *Proceedings of the International Workshop on Computer Architectures to Support Security and Persistence of Information*, Workshops in Computing, Springer-Verlag, Berlin, 1990. pp. 339–355.

[68] Lacourte, S. Exceptions in Guide, an Object-Oriented Language for Distributed Applications. In America, P. (Ed.): *ECOOP '91: European Conference on Object-Oriented Programming*, Lecture Notes in Computer Science 512, Springer-Verlag, Berlin, 1991. pp. 268–287.

[69] Lacourte, S. *Traitement des Exceptions dans un Langage à Objets*. PhD thesis, Université Joseph Fourier (Grenoble), 1991.

[70] Lacourte, S. and Riveill, M. Generic System Support for Shared Object Synchronization. In Cabrera, L.-F. and Jul, E. (Eds.): *Proceedings of the 2nd International Workshop on Object-Orientation in Operating Systems*, Dourdan, France, September 1992. IEEE, Los Alamitos, 1992. pp. 153–157.

[71] Lautier, C. Generation Automatique de Conditions de Synchronisation dans le Systeme Reparti a Objets GUIDE. Technical Report DT/SPT/SCE/200, SEPT, 1991.

[72] Lea, R., Amaral, P. and Jacquemot, C. COOL-2: An Object-Oriented Support Platform Built above the CHORUS Micro-Kernel. In Cabrera, L.-F., Russo, V. and Shapiro, M. (Eds.): *Proceedings of the International Workshop on Object-Orientation in Operating Systems*, Palo Alto, CA, USA, October 1991. IEEE, Los Alamitos, 1991. pp. 68–72.

[73] Lea, R. and Jacquemot, C. The COOL Architecture and Abstractions for Object-Oriented Distributed Operating Systems. In *Proceedings of the 5th SIGOPS European Workshop*, Le Mont Saint-Michel, France, 1992. IRISA/INRIA, Rennes, 1992.

[74] Lea, R. and Weightman, J. COOL: An Object Support Environment Co-existing with UNIX. In *Convention UNIX '91*, Paris, France, 1991. AFUU, Paris, 1991. pp 159–171.

[75] Lea, R. and Weightman, J. Supporting Object-Oriented Languages in a Distributed Environment: The COOL Approach. In Meyer, B., Korson, T. and Vaishnavi, V. (Eds.): *TOOLS 5 (Technology of Object-Oriented Languages and Systems)*, TOOLS Conference Series, Prentice-Hall, 1991. pp. 37–47.

[76] Lenormand, E. and Riveill, M. Experience with Types and Classes in the Guide Language. In Calsberg, J. and Schwartzbach, J. (Eds.): *Proceeding of the ECOOP '91 Workshop on Types, Inheritance and Assignments*, Geneva, Switzerland, 1991. Computer Science Department, Aarhus University, 1991.

[77] Lescalier, V. Rubens : un Service de Negociation Bureautique Reparti. Technical Report DT/SPT/SCE/201, SEPT, 1992.

[78] Lynch, F. Parallel Programming in DUMPS. Master's thesis, Department of Computer Science, Trinity College Dublin, 1990.

[79] Martin, M.T. TGS – A Translator Generator System. Master's thesis, Department of Computer Science, Trinity College Dublin, March 1992.

[80] McHale, C., Walsh, B., Baker, S. and Donnelly, A. Scheduling Predicates. In Tokoro, M., Nierstrasz, O. and Wegner, P. (Eds.): *Proceedings of the ECOOP '91 Workshop on Object-Based Concurrent Computing*, Lecture Notes in Computer Science 612, Springer-Verlag, Berlin, 1991. pp. 177–193.

[81] McHale, C., Walsh, B., Baker, S., and Donnelly, A. Evaluating Synchronisation Mechanisms: The Inheritance Matrix. Technical Report TCD-

CS-92-18, Department of Computer Science, Trinity College Dublin, July 1992.

[82] McHugh, C. and Cahill, V. Eiffel**: An Implementation of Eiffel on Amadeus, a Persistent, Distributed Object-Oriented Applications Support Environment. In Magnusson, B., Meyer, B. and Perrot, J.-F. (Eds.): *TOOLS 10 (Technology of Object-Oriented Languages and Systems)*, TOOLS Conference Series, Prentice-Hall, 1993. pp. 47–62.

[83] Medina, M. and Moreno, A. Security Levels Supported by the Comandos Security Architecture. In *Proceedings of the 1991 ESPRIT Conference*, Brussels, Belgium, 1991. Commission of the European Communities, Luxembourg, 1991. pp. 421–426.

[84] Meitner, H. Phasenkonzepte fuer das Risikomanagement. *Zeitschrift fuer Kommunikations- und EDV-Sicherheit KES*, 6(6):394–399, 1990.

[85] Meitner, H. Modellierung und Analyse von Ausfallrisiken in verteilten Informationssystemen. In Lippold, H., Schmitz, P. and Kersten, H.(Eds.): *Sicherheit in Informationssystemen: SECUNET '91 und 2. Deutsche Konferenz ueber Computersicherheit*, Bonn, Germany, 1991. Vieweg, Braunschweig, 1991. pp. 76–87.

[86] Meitner, H. Sicherheitsmanagement beim Einsatz von Rechnernetzen. In Bullinger, H.-J. (Ed.): *Handbuch des Informationsmanagements im Unternehmen*, C.H. Becksche Verlagsbuchandlung, Munich, 991. pp. 719–757.

[87] Meitner, H. and Steinacker, M. Sicherheitsmassnahmen fuer verteilte Systeme. *Office Management*, 40(5):6–16, 1992.

[88] Meitner, H. and Teuber, V. Werkzeuggestuetzter Aufbau und Optimierung von Netzwerken. In Warnecke, H.J. and Bullinger, H.-J. (Eds.): *Verteilte, offene Informationssysteme in der betriebliche Anwendung*, Springer-Verlag, Berlin, 1990. pp. 199–214.

[89] Meitner, H., Medina, M., Finn, E. and Persy, C. Security Facilities in Distributed Systems. In Lippold, H. and Schmitz, P. (Eds.): *Sicherheit in netzgestuetzten Informationssystemen: SECUNET '90*, Cologne, Germany, 1990. Vieweg, Braunschweig, 1990. pp. 357–371.

[90] Merciol, F. Systemes Repartis a Objets en Bureautique. Technical Report DT/SPT/SCE/98, SEPT, 1991.

[91] Meysembourg, M. *Modèle et Langage à Objets pour la Programmation d'Applications Réparties*. PhD thesis, Institut National Polytechnique (Grenoble), 1989.

[92] Mock, M. and Kroeger, R. Implementing Atomic Objects with the RelaX Transaction Facility. In Cabrera, L.-F., Russo, V. and Shapiro, M. (Eds.): *Proceedings of the International Workshop on Object-Orientation in Operating Systems*, Palo Alto, CA, USA, 1991. IEEE, Los Alamitos, 1991. pp. 190–193.

[93] Mock, M., Kroeger, R. and Cahill, V. Implementing Atomic Objects with the RelaX Transaction Facility. *Computing Systems*, 5(3):259–304, 1992.

[94] Nguyen Van, H. *Compilation et Environnement d'Exécution d'un Langage à base d'Objets.* PhD thesis, Institut National Polytechnique (Grenoble), 1991.

[95] Normand, V. A Practical Framework for Interactive Applications in Guide, an Object-Oriented Distributed System. In Bezivin, J., Meyer, B. and Nerson, J.M. (Eds.): *Proceedings of TOOLS (Technology of Object-Oriented Languages and Systems) Europe '90,* Paris, France, 1990. Angkor, Paris, 1990. pp. 737–768.

[96] Normand, V. *Le Modèle SIROCO : de la Spécification Conceptuelle des Interfaces Utilisateur à leur Réalisation.* PhD thesis, Université Joseph Fourier (Grenoble), 1992.

[97] Normand, V. and Coutaz, J. Unifying the Design and Implementation of User Interfaces through the Object Paradigm. In Lehrmann Madsen, O. (Ed.): *ECOOP '92: European Conference on Object-Oriented Programming,* Lecture Notes in Computer Science 615, Springer-Verlag, Berlin, 1992. pp. 153–169.

[98] Norrie, M.C. A Specification of an Object-Oriented Data Model with Relations. In Harper, D.J. and Norrie, M.C. (Eds.): *Specifications of Database Systems,* Workshops in Computing, Springer-Verlag, Berlin, 1992. pp. 213–227.

[99] Norrie, M.C. Supporting the Design of Object-Oriented Databases. In Cadish, B. and Ageshin, S. (Eds.): *Proceedings of the Baltic Conference on Methods of Database Design,* Riga, Latvia, 1992. FRAME Press, 1992.

[100] Norrie, M.C. An Interactive System for the Design of Object-Oriented Databases. In Cooper, R.L. (Ed.): *Proceedings of International Workshop on Interfaces to Database Systems,* Workshops in Computing, Springer-Verlag, Berlin, 1993. pp. 6–21.

[101] O'Toole, A. The Implementation of a Multi-processor Kernel. Master's thesis, Department of Computer Science, Trinity College Dublin, 1990.

[102] Pereira, J. Técnicas e Ferramentas de Suporte para um Ambiente Cooperativo de Programação Orientada para Objectos. Master's thesis, IST, Lisbon, Portugal, 1991.

[103] Rathgeb, M. and Roos, A. Office Procedure Support Systems on the Basis of Open Distributed Systems. In Bullinger, H.-J. (Ed.): *Proceedings of the 4th International Conference on Human-Computer Interaction,* Stuttgart, Germany, 1991. Elsevier Science Publishers, Amsterdam, 1991. pp. 389–394.

[104] Reim, F. *Entwicklung eines Verfahrens zur rechnerunterstuetzten Gestaltung verteilter Informationssysteme.* Springer-Verlag, Berlin, 1992.

[105] Reim, F. Organizational Integration of the Information System Design Process. In Loucopoulos, P. (Ed.): *Advanced Information Systems Engineering,* Lecture Notes in Computer Science 593, Springer-Verlag, Berlin, 1992. pp. 410–424.

[106] Reim, F. and Meitner, H. A Toolset for Administration and Management of Distributed Information Systems. In Bullinger, H.-J. (Ed.): *Proceed-*

ings of the 4th *International Conference on Human-Computer Interaction*, Stuttgart, Germany, 1991. Elsevier Science Publishers, Amsterdam, 1991. pp. 374–378.

[107] Reim, F. and Roos, A. DISDES: Ein Gestaltungswerkzeug zur Verbindung von Analyse und Gestaltung verteilter Informationssysteme. In Warnecke, H.J. and Bullinger, H.-J. (Eds.): *Verteilte, offene Informationssysteme in der betriebliche Anwendung*, Springer-Verlag, Berlin, 1990. pp. 137–154.

[108] Roos, A. and Reim, F. Ein Werkzeug fuer alle Faelle. *Net*, 44(12):532–535, 1990.

[109] Scioville, R. *Gestion des Informations Persistantes dans un Système Réparti à Objets*. PhD thesis, Université Joseph Fourier (Grenoble), 1989.

[110] Sequeira, M. EC++: Uma Linguagem para a Programação num Sistema Distribuído Orientado a Objectos. Master's thesis, IST, Lisbon, Portugal, 1991.

[111] Sequeira, M. and Alves Marques, J. Can C++ be Used for Programming Distributed and Persistent Objects? In Cabrera, L.-F., Russo, V. and Shapiro, M. (Eds.): *Proceedings of the International Workshop on Object-Orientation in Operating Systems*, Palo Alto, CA, USA, 1991. IEEE, Los Alamitos, 1991. pp. 173–176.

[112] Sequeira, M., Sousa, P. and Alves Marques, J. Distributed and Persistent Objects in C++. In *Proceedings of the ERCIM Workshop on Distributed Systems*, Lisbon, Portugal, 1991. INESC, Lisbon, 1991. pp. 93–98.

[113] Slattery, J.A. The Design and Implementation of a Communication Subsystem for a Distributed Operating System. Master's thesis, Department of Computer Science, Trinity College Dublin, June 1990.

[114] Sousa, P. Concepção e Realização de um Sistema de Suporte à Execução de Objectos. Master's thesis, IST, Lisbon, Portugal, 1991.

[115] Sousa, P., Ferreira, P., Monge, J., Zúquete, A., Sequeira, M., Guedes, P. and Alves Marques, J. IK Implementation Report. Technical Report COMANDOS-INESC-TR-0012, INESC, 1990.

[116] Sousa, P., Sequeira, M. and Alves Marques, J. Experiences and Implementation of an Object-Oriented Distributed Platform. In *Proceedings of the ERCIM Workshop on Distributed Systems*, Lisbon, Portugal, 1991. INESC, Lisbon, 1991. pp. 117–121.

[117] Sousa, P., Zúquete, A., Sequeira, M., Guedes, P. and Alves Marques, J. IK-2 Implementation Report. Technical Report COMANDOS-INESC-TR-0040, INESC, 1993. To appear.

[118] Starovic, G. The Design and Implementation of an Object-Oriented Input/Output and Storage System for a Distributed Kernel. Master's thesis, Department of Computer Science, Trinity College Dublin, September 1989.

[119] Tangney, B. and O'Toole, A. An Overview of Load Balancing in Amadeus. In Ammar, R.A. (Ed.): *Proceedings of the* 4th *ISMM/IASTED Conference on Parallel and Distributed Computing and Systems*, Washington DC, USA, 1991. Acta Press, Anaheim, 1991. pp. 144–146.

[120] Tangney, B., Cahill, V., Horn, C., Herity, D., Judge, A., Starovic, G. and Sheppard, M. Some Ideas on Support for Fault Tolerance in Comandos, an Object-Oriented Distributed System. *ACM SIGOPS Operating Systems Review*, 25(2):130–135, 1991.

[121] Walsh, B. The Type Model of Oscar-2. Master's thesis, Department of Computer Science, Trinity College Dublin, October 1992.

[122] Weiss, W. and Baur, A. Analysis of Audit and Protocol Data using Methods from Artifical Intelligence. In *Proceedings of the 13th National Computer Security Conference*, Washington DC, USA, 1990. National Institute of Standards and Technology/National Computer Security Center, 1990. pp. 109–114.

[123] White, I. The Development of Subtyping in Comandos. Master's thesis, Department of Computer Science, Trinity College Dublin, November 1989.

[124] Zúquete, A. Matos, D. Ferreira, P. and Sousa, P. IK 1.0 Instalation and Configuration Manual. Technical Report COMANDOS-INESC-TR-0023, INESC, 1991.

[125] Zúquete, A., Matos, D., Ferreira, P. and Sousa, P. IK 1.0 Users Manual. Technical Report COMANDOS-INESC-TR-0022, INESC, 1991.

E.2 Project Deliverables

[1] Comandos Consortium. Comandos-1 Evaluation Report. Deliverable D1-T3.4.3, Comandos (ESPRIT Project No. 2071), March 1990.

[2] Comandos Consortium. Design Specification for the Pilot Demonstrator. Deliverable D1-T5.1, Comandos (ESPRIT Project No. 2071), March 1990.

[3] Comandos Consortium. Implementation Specification for a Distributed System Control Facility. Deliverable D1-T4.3.1, Comandos (ESPRIT Project No. 2071), September 1990.

[4] Comandos Consortium. Implementation Specification for a Distributed System Observation Facility. Comandos (ESPRIT Project No. 2071), March 1990.

[5] Comandos Consortium. Implementation Specification of the Distributed Directory Service. Comandos (ESPRIT Project No. 2071), March 1990.

[6] Comandos Consortium. Implementation Specification of the Management Tools. Deliverable D1-T4.2.1, Comandos (ESPRIT Project No. 2071), September 1990.

[7] Comandos Consortium. Implementation Specification of the Security Tools. Deliverable D1-T4.5.1, Comandos (ESPRIT Project No. 2071), March 1990.

[8] Comandos Consortium. ODMS Prototype Specification. Deliverable D1-T3.4.1.2, Comandos (ESPRIT Project No. 2071), September 1990.

[9] Comandos Consortium. Type Manager Prototype Specification. Deliverable D1-T3.4.1.1, Comandos (ESPRIT Project No. 2071), September 1990.

[10] Comandos Consortium. Comandos Language Reference Manual. Deliverable D4-T2.3, Comandos (ESPRIT Project No. 2071), 1991.

[11] Comandos Consortium. DDS-v1 Implementation Report. Deliverable D1-T4.1.3, Comandos (ESPRIT Project No. 2071), March 1991.

[12] Comandos Consortium. Description of Comandos-2 Architecture. Deliverable D1-T2.2, Comandos (ESPRIT Project No. 2071), March 1991.

[13] Comandos Consortium. Description of Management and Security Tools and Facilities. Deliverable D1-T4.5.2, Comandos (ESPRIT Project No. 2071), March 1991.

[14] Comandos Consortium. Functional Specification of Release 2. Deliverable D1-T2.3, Comandos (ESPRIT Project No. 2071), March 1991.

[15] Comandos Consortium. Implementation Specification for the Pilot Demonstrator. Deliverable D1-T5.2, Comandos (ESPRIT Project No. 2071), March 1991.

[16] Comandos Consortium. Secure Transmission System: User Manual. Comandos (ESPRIT Project No. 2071), April 1992.

[17] Comandos Consortium. The Comandos Virtual Machine Interface – v2.0. Deliverable D3-T2.3, Comandos (ESPRIT Project No. 2071), March 1992.

[18] Comandos Consortium. Type Manager Manual. Deliverable D2-T2.5.1, Comandos (ESPRIT Project No. 2071), April 1992.

References

[Accetta et al. 1986] Accetta, M., Baron, R., Bolosky, W., Golub, D., Rashid, R., Tevanian, A. and Young, M. Mach: A New Kernel Foundation for UNIX Development. In *Proceedings of the Summer USENIX Conference*, Atlanta, GA, USA, 1986. USENIX, Berkeley, 1986. pp. 93–112.

[Almes et al. 1985] Almes, G., Black, A., Lazowska, E. and Noe, J. The Eden System: A Technical Review. *IEEE Transactions on Software Engineering*, SE-11(1):43–58, 1985.

[APM 1991] Architecture Projects Management Ltd. *ANSA: An Engineer's Introduction to the Architecture*. Architecture Projects Management Ltd., Cambridge, 1991.

[Atkinson et al. 1983] Atkinson, M.P., Bailey, P.J., Chisholm, K.G., Cockshott, W.P. and Morrison, R. An Approach to Persistent Programming. *Computer Journal*, 26(4):360–365, 1983.

[Balter and Vandome 1991] Balter, R. and Vandome, G. *Bull Response to the ORB RFP*. OMG Document 91.1.5., Object Management Group, Framingham, 1991.

[Bernstein et al. 1987] Bernstein, P.A., Hadzilacos, V. and Goodman, N. *Concurrency Control and Recovery in Database Systems*. Addison-Wesley, Reading, MA, 1987.

[Boyer 1991] Boyer, F. A Causal Distributed Shared Memory Based on External Pagers. In *Proceedings of the USENIX Mach Symposium*, Monterey, CA, USA, 1991. USENIX, Berkeley, 1991. pp. 41–57.

[Boyer et al. 1991] Boyer, F., Cayuela, J., Chevalier, P.Y., Freyssinet, A. and Hagimont, D. Supporting an Object-Oriented Distributed System: Experience with UNIX, CHORUS and Mach. In *Proceedings of the 2nd Symposium on Experiences with Distributed and Multiprocessor Systems*, Atlanta, GA, USA, 1991. USENIX, Berkeley, 1991. pp. 283–300.

[Cahill 1992] Cahill, V. *Iona Technologies' Response to the Object Services Task Force RFI*. OMG Document 92.2.13., Object Management Group, Framingham, 1992.

[Cahill et al. 1992] Cahill, V., Taylor, P., Starovic, G., Tangney,, B. and O'Grady, D. *Supporting the Amadeus Platform on UNIX*. Technical Report TCD-CS-92-25, Department of Computer Science, Trinity College Dublin, 1992.

[Canning et al. 1989] Canning, P., Cook, W., Hill, W., Olthoff, W. and Mitchell, J. F-Bounded Polymorphism for Object-Oriented Programming. In *Proceedings* *of the 4th International Conference on Functional Programming Languages and Computer Architecture*, London, UK, 1989. ACM, New York, 1989. pp. 273–280.

[Cardelli 1984] Cardelli, L. *Amber.* Technical Memorandum 11271–840924–10TM, AT&T Bell Labs., Murray Hill, New Jersey, 1984.

[Cardelli and Wegner 1985] Cardelli, L. and Wegner, P. On Understanding Types, Data Abstraction and Polymorphism. *ACM Computing Surveys*, 17(4):471–522, 1985.

[Carey et al. 1986] Carey, M.J., Frank, D., Muralkrishna, M., De Witt, D.J., Graefe, G., Richardson, J.F. and Shekita, E.J. The Architecture of the EXODUS Extensible DBMS. In *Proceedings of the 1986 International Workshop on Object-Oriented Database Systems*, Asilomar, CA, USA, 1986. IEEE, Los Alamitos, 1986. pp. 52–65.

[CCITT 1988] CCITT *X.500 Series Recommendations – The Directory.* CCITT, 1988.

[Chang and Maxemchuk 1984] Chang, J. and Maxemchuk, N. Reliable Broadcast Protocols. *ACM Transactions on Computer Systems*, 2(3):251–273, 1984.

[Cheriton 1983] Cheriton, D. Local Networking and Internetworking in the V-System. In *Proceeding of the 8th Data Communications Symposium*, North Falmouth, MA, USA, 1983. IEEE/ACM, Los Angeles, 1983. pp. 9–16.

[Comandos 1990a] Comandos Consortium *Implementation Specification of the Management Tools.* Deliverable D1-T4.2.1., Comandos Consortium, 1990.

[Comandos 1990b] Comandos Consortium *Type Manager Prototype Specification.* Deliverable D1-T3.4.1.1., Comandos Consortium, 1990.

[Comandos 1990c] Comandos Consortium *Implementation Specification for a Distributed System Control Facility.* Deliverable D1-T4.3.1., Comandos Consortium, 1990.

[Comandos 1991] Comandos Consortium *Comandos Language Reference Manual.* Deliverable D4-T2.3., Comandos Consortium, 1991.

[Cook 1989] Cook, W.R. A proposal for Making Eiffel Type Safe. *Computer Journal*, 32(4):305–311, 1989.

[Dasgupta et al. 1988] Dasgupta, P., LeBlanc, R. and Appelba, W. The Clouds Distributed Operating System. In *Proceedings of the 8th International Conference on Distributed Computing Systems*, San-Jose, CA, USA, 1988. IEEE, Los Alamitos, 1988. pp. 2–9.

[DEC et al. 1991] Digital Equipment Corporation, Hewlett-Packard Company, HyperDesk Corporation, NCR Corporation, Object Design, Inc., and SunSoft, Inc. *The Common Object Request Broker: Architecture and Specification. Revision 1.1..* OMG Document 91.12.1., Object Management Group and X/Open, Framingham and Reading, 1991.

[Decouchant et al. 1991] Decouchant, D., Le Dot, P., Riveill, M., Roisin, C. and Rousset de Pina, X. A Synchronisation Mechanism for Typed Objects in a Distributed System. In *Proceedings of the 11th International Conference on Distributed Computing Systems*, Arlington, TX, USA, 1991. IEEE, Los Alamitos, 1991. pp. 152–159.

[DoD 1985] U.S. Department of Defense *Trusted Computing System Evaluation Criteria.* 5200.28-STD, U.S. Department of Defense, 1985.

[DSG 1992] Distributed Systems Group *C** Programmer's Guide (Amadeus v2.0).* Technical Report TCD-CS-92-03, Department of Computer Science, Trinity College Dublin, 1992.

[Eager et al. 1986] Eager, D.L., Lazowska, E.D. and Zahorjan, J. Adaptive Load Sharing in Homogeneous Distributed Systems. *IEEE Transactions on Software Engineering,* SE-12(5):662–675, 1986.

[Ellis and Stroustrup 1990] Ellis, M.A. and Stroustrup, B. *The Annotated C++ Reference Manual.* Addison-Wesley, Reading, MA, 1990.

[Floyd 1981] Floyd, C. A Process-Oriented Approach to Software Development. In *Proceedings of the 6th ACM European Regional Conference,* London, UK, 1981. ACM, New York, 1981. pp. 285–294.

[Girard 1972] Girard, J-Y. *Interpretation Fonctionelle et Elimination des Coupures Dans l'Arithmétique de l'Ordre Superieur,* PhD thesis, Université Paris VII, 1972.

[Glasgow 1992] Glasgow Comandos ODMS Group *The Comandos ODMS Portable Toolkit.* Technical Report DB-92-4, Department of Computing Science, University of Glasgow, 1992.

[Golub et al. 1990] Golub, D., Dean, R., Forin, A. and Rashid, R. UNIX as an Application Program. In *Proceedings of the Summer USENIX Conference,* Anaheim, CA, USA, 1990. USENIX, Berkeley, 1990. pp. 11–15.

[Grochla 1982] Grochla, E. *Grundlagen der Organisatorischen Gestaltung.* C.E. Poeschel Verlag, 1982.

[Halstead 1985] Halstead, R. Multilisp: a Language for Concurrent Symbolic Computation. *ACM Transactions on Programming Languages and Systems,* 7(4):501–538, 1985.

[HARNESS 1991a] HARNESS Consortium *HARNESS Project Overview.* HARNESS/ACC/MI/CGI/001/1.2, HARNESS Consortium, 1991.

[HARNESS 1991b] HARNESS Consortium *HARNESS Platform: Basic Specification.* HARNESS/PSE1/DEL/COO/001/1.0, HARNESS Consortium, 1991.

[Harper and Norrie 1991a] Harper, D.J. and Norrie, M.C Data Management for Object-Oriented Systems. In Jackson, M.S. and Robinson, A.F. (Eds.): *Aspects of Databases,* Butterworth-Heinemann, Oxford, 1991. pp. 69–72.

[Harper and Norrie 1991b] Harper, D.J. and Norrie, M.C (Eds.) *The Glasgow Collection of Comandos Papers.* Technical Report CSC/91/R16, Department of Computing Science, University of Glasgow, 1991.

[ISO 1989] ISO *Proposed Working Draft for Addenda to ISO 8073 and ISO 8602 Covering Cryptographic Data Protection.* ISO, 1989.

[ISO 1991] ISO *Transport Layer Security Protocol – Draft International Standard.* ISO DIS N6779, ISO, 1991.

[Jacqmot et al. 1989] Jacqmot, C., Milgrom, E., Joosen, W. and Berbers, Y. UNIX and Load Balancing: a Survey. In *Proceedings of the EUUG Spring Conference,* Brussels, Belgium, 1989. EUUG, Buntingford, 1989. pp. 1–15.

[Jamrozik et al. 1991] Jamrozik, H., Santana, M. and Roisin, C. A Graphical Debugger for Object-Oriented Distributed Programs. In Meyer, B., Korson, T. and Vaishnavi, V. (Eds.): *TOOLS 5 (Technology of Object-Oriented Languages and Systems)*, TOOLS Conference Series, Prentice-Hall, 1991. pp. 117–128.

[Jones 1991] Jones, M.B. Bringing the C Libraries with Us into a Mutli-Threaded Future. In *Proceedings of the USENIX Winter Conference*, Dallas, TX, USA, 1991. USENIX, Berkeley, 1991. pp. 81–91.

[Kroeger et al. 1990] Kroeger, R., Mock, M. and Schumann, R. The RelaX Transactional Object Management System. In Rosenberg, J. and Leslie Keedy J. (Eds.): *Proceedings of the International Workshop on Computer Architectures to Support Security and Persistence of Information*, Workshops in Computing, Springer-Verlag, Berlin, 1990. pp. 339–355.

[LeBlanc and Mellor-Crummey 1987] LeBlanc, T.-J. and Mellor-Crummey, J.-M. Debugging Parallel Programs with Instant Replay. *IEEE Transactions on Computers*, C-36(4):471–482, 1987.

[Li and Hudak 1989] Li, K. and Hudak, P. Memory Coherence in Shared Virtual Memory Systems. *ACM Transactions on Computer Systems*, 7(4):321–359, 1989.

[Liskov and Scheifler 1983] Liskov, B. and Scheifler, R. Guardians and Actions: Linguistic Support for Robust, Distributed Programs. *ACM Transactions on Programming Languages and Systems*, 5(3):381–404, 1983.

[Lockemann and Mayr 1986] Lockemann, P.C. and Mayr, H.C. Information System Design: Techniques and Software Support. In Kugler, H.-J. (Ed.): *Proceedings of the IFIP 10th World Computer Congress*, Dublin, Ireland, 1986. Elsevier Science Publishers, Amsterdam, 1986. pp. 617–634.

[Medina and Morena 1991] Medina, M. and Moreno, A. Security Levels Supported by the Comandos Security Architecture. In *Proceedings of the 1991 ESPRIT Conference*, Brussels, Belgium, 1991. Commission of the European Communities, Luxembourg, 1991. pp. 421–426.

[Meyer 1988] Meyer, B. *Object Oriented Software Construction*. Prentice Hall, 1988.

[Meyer 1989a] Meyer, B. *Eiffel: The Language*. TR-EI-17/RM, I.S.E., 1989.

[Meyer 1989b] Meyer, B. *Static Typing for Eiffel*. TR-EI-18/ST, I.S.E., 1989.

[Meyer and Nerson 1990] Meyer, B. and Nerson, J.-M. *Eiffel: The Libraries*. TR-EI-7/LI, I.S.E., 1990.

[Miller and Choi 1988] Miller, B.-P. and Choi, J.-D. A Mechanism for Efficient Debugging of Parallel Programs. In *Proceedings of the SIGPLAN '88 Conference on Programming Language Design and Implementation*, Atlanta, GA, USA, 1988. ACM, New York, 1988. pp. 135–144.

[Mitchell and Plotkin 1988] Mitchell, J. and Plotkin, G. Abstract Types have Existential Type. *ACM Transactions on Programming Languages and Systems*, 10(3):470–502, 1988.

[Mock et al. 1992] Mock, M., Kroeger, R. and Cahill, V. Implementing Atomic Objects with the RelaX Transaction Facility. *Computing Systems*, 5(3):259–304, 1992.

[Morrison et al. 1989] Morrison, R., Brown, A.L., Connor, R.C. and Dearle, A. *Napier Reference Manual.* Programming Research Report 77, University of St. Andrews, 1989.

[Moss 1981] Moss, J.E. *Nested Transactions: An Approach to Reliable Distributed Computing.* Technical Report MIT/LCS/TR 260, MIT, 1981.

[Mullender 1985] Mullender, S. *Principles of Distributed Operating System Design.* PhD thesis, Mathematisch Centrum, Vrije Univeriseit, 1985.

[NCSC 1988] National Computer Security Center *A Guide to Understanding AUDIT in Trusted Sytems.* NCSC-TG-001 Version 2, NCSC, 1988.

[Normand 1990] Normand, V. A Practical Framework for Interactive Applications in Guide, an Object-Oriented Distributed System. In Bezivin, J., Meyer, B. and Nerson, J.M. (Eds.): *Proceedings of TOOLS (Technology of Object-Oriented Languages and Systems) Europe '90*, Paris, France, 1990. Angkor, Paris, 1990. pp. 737–768.

[Norrie 1992] Norrie, M.C. A Specification of an Object-Oriented Data Model with Relations. In Harper, D.J. and Norrie, M.C. (Eds.): *Specifications of Database Systems*, Workshops in Computing, Springer-Verlag, Berlin, 1992. pp.213–227.

[OSF 1991] Open Software Foundation *Member Survey Summary.* OSF, 1991.

[Popek and Walker 1985] Popek, G. and Walker, B. (Eds.) The LOCUS Distributed System Architecture. MIT Press, Cambridge, MA, 1985.

[PPRR 1986] Persistent Programming Research Group *PS-Algol Reference Manual – Third Edition.* Persistent Programming Research Report 12, Department of Computing Science, University of Glasgow and Department of Computational Science, University of St. Andrews, 1986.

[Puech and Trabelsi 1992] Puech, M. and Trabelsi. H. *Bull Response to the OMG Object Services Task Force RFI.* OMG Document 92.2.20., Object Management Group, Framingham, 1992.

[Rozier et al. 1988] Rozier, M., Abrossimov, V., Armand, F., Boule, I., Gien, M., Guillemont, M., Herrmann, F., Kaiser, C., Langlois, S., Léonard, P. and Neuhauser, W. CHORUS Distributed Operating Systems. *Computing Systems*, 1(4):305–370, 1988.

[Schumann et al. 1989] Schumann, R., Kroeger, R., Mock, M. and Nett, E. Recovery Management in the RelaX Distributed Transaction Layer. In *Proceedings of the 8th Symposium on Reliable Distributed Systems*, Seattle, Washington, USA, 1989. IEEE, Los Alamitos, 1989. pp. 21–28.

[Shapiro et al. 1989] Shapiro, M., Gourhant, Y., Habert, S., Mosseri, L., Ruffin, M. and Valot, C. SOS: An Object-Oriented Operating System – Assessment and Perspectives. *Computing Systems*, 2(4):287–338, 1989.

[Soley 1990] Soley, R. (Ed.) *Object Management Architecture Guide.* OMG Document 90.9.1., Object Management Group, Framingham, 1990.

[Sousa et al. 1993] Sousa, P., Zúquete, A., Sequeira, M., Guedes, P. and Alves Marques, J. *IK-2 Implementation Report.* Technical Report COMANDOS-INESC-TR-0040, INESC, *To appear 1993.*

[Steiner et al. 1988] Steiner, J.G., Neumann, C., and Schiller, J.I. Kerberos, an Authentication Service for Open Network Systems. In *Proceedings of the USENIX Winter Conference*, Dallas, TX, USA, 1988. USENIX, Berkeley, 1988. pp. 191–202.

[Stroustrup 1987] Stroustrup, B. *The C++ Programming Language*. Addison-Wesley, Reading, MA, 1987.

[Tangney and O'Toole 1991] Tangney, B. and O'Toole, A. An Overview of Load Balancing in Amadeus. In Ammar, R.A. (Ed.): *Proceedings of the 4th ISMM/IASTED Conference on Parallel and Distributed Computing and Systems*, Washington DC, USA, 1991. Acta Press, Anaheim, 1991. pp. 144–146.

[Vonthin 1987] Vonthin, R. *Spezifikation des PROFEMO-Reliable Broadcast Protokolls in UNIX 4.2BSD*. GMD-Studie 127. GMD, Sankt Augustin, 1987.

[Weinstein et al. 1985] Weinstein, M., Page, T., Livezey, B. and Popek, G. Transactions and Synchronization in a Distributed Operating System. In *Proceedings of the 10th ACM Symposium on Operating System Principles*, Orcas Island, Washington, USA, 1985. ACM, New York, 1985. pp. 115–126.

[Wileden et al. 1991] Wileden, J.C., Wolf, A.L., Rosenblatt, W.R. and Tarr, P.L. Specification Level Interoperability. *Communications of the ACM*, 34(5):72–87, 1991.

[Wirth 1988] Wirth, N. Type Extensions. *ACM Transaction on Programming Languages and Systems*, 10(2):204–214, 1988.

[X/Open 1989] X/Open Company *X/Open Preliminary Specification: Distributed Transaction Processing: The XA Specification*. X/Open Company, Reading, 1989.

[Zhou and Ferrari 1987] Zhou, S. and Ferrari, D. A Measurement Study of Load Balancing Performance. In *Proceedings of the 7th International Conference on Distributed Computing Systems*, Berlin, Germany, 1987. IEEE, Los Alamitos, 1987. pp. 490–497.

Springer-Verlag
and the Environment

We at Springer-Verlag firmly believe that an international science publisher has a special obligation to the environment, and our corporate policies consistently reflect this conviction.

We also expect our business partners – paper mills, printers, packaging manufacturers, etc. – to commit themselves to using environmentally friendly materials and production processes.

The paper in this book is made from low- or no-chlorine pulp and is acid free, in conformance with international standards for paper permanency.